BEYOND THE MARKETPLACE

Rethinking Economy and Society

SOCIOLOGY AND ECONOMICS
Controversy and Integration

An Aldine de Gruyter Series of Texts and Monographs

Series Editors

Paula England, *Department of Sociology,*
University of Arizona, Tucson
George Farkas, *School of Social Sciences,*
University of Texas, Dallas
Kevin Lang, *Department of Economics,*
Boston University

Beyond the Marketplace:
Rethinking Economy and Society
Roger Friedland and A.F. Robertson (eds.)

Social Institutions:
Their Emergence, Maintenance and Effects
Michael Hechter, Karl-Dieter Opp, and Reinhard Wippler (eds.)

BEYOND THE MARKETPLACE

Rethinking Economy and Society

Edited by

Roger Friedland and A. F. Robertson

Aldine de Gruyter
New York

ABOUT THE EDITORS

Roger Friedland is Professor of Sociology at the University of California, Santa Barbara. He is currently studying conflicts over the organization and meaning of time and space in Jerusalem (with Richard Hecht) and is developing a comparative study of corporate geographies in market economies (with Guido Martinotti).

A. F. (Sandy) Robertson is Professor of Anthropology at the University of California, Santa Barbara. Until 1985 he taught Development Studies and was Director of the African Studies Centre at Cambridge University.

Copyright © 1990 by Walter de Gruyter, Inc., New York.
All rights reserved. No part of this publication may be reproduced or transmitted in any form or by any means, electronic or mechanical, including photocopy, recording, or any information storage, and retrieval system, without permission in writing from the publisher.

ALDINE DE GRUYTER
A Division of Walter de Gruyter, Inc.
200 Saw Mill River Road
Hawthorne, New York 10532

Library of Congress Cataloging-in-Publication Data
Beyond the marketplace: rethinking economy and society/edited by
   Roger Friedland and A. F. Robertson.
      p. cm.—(Sociology and economics)
   Includes bibliographical references.
   ISBN 0-202-30370-5.—ISBN 0-202-30371-3 (pbk.)
      1. Capitalism—Social aspects.   2. Political science—Economic
aspects.   3. Family—Economic aspects.   4. Labor market.
5. Neoclassical school of economics.   I. Friedland, Roger.
II. Robertson, A. F.   III. Series.
HB501.B49   1990
306.3—dc20   89-77722
                                                        CIP

Manufactured in the United States of America

10 9 8 7 6 5 4 3 2 1

CONTENTS

v

PART IV. MARKETS IN SOCIETY

PART V. MARKETS AS SOCIETY

INTRODUCTION

Beyond the Marketplace

1

Roger Friedland and A. F. Robertson[1]

This volume brings together social scientists who have been rethinking the relationship between economy and society. Although they range in theoretical taste from marxist to marginalist, structuralist to individualist, materialist to idealist, they share a critical interest in the market. The desire to go beyond conventional understandings of the market means, for some of our authors, a reexamination of assumptions about the behavior of individuals in economic transactions. For others, it means extending the logic of market exchange to other arenas such as the household, the political party, or the state. To a third group, it means understanding the ways in which these other institutions shape the operations of markets. And to a fourth, it means interpreting markets themselves as social and cultural institutions from which the logic of individual exchange derives.

Although these essays converge on the market, there is little agreement on what markets are and do. No doubt we all gravitate to the marketplace because that is where the social and economic action is, the common empirical ground between contesting theories about the distribution of goods and services. Our focus on the market also reflects the success of one discipline, and of one doctrine within that discipline, neoclassical economics, in asserting the primacy of the market as the most important economic institution, in constituting it as object of enquiry, and in monopolizing its analysis. As a result, this resurgence of interest in the relationship between markets and society appears as a movement between an economic core and a social periphery.

Our introduction to this volume is an attempt to dislodge this center of gravity and to rechart the territory of economy and society. In editing this collection we have grouped our authors, not according to discipline, but according to our perception of two countervailing trajectories into and out of the marketplace: the pursuit of economic meaning in society and the pursuit of social meaning in the economy. We begin with four who challenge the behavioral assumptions of neoclassical economics by exploring the psychological, social, and cultural dispositions of individual behavior in markets.

The next trio consider how models of market behavior may be adjusted to analyze social institutions ranging from marital relations to democratic process, and the relations between families, firms, unions, and states. From a firmly materialist perspective, the next four authors locate the market as one among a number of interacting institutions ranging from the household to the state, each of which operates according to different principles and is the means of expressing different sorts of interest. By interpreting the complex relationships among these institutions these authors seek to explain variations in the individual life course, the structure of households, the development of the welfare states and economic policy regimes, as well as the structure and operation of markets themselves. The final group of authors construe the market as a social product, a culturally and historically constructed institution. They extend this interpretation to the discipline of economics itself, viewing it as rhetoric, as ideology, and even as a modern secular religion.

ECONOMY VS. SOCIETY

To grasp why we do not understand the relationship between economy and society, it is first necessary to understand the relationship between economists and other social scientists. In world historical time, as Hart (this volume) points out, the origins of our idea of economy are recent and regional—the Anglo-American world since the seventeenth century. The economistic view of society as an accumulation of individual transactions is even more recent. The classical social theorists of the eighteenth and nineteenth centuries analyzed the economy as a central institution structured by and structuring the social order. They were inspired to do so by the times in which they lived. The old order was crashing down about their ears as industrial capitalism transformed the processes of production, the structure of markets and enterprises, and the role of the nation state in the world economy. They were painfully aware of the social traumas of economic transformation and were animated by the desire for reform. They differed in the kinds of relationship between economy and society they considered possible and preferable, but they did not question the intimacy of the relationship, nor did they regard individual and public motives as irreconcilable.

Adam Smith, proponent of the free market, wondered how the state could check the businessmen's natural proclivities for association and manipulation of the market, and stressed the importance of social honor as a motivation for work. Vilfredo Pareto could not lay down the basis of contemporary welfare economics without scrutinizing the dynamics of power in the societies of his day. This same thinker who gave us the notion of "economic man" also pioneered study of the "circulation of elites." Marx and Engels traced the changing division of labor in the household to the logic of capitalism. Durkheim understood the emergence of ideologies of humanism and liberalism as reflections of the unfolding of a radically new division of labor. Max Weber treated the separation of household and firm accounts and the rationalization of state-financed armies in essentially the same terms. He could confidently call his magnum opus *Economy and Society* because the marginalist revolution had not yet detached economy from its social and political context.

The disruption came in the twentieth century, as the division of academic labor split the social sciences into discrete, competitive professional fields. Its close alliance with the science of mathematics allowed economics to claim intellectual supremacy, establishing the power of abstract deductive models over the more empirical disciplines. It became involved in and lent credence to the political drive of the new nation states to establish the conditions necessary for economic growth. Economists were thus encouraged to generate models whose utility could be validated through the exercise of state power. Scrutiny of the empirical adequacy of these models of "rational expectations" mattered less than crude reckoning of whether a policy could be made to work. Economists thus found themselves with the power to define simultaneously the world and their own intellectual credentials.

In the face of such robust competition, the other social science disciplines retreated from the capitalist marketplace. The rising discipline of anthropology based its credentials on association with natural history, and devoted its attention to the exotic worlds being opened up by European colonial expansion. It became preoccupied with a holistic, organic view of culture in which economy merged with religion and kinship, and in which money, markets, and sometimes economic rationality itself were regarded as intrusive. Political scientists fixed on the institutions and the dilemmas of popular participation in the expanding nation state. Sociologists, perhaps clinging to the Comptean notion that theirs was the most inclusive intellectual calling, pursued the social construction of virtually everything—except the economy. Swedberg has pointed out that in the United States the division of academic labor involved an exercise of political power in the late nineteenth century, in which the intellectual territory of the economy was ceded to the already well-organized and institutionally powerful profession of economists in exchange for survival within the American academy (Swedberg 1987).

When the other social scientists did approach the economy they adopted the role of scavenger, picking up matters of peripheral or residual interest to economists: entrepreneurial motivation, the structure of collective bargaining, ethnic and gender segregation, social mobility, the politics of economic policy-making, ideology, trust, and altruism. As economists worked in the marketplace among orderly and rational individuals, the other social sciences became embroiled in the noisy and incoherent social world beyond. Thus, Paul Samuelson could remark in 1947 that economics studied behavior that was rational while sociology studied that which was not (Swedberg 1987:101).[2]

Nevertheless, there were very few social scientists who were not strongly influenced, one way or another by economic paradigms. Although many were happy to construe the perennial problem of social order in the idiom of self-interested individuals competing in free markets, others like Polanyi took a reactive position. In his view economic activity is not confined to market, or market-like domains. Rather, Polanyi distinguished the market from other means of exchange, most particulary forms of reciprocity and redistribution conditioned by long-standing social relationships.[3] It was in those capitalist societies that had engendered the discipline of economics itself that the market as a formal and relatively autonomous institution was most highly developed. Polanyi's account of the 'substantive' meaning of economic behavior, of transactions embedded within wider social institutions, depended on a contrast with the dominant 'formal' conventions of free market exchange (Polanyi 1944, 1947; Polanyi et al. 1957; and see Hart, this volume). Within the domain that it claimed for itself, he did not dispute the theoretical adequacy of the formal market model. Marcus (this volume) argues that, whether they are "formalists" or "substantivists," anthropologists who study noncapitalist, non-Western societies depend on definitions of the economic appropriate to capitalism. As a result, the local meanings of production, consumption and exchange remain obscure.

MARKETS IN SOCIETY

The mainstream of neoclassical economics proceeds from the assumption that the market is an autonomous, self-regulating arena. The interventions of states and social classes, or the peculiar interests of men and women, or of religious and ethnic groups, are either taken as exogenous factors forming tastes, or repudiated as imperfections that distort the efficient allocation of resources. The first task is thus to return the market to its social context and to understand its social history.

To economists, Lie (1988:12) notes, "the market merely becomes a synonym for the universe of traders, since there exists no specification of its institutional features or instruments of exchange." But markets are more than the contingent aggregation of individual transactions or exchanges. As *institutions* markets make such exchanges practicable, but *because* they are institutions they transcend these transactions in both time and space, qualifying them in intricate ways. The conditions under which factors, activities, and individuals are included or excluded from such exchange are not simply shaped by what undifferentiated producers and consumers want or will tolerate. They have a social history that involves the repeated exercise of political power and the establishment and defense of property rights.[4] Because power has no place in neoclassical theory (Swedberg et al. 1987), the actual history of market forms remains outside the purview of economics.

The genesis of the market was contingent on the political actions of groups who structured it to their benefit, who defined property rights in particular ways, and who repeatedly redefined the boundaries of the institution they were making. An autonomous market did not "emerge"; it was constructed through the exercise of political and state power, not unlike the way in which Kabbalists argued that God had created the universe, by active withdrawal. That withdrawal was neither divine, nor the unintended outcome of interactions among utility-maximizing individuals. Everywhere, it required concerted action to redraw the institutional relation between state and market.

Let us consider the prototypical case of the national market as it emerged in England in the seventeenth and eighteenth centuries, as described by Lie (1988). This was not an organic coalescence of existing local markets, a new aggregation of transactions among numerous individual buyers and sellers. It was the social and political creation of new kinds of agent, primarily a small group of London-based wholesale merchants. They profited from their exclusive access to information and new national distribution networks. They used their influence in government to repeal existent legislation against middlemen merchants who, it was rightly feared, would disrupt face-to-face, normatively regulated local markets. These London-based wholesale merchants bypassed traditional local markets, in which producers and consumers traded directly, and constructed new distribution networks which had different principles of operation and different structures of market power between producers, buyers, and distributors. "The invisible hand of the national market depended on the invisibility to the populace of the minority of middlemen merchants who exploited the price differentials across regions, speculating in place and time" (Lie 1988:109). The exercise of political power was necessary to the institution of a national market that provided the wholesaler with greater market power. The national market did not emerge organically as an extension of local exchange networks; it was socially constructed *de novo* by a particular group of institutional entrepreneurs. Through their efforts, the marketplace was replaced by a placeless market in which the capacities for consumers to control prices were radically reduced. It would be difficult to explain the origins of the market as a consequence of market efficiency, if the market, as we conceive it today, did not then exist.

If the market was not formed simply by the logic of efficiency, neither was the business firm. Jung, in her revisionist social history of the rise of the Comstock mining corporations of California and Nevada, among the first joint-stock corporations in the United States, has argued that efficiency concerns had nothing to do with their formation (Jung 1988). She shows that these corporations were created by a small group of individuals who owned a substantial proportion of such mines and also the milling, timber, and quicksilver industries upon which they were dependent. Common ownership, however, was not accompanied by organizational integration. In the context of this ownership structure, corporations were formed as a way to maximize owners' profits by self-serving "transfer pricing," by securing capital from private investors, by using political power to transfer public rights, public expenditures and public lands, and by manipulating stock markets. The generation of more efficient production was, at best, a secondary concern. Because of the political and market power of the mine owners, there was no relationship between the survival of firms and their efficiency in the California/Nevada mining industry. The appearance of market competition among independent firms was used to legitimate private investment in the stock market and thereby to extract greater resources from both private investors and the state. As a result there was no relationship between movements of stock prices and actual movements in production in the mining industry because both were used to generate private profits, not corporate efficiency. Indeed, if anything, the lowest equity prices coincided with the highest levels of production (Jung 1988:213). The first corporations were thus formed to capitalize opportunistically on a market for new forms of property rights, the stock market. As Jung (1988) remarks: "If the Comstock corporations were efficient at anything it was in providing the opportunity for insiders to line their own pockets at the expense of the corporation while permitting them to violate their positions of trust at the expense of shareholders" (p. 225).

These first corporations and first stock markets, the organizational forms of which were later institutionalized, emerged as the result of inefficient, power-laden, opportunistic, malfeasance on a mass scale. Like the origins of the market in England, they depended on the collusive exercise of power derived from advantageous positions in social networks. Owners and traders brought these powers to bear on the state to redefine the parameters of exchange. It should be no surprise that the operation of markets and firms continues to depend on the exercise of these powers.

Although neoclassical economists treat the firm, including the fiduciary responsibilities of its management, as if these were derived from voluntary contracts among its "members," in fact they are legal fictions created by courts and legislatures (Clark 1985). The structure of the firm should therefore be presumed neither to be efficient nor to be changed simply by marginal negotiation among contracting parties. Change requires an investment in power. Economists refer to attempts of economic agents to move from being price-takers to price-makers as rent-seeking activity, which they tend to treat as an aberration. Rent-seeking behavior is, in effect, the pursuit of power. Yet power remains outside the corpus of neoclassical theory, reduced at best to an exogenous parameter that affects the distribution of resources in an inefficient manner.[5] Neoclassical economics can understand politics as something external that impinges on efficient markets, but it cannot understand the politics of those markets themselves. If the exercise of power is made endogenous in the marginalist model, the model becomes inoperable. Until we understand the conditions under which economic agents invest in and use power, then the conditions under which competitive and efficient markets operate will also elude us.

The pursuit of power pervades the marketplace. It draws on social relationships within and beyond the market, as well as capacities to use other institutions. But as Wallerstein (this volume) argues, the exercise of power has an economics, a calculus of mobilization and a distributional impact of its own. In his model, it is motivated by material interests such as working class uncertainty about whether the nonwage share of the product will be reinvested or not, but it is a form of collective action coordinated outside the market. Wallerstein analyzes as a dynamic game the ways in which political conflicts among unions, firms, and governments over wages and investment shape macroeconomic performance. "If the general equilibrium model is a theory of a competitive economy, the dynamic game model is a theory of a capitalist economy with strong trade unions." In such a game, patterns of wage restraint depend on the extent and manner in which wage and investment decisions are politically coordinated *outside* the marketplace. This in turn depends on how organized the workers and owners are, the modes of coordination between them, and the discounted value of future consumption, which in turn depends on the nature of state intervention and the political strength of the working class.

Legitimate economic strategy is very largely determined outside the marketplace. Neoclassical theory takes property rights as given. But it is clear that their principles are highly variable and keenly contested: witness the current struggle over the rights of shareholders, directors, and managers to control a firm's capital; between all of these and workers over the property rights involved in the labor contract; and between all these and the residents of territorial communities in which firms produce and market their goods. The contest over property rights is not one that is played out in the market, but in regulatory agencies, law courts, and legislatures. To understand how individuals work to maximize utility—the hostile take-over, dual classes of stock, "golden parachutes" granting executives certain benefits in the event of a takeover, due process rights for employees, prenotification of workers in

the event of plant closing, requirements that developers absorb public in-
frastructural costs, or environmental impact statements—requires that we
bring power, and hence the state, from the margins of economic analysis to
the very center. Because property rights attach to categories of actors and
actions, some of the most important exercises of power involve the defense
or transformation of systems of economic classification, the ways in which
people construe, categorize, and measure economic activity. Today this is
evident in the redefinition of both bonds and banks. For example, the rise of
"non-bank banks," diversified financial service corporations, has forced regulatory agencies into the adjudication of political conflicts over what constitutes a bank, demand deposits, and commercial loans (Woolley 1988).

The political resolution of these conflicts does not simply redirect the flow
of capital in quite dramatic ways, it redefines the means by which material
gains can be pursued. In her studies of California agriculture, Wells (1984)
has shown how producers of the lucrative strawberry crop sought to control
labor by redefining relations with their workforce. Faced with unionization
and the extension of protective labor legislation to farm workers, employers
introduced sharecropping—a productive relationship heavily stigmatized in
the history of American agriculture. Cast in the role of "independent contractors," agricultural workers now lost unemployment insurance and other
benefits, and found themselves deprived of the protection both of trade
unions and of legislation guaranteeing minimum wages and working conditions. Redesignating workers as tenant farmers also helped employers to
circumvent restrictions on the hiring of illegal aliens. Initially, the sharecroppers accepted their categorization as tenants. As it became clear that their
economic bargaining power was seriously curtailed, they went to court
claiming that they were the victim of illegal monopolistic practices. In the
course of the legal battle, the sharecroppers changed their position and
fought their categorization as tenants. The court found that they were in fact
"disguised workers" and thus eligible for many of the protections applicable
to wage laborers. This example shows how, through legislation and judicial
process, the state is instrumental in establishing economic categories to
which rights and obligations attach. These categorizations and the people
and activities to which they apply are repeatedly contested. Such conflicts
and their resolution may be as important as transactions in the marketplace
in shaping the organization of production and exchange.

STATES AND MARKETS

Neoclassical theory's exclusion of power, and political power in particular, derives from both normative and theoretical commitments to the institutional autonomy of the marketplace. Neoclassical economics prescribes

where the state has a chance of success by reckoning those areas in which markets are most likely to fail. It does not, and perhaps cannot, offer an explanation of where the boundary between state and market will in fact be located, or the nature of the relationship between the two. Thus, it tends to treat the state's extraction and redistribution of market resources as corrosive of the efficiency of the competitive marketplace. Although economists can explain microeconomic adaptations to its actions, they cannot explain state actions vis-à-vis the economy, much less the relationship between states and markets as a dynamic system.

Historically we cannot understand the development and operation of markets without recognizing the extent to which they have been shaped by the fiscal interests of states and forms of legitimation of state power, which have in turn been influenced by international preoccupation with military armament (Tilly 1975; Hamilton and Biggart 1988). Depending on the strategy of fiscal extraction, states have sometimes facilitated and sometimes obstructed the extension of markets (Tilly 1975; Skocpol 1985). This does not mean we should a priori accord primacy to the state. Indeed, it is striking that analysts of socialist societies, where the state is presumed to be in command, are increasingly recognizing the autonomous dynamics of "civil society" (Stark and Nee 1989). Piven and Cloward (this volume), for example, argue that state-centered analyses of welfare policies have overemphasized the role of existent governmental structures, policy precedents, and the initiative of officials concerned with the organizational capacities of the state. They argue that these state-centered analyses have neglected political conflicts over the control and cost of wage labor in accounting for the form and diffusion of the welfare state. Nonetheless, the tension between the resource requirements of the state, on whose enforcement mechanisms the economy ultimately depends, and groups that wish to maximize the return to the different resources they control in the marketplace, remains ripe for analysis. The contemporary tensions between states that wish to optimize their capacities for strategic action in a world of states, governing coalitions that must secure electoral majorities and sufficient revenues to govern, corporations that wish to achieve maximum flexibility in the allocation of capital across national boundaries and maximum profitability, and workers who wish to control the allocation of that capital in space and time and maximize their real wages over their life course are as relevant today as they were when national markets were first being created in Europe and America in the eighteenth and nineteenth centuries (Piven and Friedland 1984). As the last decade of American economic history attests, where employers adapted to sluggish growth in profits through reduced tax liability, the exercise of capitalist power continues to remain an important and underexplored alternative to productivity as a means to maximize returns on investment (Useem 1984).

If the determinants of state policies that shape costs and profitability, investment and growth, lie *outside* the marketplace, then analyses that bracket off the market are likely to be misspecified (Hibbs 1987). Domestically, for example, the growth of the welfare state has been variously attributed to the bureaucratic preoccupations of agency personnel, the electoral strength of constituencies unable to assure an adequate living from private incomes obtained in the labor market or anxious to defend what they do receive from low-wage competition, the emergence of normative commitments to a rising welfare floor below which no citizen should be allowed to fall, or as a mechanism to reproduce the patriarchal family (see Piven and Cloward, this volume, for a review). A wide variety of analysts have argued that the growth of the welfare state, driven by various forces outside the marketplace, has undercut the efficiency of both the capital and labor markets, undermined the capacity of the business cycle to prevent wage-push inflation, worsened the Keynesian trade-off between unemployment and inflation, and undercut economic growth (Korpi 1985; Piven and Cloward 1982; Cameron 1984; Gilder 1984; Wanniski 1979; Rahn 1983; Esping-Andersen 1985, but see also Wallerstein, and Myles, this volume). Certainly, the evidence indicates that different patterns of state expenditure and taxation have different impacts on short-term economic growth in the advanced western market economies (Hibbs 1987; Friedland and Sanders 1985; Korpi 1985; Lange and Garrett 1985). As Wallerstein (this volume) demonstrates formally, if workers and employers both adapt to them, taxes on incomes should not affect investment shares, only the government share; while taxes on consumption *can* be used to affect profit shares without affecting investment. Indeed, under these conditions, workers are willing to moderate wage demands because investment remains unaffected and their private wage restraint can be compensated in part through increased social wages. Wallerstein thus develops a startling conclusion: "A pro-worker government . . . could bring workers' welfare arbitrarily close to the welfare workers would enjoy if they owned the capital stock without disturbing private investment."

State monetary, fiscal and trade policies shape the international value of assets and profits denominated in a nation's currency, as well as the conditions under which factors flow into and out of the national economy. If economic analyses of these policy patterns tend toward the prescriptive, as Frieden (1989) shows, political analyses tend to be unrealistic because they fail to specify the divergent economic interests that animate state policy-making. A state's economic interests cannot be read neatly off a geopolitical map of factor endowments. Frieden argues that a state's fiscal and monetary policies are shaped by the relative power of competitive multinational corporations with overseas investments, rather than those less competitive firms that depend on the domestic market. These two kinds of owners have opposing preferences for, or interests in fiscal orthodoxy and monetary restraint as opposed to expansion, and open as opposed to protective trade policies. Competitive multinational corporations, for example, have an interest in a strong currency to protect the value of their foreign assets and can adapt to that strength by moving their production overseas. Frieden shows how American policy shifted in response to the changing balance of political power between these two sectors. Although a sectoral model of interest-group pressure is an improvement, that one can specify a model of cross-national variation in fiscal, monetary and trade policies over time *without* specifying the impacts of nonowning voters is problematic. It must assume that what benefits the multinational corporation also benefits the median voter, or that the most important parameters of economic policy are not subject to electoral influence (Moe 1989). At any rate, as our economies become increasingly open, unless we make political power endogenous to our models, we will not be able to understand fully the requisites of growth in an economic environment permeated by state action and inaction.

Patterns of state taxation, expenditure, and regulation do variously affect the growth of the economy and its distributional consequences. Although microeconomic analysis may tell us what preferences different groups will have in different state policies, it cannot provide us with an adequate explanation of the policies that the state in fact adopts. Because neoclassical economists have disregarded the role of group power relative to individual exchange, the origins and operation of politics have largely been excluded from their domain. Although economists are eager to prescribe roles for the state based on abstract models of how and whether markets operate, the real conditions under which agents might be able to follow their advice are seldom adequately explained. Economics has no theory of the state, except as a predatory firm, a necessary guarantor of property rights, a technical provider of pure public goods. In recent formulations, the effects of state policies are neutralized through the "rational expectations" of market actors.

FAMILY, GENDER, AND AGENCY

In recent decades, studies emanating from sociology, history, and anthropology have drawn attention to another social context in which the economic interests and actions of individuals are shaped and constrained. Economists have taken it for granted that 'the household' constitutes a fundamental unit for economic organization and decision-making, but why this should be so remains as vague as the definition of the unit itself. The tendency to treat the household as a "black box," a distinct modal unit of labor supply and consumer demand, tells us nothing about how its economic needs and capacities are structured by distinctions of gender and generation. Viewing it as a single managerial unit ignores the complex of interests and

motivations of which it is composed, and the fact that households depend
on many forms of collaboration that shift the locus of economic decision-
making into or out of community networks. Many recent studies have made
it clear that the failure of economic analysis to penetrate domestic relations
has debilitating consequences for macroeconomic understanding, whether
of labor migration, fiscal strategy or national development planning
(Meillassoux 1981; Murray 1981; Guyer and Peters 1985; Robertson 1987).

The "family" or "household" is highly variable in space and over time,
and contains a congeries of interests not all of which are concerned with
material welfare. A central purpose of families is the organization of reproduction, a process that has no simple economic determinants and consequences. The household is not an inert social and economic building block,
it is a set of interacting life processes, a relentlessly changing program of
needs and capacities. A disaggregated view of the household quickly reveals
this animation, and obliges us to recognize the impetus which it exerts on
economic organization.

The work of the Russian economist A. V. Chayanov earlier this century
drew attention to the significance of domestic reproductive strategies in the
formation of the peasant economy, and their active resistance to the intru-
sion of factor and commodity markets. Enthusiastically revived in the 1960s
in the West, Chayanov's ideas have been adduced to many contemporary
Third World contexts (Chayanov 1966; Sahlins 1974; Hunt 1978; Deere and
de Janvri 1981; Greenhalgh 1983). There is no reason to suppose that the
reproductive dynamism of households has lost its significance in the modern
industrial world. Nevertheless, the study of human reproduction has been
relegated to biology and demography; those who, like the sociobiologists,
pursue a serious interest in its social organization tend to be regarded as
disciplinary pariahs. Instead, reproduction is tacitly and primly assumed to
be the proper business of the domestic institution we know as "the family."
Closeted in this way, reproduction is lost to sight as an active force in society
and history. Meanwhile "the family" itself is viewed as the passive object of
economic forces, at serious risk of being put out of business by the relentless
expansion of industrial processes. Thus, the baby of reproduction is in grave
danger of draining away with the bathwater of the Western urban family.

Recently, these perceptions of reproduction and the family have been
challenged by impressive historiographic work. We now know that the small
"nuclear family" household, which was supposedly the product of industrialization, was in fact in place in Western Europe many centuries before the
Industrial Revolution began. This discovery clears the way for some startling
reversals of conventional wisdom: were family processes an instrument of
industrial transformation, rather than the converse? (Laslett 1969; Medick
1976; Levine 1977; Macfarlane 1978). Studies of more recent periods have
also made it clear that families have not simply been squeezed down to the

nuclear stereotype, stripped of influence and function. They have not only acted as economic shock absorbers in periods of rapid development, their internal processes have exerted a powerful influence on fast-growing industrial communities, shaping the organization of factories and enterprises. This is the thrust of Hareven's celebrated studies in New Hampshire early this century, further elaborated in her contribution to this volume (Hareven 1977, 1982, this volume).

It is also the implication of Myles' work (this volume) that families, gender, and life cycles are profoundly affected by the relationship between labor markets and states. The mediation of the state, and hence politics, suggests that demography is not destiny. Myles does argue that one can understand the sequence of welfare policies—poorhouse, social assistance, social security—as state-organized solutions to the changing challenges of capitalism. The third welfare state form, oriented to income security over the life course, is organized around what Myles calls a "Fordist life cycle" in which men would have high levels of employment at high wages with a retirement wage and women and children would largely depend on this wage stream for their survival. Although Myles links social security to the problem of assuring demand in capital-intensive, material production, it is a politically mediated solution, not one dictated by the logic of the marketplace itself. Indeed Myles argues that the decline of material production now opens choices about how to organize the life course in relationship to the economy, which have dramatic implications for the flexibility of the labor force in response to economic change, the extent to which people participate in the labor force at all, and the trajectory of service sector expansion. After the "Fordist life cycle," the options are clearly open.

Today, a widening group of social scientists is being persuaded of the virtues of regarding "family process" as an independent variable rather than one crudely dependent on economic process. For example, changes in the housing market and the whole pattern of savings and investment associated with pensioning arrangements are being traced to reduced fertility and increased longevity (Oppenheimer 1974; Skolnik and Skolnik 1980; Davis 1985; Anderson 1985; Elder 1985). Social responses to reproductive pressures now transcend extended families and local communities, finding expression in a much wider range of social institutions: creches and schools to assist in the process of child-rearing, banks to guarantee life savings and provide mortgages, or pension schemes to support the elderly in the closing stages of household development.

The phenomenon of the *salary* is an example of the way in which the organization of reproduction shapes economic institutions. Distinguished by a structure of rewards that rises incrementally over a *career*, the salary has been explained in terms of the increasing value of "human capital" over a lifetime of service. The implication is that the services of a 60-year-old doctor or architect are as much as 8 times more valuable than those of a 25-year-old. This is surely unreasonable: given a truly free choice, patients or clients might actually prefer the services of a freshly trained professional. Robertson (forthcoming) has suggested that the salary is an institutionalized response to *need* emanating from the organization of reproduction, rather than variable *capacity* assessed in professional competences which are often very mysterious. The steeply-rising curve of a salary responds to the accelerating demand for income to support and educate children, to buy housing, and to accumulate savings for retirement. The institution depends on middle-class power and privilege in society, and is in stark contrast to *wages,* the institutionalized structure of rewards for the working classes. In western economies these are characteristically "flat" rather than incremental, geared to piecework or hourly rates. Their effect is to leave the working class household exposed to the cyclical pressures of family development, and increase their dependence on welfare subsidies issued grudgingly by the state (see Rowntree 1922; Wynn 1970).

A closely related theme is the sexual division of labor within and between the household and the firm. Regarding this as the outcome of individual strategies for maximizing income leaves too much unexplained. A model that assumes that a household is a firm attempting to optimize output cannot account for the unchanging division of domestic labor between husband and wife in the United States, particularly the failure of men to respond to increases in the burdens of household work (Berk 1985). Households not only produce goods, they reproduce gender, the "doing" of which is inseparable from the household's productive activities (Berk 1987). Gendered divisions of labor are as important within individual firms as they are within households and in the economy at large (Bielby and Baron 1986). Alternative allocations of work among men and women, which would be materially more efficient, are evidently rejected by employers *and employees* because they would undermine the established logic and symbolism of male identity and privilege (Reskin 1987; Bielby and Bielby 1988).

The interdependence between the organization of production and reproduction as it is mediated by the state is not new. Since the nineteenth century men in the industrial world have contrived to exclude women as well as children from their domains in the labor market. They have done this both to reduce job competition and to confine women to underrated and underrewarded domestic work, the basic component of which is the organization of reproduction (Reskin 1987). Nineteenth- and early twentieth-century legislation for a "family wage" is an interesting symptom of this: in the guise of adjusting the rewards for men according to the needs of a modal household it officially reinforced the removal of women from the labor market and their confinement to the domestic domain. It is no accident that the return of women en masse to the labor market in the 1960s unleashed the political force of feminism (England and Farkas 1986).

SOCIETY AS MARKET

Some of the most important changes in the boundaries, forms, and performance of markets are located in the actions of actors who are constrained and enabled by identities, interests, and capacities located outside the market in states and households. This points to the importance of understanding society as an assemblage of institutions (Friedland and Alford 1989). Yet in the social sciences, society, viewed as either a normative or dialectical structure, seems to have lost its theoretical appeal. In Europe, the traditional haven of structuralism, social scientists no longer construct historical narratives on the grand scale. Rather, space and time are understood as "sites," "moments," "locales" or "fields" in which structure and action become fused in "micropolitics," "practice" or "structuration" (Foucault 1970; Bourdieu 1977; Giddens 1984). Some of the most extreme interpretations of culture as practice arrive, by a circuitous route, at a romantic individualism strangely similar to that of neoclassical economics (DeLeuze and Guattari 1987).

In North America, on the other hand, gravitation back toward the sovereign subject has been much more explicit. One of the great ironies is that theories developed to describe behavior within the market are now being imported wholesale for analysis of noneconomic institutions. Social structure and cultural values are extrapolated from the interactions of self-seeking individuals. The most serious doubts are about whether the egoists are smart, as in theories of public choice and "institutional" economics; or dumb, as in population ecology and its economic analogue, evolutionary economics. In the latter, the motive is survival in the frog pond rather than efficiency in the marketplace.[6] There is the heavy implication that if we have any theoretical ambitions we can expect either to be bought out or devoured by the mother discipline.

It seems perverse that economics is tightening its grip on other branches of social science at a time when an increasing number of economists are themselves questioning its theoretical adequacy. Anxieties about the meaning of rationality, the relationships between micro- and macroeconomics, discontinuities between economics and economic history, the applicability of monetary theory, or the raw empiricism of business economics contrast with the confident extension of economic models out into the realms of politics, kinship, culture, and even genetics. Theoretical doubt and dissent have exposed many social scientists to promises of redemption, and the doctrinally orthodox have responded readily with the assurance that neoclassical economics offers the prospect of theoretical unification in the social sciences.

Behavior hitherto regarded as proper to the marketplace is now to be seen as the essence of social interaction everywhere. Thus, the champion of economistic analysis, Gary Becker, argues:

> The economic approach . . . now assumes that individuals maximize their utility from
> basic preferences that do not change rapidly over time and that the behavior of different
> individuals is coordinated by explicit and implicit markets. . . . [T]he economic ap-
> proach is not restricted to material goods and wants or to markets with monetary transac-
> tions, and *conceptually* does not distinguish between major and minor decisions or
> between "emotional" and other decisions. Indeed . . . the economic approach provides
> a framework applicable to all human behavior—to all types of decisions and to persons
> from all walks of life (1981:ix).

All the mysteries of social structure—altruism, hierarchy, regulation, religious belief—can be derived from the individual pursuit of the most efficient and personally gratifying means of cooperating (Axelrod 1981, 1986).
Reflecting on Becker's "radical effort to recast all the theories of behavior
into utility theory" Daniel Bell notes that

> The crux of the argument is that where there is the pain of choice forced upon us by
> some scarce resources, we will take the most "pleasurable" route. But this hedonistic
> calculus is by itself the most narrowly culturally-bound interpretation of human behav-
> ior, ignoring the large areas of traditionalism on the one hand and moral reflection on
> the other (1981:71).

In these economistic formulations, the contours of social organization are
marked by the functional limits of individual exchange. For example, government regulation is a means for overcoming the negative externalities of
free ridership, and bureaucratic hierarchy solves the problem of opportunism and shirking. In its most open-ended formulation, the enduring structures of economic life are assumed to meet the minimum requirements of
effectiveness necessary to survive in a competitive market-like environment.
Society is to be perceived as being built from the ground up through a
multitude of individual transactions, its institutions a complex of necessary
adaptations to the technical limits of individual exchange. It is argued, for
example, that social norms evolve because of their contribution to efficiency, where the costs of search for optimal solutions would outweigh the likely
marginal benefits. However, attributing norms to a kind of bargaining inertia
makes little sense of the social "work" entailed over many decades or centuries in their production. An answer to that testing historical question "why
these norms rather than some other?" remains remote.

Rational choice theorists derive organizational arrangements—whether
party, state, household, or firm—from the rational action of individuals,
each attempting to maximize his or her utility by exchanging scarce, usually
material resources. Organizational structures such as firms, parliaments,
and municipalities are variously analyzed as unitary individual-like agents,
as market-like arenas whose structures are determined by the functional
limits of exchange, or by their efficiency in competition with other organizations.

In their quest to understand organizations, market analysts have focused on the structure of firms and of contracts. Oliver Williamson, for example, has attributed the emergence of large corporate hierarchies to the difficulties of efficient exchange where transaction costs are high, that is, where outcomes are uncertain, assets specific, actors few, and information highly localized (Williamson 1975). These corporate hierarchies emerge, Williamson argues, because they contribute to efficiency by reducing uncertainty where performance cannot be measured and individual opportunism is likely. Similarly, in agency theory organizations are analyzed as a network of voluntaristic contracts. Organizational structures derive as solutions to problems of opportunism where self-interest and the costs of surveillance might otherwise interact to produce shirking (Alchian and Demsetz 1972; Moe 1984; Perrow 1986). The transaction-cost and principal-agent theorists thus derive firm structures such as the staff-line hierarchy and multidivisional forms from the stupidity, cupidity, and lack of trust between contracting individuals. They *assume* that these forms are in fact efficient because they emerge in competitive marketplaces.

STATE AS MARKET

Application of rational-actor models has been extended from the business firm to institutions such as the household and the state. It does not seem to bother these analysts that institutions that predated the market are assumed to be animated by principles of behavior associated with a historically later institution. Thus, the limititations and failures of individual exchange are assumed to generate organizational and institutional structures, rather than vice versa. Households and states are interpreted as market analogues, as shaped by the interaction of rational agents, or as exogenous structures that pattern the costs and benefits to be obtained by these agents.

For example, public choice theorists analyze the emergence of multiple municipalities as an efficient response to the problem of delivery of public goods to differentiated residential communities. In this version of the marketplace, patterns of electoral voice and residential exit produce an equilibrium in which each municipality provides a bundle of public goods at a tax price that conforms to the preferences of the median voter (Borcherding and Deacon 1972; Deacon 1978). In the municipal marketplace, the theory assumes, for example, that the adjustment of policies to secure private capital investment and economic growth redounds to the fiscal benefit of the locality and the aggregate utility of its resident citizens (Peterson 1981). Critics have argued, on the contrary, that this theory is used to legitimate policies pursued by a coalition of economic owners whose profitability in fact depends on the growth of the locality (Molotch 1975; Friedland and

Palmer 1984). The local growth engendered is not necessarily beneficial from a fiscal, quality of life, or employment point of view for local residents (Molotch 1975; Logan and Molotch 1987; Friedland 1983).

This approach raises questions about how officials get elected and, once elected, how they actually make policy choices. In the classical formulation, for example, candidates are analyzed as vote-maximizing agents who, in a two-party, winner-take-all system of single seat constituencies, make campaign promises and ultimately government policies that approximate the preferences of the median voter (Downs 1957). Contrary to expectations that efficient elected officials would form minimum winning coalitions, it is evident that many policies are universalistic, distributed to all rather than to only those necessary to pass the legislation (Shepsle 1979). This is particularly the case with regard to 'pork barrel' policies of public goods—dams, water projects, siting of military bases—whose location will concentrate benefits in a representative's constituency. Rational-actor models of this behavior argue that candidates, given the *repeated* consideration of such issues, are always uncertain about whether they will be part of a winning coalition, hence universalistic norms are an adaptive response. This approach explains the steady increase in economic regulation as a cheap way for candidates to maximize votes because it does not impose high visible costs on the average voter. Moreover, once regulation is in force, it allows candidates to obtain campaign contributions more easily from regulated firms (Peltzman 1976).

These economistic models of policy-making have little ability to explain either dramatic shifts such as deregulation *or* things such as policy consistency in the face of unexpected shocks, the aggregation of microlevel pressures for change, or where policy preferences diverge from those likely to generate the preferred outcome (Weatherford 1988; Woolley 1988). These models suffer from a double defect: they overeconomize the polity and yet insulate it from the economy. Part of the problem is that such models assume self-interested rational exchange between materially interested constituencies, the representatives they elect, and the bureaucracies that implement the policy. In fact, voters do not act like economic maximizers (Chappell and Keech 1985; Rhoads 1985). Rather, both they and those they elect have strong normative expectations about policy consistency and the appropriate behavior for elected officials to take vis-à-vis the economy (Weatherford 1988). Thus, while it would be rational for governing regimes to engineer business cycles politically, the best available evidence indicates that they do not (Weatherford 1988). Voters in fact tend to punish office-holders who appear to manipulate the economy in order to win elections. Further, neither parties nor voters behave like individual marginalists, but act out ideological scripts for audiences of core constituents. Equally important, these models have not analyzed adequately the ways in which market changes, partially in adaptation to the policy environment, can radically destabilize the policy regime (Hammond and Knott 1988; Woolley 1988).

Weatherford (1988) argues that ideologies oriented to long-range goals are rational strategies that office-holders, and presidents in particular, develop for purposes of building coalitions. Lacking ideology, coalition members would otherwise be subject to prisoner's dilemmas if they failed to pursue their particular constituents' interests over the short term. Ideologies are functional for building the "conditional altruism" necessary to maintain the coalition's commitment to long-range economic goals. However, ideologies are more than statements about preferred objectives that shape expectations about a future flow of benefits. They also have cognitive foundations, derived from theories linking means to ends. Although critics of the idea of a value-free social science have stressed that political ideology is always implicit in social theory, it is no less important to recognize that social theory is itself embedded in practical politics. Thus, for example, the rise of economic regulation in the 1930s can be traced both to the efforts of firms in various industries to use public authority to form cartels *and* the belief that market competition had led to the depression (Hammond and Knott 1988). Coalitions are rooted not only in common interests and values, but in shared theory as well. Economic history is in part a political struggle between accounts, the truth value of which depends on their capacity to make sense of the economy. This in turn depends on the power of those who use these accounts to shape the structure and movement of the economy. In sum, the relationship between ideology, knowledge and power in the economy begs for closer study (Foucault 1970; and see Marcus, this volume).

Just as the hierarchical structure of a firm or the normative organization of professional regulation poses serious problems to an economist, political scientists see the development of bureaucratic structures as problematic for the efficient organization of representative government. Moe (1989), for example, argues that unlike the authority of firms, which derives from contractual relationships between individuals, the incumbents of public bureaucratic offices acquire preexisting "property rights"—the rights and obligations of office—which cannot be exchanged. Political scientists have increasingly applied agency theory, developed by economists to analyze the design of firms and relations among owners, managers, and workers, to the relationship between Congress and the bureaucracy. It is assumed that the same practical problems of how to control subordinates and avoid opportunism and shirking apply.

Although representatives need to get reelected, bureaucrats do not. In the case of economic regulation, political scientists argue that nonelected regulatory agencies are ultimately responsive to the electorate because agencies are either beholden to Congressional committees for their budgets, or because voters and their Congressional representatives can always produce legislation that will change their mandate or their budget, or threaten their very existence (Weingast and Moran 1983; Weingast 1984; McCubbins and Park 1987). Agencies, even with their advantages of specialized information, cannot expand their budget and authority in a manner that does not respond to the preferences of the electorate.

Moe has argued that the thesis of Congressional dominance is incorrect (1985, 1987). To apply the new 'institutional' economics, Moe (in press) suggests it is necessary to move beyond the interaction of politicians who serve ideal and passive constituencies through pliant bureaucracies toward active politicians, bureaucrats, and interest groups. He argues that the uncertainty of political property rights tends to be greater than that of economic property rights. Because there are institutionalized mechanisms within democratic polities for opponents to put public authority to uses other than a constituency intends, interest groups prefer to place programs in professional hands—in public bureaucracies highly constrained by statute, staffed with career civil servants who are insulated from appointed officials and thus from politics. Politicians contribute to the formation of such structures to distance themselves from future group conflict. Career bureaucrats also want to insulate their agencies from political intervention by relatively short-term presidents, and thereby ally themselves with the enduring interest groups who brought them into existence. "In economics, organization arises as creators find a way of governing themselves. In politics, organization arises as the creators find a way of protecting their achievements from subversion by other actors who may soon wield public authority" (Moe in press).

Moe's application of agency theory to the bureaucratic design of states is elegant and powerful, one that at last addresses the institutional specificity of the state; but it also exhibits the limits of this approach. It is striking that he uses agency theory to explain the uses of state power by the most influential interest groups. While these groups are not named, we can be certain that their interests derive from their position in the market, predominantly as owners of different kinds of capital. Thus, the typically "rent-seeking" uses of state authority, which goes unexamined and unexplained within transaction cost economics, drives an agency cost explanation of the structure of the American state. Second, political uncertainty would just as easily dictate legislative specificity as the delegation of authority to professionalized bureaucracies.[7] If public authority is in fact being used to sustain corporate profitability, this would provide an explanation of the particular form of insulation from political uncertainty. If the beneficiaries are few and/or the potential bearers of the tax or price burdens many, then such interest groups would fear the legislative process for good reason (Piven and Friedland 1984). Further, if public authority is being used to support private profitability, it is difficult to legitimate it as serving the public interest. Under these conditions, legislators who depend on the campaign contributions and investment by such interest groups will be more likely to delegate policy-making to private bureaucracies. The point is that the structure of the state is generated by something more than generic political uncertainty. To understand the structure of the firm, no less the structure of the state, one must analyze the disposition of power, the interests that are at stake, and ways in which they are promoted and defended across both market and state.

ECONOMIZING THE FAMILY

The "new household economics" has attempted to extend the logic of the market to explain family and household organization. The economization of family life undertaken by the great neoclassical dogmatist, Gary Becker, is a conspicuous example. In his *Treatise on the Family* his intention is "to analyze marriage, births, divorce, division of labor in households, prestige and other nonmaterial behavior with the tools and framework developed for material behavior." The result is a tightly constricted image of social relationships. There are very strict limits, for example, on the usefulness of regarding larger households as tradeoffs between mutual policing that discourages "shirking of duties, pilfering, and cheating" (Becker 1981:15) and the sacrifice of privacy. This is not the illumination of an elegantly simple model applied to a wider social frame of reference. It is simply a distortion.

There is no place in Becker's analysis for generalized cultural norms that structure and preempt choice. The strictly material calculus means that certain kinds of gratification have to be translated into vague notions such as "psychic income" (1981:195). Nor is the analysis sensitive to power relations that transcend and define the rubric of short-term transactions. Differences in wealth are too readily attributed to luck, imperfect information or murky notions such as "family reputation." Social class has no relevance, while ethnic differences get swallowed up in the notion of "endowed luck" and vague allusions to "genetically determined race". The fascination of such economists with Darwinian theory is often painfully evident [a chapter of Becker's *Treatise on the Family* is devoted to "Families in Nonhuman Species" (1981:202–218)]. Although Becker views marriage as the transaction of stable preferences by two free agents, the domestic division of labor is glibly taken as some sort of biological given (1981:28–31).

Such excursions may have the advantage of offering new insights into areas of study very familiar to anthropologists and sociologists. However, we should not allow Becker's imperial zeal to disguise the very real strictures that liberal application of the neoclassical paradigm places on social explanation. There *is* something to be learned from an interpretation of marriage as the self-interested transaction of productive and reproductive services. England and Kilbourne's (this volume) derivation of women's relative powerlessness in marriage from the asset-specificity and illiquidity of their skills and human capital investments is an incisive contribution to this line of thinking. But the implications of Becker's analysis are often amusing rather than instructive: a market for children would not work, he reckons, because "parents would be more likely to put their inferior children rather than their superior children up for sale or adoption if buyers were not readily able to determine quality" (1981:98–99). It is the complexities of social organization that account for the absurdity of such a counterfactual observation. No commitment, however passionate, to "the assumptions of maximizing behavior, stable preferences, and equilibrium in implicit or explicit markets" can alter that (1981:ix). More gravely, the confidence with which such reckoning is used to propose social policy can be regarded only as a public threat.

THE SOCIAL CONSTRUCTION OF ECONOMIC MAN

Neoclassical economic theory assumes that individual preferences are exogenous, ordered, and stable. How these preferences are formed is not of analytical concern because, economists argue, individuals make independent rational choices to maximize their utility. But because it does not have a theory of utility formation the neoclassical apparatus cannot take us much beyond the realm of material goods calibrated by relative prices. That realm is in fact very constricted: as Sen has pointed out, *rationality* in the model rests on the assumption that preferences are consistently ordered, *maximization* on the assumption that choices 'reveal' preferences, and *individuality* on the assumption that all acts are evaluated in terms of their anticipated consequences for the self (Sen 1977).

Recently, the premises of neoclassical economics have been called into question in a variety of ways. Experimental work by cognitive psychologists suggests that if individuals maximize utility, they often do so *within* particular contexts, rather across all contexts (Tversky and Kahneman 1981). As Frank (this volume) points out, preferences may shift dramatically depending on how choices are framed. Further, individuals treat gains and losses asymmetrically, with the latter weighing more heavily than the former. This also appears to be how voters respond to the economic performance of elected officials (Weatherford 1988). Other studies suggest that people are not always prospectively rational—basing their decisions upon an expected flow of costs and benefits—but are often retrospectively rational, justifying a prior commitment to a choice regardless of shifts in the marginal costs and benefits to be obtained from that behavior. Sunk costs, and thus *past* behavior, remain relevant to explaining current economic behavior.

Economists have made their own adaptations to the apparent adaptiveness of preferences to context, opportunity, culture, and social milieu—in short to the apparent social pliability of self. Becker, for instance, has countered by attempting to make preferences *endogenous,* arguing that we choose our preferences to maximize our utility. They have also adapted to the expressive, irrational dimensions of economic man—honor, anger, jealousy, and shame, as well as to the apparent invariance and thus "irrationality" of self. Thus, Frank (1987 and this volume) points to the functional role of "irrationality without regret." Emotions are reframed as "commitment" devices which have evolved to facilitate co-operative transactions among individuals. In both competitive and bargaining situations, emotional or ethical nonselfish behavior may lead to more efficient outcomes. This reduces the self to a form of human capital, whose hard-wired emotions and deep values are functional for exchange; attitudes are adaptive or fungible depending on their contribution to an abstract utility. The requisites of cooperation in two-person games shapes the evolution of the species. Thank God for Man Friday.

Amartya Sen has argued that we must distinguish between preferences and metapreferences, between what we want and what we think we should want. He has thus introduced a socialized individual into the utilitarian analysis, a divided and reflexive person whose choices in exchange may not reveal the bases on which he himself evaluates whether he is maximizing his utility. Such an individual can defy the logic of the marketplace, simultaneously getting more and having less. Explanation of this requires the concept of a socialized identity, an understanding of the way individual commitments are accumulated through time and reinforced through social location both inside and outside the marketplace. It thus opens the door for the nonindependence of preference formation, and an erosion of the possibilities for Pareto optimality. DiMaggio (this volume) discusses some of the ways in which the interdependence of tastes may be socially structured and how this can lead to volatility in preferences.

One of the most nettlesome aspects of the assumption of rational utility maximization is that it converts all behavior to the instrumental. The utilitarian and contractarian philosophical foundations of neoclassical economics operate with a means–ends, subject–object dualism that assumes that individuals are instrumentally rational, that they evaluate social transactions on a moment-by-moment assessment of the costs and benefits of social relations. From this perspective voting, for example, must appear a decidedly irrational form of behavior when analyzed on a cost-benefit basis, because the marginal contribution to the outcome is small, and the benefits can be enjoyed without voting. But the decision to work is no less problematic.

Work provides identities as much as it provides bread for the table; participation in commodity and labor markets is as much an expression of who you are as what you want. Although economists typically assume that work is a disutility to be traded off against leisure or income, it actually contains other kinds of utility, ranging from the expression of an identity (I am a metal worker), to relative performance (I am a good metal worker), social value (It is good to be a metal worker—or—It is good to work), gender (It is good for a man to be a metal worker), or prestige (It is better to be a metal worker than a salesperson).

When Americans are asked about whether they would work, even if they did not need the money, the overwhelming majority say yes: that nonwork brings depression, stress, and even death in its wake; and that monetary income is only roughly correlated with "job satisfaction."[8] These socially constructed utilities have an impact on the structure of wages and the operation of labor markets. Frank (this volume), for example, shows that the extent to which individuals are concerned about the absolute level of their wages as opposed to their level relative to their co-workers changes the relationship between individual wages and productivity. Certainly, the utilities that individuals derive from their participation in the economy will shape the probability that they will shirk, misrepresent their performance, or behave opportunistically. These utilities will affect the level of transaction costs and hence the need for organizational structures designed to control them.

As the term *homo economicus* implies, the rational, utilitarian individual assumed by neoclassical economics is gendered. Yet recent research indicates that *he* has also been socialized to participate in the marketplace as a condition of maleness. In their challenge to Becker's neoclassical explanation of wage differentials over the male and female life course, Bielby and Bielby (1988) found that the allocation of female effort in the workplace was much more responsive to marginal increments in their human capital than it was for men. For men, working fulfills strong normative expectations formed early in a man's life about what a male does, whereas for women the absence of such expectations means that they act more like "economic men," such that marginal material calculations have more impact on their behavior. Although the specific empirical findings are contrary to DiMaggio's predictions (this volume), they suggest the utility of his agenda of studying social variation in orientation toward exchange.

Many of the most important dimensions of economic life—material security, prestige, meaningful and gratifying work, sociability, craftsmanship—do not have explicit prices. Taken beyond priced commodities, and hence beyond the marketplace, the postulate of rational utility maximization becomes at best speculative and at worst tautologous. Even if one can derive individual "shadow" prices, one cannot derive aggregate utilities on which assessments of efficiency depend. Economic life is permeated by expressive interests that are not tradable and which cannot be rated as commensurable choices on a single schedule of preferences.[9] If preferences are formed adaptively, it means they are shaped by the market. Taken to its logical conclusion, individuals are as much the dependent objects of the market as they are its sovereign subjects. If people are retrospectively rational, if they form preferences based on the options that are open to them, it turns the premises of neoclassical welfare economics in on itself: markets aggregate utilities that have been profoundly shaped by those markets themselves.

But we would go farther. Economic life is social in more than a frictional sense. A market is not simply an allocative mechanism. It is also a system for generating and measuring value, for producing and ordering preferences that in turn become embedded in culture. Marx's labor theory of value, however flawed, must be understood not only as an effort to understand the "objective" laws of capital, but as a theory of capitalist culture. As ethnographic work has demonstrated across cultures, the commodification of social life has profound impacts on the discourse through which value is understood and measured and hence preferences formed (Taussig 1980; Marcus this volume).

If we understand that capitalist markets have powerful cultural effects, we can trace Sen's "metapreferences" to particular institutions. We may also begin to make sense of the finding that half of all Americans believe they buy more than they need, or the discovery that there is no association between marginal shifts in a society's real income and its citizens' sense of satisfaction with their lives (Rhoads 1985:158,165). On the other hand, we can also address explicitly how markets are shaped by other institutional structures. Economists have admitted patterns of social interaction into market analysis through devices such as the "demonstration effect," whereby the preferences of the influential few are diffused to the many. But as DiMaggio (this volume) and Zelizer (1989) both argue, the social organization of preferences goes deeper than this. People express identities, social relationships, and cultural systems of classification and valuation through the goods they consume.[10] Preferences are formed not simply in response to the opportunities available, but by the nature of the discourse through which people understand what choices are available, what it is legitimate or socially appropriate to want, and according to the particular metric in which its costs and benefits are to be evaluated (for example, income, efficiency, profitability, productivity, production, power, security, autonomy, visibility, prestige, calories, pleasure). The ways in which markets shape and are shaped by processes of social measurement are a promising avenue for investigation. It requires, however, that we do not limit ourselves to such market-derived measures as "psychic income" or "revealed preferences."

ATOMIC MAN

The failure to explain the formation of preferences is linked to the assumption that the economy is engendered by autonomous individuals who interact instrumentally through exchange. It is arguable that a market economy could not operate efficiently if individuals were truly instrumentally egoistic, participating lawfully only when the probable benefits of guile are outweighed by its costs. Thus, Shapiro (1987) has drawn attention to the efficiency of trust for exchange, and the ways in which attempts to commodify trust lead to inefficiency and escalating costs. The reality of economic life is that most actors interact repeatedly over time and thus form expectations about each other's behavior, constructing patterns of association that are not only valued in themselves but become mechanisms for the dissemination of information and for the control of each other's behavior.

As Granovetter (1985 and this volume) has forcefully argued, in market exchange—particularly in labor and capital markets—actors are embedded in interpersonal social networks. Individuals take up particular positions in those networks and the networks themselves are structured in particular ways. Granovetter argues that "dense" networks facilitate the flow of information and the formation and enforcement of norms. Thus, for example, Baker (1984) found that as the number of traders in stock options increased, price volatility also increased. Reduction in network density diminished the conformity of members' behavior. These social networks are resources that individuals can exploit for market advantage, as well as sources of constraint on the strategies and even the preferences that individuals adopt. Thus, Granovetter points to the ways in which the formation and efficiency of firms are generated not out of fields of atomized individuals, but out of denser social networks in which the commitments are neither too extensive nor too diffuse.[11] Neoclassical economics, of course, assumes that information asymmetries are inimical to efficient markets. If social networks shape the flow of information, then study of their incidence, structure, and reproduction is a prerequisite to understanding the conditions for such markets to obtain.

Not surprisingly, because established social networks are resources of value in exchange, particularly with respect to the dissemination of information, individuals act instrumentally in their patterns of association. Similarly, it has been shown how corporations shape the private social and public political lives of their top personnel (Kanter 1977). Indeed, the behaviors that constitute an individual's most "private" identity—what and how they eat, their clothes, their leisure and language, the movies they watch—have been adduced by Bourdieu, in his own non-neoclassical, nonmaterialist economization of "cultural capital" in which upwardly mobile individuals invest in order to achieve positions of economic power (Bourdieu 1977).

As one ascends the corporate hierarchy and as markets become more concentrated, strategic information becomes increasingly relevant to profitability. Personal trust is critical to the transmission of such information across firm boundaries because this information cannot be easily validated, its transmission may even be illegal, and access to it may be strictly regulated (Friedland and Palmer, forthcoming). It is thus not surprising that social homogeneity in general, and membership in elite or upper class social institutions in particular, become increasingly important for access to those positions and industries, notably in banks in which the exchange of information requires trust (Useem 1984; Friedland and Palmer, forthcoming). Social class then helps to reproduce asymmetrical information flows. Similarly, intense market dependencies between firms do not remain impersonal exchanges for long. This is particularly true where firms with low market power depend on firms with high market power. Such market dependencies tend to be overlaid by patterns of interlocking directorates, which have some impact on corporate profitability and capital allocation (Burt 1983; Mintz and Schwartz 1985; Pfeffer 1987).

But social networks are not simply resources to be exploited contingently by individuals and firms. Their structure endures over time and has an impact on the prevalence of different economic forms and perhaps other aggregate outcomes as well. Social interaction is less costly and more conducive to trust when individuals are physically close to one another, can observe each other repeatedly in both public and private, or can garner information from others who also have such access. This suggests that the geographic distribution of firms will affect the adoption of other forms intended to otherwise internalize market uncertainty (Palmer, Friedland and Singh 1986). Friedland and Palmer (forthcoming) argue that because the centers of corporate decision-making were and continue to be more dispersed in the United States, capitalists were less cohesive socially and politically, and as a result, multidivisional structures were adopted earlier and more extensively and family control became more attenuated than in France, Britain, and Japan. In these latter countries, private and public capital is concentrated in Paris, London, and Tokyo, interlocking tends to coincide with ownership linkages, there is a greater incidence of holding companies, corporate capital is more cohesive both socially and politically, and there is more informal coordination with the state. The concentrated and coincident geography of corporate and state capital thus produces social networks that substitute for the forms of market internalization and interfirm coordination found in the United States. The general point is that social networks may facilitate interfirm exchange under conditions in which transaction cost economics would predict internalization through hierarchy. To understand the relative performance of different organizations of production and exchange, it is necessary to understand not only the microeconomics of social life, but the social structure of economic life.

MARKETS AND INSTITUTIONS

Most neoclassical economists derive the norms and forms of the economy from the technical limits of exchange and the costs of arranging transactions.

A number of scholars in what can rightfully be called the institutionalist school of organizational research argue that this simply is not so. It is certainly not the case outside the capitalist west, where, in Korea, Taiwan, and Japan, organizational forms appear to mirror patterns of authority found in the state and family (Hamilton and Biggart 1988).[12] Nor is it the case where means–ends relationships are opaque, as in public institutions such as schools or police departments (Meyer and Rowan 1977). But even with regard to the development of the American marketplace, the institutionalists argue that multidivisional structures, insurance, and even contracts diffuse among a population of firms not because they are efficient, but because they are perceived to be an 'appropriate' form of organization given the tasks at hand. As a result, other actors are more likely to transact with those firms who use the 'appropriate' form and thereby assure their effectiveness as measured by control over resources (DiMaggio and Powell 1983; DiMaggio this volume; Powell this volume). Thus, a contract may not be a source of trust in the sense that it is enforceable by the state in the event of breach, but because it indicates an agent who is trustworthy precisely because he is willing to sign a contract (Zucker 1986). Legitimacy breeds effectiveness just as much as the reverse.

Actions are not simply embedded in social networks; they are embedded, Molotch (forthcoming) argues, in institutions. This assumes an order of individual rationality different from the formal sort relied on by economic models. People exhibit a "practical rationality," that is, their behavior is premised on their knowledge of the way in which an institution, like a restaurant, works and what must be done, in a specific context, to get the job done. Thus, Molotch argues, people leave tips in restaurants to which they will never return, "not because they are nice but because they are rational". In this practical rationality, there is a need to appear socially competent. "That life is hard is evidence that the essence of rationality is not the ability to follow rules or atomistic greed, but the capacity to appear appropriate under diverse settings and ever-changing circumstance". Thus, within the institution of the marketplace, displays of atomistic rationality are done, in part, to appear competent.

This approach suggests that definitions of risk, normal levels of profitability, assets, liabilities, valuation and measurement of time, credit worthiness, and even productivity are culturally specific, institutionalized through categories and norms that are reproduced through the routines of states, financial intermediaries, and major corporations. These definitions or "labelings" have real material consequences, whether it be the determination by the underwriters of corporate paper that loans to smaller, younger companies constitute "junk" bonds; changes in accounting *conventions* (Montagna 1986) such that, for example, bank assets can no longer be valued at their original purchase price; or as Marcus (this volume) discusses, that a national budget adequately represents its economy.[13] In Keynes' economics, it was the failure of representation—of money to reflect value, and the tendency of workers to respond to nominal as opposed to real wages, that had such perverse consequences for that sublime solution of full-employment equilibrium. Social measurement is a textual and frequently contested dimension of all institutions, including the economy. The very accounting schemes by which we measure our national product shape the economy they purport to represent because they provide criteria by which governments are evaluated and the bases by which owners of capital make judgments about the likely impact of future policies.

Block (forthcoming) argues that the datum of Gross National Product, for example, increasingly fails to measure either productivity or aggregate welfare. The government's contribution to this measure of output is measured only by its purchase of goods and services. The ways in which the provision of new public goods is necessary for the use of new technologies, for example, fail to register. The GNP measure also fails to capture capital savings (which become increasingly important in the postindustrial economy), the movement of activities into and out of the marketplace, the value of "free" time, quality as opposed to price changes, and a host of positive and negative externalities. Yet decision-makers in both the private and public sector base their decisions about capital flows and public policy on marginal movements in this magical number. In the postindustrial world, the entire distinction between investment and consumption is breaking down. Consumption contributes increasingly to productivity and production, and, conversely, work is becoming for many people a form of consumption. The implication of Block's analysis is that the categories by which we measure value, our representations of the economy, are integral to its operation. Systems of classification are not simply legitimation, although they may be that too. They are material forces.

We can perhaps see this most clearly in the transformation of socialist economies currently under way. Stark (forthcoming) has made an ethnographic study of a Hungarian work partnership composed of workers who use their skills, contacts, and positions in the Party outside of regular hours in a form of subcontracting within socialist enterprises. He shows how conflicts over institutional boundaries are coincident with conflicts over evaluative criteria, and, thus, the returns to these various forms of capital. During socialist factory hours the workers sold their time; but while working in partnership, at first they sold their skills and later the product of their labor. Stark shows that although the skilled workers who formed the partnership were motivated by the chance to make more income, they were also motivated by the opportunity to demonstrate their skill, which was underutilized and rewarded in ways that required them to act dishonorably during regular working hours. The effort to seek conditions for efficiency was inseparable from efforts to realize an identity as a skilled worker, to be properly honored and rewarded materially for it, and to demonstrate the impropriety of the distribution of power and income during regular hours. That struggle required that the partnership confine its membership to nonmanagerial and nontechnical personnel. When it was forced to negotiate as a result of its conflict with the socialist factory's management, the partnership ultimately "hired" an outsider, an engineer, to protect its identity as a collective entrepreneur composed of skilled workers and to avoid having to validate a manager as its "representative" or "emblem."

Utility formation is institutionally specific. It is not simply that individuals are either inherently rational or irrational, self- or other-regarding; rather it is that the institutional contexts in which individuality and rationality are appropriate are learned. Efforts to analyze all activities in the idiom of the market imply that values are transacted with full cognizance of costs and benefits. Markets reduce values to a common metric, but other institutions—households, states, or churches—generate values, and hence utilities, which cannot be traded off against each other. Relativization through the mechanism of price undercuts the bases of those values. Thus, the instrumentalization of the relationship between citizen and state has pushed the state to legitimate its behaviors in terms of their economic consequences rather than, for example, their procedural legitimacy (Hall 1982).

Individuals are still confronted with instrumental choices within each institutional realm, but one of the reasons why they are distinct institutions is because values are *not* freely transferable between them. The values associated with the relationships between parents and children, states and citizens, priests and laity, neighbors, friends and enemies are transferable only in the most restricted, metaphoric sense. An individual would be at grave risk if he were unable to discriminate the expressive as well as the instrumental behavior appropriate to each context. In our society, for example, we jeopardize our long-term interests if we confuse gifts with commercial transactions—a dilemma which can quickly lead to charges of graft and corruption. According to the anthropologist Malinowski (1961), Melanesians were likewise appalled by people who approached the ritual exchanges of the *kula* in the same idiom as the trading relationship known as *gimwali*. The two sorts of exchange would be conducted between the two partners almost concurrently, but although exchange of *kula* valuables would appear almost casual, *gimwali* in ordinary commodities could involve intense bargaining.

As we have seen, economists' bold efforts to understand institutions consist largely in extending the logic of the efficient market to everything from private property to norms of reciprocity and family life. Institutions emerge as solutions that solve problems of externalities while economizing on transaction costs (Oberschall and Leifer 1986:233; Mueller 1984). The resulting formalistic images cannot represent the enduring qualities of institutions which are simultaneously composed of a corpus of categories, theories, symbols, and values (or "social cognition" as DiMaggio calls culture) and the social structures through which they are made manifest. It is by virtue of these meanings and powers that families or friendships are formed and dissolved, that regimes rise and fall, and that some states identify others as enemies and go to war. Viewing them as bargaining equilibria, teetering from one transaction to another, leaves too much unsaid.

TIME AND THE MARKETPLACE

Time, economists like to tell each other, is a device to prevent everything from happening at once. No transaction is instantaneous, and even the most rapid bargaining process is a sequence of events that qualify each other. Thus, in a polemic against the static, objectivized, product-oriented understanding of "the market," Brenner points out that time does not simply separate one transaction from another, it distinguishes new products, services or agents from old ones. "The difficulty with the definition of markets arises because of *innovations*," he declares, "innovations that change the number and quality of goods perceived as good substitutes, and because of different perceptions of demands for new products" (1987:3). However, these things are largely what business is about.

Political, religious, familial, and other processes all have different periodicities (and spatialities) through which actions are imbued with distinct meanings. Trying to subordinate our comprehension of all of these to the peculiarly narrow temporal logic of economic analysis presents serious difficulties. Economists, for example, have long struggled to explain how such things as savings behavior, income flows, or the accumulation of "human capital" are structured by variations over an individual's life course (Lydall 1955; Ando and Modigliani 1963; Atkinson 1971; Heckman 1975). Once again, a rational actor is excised from social time and space. Especially if this lifetime is viewed in the distorting mirror of synchronic, cross-section analysis (see Browning 1985), it is robbed of its meaning within the context of human reproduction, a process which transcends individual lives in many ways (Robertson 1987, and forthcoming). Our understanding of decisions about child-rearing are complicated not only by the fact that costs and benefits are distributed over many decades, but because we are simply unable to distinguish the material calculus from the many other values and motives, which are not accountable in the idiom of rational choice. If our analytical horizons are confined to the rhythms and locales of economic activity (the cycles of crop production, trade, or industrial manufacturing) how can we even perceive those interests that derive from the formation and dissolution of households, and that link one generation through several decades to the next?

England, in her collaboration here with Kilbourne and elsewhere with Farkas (1986), has argued that cultural values shape the power differentials in gender, as expressed in the sexual division of labor, the devaluation of the female sphere, and women's tendencies to be less self-oriented and more child-oriented than men. Although England and Kilbourne (this volume) insist that values are "endogenous" to an individual's "structural role," their analysis remains premised on a decidedly economistic view of the institution of marriage. Reduced to the static image of an "implicit contract" the social institution becomes amenable to appraisal in the neoclassical idiom. Why, England and Kilbourne wonder, do women not seek to consolidate their interests in "formal" written contracts before marriage? The answer is as old as time: Because marriage is not a state but a lengthy process, a sequence of eventualities extending through child rearing and career promotions into old age, all of which can be anticipated only in the vaguest nuptial vows.[14] This is well known to the Nuer of the Sudan, whose "wedding" is not a single event but extends over many years, involving a sequence of transactions of sexual services, children, and cattle. Their celebrated ethnographer, Evans-Pritchard, was able to perceive this because he understood Nuer marriage as an institutionalized process, not just as a transaction bound by a single contract (Evans-Pritchard 1951; see also Oberschall and Leifer 1986; Marsden 1984).

It was the social nature of time, the importance of expectations about the future, that led economists like Keynes to recognize that full employment equilibria were not a "natural" state of affairs. Unless we are to succumb to the current fantasy of rational expectations where actors are all economists and actuaries to boot, we must recognize that socially and culturally conditioned expectations about the future shape that future. Time is what we make it. Together with space, time is the medium in and through which exchanges, as well as the arenas in which they occur, take on the characteristics of *social institutions:* They become repositories of information and meaning, which in turn advise economic decisions, and they acquire those social encumbrances that are an embarrassment to models of individual economic rationality.[15] But without this social apparatus we cannot as rational individuals make reliable distinctions among people, objects and relationships; we cannot know whom we can trust or respect; and we cannot exert authority over one another.

CULTURE AND ECONOMIC CRITIQUE

For most economists social institutions are too distant from the transactions of individuals to be of interest or analytical use. Sociologists concerned to bridge this gap between action and culture have found a promising tactic in the notion of *social networks*. The implication in Granovetter's approach to the "embeddedness" of networks (this volume) is that reiterated transactions will congeal into statistical norm and thence be translated (precisely how remains unclear) into cultural norm. Wending his way between economic and social "overdetermination" he seems intent on reconciling those who would wish to draw other institutions into the economic domain and those who would prefer to draw the economy—and economics—into culturally grounded social institutions.

In his polemic on "Culture and Practical Reason" (1976), the anthropologist Marshall Sahlins has proposed what Granovetter might call a "socially overdetermined" version of the institutionalist position. Insisting that custom is not "fetishized utility," he "takes as the decisive quality of culture . . . not that this culture must conform to material constraints, but that it does so according to a definite symbolic scheme which is never the only one possible." Hence, he declares, "it is culture which constitutes utility" (pp.x, viii).

> The unity of cultural order is constituted by . . . meaning. And it is this meaningful system that defines all functionality; that is, according to the particular structure and finalities of the cultural order . . . [F]or functional value is always relative to the given cultural scheme.
> . . . no cultural form can ever be read from a set of 'material forces,' as if the cultural were the dependent variable of an inescapable practical logic (Sahlins 1976:206).

For most economists this will be pure mumbo-jumbo. How can we prove the "unity and distinctiveness of culture as a symbolic system" (p.206)? How can we *know* this unified culture? Is it in one brain or a million? Or must we take it on trust that it is "out there" in some other, metaphysical sense? For many it will appear that Sahlins has fetishized meaning instead of practical utility, and replaced one causal loop (economic transactions make economic transactions) with another (culture makes meaning makes culture). Once again we have the clearest impression that the argument is structured antithetically by economics, the mother discipline we love to hate.

Sahlins' critique is directed mainly against Marxian materialism, so often seen as the radical alternative to the functionalism of the Western liberal tradition. If we are seeking a view of economy from society that offers a clear conception of power, agency, history, and ideology, it would seem that we need look no further than the dialectical materialism of Marx, a "scientific theory of history" centered on the forces, factors, and relations of production. Alas, in offering an escape from the marketplace, it proposes its own 'overdetermined' theory of production coupled to a teleology that many find both rationally and morally unacceptable (Dunn 1979:80ff). In reality these political aspirations for communism have progressed no further than state socialism, in which rigorous management of the economy is starved of vital information about supply and demand. Periodically, these failures revive enthusiasm for the competition of free men and free markets. Meanwhile in the capitalist states, liberalism engenders a different sort of disgust, and a periodic plea for more equitable means of distribution than the invisible hand. In these periods of intellectual disillusionment in the West, historical materialism has filled the vacuum, producing a flurry of Marxisms. However, to the extent these revisions stray too far from the history of production toward the logic of exchange, they lose their Marxist credentials. Situated so resolutely beyond the marketplace, Marxist theories leave too much unexplained; and so the pendulum swings back again in favor of the liberal intellectual tradition.

This dialectic continues to divide the modern world, creating a partisanship in the academy that admits little in the way of compromise or synthesis. Each swing of the pendulum confronts us again with that ancient ideological impasse: how are the feral, selfish instincts of individual human beings moderated and constrained by the aggregations in which they live?

This issue lay behind the debates about nature and nurture, heredity and environment, personality and culture, individual freedom and public constraint. It persists in numerous analytical dichotomies: macro and micro, psychology and sociology, the "bottom-up" vs. the "top-down" view of society and social behavior. Doctrinally, this disposes some people to view society as a composite of individual actions, and others to view individual interaction as expressions of elaborate social programs. It has tended to produce one-sided obsessions with the importance of production as against exchange, class as against money, conflict as against consensus, the necessity of planning as against the "invisible hand." These dialectics only exacerbate the polarity between explanation of the economy as individual initiative and of society as collective interest.[16] It also cripples our understanding of the institutional differences between modern capitalisms and socialisms.

For Sahlins, no materialist theory, whether marxist or liberal, has made meaning central to the interpretation of economic life. Actions have to be meaningful to be efficient, but institutions have to be efficient, or at least effective, to give meaning to action. Again there is the integral relationship of truth and power. Institutions are a kind of shorthand: sets of information that individuals can learn, use and pass on to others *without* fretting too much about *all* the details. They are abstractions about behavior, built up over time, expressive of power, categories, values, and all manner of affective relations, and in some sense slotting together into that omnibus abstraction we call "culture." It is this very conciseness, their summary qualities, and their consistency within a broader cognitive and normative framework that give institutions much of their power in our lives. Their capacity to aggregate and simplify is of the very greatest significance in understanding how and why people behave as they do in marketplaces.

We need not assume that social norms are stable or consensual. Rather they are transacted in daily life and are often bitterly contested. The multiple logics of different institutions present individuals with different vocabularies of motive (loyalty, acquisitiveness, faith) and symbolic systems by which to create and measure value (nation, money, religion). They also find expression in different techniques for producing and distributing these values (national armies, markets, churches). Some of the most important conflicts in society are over institutional boundaries and the criteria by which different activities are to be organized (Friedland and Alford 1989). Every marketplace is assaulted, from time to time, by conflicting logics. Is the supply of oil, for example, to be regulated by profit-maximizing transnational corporations, by states seeking to conserve strategic resources, or according to the needs of people in households for heat, power and, transportation? In what sense is water a "public good" if the problem of scarcity is resolved by raising tariffs rather than by equitable rationing?

The resolution of such conflicts has enormous consequences for material production and allocation, but they also matter for the cultural order of our societies. The market itself cannot offer an explanation of its own boundaries. Because individuals are whole persons whose lives transect different institutions, they not infrequently attempt to transfer the logic of one institution to secure their interests in another. This is not to say, as Piven and Cloward (this volume) show in the case of family values and the design of welfare state, that they do not also use the logic of other institutions as pure legitimation of action that has another purpose altogether. However, a good example of its effective use is contemporary China, where individuals, particularly those disadvantaged in the market and state bureaucracy, attempt to control those with resources through Confucian kinship ethics and the artful manipulation of *quanxi,* or gift-giving (Yang 1989). Closer to home, workers in the capitalist West have consistently extended the logic of citizenship to the economy where they bargain about entitlements to particular living standards, working conditions, minimum wages, terms of employment, access to due legal process, and control over capital investment (Edelman 1985; Marshall 1964; Esping-Andersen 1985). Just as some push to make the state, including its courts, behave in a market-like manner, others push to make the market operate more like a democracy wherein all are granted various rights of social and economic citizenship.[17]

It is not only economists who reach for their guns when the word "culture" is mentioned. The idea is just too vague for minds craving scientific exactitude, too redolent of idealism for the materialist. "When all other explanations fail" Caiden and Wildavsky remark, "the analyst can always try to save the situation by saying that some amorphous glob called culture is responsible for the phenomenon he cannot explain" (1974:xvi). Those who insist on the cultural viewpoint too rarely have hard proof of its salience in economic transactions. Moreover, they keep one card up their sleeves, which seems to put orderly discussion itself in jeopardy: the discipline of economics is itself a cultural artifact, an unselfconscious victim of its own narrow discourse. It would, of course, be easy to turn the tables, and point out that the cultural critics are themselves have no better grip on their own discourse. The suspicion hardens as proponents of "cultural man" delight in the "free play" of various postmodernisms which deny any form of discipline or convergent analysis (see Lyotard 1984).

This cultural relativization of economics is emotionally colored by an antipathy to what Zelizer (1989) characterizes as "the boundless market," a predatory and alienating force that offends the populist temperament of many social scientists. Many of them would prefer to see the market—and the economic theory which justifies it—as "subordinate" (Zelizer) to other sorts of social value. In a bold essay on 'Economics as Culture,' Gudeman makes the point that "Any set of economic constructions is a kind of mystification or ideology" (1986:154). The Cobb–Douglas production function is as much a cultural artifact as the theory of natural and supernatural regeneration that Melanesian islanders use in their horticulture. "I would base a cultural economics upon the direct comparison and contrast of metaphors and models of livelihood" (p.ix). Gudeman, it seems, is prepared to suspend disbelief and give every folk theory a sporting chance. This boundless populism proceeds from an unhappiness about "our" economic models, which he sees as emanating from the work of David Ricardo: mathematical in their structure, Euclidian and "derivational" in their linear argument, and "universal" in their intended application. We have no basis for presuming, Gudeman argues, that they are better or truer than the economic models of "the exotics." An economics comprising some sort of common denominator embracing the ideas of Africa, Melanesia and Wall Street is very hard to imagine. In pursuing this, Gudeman evidently fails to recognize the real power of Western economics: that it was devised to generalize about a general phenomenon, the industrial capitalist transformation of the world. It is no accident that Gudeman's own Panamanian peasants are trading their less effectual economic rationales for ones more familiar to ourselves. For reasons fair or foul, the latter simply afford a better purchase on the opportunities and problems confronting modern Panamanians. Our economics now "works" in ways that theirs does not. But we would argue that neoclassical economics cannot explain *why* it works, for it must convert capital, labor, technology and money into *things*, when in fact their nature is dependent on particular kinds of social relationships. Neither the market, nor economics, can represent the social relationships that make the use of those "things" possible.

We have, however roughly, mapped a territory; we have not produced the tools to explore it. The contributions to this volume make it clear that our visions of economy and society, and our analytical methods, are still configured by the rival disciplines of the social sciences. Disciplinarity itself is no vice—it is merely the division of academic labor. But if disciplines close off access to domains within the broad field of economy and society, *and* then proceed to claim universality for the explanations they devise (the "over-determination" of which Granovetter warns us here), something is seriously amiss. Central issues in one domain become marginalia in another: power or culture becomes an "imperfection" for the economist, bargaining among individuals is lost in the normative and classificatory schemes of the cultural anthropologist. We should not have to choose between a cultural theory stripped of agency and an atomized and deracinated world of incessant contract makers, each seeking marginal advantage.

Ultimately, our dissatisfaction with economic paradigms and with our own efforts to rectify them turns on what we believe makes "good theory." Again, standards vary according to discipline and individual temperament. Theorizing is always in some measure an act of faith; but as Hart (this volume) points out we have good reason to suspect an economics which has become a secular religion whose epistemology, like Newtonian mechanics, is rooted in a preindustrial world of handicrafts and agriculture. Fervent belief in the "invisible hand" is no substitute for a precise understanding of how and *why* that hand works.

One way in which theoretical temperaments vary is in their modesty or grandiloquence. Too often what is merely an *explanation* is touted as a *theory*. Some "theories," such as social networks, are more truthfully meth-ods of enquiry. To earn its keep a theory must be bigger than that: it must move beyond proximate causes and middle-level explanations, make many more connections, and move freely and brightly from one context another. If our grand theories are crumbling we can either patch them up or look for something better. Today it seems that if we are not doctrinal die-hards, we are too easily seduced by some flashy explanation masquerading as grand theory.

A more sober and conservative response, evident in many of the contribu-tions to this volume, is to insist on more catholic use of what we already know, and to pay more attention to its empirical validation. Neoclassical economics has a poor reputation in this regard—it is a consumer rather than a producer of hard facts (Hirsch et al. 1987). More than one critic has underscored its rhetorical qualities. But again, we should not be enthralled by scientism, or worse statisticism: only knowing what we can prove can extinguish originality, the speculative approach to economy and society that has, in the past, afforded vital flashes of illumination. As an antidote to positivism, Marcus and others pin their hopes on the "postmodern" enthusi-asm for *interpretation*. This is a frame of mind which suspects *any* theory of hegemonic tendencies, and wants to scrutinize how we think before we think. Skeptics would say that if we become so self absorbed we shall end up like the proverbial centipede, unable to walk, far less make any sense of the world about us.

If one of our problems is the extent to which our disciplines have divided us, then we should indeed make a virtue of interdisciplinarity (Eichner 1983). It is probably wrong to think of the development of social science as increasing compartmentalization. Periods of intellectual growth have in fact been marked by a studious transgression of boundaries. But they have been initiated by movements outside the academy: the excitement and trauma of the industrial revolution, disillusionment in the face of the barbarism of imperial war, fascism, depression, decolonization, and persistent poverty in the Third World. We face our own challenges, many of which hinge on the problematic relationship between economy and society on various spatial and temporal scales. If we are galvanized by some urgent desire to put the world to rights, maybe we will find a motive for collaboration other than the internal scholastic rumblings of discontent that draw us into arenas, like the one represented in this volume, today.

NOTES

1.   The conference from which these essays are drawn grew out of the Economy and Society seminar at the University of California at Santa Barbara. Our introduction draws on the discussions of this seminar, whose faculty participants included William Bielby, Stephen LeRoy, Harvey Molotch, Stephen Weatherford, John Woolley, and Mayfair Yang. We are indebted to Charles Maier for his virtuoso performance in the role of rapporteur and clearer of the bases, and to Cliff Kono who made sure that the papers moved expeditiously among the players. Michael Burawoy, Jeff Frieden, Terry Moe, Victor Nee and Viviana Zelizer all made valuable contributions to the conference. Their papers are being published elsewhere (see Frieden 1989; Moe 1989; Nee, forthcoming; Zelizer 1988). As a small and fragile society of scholars, we are grateful to the College of Letters and Science at UCSB, and Provost David Sprecher in particular, for their economic support for both ventures. We are especially grateful to Paul DiMaggio, David Stark, and John Sutton for their comments on this introduction.

2.   Albion Small of the sociology department of the University of Chicago complained at the time that sociology had become "a convenient label for leftovers" (Swedberg 1987:19).

3.   More recently Ouchi (1980) has made a similar distinction between market, bureaucracy, and clan, governed respectively by prices, rules, and tradition.

4.   Nee (forthcoming), in the paper presented at the conference, demonstrates empirically the ways in which the rise of the market shifted the balance of power within the Chinese economy.

5.   Thus, for example, transaction cost theorists argue that new organizational forms and particular definitions of property rights emerge because of their contribution to efficiency (Williamson 1975; Alchian and Demsetz 1973). Whether the forms are more efficient is rarely, if ever measured. It is simply assumed because, given their location in a market environment, they continue to survive and diffuse. The exercise of power, while recognized empirically, is treated as an exogenous phenomenon, unimportant in the explanation of organizational change (Williamson and Ouchi 1981).

6.   Population ecology and evolutionary economics analyze the market, but not as an efficient series of exchanges tending toward equilibrium.

7.   We are indebted to John Woolley for this point.

8. See Block (forthcoming), as well as Burawoy (1979), who points to the critical role of task execution or "making out" as a meaningful game that motivates work effort and the flow of production.

9. Those who study individual behavior in precapitalist, prestate societies or in nonmarket, nonstate institutional arenas often attempt to save the premise of individual instrumental rationality by expanding the sources of utility that individuals try to optimize: prestige, honor, power, holiness, security, wives, or whatever (see Hatch 1989).

10. Sidney Mintz's essay (1985) on sugar is a remarkable exposition of the ways in which tastes are formed and consumption socially organized over lengthy periods of history.

11. Thus, for example, anthropologists and agricultural economists have discovered that parents and children can be more guarded in their economic transactions than they would be with strangers. Heady and Kehrberg (1952) discovered that farmers in Iowa often preferred to tie a close relative down to formal, fixed-rent contracts, while forming more flexible sharecropping arrangements with strangers. With formal wage or leasing agreements a father can secure his own interests by bringing the constraints of the marketplace to bear on his relations with his son. Conversely, trustworthiness is vital in assessing a nonrelative, who may then be addressed as "son" or "brother" as the economic partnership matures (Robertson 1987).

12. They conclude: 'This suggests further that the economic theory of the firm may in fact be a theory based on, and only well suited to, the American firm as it has developed historically in American society' (Hamilton and Biggart 1988:87–88).

13. The boundaries and media of trade may be defined by highly relative cultural values. A striking example of this is the notion of "bad money"—the "tainting" of the medium of exchange by its involvement in particular transactions—wage labor, dope dealing, bribery, usury among friends, etc. (Taussig 1980; Shipton 1989).

14. It is now well known that modern pre-nuptial contracts are much less concerned with the organization of conjugal life than with "postnuptial" matters such as the deposition of goods, the placement of children, and all other responsibilities in the single eventuality of divorce.

15. Thus, institutionalization can be understood as the reproduction of social relationships across space and time—a form of "distanciation," in Giddens' (1985) felicitous phrase.

16. Efforts to close this gap always seem to come from the margins of social science. Action is socially structured, and institutions are social processes, not immutable normative states, which is why they *must* admit the notion of transaction. "Ethnomethodology" is a peculiarly frenetic effort to establish "real" connections between doing and knowing, between the pragmatic behavior of individuals and the grand cultural repositories of social values (Garfinkel 1967). Unlike the analysis of networks, the ambition is to cover all the ground between ideas and actions, means and ends, and cultural ideals versus the reality of individual "ad-hocing." The intention is to show the layers of norm, pragmatism, and implicitness that give meaning to all action. Nevertheless, ethnomethodological enquiry tends to contract to those 'contextual rationales' (talking, telephoning, banking) which lie somewhere between the "shot in the brain" of socialization and cynical manipulation (as Harvey Molotch put it at our conference. The danger of such endeavors is not only that they become overburdened with detail, they tend to conflate action and structure, leaving us no better informed about behavioral rationales or the meaning of institutions.

17. This does not mean that there are no constraints on the extension of the logic of one institution to another. Indeed, Esping-Andersen (1985, 1986) argues that attempts to unhinge social policies from the labor market, to "decommodify" them, can be understood as an extension of citizenship rights to the economy. But, he shows, that in the Scandinavian countries, where decommodification has gone furthest, the political coalitions necessary to sustain this extension have unraveled due to the inability to maintain full employment, increased tax burdens on workers, and the failure to control the investment of capital and thus the supply of jobs.

REFERENCES

Alchian, Armen and Harold Demsetz. 1972. "Production, Information Cost, and Economic Organization." *American Economic Review* 62(5):777–795.

———. 1973. "Property Rights Paradigm." *Journal of Economic History* 33:16–27.

Alford, Robert R. and Roger Friedland. 1985. *Powers of Theory: Capitalism, the State and Democracy*. Cambridge: Cambridge University Press.

Anderson, Michael. 1985. "The Emergence of the Modern Life Cycle in Britain." *Social History* 10:69–87.

Ando, A., and F. Modigliani. 1963. "The Life Cycle Hypothesis of Saving: Aggregate Implications and Tests." *American Economic Review* 53:55–84.

Atkinson, A. B. 1971. "The Distribution of Wealth and the Individual Life Cycle." *Oxford Economic Papers* 23:239–254.

Axelrod, Robert M. 1981. "The Emergence of Cooperation Among Egoists." *American Political Science Review* 75:306–318.

Axelrod, Robert M. 1986. "An Evolutionary Approach to Norms." *American Political Science Review* 80:1095–1111.

Baker, Wayne. 1984. "The Social Structure of a National Securities Market." *American Journal of Sociology* 89(4):775–811.

Becker, Gary S. 1981. *A Treatise on the Family*. Cambridge: Harvard University Press.

Bell, Daniel. 1981. "Models and reality in Economic Discourse." Pp. 46–80 in *The Crisis in Economic Theory*, edited by Daniel Bell and Irving Kristol. New York: Basic Books.

Bell, Daniel and Irving Kristol (eds.) 1981. *The Crisis in Economic Theory*. New York: Basic Books.

Berk, Sarah Fenstermaker. 1987. *The Gender Factory*. New York: Plenum.

Bielby, William T. and James N. Baron. 1986. "Men and Women at Work: Sex Segregation and Statistical Discrimination," *American Journal of Sociology* 91:759–799.

Bielby, Denise and William Bielby. 1988. "She Works Hard for the Money: Household Responsibilities and the Allocation of Work Effort." *American Journal of Sociology* 93:1031–1059.

Block, Fred. Forthcoming. *The Economic Sociology of Postindustrialism*. Berkeley: University of California Press.

Borcherding, T. E. and R. T. Deacon. 1972. "The Demand for the Services of Non-Federal Government." *American Economic Review* 62:891–901.

Bourdieu, Pierre. 1977. *Outline of a Theory of Practice*. Cambridge: Cambridge University Press.

Brenner, Reuven. 1987. *Rivalry. In Business, Science, Among Nations*. Cambridge: Cambridge University Press.

Browning, Mark. 1985. Time-series, cross-sections and pooling. Pp 149–170 in *Fertility in developing countries*, edited by Ghazi M. Farooq and George B. Simmons. New York: St Martin's Press.

Burawoy, Michael. 1979. *Manufacturing Consent: Changes in the Labor Process Under Monopoly Capitalism*. Chicago: University of Chicago Press.

————. 1985. *The Politics of Production: Factory Regimes Under Capitalism and Socialism.* London: Verso.

————. 1983. "Between the Labor Process and the State: The Changing Face of Factory Regimes Under Advanced Capitalism." *American Sociological Review* 48:587–605.

Burt, Ronald. 1983. *Corporate Profits and Cooptation: Networks of Market Constraints and Directorate Ties in the American Economy.* New York: Academic Press.

Caiden, Naomi and Aaron Wildavsky. 1974. *Planning and Budgeting in Poor Countries.* New York: Wiley.

Cameron, David. 1984. "The Politics and Economics of the Business Cycle." Pp. 236–262 in *The Political Economy,* edited by Thomas Ferguson and Joel Rogers. Armonk: M. E. Sharpe.

Chappell, Henry W. and William R. Keech. 1985. "A New View of Political Accountability for Economic Performance." *American Political Science Review* 79:10–27.

Chayanov, A. V. 1966. *On the Theory of Non-Capitalist Economic Systems.* Pp. 29–269 in *A. V. Chayanov on the Theory of Peasant Economy,* edited by Daniel Thorner, Basile Kerblay and R. E. F. Smith. Homewood, IL: Irwin.

Clark, Rolbert C. 1985. "Agency Costs Versus Fiduciary Duties." Pp. 55–79 in *Principles and Agents: The Structure of Business,* edited by John H. Pratt and Richard J. Zeckhauser. Boston: Harvard Business School Press.

Davis, Kingsley, 1985. *Contemporary Marriage: Comparative Perspectives on a Changing Institution.* New York: Russell Sage Foundation.

Deacon, R. T. 1978. "A Demand Model for the Local Public Sector," *Review of Economics and Statistics* 50:184–192.

Deere, Carmen D. and Alain de Janvri. 1981. "Demographic and Social Differentiation Among Northern Peruvian Peasants." *Journal of Development Studies* 8:335–366.

Deleuze, Gilles and Felix Guattari. 1987. *A Thousand Plateaus: Capitalism and Schizophrenia* Minneapolis: University of Minnesota Press.

DiMaggio, Paul and Walter W. Powell. 1983. "The Iron Cage Revisited: Institutional Isomorphism and Collective Rationality in Organizational Fields." *American Sociological Review* 48:147–160.

Downs, Anthony. 1957. *An Economic Theory of Democracy.* New York: Harper.

Dunn, John. 1979. *Western Political Theory in the Face of the Future.* Cambridge: Cambridge University Press.

Edelman, Lauren. 1985. *Organizational Governance and Due Process: The Expansion of Rights in the American Workplace.* Stanford University: Unpublished doctoral dissertation.

Eichner, Alfred S. 1983. *Why Economics is Not Yet a Science.* Armonk, NY: M. E. Sharpe.

Elder, Glen H. (ed.) 1985. *Life Course Dynamics: Trajectories and Transitions, 1968–1980.* Ithaca: Cornell University Press.

Ellman, Michael. 1979. *Socialist Planning* Cambridge: Cambridge University Press.

England, Paula and George Farkas. 1986. *Households, Employment, and Gender.* New York: Aldine.

Esping-Andersen, Gosta. 1985. *Politics Against Markets: The Social Democratic Road to Power.* Princeton: Princeton University Press.

————. 1986. "Citizenship and Socialism: De-Commodification and Solidarity in the Welfare State." Pp. 78–101 in *Stagnation and Renewal in Social Policy: The Rise and Fall of Policy Regimes,* edited by Martin Rein, Gosta Esping-Andersen and Lee Rainwater. Armonk, NY: M. E. Sharpe.

Evans-Pritchard, E. E. 1951. *Kinship and Marriage among the Nuer.* Oxford: Clarendon Press.

Foucault, Michel. 1970. *The Order of Things: An Archaeology of the Human Sciences.* New York: Random House.

Frank, Robert H. 1987. "If *Homo Economicus* Could Choose His Own Utility Function, Would He Want One with a Conscience?" *American Economic Review* 77:593–604.

Frieden, Jeffry A. 1989. "Capital Politics: Creditors and the International Political Economy." *Journal of Public Policy* 8(3):265–286.

Friedland, Roger. 1983. *Power and Crisis in the City.* New York: Schoken.

Friedland, Roger and Robert Alford. Forthcoming. "Bringing Society Back In: Symbols, Practices; and Institutional Contradictions." In *The New Institutionalism in Organizational Analysis,* edited by Walter W. Powell and Paul DiMaggio. Chicago: University of Chicago Press.

Friedland, Roger and Donald Palmer. Forthcoming. "Class, Corporation and Space." In *Now/here: Space, Time and Social Theory,* edited by Roger Friedland and Deirdre Boden.

Friedland, Roger and Donald Palmer. 1984. "Park Place and Main Street: Business and the Urban Power Structure." *Annual Review of Sociology* 10:393–416.

Friedland, Roger and Jimy Sanders. 1988. "Capitalism and the Welfare State: The Politics of Wages and Growth." Pp. 29–57 in *Remaking the Welfare State: Retrenchment and Social Policy in America and Europe,* edited by Michael K. Brown. Philadelphia: Temple University Press.

Friedland, Roger and Jimy Sanders. 1985. "The Public Economy and Economic Growth in Western Market Economies." *American Sociological Review* 50:421–437.

Garfinkel, Harold. 1967. *Studies in Ethnomethodology.* Englewood Cliffs, N.J.: Prentice Hall.

Giddens, Anthony. 1984. *The Constitution of Society. Outline of the Theory of Structuration.* Berkeley and Los Angeles: University of California Press.

————. 1985. *The Nation State and Violence.* Berkeley and Los Angeles: University of California Press.

Gilder, George. 1984. *The Spirit of Enterprise.* New York: Simon and Schuster.

Granovetter, Mark. 1985. "Economic Action and Social Structure: the Problem of Embeddedness." *American Journal of Sociology* 91:481–510.

Greenhalgh, Susan. 1983. "Is Inequality Demographically Induced?" *American Anthropologist* 87:571–594.

Gudeman, Stephen. 1986. *Economics as Culture: Models and Metaphors of Livelihood.* London: Routledge.

Guyer, J., and P. Peters (ed.). 1985. *Conceptualizing the Household: Issues of Theo-*

ry, *Method and Application*. Cambridge: Joint Committee of African Studies, Harvard University.

Hall, Peter. 1982. "Economic Planning, and the State: The Evolution of Economic Challenge and Political Response in France." Pp. 175–214 in *Political Power and Social Theory,* edited by Maurice Zeitlin. Greenwich: JAI Press.

Hamilton, Gary G. and Nicole Woolsey Biggart. 1988. "Market, Culture and Authority: A Comparative Analysis of Management and Organization in the Far East." *American Journal of Sociology* 94 (S):52–94.

Hammond, Thomas H. and Jack H. Knott. 1988. "The Deregulatory Snowball: Explaining Deregulation in the Financial Industry." *Journal of Politics* 50:3–30.

Hareven, Tamara K. 1977. "Family Time and Historical Time." *Daedalus* 106:57–70.

——— 1982. *Family Time and Industrial Time. The Relationships Between the Family and Work in a New England Industrial Community.* Cambridge: Cambridge University Press.

Hatch, Elvin 1989. "Theories of Social Honor." *American Anthropologist* 91:341–353.

Heady, Earl O. and Earl W. Kehrberg. 1952. "Relationship of Crop-share and Cash Leasing Systems to Farming Efficiency." Iowa State College Agricultural Experiment Station Research Bulletin 386:634–683.

Heckman, James J. 1975. Estimates of a human capital production function embedded in a life-cycle model of labor supply. Pp. 227–264 in *Household Production and Consumption,* edited by Nestor E. Terlecky. National Bureau of Economic Research, New York, 1975.

Hibbs, Douglas A., Jr. 1987. *The Political Economy of Industrial Democracies.* Cambridge: Harvard University Press.

Hirsch, Paul, Stuart Michaels and Ray Friedman. 1987. "'Dirty Hands' versus 'Clean Models': Is Sociology in Danger of Being Seduced by Economics?" *Theory and Society* 16(3):317–336.

Hunt, Diana. 1978. "Chayanov's Model of Peasant Household Resource Allocation and its Relevance to Mbere Division, Eastern Kenya." *Journal of Development Studies* 15:59–86.

Jung, Maureen. 1988. *Corporations and the Structure in Markets: The Comstocks and the Mining Economy in the Far West, 1848–1900.* Unpublished doctoral dissertation. Santa Barbara, California: University of California, Santa Barbara.

Kanter, Rosabeth Moss. 1977. *Men and Women of the Corporation.* New York: Basic Books.

Korpi, Walter. 1985. "Economic Growth and the Welfare State: Leaky Bucket or Irrigation System?" *European Sociological Review* 1(2):97–118.

Lange, Peter and Geoffrey Garrett. 1985. "The Politics of Growth." *Journal of Politics* 47:792–827.

Laslett, Peter and Richard Wall (eds.) 1972. *Household and Family in Past Time.* Cambridge: Cambridge University Press.

Levine, David. 1977. *Family Formation in an Age of Nascent Capitalism.* New York: Academic Press.

Lie, John. 1988. *Visualizing the Invisible Hand: From Market to Mode of Exchange.*

46 Roger Friedland and A. F. Robertson

Department of Sociology: Unpublished doctoral dissertation. Cambridge: Harvard University.

Logan, John and Harvey Molotch. 1987. *Urban Fortunes.* Berkeley: University of California Press.

Lydall, Harold. 1955. "The Life Cycle in Income, Saving, and Asset Ownership." *Econometrica* 23:133–150.

Lyotard, Jean-Francois. 1984. *The Postmodern Condition: a Report on Knowledge.* Minneapolis: University of Minnesota Press.

McCubbins, Mathew D. and Talbot Page. 1987. "A Theory of Congressional Delegation." Pp 409–425 in *Congress: Structure and Policy,* edited by Mathew D. McCubbins and Terry Sullivan. Cambridge: Cambridge University Press.

McCubbins, Mathew D. & Thomas Schwartz 1984 Congressional oversight overlooked: police patrols versus fire alarms *American Journal of Political Science* 28:165–179.

Macfarlane, Alan. 1978. *The Origins of English Individualism: The Family, Property and Social Transition.* Oxford: Blackwell.

Malinowski, Bronislaw. (1922) 1961. *Argonauts of the Western Pacific.* New York: Dutton.

Marsden, David. 1984. "Homo Economicus and the Labour Market." Pp. 121–158 in *Economics in Disarray,* edited by Peter Wiles and Guy Routh. New York: Basic Books.

Marshall, T. H. 1964. *Class, Citizenship and Social Development.* New York: Doubleday.

Medick, Hans. 1976. "The Proto-industrial Family Economy." *Social History* 3:291–315.

Meillassoux, Claude. 1981. *Maidens, Meal and Money: Capitalism and the Domestic Community.* Cambridge: Cambridge University Press.

Meyer, John and Brian Rowan. 1977. "Institutionalized Organizations: Formal Structure as Myth and Ceremony." *American Journal of Sociology.* 83:66–94.

Mintz, Beth and Michael Schwartz. 1985. *Power Structure of American Business.* Chicago: University of Chicago Press.

Mintz, Sidney. 1985. *Sweetness and Power: The Place of Sugar in Modern History.* New York: Viking Penguin.

Moe, Terry. 1984. "The New Economics of Organization." *American Journal of Political Science* 78:738–777.

———. 1985. "Control and Feedback in Economic Regulation: The Case of the NLRB." *American Political Science Review* 79:1016–1040.

———. 1987. "An Assessment of the Positive Theory of 'Congressional Dominance.'" *Legislative Studies Quarterly* 12:475–520.

———. In press. "Bureaucratic Autonomy and Political Choice. Toward a Theory of Public Bureaucracy." In *Organization Theory: From Chester Barnard to the Present and Beyond,* edited by Oliver E. Williamson, Oxford University Press, New York.

Molotch, Harvey. Forthcoming. "Sociology and the Economy." In *Sociology in America* edited by Herbert Gans. New York: Russell Sage.

———. 1975. "The City as a Growth Machine: Towards a Political Economy of Place." *American Journal of Sociology* 82:309–331.

Montagna, Paul. 1986. "Accounting Rationality and Financial Legitimation." *Theory and Society* 15:103–138.

Mueller, Dennis. 1984. "Further Reflections on the Invisible Hand Theorem." Pp. 159–189 in *Economics in Disarray,* edited by Peter Wiles and Guy Routh. New York: Basic Books.

Murray, Colin. 1981. *Families Divided: The Impact of Migrant Labour in Lesotho.* Cambridge: Cambridge University Press.

Nee, Victor. Forthcoming. "A Theory of Market Transition: From Redistribution to Markets in State Socialism." *American Sociological Review.*

Oberschall, A., and E. M. Leifer. 1986. "Efficiency and social institutions: uses and misuses of economic reasoning in sociology." *Annual Review of Sociology* 12:233–253.

Oppenheimer, Valerie. 1974. "The Life Cycle Squeeze: The Interaction of Men's Occupational and Family Life Cycles." *Demography* 11:227–245.

Ouchi, William. 1980. "Markets, Bureaucracies and Clans." *Administrative Science Quarterly* 25:129–141.

Palmer, Donald, Roger Friedland and Jitendra Singh. 1986. "The Ties That Bind: Organizational and Class Determinants of Stability in a Corporate Interlock Network." *American Sociological Review* 51:781–796.

Peltzman, Sam. 1976. "Toward a More General Theory of Regulation." *Journal of Law and Economics* 19:211–240.

Perrow, Charles. 1986. "Economic Theories of Organization." *Theory and Society* 15:11–45.

Peterson, Paul E. 1981. *City Limits.* Chicago: University of Chicago Press.

Pfeffer, Jeffrey. 1987. "A Resource Dependence Perspective on Intercorporate Relations." Pp. 25–55 in *Intercorporate Relations: The Structural Analysis of Business,* edited by Mark S. Mizruchi and Michael Schwartz. Cambridge: Cambridge University Press.

Piven, Frances Fox and Richard Cloward. 1982. *The New Class War.* New York: Pantheon.

Piven, Frances Fox and Roger Friedland. 1984. "Public Choice and Private Power: A Theory of Fiscal Crisis." Pp. 390–420 in *Public Service Provision and Urban Development,* edited by Andrew Kirby, Paul Knox and Steven Pinch. London and New York: Croom Helm and St. Martin's Press.

Polanyi, Karl. 1944. *The Great Transformation.* New York: Rinehart.

———. 1947. "Our Obsolete Market Mentality." *Commentary* 13:109–117.

Polanyi, Karl, C. M. Arensberg and H. W. Pearson (eds.) 1957. *Trade and Market in the Early Empires* Glencoe: The Free Press.

Rahn, Richard W. 1983. "Supply-Side Economics: The U.S. Experience." Pp. 53–58 in *Reaganomics: A Midterm Report,* edited by William Craig Stubblebine and Thomas D. Willett. San Francisco: Institute for Contemporary Studies.

Reskin, Barbara. 1987. "Bringing Men Back In: Sex Differentiation and the Devaluation of Women's Work." Paper presented at the Department of Sociology, UC Santa Barbara. Forthcoming in *Gender and Society.*

Rhoads, Steven E. 1985. *The Economist's View of the World: Government, Markets, and Public Policy.* Cambridge: Cambridge University Press.

Robertson, A. F. 1984. *People and the State: an Anthropology of Planned Development*. Cambridge: Cambridge University Press.

———. 1987. *The Dynamics of Productive Relationships: African Share Contracts in Comparative Perspective*. Cambridge: Cambridge University Press.

———. Forthcoming. "Reproduction and the Making of History: Time, The Family and the Rise of Capitalism." In *Now/here: Space, Time and Modernity*, edited by Roger Friedland and Deirdre Boden.

Rowntree, Seebohm. 1922. *Poverty: A Study of Town Life*. New York: Fertig.

Sahlins, Marshall. 1974. *Stone Age Economics*. London: Tavistock.

———. 1976. *Culture and Practical Reason*. Chicago: University of Chicago Press.

Sen, Amartya. 1977. "Rational Fools: a Critique of the Behavioral Foundations of Economic Theory." *Philosophy and Public Affairs* 6(4):317–344.

Shapiro, Susan. 1987. "The Social Control of Impersonal Trust." *American Journal of Sociology* 93:623–658.

Shepsle, Kenneth A. 1979. "Institutional Arrangements and Equilibrium in Multidimensional Voting Models." 1979. *American Journal of Political Science*. 23:27–60.

Shipton, Parker. 1989. *Bitter Money: Cultural Economy and Some African Meanings of Forbidden Commodities*. Washington DC: American Ethnological Society.

Skocpol, Theda. 1985. "Bringing the State Back In: Strategies of Analysis in Current Research." Pp. 3–37 in *Bringing the State Back In*, edited by Peter Evans, Dietrich Rueschemeyer and Theda Skocpol. Cambridge: Cambridge University Press.

Skolnik, Arlene and Jerome Skolnik (eds). 1980. *Family in Transition: Rethinking Marriage, Sexuality, Childrearing and Family Organization*. Boston: Little, Brown.

Stark, David. Forthcoming. "Work, Worth and Justice in a Socialist Mixed Economy." *Actes de la Recherche en Sciences Sociales*.

Stark, David and Victor Nee. 1989. "Towards an Institutional Analysis of State Socialism." Pp. 1–31 in *Remaking the Economic Institutions of Socialism: China and Eastern Europe*, edited by Victor Nee and David Stark. Stanford: Stanford University Press.

Swedberg, Richard. 1987. *Economic Sociology: Past and Present*, Newbury Park: Sage.

Swedberg, Richard, Ulf Himmelstrand, and Goran Brulin, "The Paradigm of Economic Sociology: Premises and Promises." 1987. *Theory and Society* 16(2):169–214.

Taussig, Michael. 1980. *The Devil and Commodity Fetishism in South America*. Chapel Hill: The University of North Carolina Press.

Tilly, Charles. 1975. *The Formation of National States in Western Europe*. Princeton, N.J.: Princeton University Press.

Tversky, Amos and Daniel Kahneman. 1981. "The Framing of Decisions and the Psychology of Choice," *Science* 21:453–458.

Useem, Michael. 1984. *The Inner Circle: Large Corporations and the Rise of Business Political Activity in the U.S. and U.K.* New York: Oxford University Press.

Wanniski, J. 1979. "Taxes, Revenues and the 'Laffer Curve.'" Pp. 7–12 in *The Economics of the Tax Revolt*. edited by A. B. Laffer and J. P. Seymour. New York: Harcourt Brace and Jovanovich.

Weatherford, Stephen M. 1988. *"An Economic Theory of Democracy* as a Theory of Policy."* Paper presented at the Conference on "Anthony Downs' Economic Theory of Democracy Thirty Years After," October, 1988. Irvine, California.

Weingast, Barry R. 1981. "Regulation, Reregulation and Deregulation: The Political Foundations of Agency Clientele Relations." *Law and Contemporary Problems* 44:147–177.

———. 1984. "The Congressional-Bureaucratic System: A Principal-Agent Perspective (with Applications to the SEC)." *Public Choice* 44:147–191.

Weingast, Barry R. and Mark J. Moran. 1983. "Bureaucratic Discretion or Congressional Control? Regulatory Policymaking by the Federal Trade Commission." *Journal of Political Economy* 91:765–800.

Wells, Miriam J. 1984. "The Resurgence of Sharecropping." 1984. *American Journal of Sociology* 90 (1):1–29.

Wells, Miriam J. 1987. "Legal Conflict and Class Structure: The Independent Contractor-Employees Controversy in California Agriculture." *Law and Society Review* 21 (1):49–82.

Williamson, Oliver. 1975. *Markets and Hierarchies.* New York: The Free Press.

———. 1981. "The Modern Corporation: Origins, Evolution, Attributes." *Journal of Economic Literature* 19:1537–1568.

Williamson, Oliver and William Ouchi. 1981. "The Markets and Hierarchies and Visible Hand Perspective." Pp. 348–370 in *Perspectives on Organizational Design and Behavior,* edited by Andrew Vande Ven and William R. Joyce. New York: John Wiley.

Woolley, John T. 1988. "When Regulators Disagree: Financial Regulatory Conflict in Light of the Congressional Dominance Hypothesis." Paper prepared for the American Political Science Association, Washington D.C.

Wynn, Margaret. 1970. *Family Policy* London: Michael Joseph.

Yang, Mayfair Mei-Hui. 1989. "The Gift Economy and State Power in China." *Comparative Studies in Society and History.* 31(1):25–54.

Zelizer, Viviana. 1988. "Beyond the Polemics of the market: Establishing a Theoretical and Empirical Agenda." *Sociological Forum* 3(4):614–634.

Zucker, Lynne G. 1986. "The Production of Trust: Institutionalized Sources of Economic Structure, 1840–1920." Pp. 87–138 in *Research in Organizational Behavior,* edited by Barry M. Staw and L. L. Cummings. Greenwich: JAI Press.

INDIVIDUALS AND MARKETS

II

Rethinking Rational Choice 2

Robert H. Frank

Cornell University has two sets of faculty tennis courts, one outdoor and the other indoor. Membership in the outdoor facility is available for a fixed fee per season. There is no additional charge based on actual court use. The indoor facility, by contrast, has not only a seasonal fee, but also a $12 per hour charge for court time. The higher charges of the indoor facility reflect the additional costs of heat, electricity, and building maintenance. The indoor facility opens in early October, a time when the Ithaca weather can be anything from bright sunshine and mild temperatures to blowing sleet and snow. The outdoor courts remain open, weather permitting, until early November. During good weather, almost everyone prefers to play on the outdoor courts, which are nestled in one of Ithaca's scenic gorges.

Demand on the indoor facility is intense, and people who want to play regularly must commit themselves to buy a specific hour each week. Having done so, they must pay for the hour whether they use it or not.

Here is the problem: You are committed to an indoor court at 3:00 PM on Saturday October 20, the only hour you are free to play that day. It is a warm, sunny autumn afternoon. Where should you play, indoors or out?

I find that surprisingly many of my noneconomist partners balk when I say that playing on the outdoor courts is the only sensible thing to do. "But we've already paid for the indoor court," they invariably complain. I ask, "If both courts cost the same, which would you choose?" They immediately respond "outdoors." I then explain that both courts *do* cost the same—because our fee for the hour is going to be $12 no matter which place we play—indeed, no matter whether we play at all. The $12 is a sunk cost, and should have no effect on our decision. Yet, even at this point, many people seem to feel uncomfortable about wasting the indoor court we have paid for. The alternative, however, is to waste an opportunity to play outdoors, which we all agree is something even more valuable! True enough, it is bad to be wasteful, but *something* is going to be wasted, no matter which place we play.

Eventually, most people come around to the notion that it is more sensible

53

to abandon the indoor court, even though paid for, and play outdoors on sunny fall days. The rational choice model says unequivocally that this is what we should do. But it does not seem to be the natural inclination of most people. On the contrary, in the absence of a prodding economist, most people who have paid for an indoor court end up using it, even on the most pleasant days.

The standard economic model of rational choice assumes that consumers maximize well-defined utility functions. When questions arise about what goes into these functions (that is, questions about what people really care about), most economists quickly defer to psychologists, sociologists, and philosophers. As a practical matter, however, economists seldom consult outside sources for guidance on how to portray people's tastes. Rather, they are content to assume that the consumer's overriding objective is the consumption of goods, services, and leisure—in short, the pursuit of material self-interest. Economists also assume that the consumers act efficiently in the pursuit of their objectives.

This approach to the study of consumer behavior has extraordinary power. It helps us understand why car pools form in the wake of sharp increases in gasoline prices, why divorce rates are higher in states that provide liberal welfare benefits, why manual transmissions now have five speeds instead of three or four, why paper towels are replacing electric hand driers in public restrooms, why airline food is much worse than food served in restaurants, why certain kinds of taxes discourage economic growth while others do not, and so on.

For all of its strengths, however, the rational choice model is incomplete in several important respects. One difficulty is its implicit assumption that people are efficient processors of information. The problem is not merely that people must make decisions on the basis of incomplete information. The spring, 1988 edition of the Sears catalog alone has over 100,000 items in it. Economists are well aware that it would not be rational, let alone possible, for consumers to make decisions with full information about all of the potentially relevant alternatives. What many economists have been slower to recognize, however, is that we often make very poor use of the information we have right at our fingertips. The problem is not just that we make random computational mistakes; rather, it is that our judgmental errors are often systematic. If people are asked, for example, whether there are more murders than suicides in New York State each year, almost everyone confidently answers yes. And yet there are always more suicides.

Systematic judgmental errors give rise to a host of behaviors that contradict some of the most cherished predictions of the rational choice model. Actions that fall into this category may be called "irrational behavior with regret," because people usually want to act differently once the consequences of their behavior have become clear to them. The tennis example with which I began falls into this category.

A second difficulty with the rational choice model is that it ignores the fact that we are creatures not only of reason but also of passion. Our rational deliberations have important effects on our behavior, to be sure. But they are only one of several important forces that motivate us. The strict self-interest model has a difficult time explaining behaviors like tipping on the road or returning lost wallets to their owners. Unlike the behaviors that arise from judgmental errors, these behaviors may be called "irrational behavior without regret." If a rationalist were to point out that there is no way a waiter in a distant city could retaliate for not having been left a tip, most of us would respond, "So what?" We would not suddenly regret having left tips all our lives.

In this paper I will describe why both types of departure from the rational choice model—that is, irrational behavior both with and without regret—are important. In the purely descriptive realm, I will argue that by taking account of recent developments in other disciplines, economists can do a much better job of predicting people's behavior. And at the normative level as well, these developments suggest important qualifications to many of the prescriptions of the rational choice model. Paradoxically, to do well in the material world, it is often necessary to cast aside concerns about self-interest.

IRRATIONAL BEHAVIOR WITHOUT REGRET[1]

The Commitment Problem

Ever since Adam Smith's invisible hand mechanism appeared over two hundred years ago, economists have stressed that the pursuit of self-interest often promotes not only the welfare of each individual, but also of society as a whole. In this century, increasing attention has been given to exceptions to this claim. Modern textbooks now include an obligatory chapter on market failures, cases in which individual and social interests conflict.

One of the most frequently discussed examples is the familiar prisoner's dilemma. Thomas Schelling (1960) provides a vivid illustration of another class of problems in which the purely rational, self-interested person fares poorly. Schelling describes a kidnapper who suddenly gets cold feet. He wants to set his victim free, but is afraid he will go to the police. In return for his freedom, the victim gladly promises not to do so. The problem, however, is that both realize it will no longer be in the victim's interest to keep this promise once he is free. And so the kidnapper reluctantly concludes that he must kill him. The kidnapper's belief that the victim will act in a rational, self-interested way spells apparent doom for the victim.

Schelling suggests the following way out of the dilemma: "If the victim has committed an act whose disclosure could lead to blackmail, he may confess it; if not, he might commit one in the presence of his captor, to create a bond that will ensure his silence" (1960:43,44). (Perhaps the victim could allow the kidnapper to photograph him in the process of committing some unspeakably degrading act.) The blackmailable act serves here as a *commitment device*, something that provides the victim with an incentive to keep his promise. Keeping it will still be unpleasant for him once he is freed, but clearly less so than not being able to make a credible promise in the first place.

In everyday economic and social interaction, we repeatedly encounter commitment problems like the prisoner's dilemma, or like the one confronting Schelling's kidnapper and victim. The solution suggested by Schelling tries to eliminate the problem by altering the relevant material incentives. Unfortunately, however, this approach will not always be practical.

An alternative approach is to alter the psychological rewards that govern behavior. Emotions that urge people to behave in non-self-interested ways can sometimes accomplish this. Suppose, for example, the kidnap victim was known to be a person who would feel bad if he broke a promise. Such a feeling, if sufficiently strong, would deter him from going to the police even after it became in his material interests to do so.

Here are some further examples of commitment problems and of how emotional predispositions can help solve them:

The Cheating Problem.   Two persons, Smith and Jones, can engage in a potentially profitable venture, say, a restaurant. Their potential for gain arises from the natural advantages inherent in the division and specialization of labor. Smith is a talented cook, but is shy and an incompetent manager. Jones, by contrast, cannot boil an egg, but is charming and has shrewd business judgment. Together, they have the necessary skills to launch a successful venture. Working alone, however, their potential is much more limited.

Their problem is this: Each will have opportunities to cheat without possibility of detection. Jones can skim from the cash drawer without Smith's knowledge. Smith, for his part, can take kickbacks from food suppliers.

If only one of them cheats, he does very well. The noncheater does poorly, but isn't sure why. His low return is not a reliable sign of having been cheated, since there are many benign explanations why a business might do poorly. If the victim also cheats, he, too, can escape detection, and will do better than by not cheating; but still not nearly so well as if both had been honest. Once the venture is under way, self-interest unambiguously dictates cheating. If both Smith and Jones were emotionally predisposed not to cheat—that is, if they were honest—they would both be better off.

The Deterrence Problem.   Now suppose Jones has a $200 leather brief-case that Smith covets. If Smith steals it, Jones must decide whether to press charges. If he does, he will have to go to court. He will get his briefcase back and Smith will spend 60 days in jail, but the day in court will cost him $300 in lost earnings. Since this is more than the briefcase is worth, it would clearly not be in his material interest to press charges. (To eliminate an obvious complication, suppose Jones is about to move to a distant city, so there is no point in his adopting a tough stance in order to deter future theft.) Thus, if Smith knows Jones is a purely rational, self-interested person, he is free to steal the briefcase with impunity. Jones may threaten to press charges, but his threat would be empty.

But now suppose that Jones is *not* a pure rationalist; that if Smith steals his briefcase, he will become outraged, and think nothing of losing a day's earnings, or even a week's, to see justice done. If Smith knows this, he will let the briefcase be. If people *expect* us to respond irrationally to the theft of our property, we will seldom *need* to, because it will not be in their interests to steal it. Being predisposed to respond irrationally serves much better than being guided only by material self-interest.

The Bargaining Problem.   In this example, Smith and Jones again face the opportunity of a profitable joint venture. There is some task that they alone can do, which will net them $1000 total. Suppose Jones has no pressing need for extra money, but Smith has important bills to pay. It is a fundamental principle of bargaining theory that the party who needs the transaction least is in the strongest position. The difference in their cir-cumstances thus gives Jones the advantage. Needing the gain less, he can threaten, credibly, to walk away from the transaction unless he gets the lion's share of the take, say $800. Rather than see the transaction fall through, it will then be in Smith's interest to capitulate.

But suppose Jones knows that Smith cares not only about how much money he receives in absolute terms, but also about how the total is divided between them. More specifically, suppose Jones knows that Smith is committed to a norm of fairness that calls for the total to be divided evenly. If Smith's emotional commitment to this norm is sufficiently strong, he will refuse Jones's one-sided offer, even though he would do better, in purely material terms, by accepting it. The irony is that if Jones knows this, he will not confront Smith with a one-sided offer in the first place.

The problems described in these examples are by no means contrived or unimportant. In joint ventures, practical difficulties almost always stand in the way of being able to monitor other people's performance. Again and again, cheating on all sides leads to a worse outcome for everyone. In these situations, having the means to make binding commitments not to cheat would benefit every party. In competitive environments, similarly, opportunities for predation are widespread. And where such opportunities exist, there is a ready supply of cynical people to exploit them. To be able to solve the deterrence problem would be an asset of the first magnitude. Bargaining problems, finally, are no less important. People must repeatedly negotiate with one another about how to divide the fruits of their collective efforts. Those who can deal successfully with these problems would have an obvious advantage.

Being known to experience certain emotions enables us to make commitments that would otherwise not be credible. The clear irony here is that this ability, which springs from a *failure* to pursue self-interest, confers genuine advantages. Granted, following through on these commitments will always involve avoidable losses—not cheating when there is a chance to, retaliating at great cost even after the damage is done, and so on. The problem, however, is that being unable to make credible commitments will often be even more costly. Confronted with the commitment problem, a purely rational, self-interested person fares poorly.

By themselves, however, emotional predispositions are not sufficient to solve the commitment problem. For the noncheater to benefit in material terms, others must thus be able to recognize her as such, and she, in turn, must be able to recognize other noncheaters. Otherwise, she has no way to protect herself from being exploited by cheaters. The impulse to seek revenge or justice is likewise counterproductive unless others have some way of discerning that one has it. The person in whom this sentiment lies undetected will fail to deter potential predators. And if one is going to be victimized anyway, it is better *not* to desire revenge. It is the worst of both worlds, after all, to end up spending $300 to recover a $200 briefcase. For similar reasons, a commitment to fairness will not yield material payoffs unless it can be somehow communicated clearly to others.

But how to communicate something so subjective as a person's innermost feelings? Surely it is insufficient merely to declare them. ("I am honest. Trust me.") Posture, the rate of respiration, the pitch and timbre of the voice, perspiration, facial muscle tone and expression, movement of the eyes, and a host of other signals guide us in making inferences about people's feelings. We quickly surmise, for example, that someone with clenched jaws and a purple face is enraged, even when we do not know what, exactly, may have triggered his anger. And we apparently know, even if we cannot articulate, how a forced smile differs from one that is heartfelt.

At least partly on the basis of such clues, we form judgments about the emotional makeup of the people with whom we deal. Some people we feel we can trust, but of others we remain ever wary. Some we feel can be taken advantage of, others we know instinctively not to provoke.

Being able to make such judgments accurately has always been an obvious advantage. But it is often no less an advantage that others be able to make similar assessments about our own predispositions. A blush may reveal a lie and cause great embarrassment at the moment, but in circumstances that require trust, there can be great advantage in being known to be a blusher.

The Problem of Mimicry

If there are genuine advantages in being vengeful or trustworthy and perceived as such, there are even greater advantages in appearing to have, but not actually having, these qualities. A liar who appears trustworthy will have better opportunities than one who glances about furtively, sweats profusely, speaks in a quavering voice, and has difficulty making eye contact.

In most people, at least some of the outwardly visible symptoms of emotion are beyond deliberate control. We do know, however, that there are people who can lie convincingly. Adolf Hitler was apparently such a person. In a September, 1938, meeting, Hitler promised British Prime Minister Neville Chamberlain that he would not go to war if the borders of Czechoslovakia were redrawn to meet his demands. Following that meeting, Chamberlain wrote in a letter to his sister: "in spite of the hardness and ruthlessness I thought I saw in his face, I got the impression that here was a man who could be relied upon when he gave his word" (Ekman 1985:15,16).

Clues to behavioral predispositions are obviously not perfect. Even with the aid of all of their sophisticated machinery, experienced professional polygraph experts cannot be sure when someone is lying. Some emotions are more difficult to simulate than others. Someone who feigns outrage, for example, is apparently easier to catch than someone who pretends to feel joyful. But no matter what the emotion, we can almost never be certain.

Indeed, the forces at work are such that it will always be possible for at least some people to succeed at deception. In a world in which no one cheated, no one would be on the lookout. A climate thus lacking in vigilance would obviously create profitable opportunities for cheaters. So there will inevitably be a niche for at least some of them.

The inevitable result is an uneasy balance between people who really possess these traits and others who merely seem to. Those who are adept at reading the relevant signals will be more successful than others. There is also a payoff to those who are able to send effective signals about their own behavioral predispositions. And, sad to say, there will also be a niche for those who are skillful at pretending to have feelings they really lack.

Indeed, at first glance it might appear that the largest payoff of all will go to the shameless liar—the person who can lie with a straight face. In specific instances, this may well be true, but we must also bear in mind the special contempt we reserve for such persons. Most of us will go to great trouble to inform others when we stumble on someone who lies with apparent sincerity. Even if such persons are caught only very rarely, it is on this account far from clear that they command any special advantage.

The critical assumption in the examples discussed above is that people can make reasonable inferences about character traits in others. How plausible is this assumption? Perhaps the following simple thought experiment will be helpful in coaxing out your beliefs on this issue.

Imagine you have just gotten home from a crowded concert and discover you have lost $1000 in cash. The cash had been in your coat pocket in a plain envelope with your name written on it. Do you know anyone, not related to you by blood or marriage, who you feel certain would return it to you if he or she found it?

For the sake of discussion, I will assume that you are not in the unenviable position of having to answer "no." Think for a moment about the person you are sure would return your cash; call her "Virtue." Try to explain *why* you feel so confident about her. Note that the situation was one in which, if she had kept the cash, you could not have known it. On the basis of your other experiences with her, the most you could possibly know is that she did not cheat you in *every* such instance in the past. Even if, for example, she returned some lost money of yours in the past, that would not prove she did not cheat you on some other occasion. (After all, if she *had* cheated you in a similar situation, you would not know it.) In any event, you almost certainly have no logical basis in experience for inferring that Virtue would not cheat you now. If you are like most participants in this thought experiment, you simply believe you can fathom her inner motives: You are sure she would return your cash because you are sure she would feel terrible if she did not.

For emotional predispositions to serve as commitment devices, it is not necessary to be able to predict other people's emotional predispositions with certainty. Just as a weather forecast of 20% chance of rain can be invaluable to someone who must plan outdoor activities, so can probabilistic assessments of character traits be of use to people who must choose someone to trust. It would obviously be nice to be accurate in every instance. But it will often suffice to be right only a fraction of the time. And most people firmly believe they can make reasonably accurate character judgments about people they know well. If you share this belief, you are in a position to see clearly why the unbridled pursuit of self-interest will often be a self-defeating strategy.

For convenience, I will use the term **commitment model** as shorthand for the notion that seemingly irrational behavior is sometimes explained by emotional predispositions that help solve commitment problems. The model describes an equilibrium in which there is an ecological balance between more and less opportunistic strategies. This balance is at once in harmony with the view that self-interest underlies all action and with the opposing view that people often transcend their selfish tendencies. As Zen masters have known all along, the best outcome is sometimes possible only when people abandon the chase.

The Importance of Tastes

The self-interest model is widely used by economists and other social scientists, game theorists, military strategists, philosophers, and others. Its results influence decisions that affect all of us. In its standard form, it assumes purely self-interested tastes; namely, for present and future consumption goods of various sorts, leisure, and so on. Envy, guilt, rage, honor, sympathy, love, and the like typically play no role.

The examples discussed above, by contrast, emphasize the role of these emotions in behavior. The rationalists speak of tastes, not emotions, but for analytical purposes, the two play exactly parallel roles. Thus, for example, a person who is motivated to avoid the emotion of guilt may be equivalently described as someone with a "taste" for honest behavior.

Tastes have important consequences for action. The inclusion of tastes that help solve commitment problems substantially alters the predictions of self-interest models. We saw that it may pay people to feel concerned about fairness for its own sake, because feeling that way makes them better bargainers. Without taking concerns about fairness into account, we cannot hope to predict what prices stores will charge, what wages workers will demand, how long business executives will resist a strike, what taxes governments will levy, how fast military budgets will grow, or whether a union leader will be reelected.

The presence of conscience also alters the predictions of self-interest models. These models predict clearly that when interactions between people are not repeated, people will cheat if they know they can get away with it. Yet evidence consistently shows that most people do not cheat under these circumstances. Self-interest models also suggest that the owner of a small business will not contribute to the lobbying efforts of trade associations. Like one man's vote, her own contribution will seem too small a part of the total to make any difference. Yet many small businesses do pay dues to trade associations, and many people do vote. Charitable institutions also exist on a far grander scale than would ever be predicted by self-interest models.

Illustration: Fairness and Bargaining

The commitment model argues that an intrinsic concern about fairness can be advantageous, even though it may sometimes lead people to reject one-sided, but nonetheless profitable, transactions. German economists

Werner Guth, Rolf Schmittberger, and Bernd Schwarze (1982) have performed an elegant test of the hypothesis that many people are indeed inclined to reject such transactions.

Their basic experiment is the so-called "ultimatum bargaining game." The game involves two players, an "allocator" and a "receiver." It begins by giving the allocator a fixed sum of money, say $20. The allocator must then make a proposal about how the money should be allocated between him and the receiver—for example, he might propose $10 for himself and $10 for the receiver. The receiver's task is then either to accept or reject the proposal. If he accepts it, then they each receive the amounts proposed. If he rejects it, however, each player receives nothing. The $20 simply reverts to the experimenters. The players in the game are strangers to one another and will play the game only once.'

What does the self-interest model predict will happen here? To answer this question, we begin by assuming that each of the players cares only about his final wealth level, not about how much the other player gets. Now suppose the allocator proposes to keep P_A for himself and give the remaining $20 − P_A to the receiver, and that the receiver accepts this proposal. If M_A and M_R were their respective wealth levels before the experiment, their final wealth levels will then be $M_A + P_A$ and $M_R + \$20 − P_A$.

If, on the other hand, the receiver rejects the allocator's proposal, then their final wealth levels will be M_A and M_R. Knowing this, the allocator can conclude that the receiver will get a higher wealth level by accepting the proposal than by rejecting it, provided only that P_A is less than $20. If the money cannot be divided into intervals any smaller than one cent, the self-interest model thus predicts unequivocally that the allocator will propose to keep $19.99 for himself and give the remaining one cent to the receiver. The receiver may not be pleased about this one-sided offer, but the self-interest model says he will accept it nonetheless because $M_R + \$.01 > M_R$. By the logic of the self-interest model, the receiver reasons that although a gain of one cent is not much, it is better than nothing, which is what he would get if he refused the offer. Because the game is played only once, there is no point in refusing in the hope of encouraging a more favorable offer next time.

The findings from one version of their experiment are reproduced in Table 1, which shows that the allocator rarely employed the rational strategy. That is, he almost never proposed an extremely one-sided division. A 50–50 split was the most common allocation proposed, and in only 6 of 51 cases did the allocator demand more than 90% of the total. On the occasions when the allocator did claim an egregiously large share for himself, the receiver usually responded not as a self-interested rationalist, but in the manner predicted by the commitment model. In five of the six cases where the allocator claimed more than 90%, for example, the receiver chose to settle for nothing.

Actions motivated by concerns about fairness are by no means limited to

Table 1. The Ultimatum Bargaining Game[a]

	Actual	Predicted by rational choice model
Average percentage of total demanded by the allocator ($N = 51$)	67.1	99+
Percentage of proposed 50–50 splits ($N = 13$)	25.5	0
Percentage of total proposals rejected by the receiver ($N = 11$)	21.5	0
Average percentage demanded by the allocator in rejected proposals ($N = 11$)	85.3	100
Average percentage demanded by the allocator in accepted proposals ($N = 40$)	61.0	99+
Percentage of allocator demands greater than 90% ($N = 6$)	11.8	100

[a]Source: Guth et al. (1982, Table 3–5).

participants in laboratory experiments. As Kahneman et al. (1986a,b) have shown, such concerns motivate similarly costly actions on the part of both consumers and firms.

Illustration: The Internal Wage Structure

Another powerful illustration of how changes in tastes alter the predictions of the traditional model is the case of the wage structure within competitive firms. Concerns about fairness are here reflected in the sacrifices that workers must make to occupy high-ranked positions among their co-workers. The traditional model, which assumes that workers do not care about the wages earned by their co-workers, says that each employee will be paid the value of his or her marginal product. Once we introduce concerns about relative wages, however, this conclusion no longer follows.[2] The argument rests on two simple assumptions: (1) most people prefer high-ranked to low-ranked positions among their co-workers; and (2) no one can be forced to remain in a firm against his wishes.

By the laws of simple arithmetic, not everyone's preference for high rank can be satisfied. Only 50% of the members of any group can be in the top half. But if people are free to associate with whomever they please, why are the lesser ranked members of groups content to remain? Why don't they all leave to form new groups of their own in which they would no longer be near the bottom? Many workers undoubtedly do precisely that. And yet we also observe many stable, heterogeneous groups. Not all accountants at General Motors are equally talented; and in every law firm, some partners attract much more new business than others. If everyone prefers to be near the top of his or her group of co-workers, what holds these heterogeneous groups together?

The apparent answer is that their low-ranked members receive extra compensation. If they were to leave, they would gain by no longer having to endure low status. By the same token, however, the top-ranked members would lose. They would no longer enjoy high status. If their gains from having high rank are larger than the costs borne by members with low rank, it does not make sense for the group to disband. Everyone can do better if the top-ranked workers induce their lesser ranked colleagues to remain by sharing some of their pay with them.

Not everyone assigns the same value to having high rank. Those who care relatively less about it will do best to join firms in which most workers are more productive than themselves. As lesser ranked members in these firms, they will receive extra compensation. People who care most strongly about rank, by contrast, will want to join firms in which most other workers are less productive than themselves. For the privilege of occupying top-ranked positions in those firms, they will have to work for less than the value of what they produce.

Workers are thus able to sort themselves among a hierarchy of firms in accordance with their demands for within-firm status. Figure 1 depicts the menu of choices confronting workers whose productivity takes a given value, M. The heavy lines represent the wage schedules offered by three different firms. They tell how much a worker with a given productivity would be paid in each firm. The average productivity level is highest in firm 3, next highest in firm 2, and lowest in firm 1. The problem facing persons with productivity level M is to choose which of these three firms to work for.

Workers who care most about status will want to "purchase" high-ranked positions like the one labeled "A" in Firm 1. In such positions, they work for less than the value of what they produce. By contrast, those who care least about status will elect to receive wage premiums by working in low-ranked positions like the one labeled "C" in Firm 3. Workers with moderate concerns about local rank will be attracted to intermediate positions like the one labeled "B" in Firm 2, for which they neither pay nor receive any compensation for local rank.

Note also in Figure 1 that even though not every worker in each firm is paid the value of what he or she produces, workers taken as a group nonetheless do receive the value of what they produce. The extra compensation received by each firm's low-ranked workers is exactly offset by the shortfall in pay of its high-ranked workers.

The self-interest model, by contrast, says that *every* worker is paid the value of what he or she produces. Yet in every firm and occupation for

Wage

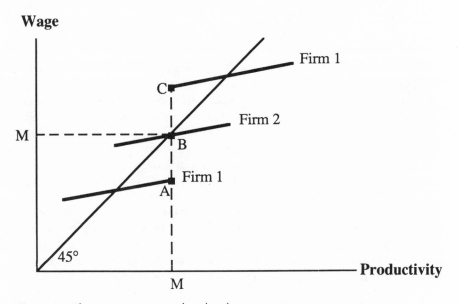

Figure 1. The wage structure when local status matters.

which the relevant data are available, high-ranked workers are paid less—often substantially less—than the value of what they produce, while low-ranked workers are paid more. The difference, in large measure, represents the price a high (low)-ranked worker pays (receives) for the position he or she occupies in the firm's internal hierarchy.

Once we modify the traditional utility function by introducing sympathy, anger, or concerns about relative position, we modify the conclusions of traditional models in fundamental ways. There is nothing mystical about the emotions that drive these behaviors. On the contrary, they are an obvious part of most people's psychological makeup. And their presence is in perfect harmony with the underlying requirements of a coherent theory of rational behavior.

IRRATIONAL BEHAVIOR WITH REGRET

All of the behaviors discussed in the preceding section were ones that, although inconsistent with the prescriptions of the rational choice model, did not summon expressions of regret. I will now discuss the second class of behaviors in tension with the rational choice model, namely, ones that people seem motivated to alter once their incompatibility with self-interest is made clear.[3]

Mental Accounting

One of the most cherished tenets of the rational choice model is that wealth is fungible. Fungibility implies, among other things, that our total wealth, not the amount we have in any particular account, determines what we buy. Cognitive psychologists Tversky and Kahneman (1981), however, provide a vivid experimental demonstration to the contrary. They tell one group of people to imagine that, having earlier purchased tickets for $10, they arrive at the theater to discover they have lost them. Members of a second group are told to picture themselves arriving just before the performance to buy their tickets when they find that they have each lost $10 from their wallets. People in both groups are then asked whether they will continue with their plans to attend the performance. In the rational choice model, the forces governing this decision are the same for both groups. Losing a $10 ticket should have precisely the same effect as losing a $10 bill. And yet, in repeated trials, most people in the lost-ticket group say they would not attend the performance, while an overwhelming majority— 88%—in the lost-bill group say they would.

Tversky and Kahneman explain that people apparently organize their spending into separate "mental accounts" for food, housing, entertainment, general expenses, and so on. People who lose their tickets act as if they debit $10 from their mental entertainment accounts, while those who lose $10 debit their general expense account. For people in the former group, the loss makes the apparent cost of seeing the show rise from $10 to $20, whereas for those in the second it remains $10.

The rational choice model makes clear that the second group's assessment is the correct one. And on reflection, most people do, in fact, agree that losing a ticket is no better reason not to see the performance than losing a $10 bill.

The Asymmetric Value Function

The rational choice model says that people should evaluate events, or collections of events, in terms of their overall effect on total wealth. Suppose A is the event that you get an unexpected gift of $100 and B is the event that you return from vacation to find an $80 invoice from the city for the repair of a broken water line on your property. According to the rational choice model, you should regard the occurrence of these two events as a good thing, because their net effect is a $20 increase in your total wealth.

Tversky and Kahneman (1974) find, however, that people seem to weigh each event separately, and attach considerably less importance to the gain than to the loss—so much less that many people actually refuse to accept pairs of events that would increase their overall wealth!

Utility

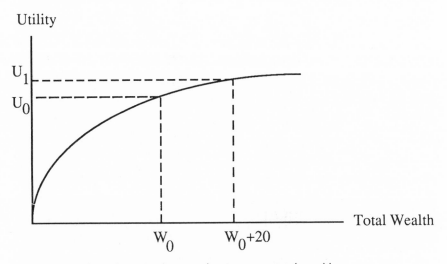

Figure 2. Utility of a pair of events that increases total wealth.

In the rational choice model, this of course can never happen. Confronted with the two events A and B described above, a person with an initial wealth level of W_0 knows exactly how to react. The combined effect of A (a \$100 gain) and B (a \$80 loss) is to increase his wealth to $W_0 + 20$. And since utility is an increasing function of total wealth, the two events taken together cause utility to increase from U_0 to U_1, as shown in Figure 2.

Tversky and Kahneman (1974) propose that people evaluate alternatives not with the conventional utility function, but instead with a **value function** that is defined over *changes* in wealth. One important property of this value function is that it is much steeper in losses than in gains. In Figure 3, for example, note how it assigns a much larger value, in absolute terms, to a loss of \$80 than to a gain of \$100. Note also that the value function is concave in gains and convex in losses. This property is the analog of diminishing marginal utility in the traditional model. It says that the impact of incremental gains or losses diminishes as the gain or loss becomes larger.

Tversky and Kahneman (1974) emphasize that their value function is a purely descriptive device. They are trying to summarize regularities in the ways people actually seem to make choices. They make no claim that people *should* choose in the ways predicted by their value functions.

According to Tversky and Kahneman (1974) it is very common for people to evaluate each item of a collection of events separately, then make decisions of the basis of the sum of the separate values. In this example, $V(100)$ is much smaller, in absolute terms, that $V(-80)$. Because the algebraic sum of the two is less than zero, anyone who employs this decision mechanism will

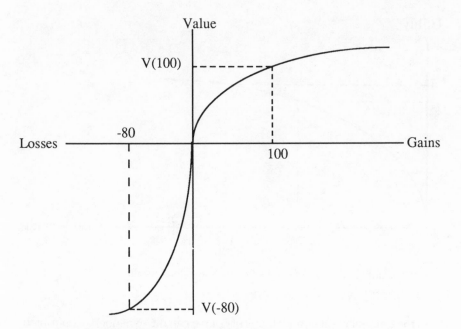

Figure 3. The Kahneman–Tversky value function.

refuse the pair of opportunities A and B, even though their net effect is to increase total wealth by $20.

There are really two important features of the Kahneman and Tversky value function. One is that people treat gains and losses asymmetrically, giving the latter much heavier weight in their decisions than the former. The second is that people evaluate events first, then add the separate values together. The first of these features does not necessarily imply irrational behavior. There is nothing inconsistent, after all, about feeling that a loss causes more pain than the happiness caused by a gain of the same magnitude. What *does* often appear irrational is the second step—treating each event separately, rather than considering their combined effect.

This is essentially a question about how to frame events. If someone pointed out to a person that the net effect of two events A and B was to increase her wealth by $20 she would probably quickly agree to allow the events to happen. Framed as an entity, they are obviously an improvement over the status quo. The problem is that, in actual decisions, it may seem more natural to frame the events separately.

Sunk Costs

Another basic tenet of the rational choice model is that sunk costs should be ignored in decisions. In the tennis example discussed earlier, we saw that it is this principle, not sunk costs, that is sometimes ignored. Cornell economist Richard Thaler (1980) argues that such examples are not isolated, that people in fact show a general tendency not to ignore sunk costs. He offers several vivid illustrations of the pattern.

One is a thought experiment in which you are asked first to imagine that you have bought a pair of very fashionable shoes for $200, only to discover that they are painfully tight. They improve slightly after being broken in, but still cause considerable discomfort. What do you do with these shoes, continue wearing them or give them away? Would your response be any different if you had not bought the shoes but instead had received them as a gift?

Under the rational choice model, it should not matter whether you bought the shoes or were given them. Either way, you own them now, and the only question is whether the discomfort they cause is serious enough to discontinue wearing them. People in both categories should be equally likely to discontinue wearing the shoes. Contrary to this prediction, however, people are much more likely to say they would abandon the shoes if they received them as a gift. Having shelled out $200 apparently makes many people determined to endure them.

Out-of-Pocket Costs vs. Opportunity Costs

Thaler suggests that our tendency not to ignore sunk costs may be given a simple interpretation in terms of the Kahneman and Tversky value function. In terms of the tennis example, failure to play on the outdoor courts on a nice day is coded mentally as a foregone gain, whereas not playing on the $12 indoor court you have already paid for is coded as a loss. Even though the gain is larger than the loss here, the greater steepness of the value function in the loss domain creates a bias in favor of the indoor court.

Much the same interpretation is supported by a number of other plausible examples (Thaler 1980). Consider a person who in 1955 bought a case of wine for $5/bottle. Today the very same wine sells for $100/bottle. His wine merchant offers him $60/bottle for it and he refuses, even though the most he would pay for the same wine today is $35/bottle. The rational choice model rules out such behavior. But if out-of-pocket expenses (e.g., for the purchase of additional wine) are coded as losses, while opportunity costs (e.g., of not selling the wine to the merchant) are coded as foregone gains, then the asymmetric value function allows for just such a response.

An even more common example occurs in the case of tickets to premium entertainment events. Tickets to the 1988 Super Bowl sold for $100 through official channels, but in the open market went for prices as high as $2000. Thousands of fans used their $100 tickets to attend the game, thus passing up the opportunity to sell them for $2000. Very few of these fans, however, would have spent $2000 to buy a ticket for the game. This behavior is also consistent with the notion that out-of-pocket expenses are coded as losses, opportunity costs as foregone gains.

Choice Under Uncertainty

The standard model of rational choice under uncertainty is the von Neumann–Morgenstern expected utility model. Its central assumption is that people attempt to maximize the weighted sum of utilities under different possible states of the world, where the weights are the subjective probabilities they assign to each state. This model provides valuable *guidance* about how best to choose between uncertain alternatives. But Tversky and Kahneman (1974) have shown that it does not always provide a good *description* of the way people actually decide. To illustrate, they posed a series of choices to a group of volunteer subjects. They began with the following problem, which elicited responses that were perfectly consistent with the expected utility model:

Problem 1. Choose between
      A: A sure gain of $240   (84%)
and

      B: A 25% chance of getting $1000 and a 75% chance of
      getting $0.   (16%)

The numbers in parentheses indicate the percentage of subjects who picked each alternative. Here, most people chose the sure gain of $240, even though the expected value of the lottery, at $250, was $10 higher. This pattern is consistent with the expected utility model under the plausible assumption that most people are risk-averse.

Subjects were then asked to consider an apparently very similar problem:

Problem 2: Choose between
      C: A sure loss of $750   (13%)
and

      D: A 75% chance of losing $1000 and a 25% chance of
      losing $0.   (87%)

This time the lottery has the same expected value as the sure option. Under the expected utility model, risk-averse subjects therefore ought to chose the sure alternative once again. But this time we see a dramatic reversal. More than six times as many people choose the lottery as chose the sure loss of $750.

Finally, the subjects were asked to consider the following problem:

Problem 3. Choose between
  E: A 25% chance of getting $240 and a 75% chance of
 losing $760   (0%)
and

  F: A 25% chance of getting $250 and a 75% chance of losing
 $750.   (100%)

Viewed in isolation, the responses to problem 3 are completely unsurprising. The lottery in F is simply better in every way than the one in E, and every sensible person would surely choose it. But note that lottery E is what we get when we combine choices A and D from problems 1 and 2; and that similarly, lottery F is the result of combining choices B and C from the two earlier problems. In the first two problems, the combination of B and C was chosen by fewer subjects (3%) than any other, whereas the combination A and D was by far the most popular (chosen by 73% of all subjects)—even though the combination of A and D is strictly dominated by the combination of B and C. Such findings, needless to say, pose a sharp challenge to the expected utility model.

Tversky and Kahneman (1974) argue that the observed pattern is exactly what would have been predicted using their asymmetric value function. In problem 1, for example, note that the choice is between a certain gain and a lottery whose possible outcomes are nonnegative. Since the value function is risk-averse in gains, and since the expected value of the lottery is only slightly larger than the sure alternative, it predicts the choice of the latter.

In problem 2, by contrast, the choice is between a certain loss, on the one hand and, on the other, a lottery each of whose outcomes is a loss. Since the value function convex in losses, it predicts risk-seeking behavior with respect to such a choice, and this, of course, is just what we saw. Because problem 3 forced people to amalgamate the relevant gains and losses, subjects were easily able to see that one pair of alternatives dominated the other, and chose accordingly.

It is tempting to suppose that violations of the expected utility model occur only when the problem is sufficiently complicated that people have difficulty computing what the model prescribes. But Tversky and Kahneman (1974) have shown that the outcomes of even the simplest of decisions can be manipulated by framing the alternatives slightly differently.

For example, they asked a group of subjects to choose between various policy responses to a rare disease that would claim 600 lives if we did nothing. One group was asked to choose either program A, which would save 200 lives with certainty, or program B, which would save 600 lives with probability ⅓ and zero lives with probability ⅔. Here, 72% of all subjects chose program A. A second group was asked to choose either program C, under which 400 people would die, or program D, under which there is a ⅓ chance no one will die and a ⅔ chance that all 600 will die. This time, 78% of all subjects chose program D.

A moment's reflection reveals that programs A and C are exactly the same, as are programs B and D. And yet subjects from the two groups chose dramatically differently. Tversky and Kahneman (1974) explain that the first group coded "lives saved" as gains, and were therefore risk-averse in choosing between A and B. Similarly, the second group coded deaths as losses, which led them to be risk-seeking in the choice between C and D.

It is also tempting to suppose that behavior inconsistent with the prescriptions of the expected utility model is largely confined to situations involving novice decision makers, or where little of importance is at stake. Tversky and Kahneman (1974) have found, however, that even experienced physicians make similarly inconsistent recommendations about treatment regimens when the problems are framed in slightly different ways. The moral is that we are all well advised to be cautious when making decisions under uncertainty. We should try framing the relevant alternatives in different ways and see if it makes any difference. And if it does, we should try to reflect on which of the formulations best captures our underlying concerns.

Judgmental Heuristics and Biases

Many of the examples we have considered so far make it clear that even when people have precisely the relevant facts at their fingertips, they often fail to make rational decisions. There is yet another difficulty confronting the rational choice model, namely, that we often draw erroneous inferences about what the relevant facts are. More important, many of the errors we make are systematic, not random. Tversky and Kahneman (1974) have identified three particularly simple heuristics, or rules of thumb, that people use to make judgments and inferences about the environment. These heuristics are efficient in the sense that they help us economize on cognitive effort and give roughly correct answers much of the time. But they also give rise to large, predictable errors in many cases. Let us consider each of the three heuristics in turn.

Availability. We often estimate the frequency of an event, or class of events, by the ease with which we can summon examples from memory. Much of the time, there is a close positive correlation between the ease with which we can do so and the true frequency of occurrence. It is easier, after all, to recall examples of things that happen often.

But frequency of occurrence is not the only factor that determines ease of recall. Recall the example about the number of murders and suicides each year in New York State. Most people feel confident that there are substantially more murders than suicides, even though, in fact, there are more suicides. Tversky and Kahneman (1974) explain that we think there are more murders because murders are more "available" in memory. Memory research demonstrates that it is much easier to recall an event the more vivid or sensational it is. Even if we have heard about equally many suicides as murders, it is on this account likely that we will be able to remember a much larger proportion of the murders.

Other elements in the mechanics of memory can also affect the availability of different events. Ask yourself, for example, whether there are more words in the English language that start with the letter r than there are words that have r as their third letter. Most people answer confidently that there are many more words that start with r, but in fact there are many more words with r as their third letter. We store words in memory much as they are stored in a dictionary—alphabetically, beginning with the first letter. We know plenty of words with r as their third letter, but they are no easier to remember than it would be to find them in a dictionary.

Events also tend to be more available in memory if they have happened more recently. A large body of research indicates that people tend to assign too much weight to recent information when making assessments about relative performance. In baseball, for example, a player's lifetime batting average against a certain pitcher is the best available predictor of how he will do against that pitcher in his next time at bat. It is apparently not uncommon, however, for a manager to bench a hitter against a pitcher he has performed poorly against the last couple of times out, even though he hit that same pitcher very well during a span of many years. The problem is that the manager estimates the player's performance by examples of it that spring easily to mind. And the most recent examples are the easiest ones to think of.

Economically, the availability bias is important because we often have to estimate the relative performance of alternative economic options. Managers of companies, for example, must weigh the merits of different employees for promotion. The most effective managers will be those that guard against the natural tendency to put too much weight on recent performance.

Representativeness.   Tversky and Kahneman (1974) have also discovered an interesting bias in the way we attempt to answer questions of the form, "What is the likelihood that object A belongs to class B?" For example, suppose that Steve is a shy person and we want to estimate the likelihood that he is a librarian rather than a salesperson. Most people are eager to respond that Steve is much more likely to be a librarian, because shyness is a representative trait for librarians, but rather an unusual one among salespersons. Such responses are often biased, however, because the likelihood of belonging to the category in question is influenced by many other important factors besides representativeness. Here it is heavily influenced by the relative frequencies of salespersons and librarians in the overall population.

A simple example conveys the essence of the problem. Suppose that 80% of all librarians are shy, but only 20% of all salespeople. Suppose further that there are nine salespeople in the population for every librarian. Under these reasonable assumptions, if we know that Steve is shy and that he is either a librarian or a salesman, what is the probability that he is a librarian? The relevant numbers for answering this question are displayed in Figure 4. There, we see that even though a much larger proportion of librarians is shy, there are more than twice as many shy salespersons as there are shy librarians. The reason, of course, is that there are so many more salespeople than librarians. Out of every 100 people here, there are 26 shy persons, 18 of them salespersons, 8 of them librarians. This means that the odds of a shy person being a librarian are only 8/26, or just under one-third. Yet most people who confront this example are reluctant to say that Steve is a salesperson, because shyness is so unrepresentative of salespersons.

Another example of the representativeness bias is the statistical phenomenon known as the regression effect, or regression to the mean. Suppose a standard IQ test is administered to 100 people and that the 20 who score highest have an average score of 122, or 22 points above the average for the population. If these same 20 people are then tested a second time, their average score will almost always be substantially smaller than 122. The reason is that there is a certain amount of randomness in performance on IQ tests, and the people who did best on the first test are likely to include

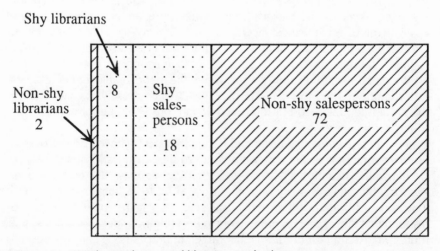

Figure 4. Distribution by type of librarians and salespersons.

disproportionately many whose performances happened to be better than usual on that particular test.

We have substantial first hand experience with regression effects in our daily lives (e.g, the sons of tall fathers tend to be shorter than their fathers). Tversky and Kahneman (1974) note, however, that we often fail to make adequate allowance for it in our judgments. The reason, they conjecture, is that we feel intuitively that an output (e.g., an offspring) should be representative of the input (e.g., the parent) that produced it.

It has long been observed that the rookie of the year in major league baseball (and in other sports as well) often has a mediocre second season. This has been attributed to the so-called "sophomore jinx." A related phenomenon is the so-called Sports Illustrated jinx, which holds that an athlete whose picture appears on the cover of Sports Illustrated one week is destined to do poorly the next. Shirley Babashoff, the Olympic swimming medalist, was once said to have refused to have her picture on the cover of SI for fear of the jinx (Gilovich 1987). Both of these supposed jinxes, however, are easily explained as the result of regression to the mean. Someone gets to be rookie of the year only after having an extraordinarily good season. Similarly, athletes appear on the cover of Sports Illustrated only after an unusually strong performance. Their subsequent performance, even if still well above average, will almost inevitably fall below the standard that earned them their accolades.

An especially pernicious consequence of our failure to take regression to the mean into account is the effect it has on our estimates of the relative efficacy of praise and blame. Psychologists have long demonstrated that praise and other forms of positive reinforcement are much more effective than punishment or blame for teaching desired skills. But people would be unlikely to draw this inference from experience if they were unmindful of the importance of regression to the mean.

The reason is that, quite independently of whether a person is praised or blamed, a good performance is likely to be followed by a lesser one, and a bad performance by a better one. Someone who praises good performances is therefore likely to conclude, erroneously, that praise perversely *causes* worse performance. Conversely, someone who denigrates poor performance is likely to spuriously attribute to his action the improvement that in fact results from regression effects. The co-movements of praise, blame, and performance would convince all but the most sophisticated analyst that blame works and praise does not. Managers who are trying to elicit the most effective performances from their employees can ill afford to overlook this lesson.

Anchoring and Adjustment. In one common strategy of estimation, known as "anchoring and adjustment," people first choose a preliminary estimate—an anchor—and adjust it in accordance with whatever additional information they have that appears relevant. Tversky and Kahneman (1974) discovered that this procedure often leads to biased estimates, for two reasons. First, the initial anchor may be completely unrelated to the value to be estimated. And second, even when it is related, people tend to adjust too little from it.

To demonstrate the anchoring and adjustment bias, Tversky and Kahneman (1974) asked a sample of students to estimate the percentage of African countries that are members of the United Nations. Each person was first asked to spin a wheel that generated a number between 1 and 100. The student was then asked whether his estimate was higher or lower than that number. And finally, the student was asked for his numerical estimate of the percentage. The results were nothing short of astonishing. Students who got a 10 on the spin of the wheel had a median estimate of 25%, whereas the corresponding figure for those who got a 65 was 45%.

Each of these students surely *knew* that the initial random number had no possible relevance for estimating the percentage of African nations that belong to the U.N. Nonetheless, the numbers had a dramatic effect on the estimates they reported. In similar problems, any number close at hand seems to provide a convenient starting point. Tversky and Kahneman (1974) report that giving the students monetary payoffs for accuracy did not alter the size of the bias.

An important economic application of the anchoring and adjustment bias is in estimating the failure rates of complex projects. Consider, for example, the starting of a new business. To succeed, it is necessary that each of a large number of events happen. Satisfactory financing must be obtained, a workable location found, a low-cost production process designed, sufficiently skilled labor hired, an effective marketing campaign implemented, and so on. The enterprise will fail if any one of these steps fails. When there are many steps involved, the failure rate is invariably high, even when each step has a high probability of success. For example, a program involving 10 steps, each with a success rate of 90%, will fail 70% of the time. When estimating failure rates for such processes, people tend to anchor on the low failure rate for the typical step, from which they make grossly insufficient adjustments. Thus, the anchoring and adjustment bias may help explain why the overwhelming majority of new businesses fail.

The Psychophysics of Perception

There is yet another pattern to the way we perceive and process information that has importance in economic applications. It derives from the so-called Weber–Fechner law of psychophysics. Weber and Fechner set out to discover how large the change in a stimulus had to be before we could perceive the difference in intensity. Most people, for example, are unable to distinguish a 100-watt light bulb from a 100.5-watt light bulb. But how large does the difference in brightness have to be before people can reliably identify it? Weber and Fechner found that the minimally perceptible difference is roughly proportional to the original intensity of the stimulus. Thus, the more intense the stimulus is, the larger the difference has to be, in absolute terms, before we can tell the difference.

Thaler (1980) has suggested that the Weber–Fechner law seems to be at work when people decide whether price differences are worth worrying about. Suppose, for example, you are about to buy a clock radio in a store for $25 when a friend informs you that the same radio is selling for only $20 in another store only 10 minutes away. Do you go to the other store? Would your answer have been different if you had been about to buy a television for $500 and your friend told you the same set was available at the other store for only $495? Thaler (1980) found that most people answer "yes" to the first question, "no" to the second.

In the rational choice model, it is inconsistent to answer differently for the two cases. A rational person will travel to the other store if and only if the benefits of doing so exceed the costs. The benefit is $5 in both cases. The cost is also the same for each trip, whether it is to buy a radio or a television. If it makes sense to go in one case, it also makes sense in the other.

The Difficulty of Actually Deciding

In the rational choice model, there should be no difficult decisions. If the choice between two alternatives is a close call—that is, if the two alternatives are predicted to yield approximately the same utility—then it should not make much difference which is chosen. Alternatively, if one of the options clearly has a higher expected utility, the choice should again be easy. Either way, the chooser has no obvious reasons to experience anxiety and indecision.

In reality, of course, we all know that difficult decisions are more often the rule than the exception. There are many pairs of alternatives over which our utility functions just do not seem to assign clear, unambiguous preference rankings. The difficulty is most pronounced when the alternatives differ along dimensions that are hard to compare. If the three things we care about in a car are, say, comfort, fuel economy, and safety, it will be easy to decide between two cars if one is safer, more comfortable, and has better gas mileage than the other. But what if one is much more comfortable and has much worse gas mileage? In principle, we are supposed to have indifference curves that tell us the rate at which we would be willing to trade one characteristic for the other. In practice, however, we often seem to find it difficult to summon the information implicit in these curves. And the very act of trying to do so often seems to provoke disquiet. For instance, it is not uncommon for people to dwell on the possibility that they will regret whichever choice they make. ("If I pick the more comfortable car, what will happen if I then get transferred to a job that requires a long daily commute?")

Such difficulties appear to cast doubt on a fundamental axiom of rational choice theory, namely, that choices should be independent of irrelevant alternatives. This axiom is often illustrated by a story like the following. A man comes into a delicatessen and asks what kind of sandwiches there are. The attendant answers that they have roast beef and chicken. The patron deliberates for a minute and finally asks for a roast beef. The counterman says, "Oh, I forgot to mention, we also have tuna." To this the patron responds, "Well, in that case I guess I'll have chicken." According to the rational choice model, the availability of tuna should matter only if it is the alternative the patron most prefers. There is no intelligible basis for its availability to cause a switch from roast beef for chicken.

Tversky has performed some intriguing experiments that suggest choice may not, in fact, always be independent of irrelevant alternatives. One of his examples is the choice between apartments that differ along two dimensions, monthly rent and distance from campus. From a student's point of view, an apartment is more attractive the closer it is to campus and the lower its monthly rent. A group of students was asked to choose between two apartments like the pair shown in Figure 5. Notice in the figure that neither apartment dominates the other. A is more expensive, but B is farther from campus. We expect that students who are relatively more concerned about rent will choose apartment B, while those who care primarily about commuting time will pick A. By manipulating the distance and rent, it is easy to get a group of students to divide roughly 50–50 between the two apartments.

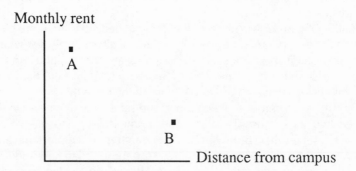

Figure 5.   Choosing between two apartments.

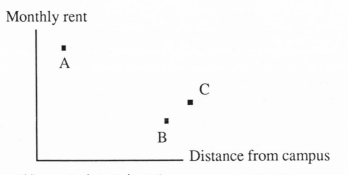

Figure 6. Adding an irrelevant alternative.

So far, no surprises. But now Tversky adds a third apartment, C, to the list of choices, giving us the set depicted in Figure 6. Notice that C is dominated by B—that is, it is both farther from campus *and* more expensive than B. In terms of the rational choice model, it is a classic example of an irrelevant alternative. Faced with the choice between A, B, and C, no rational consumer would ever choose C. And indeed, in actual experiments, hardly anyone ever does.

The surprise is that options like C turn out to affect people's choices between the remaining options. Tversky and his colleagues discovered that when an apartment like C is added to the pair A and B, the effect is to shift people's choices substantially in favor of B. Before C was available, students divided 50–50 between A and B. Once C was added, however, more than 70% of students chose B, the option that dominates C.

Many people apparently find the original choice between A and B a difficult one to make. The appearance of C gives them a comparison they can make comfortably, namely the one between B and C. Tversky hypothesizes that this creates a halo effect for B, which makes it much more likely to be chosen over A. Perhaps a similar effect might cause the availability of tuna to cause someone to switch his decision from roast beef to chicken. Whatever the reason for such behavior, it is clear that it violates the axiom that choice is independent of irrelevant alternatives.

The Self-Control Problem

An additional category of irrational behavior with regret is seen in how difficult it often is for people to carry out plans they believe to be in their own interests. Today most cigarette smokers say they want to quit. Many of them, with great effort, have done so. Many more, however, have tried to quit and failed.

Within the last decade, there has emerged a substantial scholarly literature on the topic of self-control (Ainslie 1975; Elster 1979; Schelling 1980; Thaler and Shefrin 1981; Herrnstein 1981; Winston 1980). Virtually every author mentions the example of Homer's Ulysses, who was faced with having to sail past dangerous reefs where the sirens lay. Ulysses realized that once he was within earshot of the sirens' cries, he would be drawn irresistibly toward them and sail to his doom on the reefs. Able to foresee this temporary change in his preferences, he came up with an effective commitment device: He instructed his crewmen to strap him tightly to the mast and not to release him, even though he might beg them to, until they had sailed safely past.

Similar sorts of commitment devices are familiar in modern life. Fearing they will be tempted to spend their savings, people join "Christmas clubs," special accounts that prohibit withdrawals until late autumn; and they buy whole-life insurance policies, which impose substantial penalties on withdrawals before retirement. Fearing they will spoil their dinners, they put the cashew jar out of easy reach. Fearing they will gamble too much, they limit the amount of cash they take to Atlantic City. Fearing they will stay up too late watching TV, they move the television out of the bedroom. Many of us are addicts of a sort, battling food, cigarettes, alcohol, TV sportscasts, detective novels, and a host of other seductive activities. That our psychological reward mechanism tempts us with pleasures of the moment is simply part of what it means to be a person. In the face of the behavioral evidence, it seems hardly far-fetched to suppose that rational assessments, by themselves, might often fail to assure behaviors whose rewards come mostly in the future.

The importance of impulse-control problems suggests several qualifications to the traditional economic models of savings. Saving, like dieting, is an act of self-denial. As Thaler and Shefrin (1981) emphasize, it requires discipline and self-control. A large literature documents the importance of so-called "demonstration effects" in consumption (Duesenberry 1949; Runciman 1966; Hirsch 1976; Sen 1983; Frank 1985; Kosicki 1988). For present purposes, the important message of this literature is that a person's savings rate at any moment is negatively related to the amount of time he spends in the presence of persons who consume more than he does. Other things equal, the lower a person's position in the income distribution, the greater share of his time he will spend in the presence of people who earn more than he does. Accordingly, the clear prediction of the self-control model is that personal savings rates will rise with position in the income distribution.

The standard economic model of rational savings is the life-cycle model of Modigliani and Brumberg (1953). This model implies, among other things, that the savings rate will be independent of a person's income level. As an empirical matter, however, this prediction is strongly contradicted: in every country for which the relevant data are available, savings rates rise sharply with income. The difficulties people have in executing rational savings plans suggest one reason for the contradiction.

The Positional Arms Race

As an example of yet another class of irrational behavior with regret, consider the worker's implicit decision about how much of his total compensation to "spend" on workplace safety.[5] Economists frequently argue that government makes us worse off when it requires us to spend more on job safety than we would choose to spend as individuals (Friedman and Friedman 1979). By this argument, the competitive labor market offers the worker a choice between relatively safe jobs at one wage and riskier jobs at higher wages. Workers who are most concerned about safety will choose the safer jobs; and the higher wages of riskier jobs will supposedly fully compensate the others for the extra risks they take.

But if people care about relative position, the incentives for choosing between such pairs of jobs are distorted. From each individual's perspective, the riskier jobs promise an upward movement along the economic totem pole. Yet the laws of simple arithmetic stand in the way of *everyone* moving upward in relative terms. For when everyone gets higher pay for performing riskier tasks, relative position remains unchanged. As in the familiar stadium metaphor, everyone leaps to his feet to get a better view, only to find the view no better than when all were seated. Here, an emotion (envy) helps solve one commitment problem (the bargaining problem), only to create another. The quest for relative advancement is a prisoners' dilemma, one that leads individual workers to purchase too little safety even when labor markets are perfectly competitive. By regulating safety, we attempt to solve this prisoner's dilemma (Frank 1985: Chapter 7).

Similar concerns help us understand why we regulate the length of the workweek. The Fair Labor Standards Act currently requires employers to pay premium wages to hourly employees who work more than 40 hours per week. The effect of this requirement has been to cause most firms to adopt a standard 40-hour workweek. Without it, workers would confront yet another prisoner's dilemma in their decisions about how many hours to work. By working an extra hour, a worker could increase his pay and provide additional material advantages for his or her family. But if some people work longer hours, others will feel compelled to do likewise, lest their families fall behind in relative terms. Yet when all work longer hours, relative position is left unchanged. By regulating the length of the workweek, we curtail yet another "positional arms race."

The invisible hand mechanism rests on the self-interest model's assumption that one person's income confers satisfaction irrespective of the income of others. But because many economic goals are inherently positional in character, we must reject this assumption—and with it the notion that the pursuit of self-interest is generally in harmony with overall social welfare.

The Impulse to Equate Average, Not Marginal, Returns

Consider one final category of irrational behavior with regret. The general rule for allocating a resource efficiently across different production activities is to choose the allocation for which the marginal product of the resource is the same in every activity. Psychologists Richard Herrnstein and James Mazur (1987) argue, however, that people often display a powerful impulse to equate average, not marginal, products.

Herrnstein and Mazur make their point with the following example involving the optimal selection of lobs and passing shots in tennis. When your tennis opponent comes to the net, your best response is either to lob (hit the ball over his head), or pass (hit the ball out of reach on either side). Each type of shot is more effective if it catches your opponent by surprise. Suppose that someone who lobs all the time will win a given point only 10% of the time with a lob, but that someone who virtually never lobs wins the point on 90% of the rare occasions when he does lob. Similarly, suppose that someone who tries passing shots all the time wins any given point only 30% of the time with a passing shot, but that someone who virtually never tries to pass wins 40% of the time when he does try. Suppose, finally, that the rate at which each type of shot becomes less effective with use declines linearly with the proportion of times a player uses it. What is the best proportion of lobs and passing shots to use when your opponent comes to the net?

The payoffs from the two types of shots are summarized graphically in Figure 7. Here, the "production" problem is to produce the greatest possible percentage of winning shots when your opponent comes to the net. $F(L)$ tells you the percentage of points you will win with a lob as a function of the proportion of times you lob (L). $F(L)$ is thus, in effect, the average product of L. $G(L)$ tells you the percentage of points you will win with a passing shot, again as a function of the proportion of times you lob. The negative slope of $F(L)$ reflects the fact that lobs become less effective the more you use them. Similarly, the positive slope of $G(L)$ says that passing shots become more effective the more you lob. Your problem is to choose L^*, the best proportion of times to lob.

To find the optimal value of L, we must first discover how the percentage of total points won, denoted P, varies with L. For any value of L, P is simply a weighted average of the percentages won with each type of shot. The weight used for each type of shot is simply the proportion of times it is used. Noting that $(1-L)$ is the proportion of passing shots when L is the proportion of lobs, we have

Shots won (%)

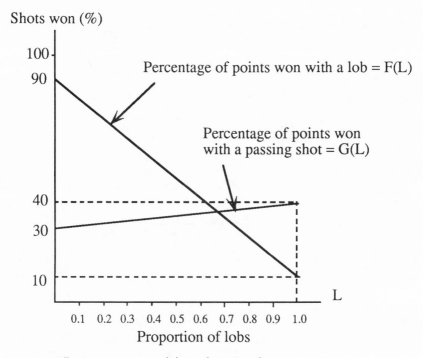

Figure 7. Effectiveness vs. use, lobs and passing shots.

$$P = LF(L) + (1-L)G(L) . \tag{1}$$

The expression $LF(L)$ is the percentage of total points won on lobs. $(1-L)G(L)$, similarly, is the percentage of total points won on passing shots. From Figure 8, we see that the algebraic formulas for $F(L)$ and $G(L)$ are given by $F(L) = 90 - 80L$ and $G(L) = 30 + 10L$. Substituting these relations into Eq. (1) gives

$$P = 30 + 70L - 90L^2, \tag{2}$$

which is plotted in Figure 8. The value of L that maximizes P turns out to be $L^* = 0.389$, and the corresponding value of P is 43.61%.[6]

Note in Figure 9 that at the optimal value of L, the likelihood of winning with a lob is almost twice as high (58.9%) as that of winning with a passing shot (33.9%). Many people seem to find this state of affairs extremely uncomfortable—so much so that they refuse to have anything to do with it. In extensive experimental studies, Herrnstein and Mazur have found that people tend to divide their shots not to maximize their overall chances of winning, but to equate the *average product* of each type. Note in Figure 9 that this occurs when $L = \frac{2}{3}$, at which point the percentage of points won

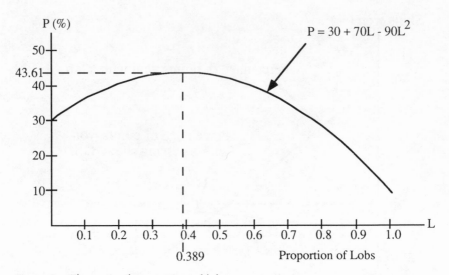

Figure 8. The optimal proportion of lobs.

with either shot is 36.7. At this value of *L*, however, the *marginal product* of a passing shot will be much higher than for a lob, because it will so strongly increase the effectiveness of all your *other* lobs. (Of course, an extra passing shot will also reduce the effectiveness of your other passing shots, but by a much smaller margin.)

Psychologists have long known that animals show a strong tendency to equate average returns when they allocate their efforts over alternative productive activities. Herrnstein and Mazur argue that the same tendency is present in people.

CONCLUDING REMARKS

In this paper, I have tried to call attention to some of the failures of the self-interest model as it is most commonly formulated. I suggested that the model often fails to predict behavior for either of two general reasons. The first is that people often adopt proximate goals—such as doing their duty—that are incompatible with the unfettered pursuit of self-interest. Discrepancies of this sort come under the rubric of irrational behavior without regret.

In addition, the self-interest model often fails to predict behavior because cognitive limitations stand in the way of rational choices. Such cases come under the heading of irrational behavior with regret. Other behaviors under the same heading include the lack of willpower to carry out intended actions as well as intended behaviors that produce unintended consequences (as, for example, in the case of the positional arms race).

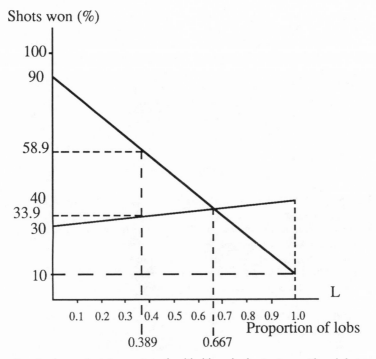

Figure 9. At the optimizing point, the likelihood of winning with a lob is much greater than of winning with a passing shot.

In calling attention to these examples, it has not been my intention to deny the obvious elegance and power of the self-interest model. On the contrary, much of the model's apparent difficulty is the result of our simply having focused its lens too narrowly. Even our cognitive failures are a testament to the self-interest model's usefulness, for without its guidance, we would never have had any way of knowing we were behaving less than optimally.

ACKNOWLEDGEMENTS

Research support for this paper was provided in part by National Science Foundation Grants SES-8707492 and SES-8605829.

NOTES

1. This section draws heavily on material from *Passions within Reason* (Frank 1988).
2. The discussion that follows is developed more fully by Frank (1985).

3. This section draws heavily on chapter 8 of *Microeconomics and Behavior* (Frank 1989).

4. Tversky and Kahneman (1981), and see also Thaler (1985).

5. I write "spend" in quotation marks here because it is the employer who makes the actual purchase of safety equipment. But the cost of this equipment comes ultimately out of the worker's pocket, not the employer's.

6. L^* is found by solving

$$dP/dL = 70 - 180L = 0,$$

which yields $L^* = \frac{7}{18} = 0.389$.

REFERENCES

Ainslie, George. 1975. "Specious Reward: A Behavioral Theory of Impulsiveness and Impulse Control." *Psychological Bulletin* 21:485–489.

Duesenberry, James. 1949. *Income, Saving, and the Theory of Consumer Behavior.* Cambridge: Harvard University Press.

Ekman, Paul. 1985. *Telling Lies.* New York: Norton.

Elster, Jon. 1979. *Ulysses and the Sirens.* Cambridge: Cambridge University Press.

Frank, Robert H. 1985. *Choosing the Right Pond.* New York: Oxford University Press.

———. 1988. *Passions within Reason: The Strategic Role of the Emotions.* New York: Norton.

———. 1989. *Microeconomics and Behavior,* preliminary edition. New York: McGraw-Hill.

Friedman, Milton and Rose Friedman. 1979. *Free to Choose.* New York: Harcourt, Brace Jovanovich.

Gilovich, Thomas. 1987. *How We Know What Isn't So.* Unpublished manuscript, Cornell University.

Guth, Werner, Rolf Schmittberger, and Bernd Schwarze. 1982. "An Experimental Analysis of Ultimatum Bargaining." *Journal of Economic Behavior and Organization* 3:367–388.

Herrnstein, Richard J. 1981. "Self-Control as Response Strength." In *Quantification of Steady-State Operant Behaviour,* edited by C. M. Bradshaw, E. Szabadi, and C. F. Lowe. Amsterdam: Elsevier/North Holland Biomedical Press.

Herrnstein, Richard J. and James Mazur. 1987. "Making Up Our Minds: A New Model of Economic Behavior." *The Sciences* Nov./Dec.:40–47.

Hirsch, Fred. 1976. *Social Limits to Growth.* Cambridge: Harvard University Press.

Kahneman, Daniel, Jack Knetsch, and Richard Thaler. 1986a. "Fairness and the Assumptions of Economics." *Journal of Business* S285–S300.

———. 1986b. "Perceptions of Unfairness: Constraints on Wealth Seeking." *American Economic Review* 76:728–741.

Kosicki, George. 1987. "Savings as a Nonpositional Good." *Southern Economic Journal* 422–34.

Modigliani, Franco and R. Brumberg. 1953. "Utility Analysis and the Consumption Function: An Interpretation of Cross-Section Data." In *Post-Keynesian Economics,* edited by K. Kurihara. London: Allen & Unwin.

Runciman, W. G. 1966. *Relative Deprivation and Social Justice*. New York: Penguin.
Schelling, Thomas. 1960. *The Strategy of Conflict*. Cambridge: Harvard University Press.
———. 1980. "The Intimate Contest for Self-Command." *The Public Interest* Summer:94–118.
Sen, Amartya. 1983. "Poor, Relatively Speaking." *Oxford Economic Papers* 153–167.
Thaler, Richard. 1980. "Toward a Positive Theory of Consumer Choice." *Journal of Economic Behavior and Organization*. 1:39–60.
Thaler, Richard. 1985. "Mental Accounting and Consumer Choice." *Marketing Science* 4:Summer, 199–214.
Thaler, R. and H. Shefrin. 1981. "An Economic Theory of Self-Control." *Journal of Political Economy* 89:392–405.
Tversky, Amos and Daniel Kahneman. 1974. "Judgment Under Uncertainty: Heuristics and Biases." *Science* 185:1124–1131.
———. 1981. "The Framing of Decisions and the Psychology of Choice." *Science* 211:453–458.
Winston, Gordon. 1980. "Addiction and Backsliding: A Theory of Compulsive Consumption." *Journal of Economic Behavior and Organization* 1:295–394.

The Old and the New Economic Sociology: A History and an Agenda   3

Mark Granovetter

In this paper I first trace the ups and downs of economic sociology in the twentieth century and then present my own perspective on the subject, and the agenda for research that it entails.

THE CHECKERED HISTORY OF ECONOMIC SOCIOLOGY

Accommodation and Separation: 1890–1970

In the late nineteenth century, economics moved away from its earlier broad institutional interests to a narrow concern with the marginal analysis of markets. The ascent of the "marginalists" in the 1890s initiated a period, lasting until the 1970s, during which the analysis of institutions was considered unscientific and thus foreign to orthodox economics. The loss of interest in institutions solidified the attitude that was already common among economists, that sociology was a pseudoscience that had nothing to offer them.[1]

Nor was it incorrect to believe, during this period, that sociologists had little to contribute to the subject areas studied by orthodox or "neoclassical" economics. This resulted in part from the academic politics surrounding the establishment of sociology as a discipline. At the turn of the century, to get a place in the university, sociologists had to persuade existing disciplines that they would not poach on their territory (see Swedberg 1987, pp. 17–20). Thus, sociology became what early Chicago sociologist Albion Small called the "science of leftovers," backing off of the economic and political spheres and focusing on such unclaimed subjects as the family, deviance, crime, and urban pathology.

Thus, from 1890 to 1970 the disciplines covered quite separate subject

89

matters. Sociologists trod lightly if at all on economic subjects while orthodox economists neglected institutions or noneconomic aspects of social life. Each discipline conceded the adequacy of the other for study of its chosen subject area.

In the "classical period," Emile Durkheim and Max Weber had similar influences on the attitude of sociologists toward economic life. Though somewhat disdainful toward pure economic theory, neither attacked it directly; both were more interested in those sociological elements that formed the preconditions for markets and capitalist organization than in the everyday workings of the economy.

Durkheim's *Division of Labor in Society* (1893/1984) asserts that when objects of study have both economic and sociological significance, the former might be more transparent but the latter are more interesting. Thus, the economic services rendered by the division of labor "are insignificant compared with the moral effect that it produces, and its true function is to create between two or more people a feeling of solidarity" (p. 17). As a result, individuals "are . . . solidly tied to one another and the links between them function not only in the brief moments when they engage in an exchange of services, but extend considerably beyond" (p. 21). Thus, Durkheim rejects the spot-market view of economic life fostered by the marginal revolution, in which economic relations are transitory and impersonal.

Weber occasionally notes, but only in passing, his skepticism of "pure economics" whose "explanatory methods . . . are as tempting as they are misleading" (1921/1968:115). But he has little to say in detail about the routine operation of markets. His main interests lie rather in the broad institutional questions that economists had abandoned. There was thus little of interest for them in Weber or in Durkheim, whose impact on sociology was therefore to define economic sociology as a field that did not mainly concern the day-to-day workings of the economy.

Thus, by 1920, both European and American sociologists were occupied with subjects far removed from the core concerns of economics. The separation of the disciplines was well underway before Talcott Parsons came on the scene, but Parsons's influence reinforced and solidified that separation.

Himself a renegade economist, much of Parsons's early work concerned the relation between economics and sociology, the scope of sociology, and its place within the social sciences.[2] He approved Lionel Robbins's now standard 1932 definition of economics as "the science which studies human behaviour as a relationship between ends and scarce means which have alternative uses" (Robbins 1932/1984:15), and strongly opposed the program of institutional economics associated with Veblen, Commons, Ayres, and Mitchell as insufficiently analytical, objecting that it proposed to throw out all that was useful in orthodox economics, and had no sense of where the boundaries of economics lie; instead it sought to incorporate biological, political, legal, and sociological issues in a fruitless and ad hoc attempt at encyclopedic coverage.

The proper division of labor, Parsons urged, was for economics to concentrate on the part of the means—ends chain involving rational adaptation of scarce means to alternative ends, and sociology on that part of the chain involving ultimate values. Such a division of labor would solve the problem that "in the theoretical sense, there has been both too much sociology (as well as biology, psychology, etc.) in economics and too much economics in sociology. There is, however, a vast field for their fruitful cooperation" (1935:666).

This argument was a central theme in *The Structure of Social Action* (1937), where Parsons asserted that "there seems to be no possibility that scientific work on a high level can be done by a man in any one . . . [discipline] who does not have a working knowledge of the others" (1937:771). Yet his argument helped solidify the separation between economics and sociology. If economics was fully adequate within its own domain, one separate from that of sociology which was to treat value systems and the institutional preconditions of economic action, there was little motive for economists to pay attention to sociology unless they were concerned with such matters, as few were in this period. And if the role of sociology in the understanding of the economy was external to its day-to-day workings, and concerned only the institutional underpinnings, it is unclear why sociologists needed to keep abreast of technical economics, and neither Parsons (see Parsons 1970) nor others did so in the period from 1940 to 1970.

And by his attacks on the institutional economists Parsons contributed to the failure of any alliance between them and economic sociologists. This failure has deprived both groups of a source of vitality, and helps account for the intellectually marginal position of current institutional economics.[3]

In the 1940s, Parsons entered his "structural functional" period, aiming to specify what structures fulfilled the functions required for a social system to persist. Since some functions were obviously economic, the economy, rather than being out of the domain of sociologists, now appeared to be a "subsystem differentiated from other sub-systems of a society. The specifically economic aspect of the theory of social systems, therefore, is a special case of the general theory of the social system" (Parsons and Smelser, 1956:6). It followed that economic theory could be derived from the general theory by introducing some logical restrictions (Parsons and Smelser 1956: 7).

Parsons and Smelser's *Economy and Society* thus undertook to analyze the economy as a Parsonian social system. That one could indeed describe the economy in Parsonian categories was taken to be a "striking fact" since these categories were "arrived at in work on the level of general theory independently, without the economic categories in mind at all" (Parsons and Smelser 1956:28). But this implies that it is the general theory that needs validation, whereas the economic theory is taken as already valid. This deferential attitude was clear in Parsons's "Marshall Lectures" at the University of Cambridge in 1953, on "The Integration of Economics and Sociology," given to an audience composed heavily of economists. Parsons offered the following reassurance: "Some may fear that the program I envisage calls for a radical reconstruction of economic theory. It seems to me that, precisely in contrast, for instance, with the program of the institutionalists, this is not the case. The farther I have gone, the more convinced I have become of the essential soundness, from a sociologist's point of view, of the main core tradition of economic theory" (1953:68).

Perhaps economists appreciated this respect, but it could hardly motivate their serious interest in a theory that offered them no important insights or modifications. What did they care whether Parsons could fit their arguments into his general theory of social systems, if he could not show them what the payoff was for them? And they generally were not interested, as he acknowledged 12 years after the publication of the Parsons–Smelser synthesis (Parsons 1968:vii n). Nor did this complex synthesis much affect sociology. Two books did try, within the structural–functional tradition, to sum up economic sociology: Wilbert Moore's Economy and Society (1955) and Neil Smelser's Sociology of Economic Life (1963). But Parsons's "economy and society" perspective produced few later followers.

Another line of economic sociology arose more or less independently of theoretical economics or sociology, when psychologists, sociologists, and anthropologists began studying the actual events in industrial plants. Sociologists first became serious about such work in the 1940s, the first textbooks appearing in the late 1940s and early 1950s.[4]

"Industrial sociology" was narrowly focused on manufacturing plants, especially on piecework, even though no more than 30% of production workers were ever paid by the piece. Part of this emphasis resulted from management's interest in the determinants of productivity in piece-rate settings, and in ways to overcome the restriction of output found in the classic studies. Thus, even left-leaning researchers found themselves chided by friends for practicing "moo sociology"—whose outcome would be to "milk" the worker (Form 1985).

Despite a series of brilliant studies from 1940 to 1965—Whyte (1955, 1961), Dalton (1959), Crozier (1964)—the focus remained narrow. Because sociological theory in this period had little direct concern with day-to-day economic processes, industrial sociology had to fend for itself theoretically, resulting in a seat-of-the-pants inductivism. The complex theoretical scheme that Parsons had erected by the 1950s did not seem relevant to industrial sociology, though an occasional figure like Wilbert Moore did try to bridge these two worlds (Moore 1955). Instead, scholars like William Foote Whyte drew on the interactionist formulations of George Homans's The Human

Group (1950), grounded in the ideas of "interaction," "sentiments," and "activities," to which Whyte added "symbols."

But as Homans himself later argued (1961), the generalizations in The Human Group were not themselves rooted in a larger theoretical scheme; correspondingly, much of the theoretical development in industrial sociology consisted of fitting observed events into Homans's categories (e.g., Whyte 1961). In my view, industrial sociology's emphasis on interaction, and its ramifications through a social system, was a move in the right direction, but there was no theoretical framework available in which the analysis could be pushed very far.

Industrial sociology was separated not only from theoretical sociology but also from economics. Economists were not interested in part because, like other sociology, industrial sociology shied away from the central neoclassical issues of economizing in production processes, and instead concentrated on what determined sentiments of cooperation and what led to conflict, within and between work groups and between workers and management. Even labor economists, few of whom in this period accepted orthodox economics, paid little attention to industrial sociology. I conjecture that this failure stemmed from the general attachment of labor economics to the broader tradition of institutional economics, which had never established any systematic linkage to sociology.

And so it happened that by the late 1960s, the two most promising traditions in economic sociology, industrial sociology and the structural–functional "economy and society" perspective, had become effectively defunct. Industrial sociology ran into diminishing returns on its "human relations in industry" program of research, and its lack of attention to organizational structure and the social environment beyond the organization became crippling liabilities. But in trying to push beyond this focus, industrial sociology found itself with no distinctive theoretical framework, and so was ultimately absorbed into organizational sociology, which, however, had even less concern than industrial sociology for the traditional problems of the economic theory of the firm.

The "economy and society" perspective fell, in part, of its own weight, as the stratospheric Parsonian categories failed to stimulate empirical research. But the perspective was further crippled when, from the mid-1960s on, Talcott Parsons began to lose his dominant position in sociological theory, for reasons related not only to intellectual life but to political developments that made many sociologists impatient with a theory that stressed value consensus and in which change was seen as an adaptive reequilibration to strains on the social system.

The period around 1970 was thus a nadir for interest in economic sociology, for the interest of orthodox economists in institutions, and for contact between the disciplines, with no obvious opening for interdisciplinary work. Yet, in both economics and sociology, internal developments were creating new concerns that would soon lead to a quite different situation. The "New Institutional Economics" was beginning to emerge from neoclassical work, and what I will call the "new sociology of economic life" was taking shape in sociology.

The New Institutional Economics and the New Sociology of Economic Life: 1970–

As Parsons recognized, institutional economics had no distinctive theoretical framework. Even such outstanding scholars as Veblen, Commons, Slichter, Mitchell, and Dunlop proceeded in an ad hoc fashion, using historical and legal arguments in ways that were impressive but not cumulative. The success of mathematical economics increasingly put the institutionalists on the defensive. They held sway longer in labor economics than elsewhere, but even there were fighting a losing battle by the 1950s; labor economics is now dominated by orthodox neoclassical views.

This orthodox penetration into labor studies is part of a broad movement—the "New Institutional Economics"—the emergence from the 1960s on of a new interest not only in economic institutions but even in such apparently noneconomic matters as marriage and divorce, crime, fertility, animal behavior, and altruism. The virtual demise of a vigorous, non-neoclassical institutional economics has thus produced an odd simultaneous narrowing of the conceptual apparatus accompanied by a broadening of the subject matter.

In the New Institutional Economics, all manner of economic, political, and legal institutions are interpreted as the efficient outcome of rational individuals pursuing their self-interest. The level of ambition displayed in this new economic imperialism is indicated by the optimistic claim of Jack Hirshleifer that "economics really does constitute the universal grammar of social science" (1985:53).

While orthodox economists were rediscovering institutions, sociologists took a new look at the economy. This new interest was largely detached from industrial sociology or the economy and society perspective, and was especially spurred by Marxist work such as Harry Braverman's *Labor and Monopoly Capital* (1974). A revival of industrial sociology followed, but in a Marxist key (Burawoy 1979, 1985; Clawson 1980; Stark 1986). Subsequently, interest in interlocking directorates and the power of finance capital led to important new work on capital markets (Mintz and Schwartz 1985; Stearns 1986).

Meanwhile, students of stratification and organizations increasingly came to see the workings of labor and product markets, and interorganizational relations, as central in explaining outcomes (Berg 1981; Farkas and England

1988). And social network analysts moved into economic sociology (White 1981; Burt 1983; Granovetter 1985; Mizruchi and Schwartz 1988). Many such analysts are mathematically inclined and thus not scared off by the technicalities of microeconomics; and since network analysis often takes the individual as a fundamental unit of analysis, it is methodologically more individualist than some other sociological traditions. But the underlying conception of network arguments lends itself to a fundamental critique of the atomized conception of action in neoclassical theory. Thus, this group, close enough to appreciate economic arguments but different enough to offer a basic critique, has been in a structurally strategic position.

Ironically, a main spur to the resurgence of sociological interest in economic life has been economic imperialism. Though some sociologists have accepted microeconomic arguments, many have come to see them, especially in the simple and stark form outlined by Gary Becker (1976, 1981), as useful foils against which to illuminate the distinctive contributions of the classical sociological tradition. One of the main differences between the old and the new sociology of economic life is thus exactly that the newer work reverses economic imperialism by offering sociological accounts of core economic subjects such as markets, contracts, money, exchange, and banking. In doing so, it is much less accepting of orthodox economic theory than the older tradition that focused on the institutional preconditions for economic life, and thus never needed to offer an alternative account of everyday economic activity.[5]

Locating my own work squarely within this "new sociology of economic life," I argue that orthodox neoclassical theory, and its recent work on economic and social institutions, are flawed in ways that a sociological perspective can highlight and help remedy. The brilliant achievements of neoclassical arguments in illuminating the efficient pursuit of well-defined preferences must be accompanied by an appreciation of the extent to which such pursuit is intertwined with noneconomic goals, and deeply embedded in structures of social interaction that extend backward in time and outward in space.

In the second part of this paper I describe my own conception of the sociology of economic life and the research agenda it entails.

THE SOCIAL CONSTRUCTION OF ECONOMIC INSTITUTIONS

The Problem of Embeddedness

My approach to economic sociology draws on two fundamental sociological propositions: (1) action is always socially situated and cannot be explained by reference to individual motives alone, and (2)social institutions do not arise automatically in some inevitable form but rather are "socially constructed" (Berger and Luckmann 1966). Both are inconsistent with the main thrust of neoclassical economic arguments.

The first proposition leads to what I call the "problem of embeddedness": the question to what extent economic activity is mediated by—or as I say, "embedded in"—networks of personal relations. This discussion will lead me into my argument about the "social construction of economic institutions."

Sociologists, anthropologists, and historians have generally argued that economic action was heavily embedded in "primitive" or "premarket" societies but has become much more autonomous with modernization: that the modern economy is more a separate sphere, where economic transactions are no longer determined mainly by the social or kinship obligations of transactors, but by rational pursuit of individual gain.

But most economists never accepted the premise of a sharp break between earlier and modern societies, asserting that embeddedness is low in both; Adam Smith set the tone, postulating "a certain propensity in human nature . . . to truck, barter and exchange one thing for another," and assuming that in primitive society, with labor the only factor of production, people must have exchanged goods in proportion to their labor cost, as rational actors would. This view has gained new adherents as recent work in anthropology, political science, and history has converged with the "New Institutional Economics" to argue that in all periods, behavior that appears to result from political, social, or legal factors is better interpreted as the outcome of rational individuals pursuing their own self-interest.

My own view differs from both. Although I agree with the economists (and their fellow travelers) that the transition to modernity did not much change the level of embeddedness, I also argue that it has always been and remains substantial: less all-encompassing in the earlier period than claimed by "substantivists," "development theorists," and evolutionists, but more so in the later period than supposed by them or by economists.

Over- and Undersocialized Conceptions of Human Action

In his 1961 article, "The Oversocialized Conception of Man in Modern Sociology," Dennis Wrong complained of the tendency of sociologists to see people as so overwhelmingly sensitive to the opinions of others that they automatically obeyed generally agreed upon norms for behavior. To the extent this was a valid complaint, it resulted from sociologists' overreaction to the neglect of social effects in what Parsons (1937) called the "utilitarian tradition"—a tradition whose view of economic action I will call "undersocialized." As Hirschman (1982) pointed out, traders in competitive markets are price-takers and thus interchangeable. The details of their social relations are irrelevant.

When the classical writers treated these relations at all, it was as a drag on perfect competition. Thus Adam Smith denounced the use of social occasions by traders to raise or fix prices. Implicitly he recognized that his image of competitive markets was at variance with a world where economic actors know one another personally well enough to collude.

A few recent economists have taken social relations as more than frictional drag. But they embrace a conception of social relations curiously similar to that criticized by Dennis Wrong as "oversocialized." So James Duesenberry (1960) quipped that "economics is all about how people make choices; sociology is all about how they don't have any choices to make"; and E. H. Phelps Brown (1977) described the "sociologists' approach to pay determination" as assuming people to act in "certain ways because to do so is customary, or an obligation, or the 'natural thing to do', or right and proper, or just and fair."

This conception of "social influences" is oversocialized because it assumes that people acquire customs, habits, or norms that they follow automatically and unconditionally; nearly all economists' treatment of "norms" has this flavor. But this brings into view an important theoretical irony: the oversocialized approach has in common with the undersocialized the assumption that actors are not influenced by existing social relations—that they are atomized. In the undersocialized account atomization results from the narrow pursuit of self-interest; in the oversocialized one—which originated as a corrective to the undersocialized—atomization results nevertheless because behavioral patterns are treated as having been internalized and thus unaffected by ongoing social relations.

This surprising convergence of under- and oversocialized views helps explain why economists who try to incorporate social influences on economic action fall so easily into oversocialized arguments. Thus, economists such as Michael Piore (1975) or Samuel Bowles and Herbert Gintis (1976) attribute distinctive styles of decision-making to members of different social classes, as the result either of class cultures or of each class's distinctive experience in the educational system. But this conception of how society influences individual economic action is too mechanical: once we know someone's social class, everything else in his behavior is automatic, since he is so well socialized—I would say "oversocialized."

I will thread my way between under- and oversocialized views by analyzing how action and institutions are embedded in concrete, ongoing systems of social relations. I first develop a general argument about "embeddedness" and then offer a series of empirical examples.[6]

Embeddedness and Economic Action: The Concepts and the Agenda

I distinguish three levels of economic phenomena. The first is "individual economic action," for which I take Max Weber's definition: action oriented to the provision of needs as individuals define them, in situations of scarcity (1921/1968:339).[7] With such a definition I could logically go on to many subjects, including those where economists have recently invaded territory previously held by sociologists—marriage, divorce, crime, and the allocation of time. Instead I confine attention to the "hard core" of economics— the provision of goods and services. I do so in part to limit my subject matter, but also for a polemical reason: even if successful in showing that typically sociological subjects are vitally affected by their embeddedness in webs of social relations, I would at best restore the *status quo ante bellum*— the intellectual situation before economists began applying their concepts to the sociological realm. I mean to suggest instead that neoclassical arguments would be strengthened even in their most familiar terrain, by the addition of a sociological perspective. A successful demonstration of this assertion would carry over a fortiori to the more peripheral subjects of recent "economic imperialism."

I also want to explain patterns beyond the actions of individuals—what I call "economic outcomes" and "economic institutions." Examples of "outcomes" would be the formation of stable prices for a commodity or of wage differentials between certain classes of workers. So these "outcomes" are regular patterns of individual action. Institutions are different from these "outcomes" in being larger complexes of action and in taking on a sense that this is how things *should* be done. Institutions often convey, as is well captured in the sociology of knowledge literature, an impression of solidity: they become reified, experienced as external and objective aspects of the world rather than as the social constructions that they really are (see, e.g., Berger and Luckmann 1966).

This social-constructionist perspective is rarely applied to economic institutions, but is just as relevant there as for any other kind. Examples of economic institutions are systems of economic organization, such as capitalism, or, at lower levels, the way particular organizations, industries, or professions are constituted.

By "embeddedness" I mean that economic action, outcomes, and institutions are affected by actors' personal relations, and by the structure of the overall network of relations. I refer to these respectively as the relational and the structural aspects of embeddedness. The structural aspect is especially crucial to keep in mind because it is easy to slip into "dyadic atomization," a kind of reductionism, as if relations among pairs of people mattered but not the way these pairs are themselves embedded in higher order structures as in, for example, the treatment of husbands and wives by Gary Becker (1981) or of employers and employees by Harvey Leibenstein (1976). This atomization makes it impossible to see the central role in outcomes of network cohesion and fragmentation.

It is also important to avoid temporal reductionism—treating relations and structures of relations as if they had no history. In ongoing relations, human beings do not start fresh each day, but carry the baggage of previous interactions into each new one. Built into our cognitive equipment is a remarkable capacity, depressingly little studied, to file away the details and especially the emotional tone of past relations for long periods, so that even when one has not had dealings with a certain person for many years, a reactivation of the relationship does not start from scratch, but from some set of previously attained common understandings and feelings. It follows that the characteristics of structures of relations also result from processes over time, and can rarely be understood except as accretions of these processes.

Embeddedness and Individual Economic Action

Relational embeddedness has typically quite direct effects. How a worker and supervisor interact is determined not only by the meaning of these categories in the division of labor, but also by the personal relationship they have, determined largely by a history of interactions and consequent mutual expectations. Thus, I may deal with you fairly in part because we have been close for so long that we expect fair treatment of one another, and I would be mortified and distressed to have cheated you—even if you did not find out.

Structural embeddedness has typically more subtle and less direct effects on economic action. A worker can more easily maintain a good relationship with a supervisor who has good relations with most other workers. If the supervisor is at odds with the others, and especially if those others are friendly with one another, they will be able to make life very difficult for the one worker who is close to the supervisor; pressures will be strong to edge away from this closeness. If the other workers do not form a cohesive group, such pressures can be mounted only with difficulty.

Consider also the impact of structural embeddedness on whether I cheat my friend. My mortification at doing so may be substantial even when undiscovered. It may increase when the friend becomes aware of it. But it may become most unbearable when our mutual friends uncover the deceit and tell one another. Whether they do so will depend on the structure of the network of relations—especially on the extent to which the mutual friends of this pair are connected to one another. When these connections are many—what is called "high network density"—the news will spread quickly; when they are isolated from one another, much less so. So we can expect greater pressure against such cheating in the denser network. This pressure arises not only on account of information spread but also because such cohesive groups are more efficient at generating normative, symbolic, and cultural structures that affect our behavior. Thus, in such a group, it may never even occur to me to cheat my friend, since I have absorbed a set of standards from the group that literally makes it unthinkable.

But here I teeter on the brink of a functionalist argument that networks of relations always lead to trust and order. Such relations do not only prevent malfeasance, however; they may also facilitate it. Those implicated in insider-trading violations are monotonously likely to be close friends or old college roommates. Malfeasance is poorly executed by those who cannot trust one another. And members of groups engaged in malfeasance persuade one another that it is routine and acceptable; they often develop a language to describe it that has a neutralizing effect, as in the OPM leasing company, where the practice of pledging the same collateral for many different loans was referred to internally as "double discounting" (Gandossy 1985; see Sykes and Matza 1957 on "neutralization"), or as in Paul Hirsch's (1986) account of how the language in which unfriendly corporate takeovers are described evolved over time in such a way as to redefine what was taken to be malfeasance. Atomized economic actors could not evolve these consequential linguistic conventions.

Embeddedness and Economic Outcomes

Individuals' economic actions may accumulate in ways that result in larger economic outcomes or institutions—but they need not. Whether this occurs and what shape the outcomes and institutions take when it does are strongly channeled by the content and structure of relations in which economic action is embedded. A simple example is the determination of prices.

In general equilibrium theory, markets become more competitive and prices more stable the greater the number of traders. But in his study of stock option trading, Baker (1984) found that price volatility increased with the size of the trading group. This occurred because as group size increased, the number of personal trading relations that the average trader could sustain did not. In a larger group it was thus harder to know about all trades; information flow was reduced by the size and resulting fragmentation of the trading network, and convergence to a single equilibrium price became problematic. The imperfect movement of information that caused this resulted from fundamental cognitive limitations of human actors in conjunction with the necessary embeddedness of trading in networks of personal relations.

This example, like those on cheating and malfeasance, involves the general principle that fragmentation of a network reduces the homogeneity of behavior. The principle is purely structural, and does not in itself predict which prices different group fragments will approach, or whether cohesive groups will forbid or facilitate malfeasance. Similarly, social psychological studies show that cohesive groups are in agreement on norms, without being able to explain by cohesion alone which norms they hold (cf. Festinger et al. 1948; Seashore 1954).

More generally, many kinds of prices are affected because transactions occur not in spot markets but between traders of long acquaintance. Anthropologists report that peasant and tribal markets are typically clientelized—that is, buyers and sellers have long-term continuing relations.[8] This leads to sticky prices, as buyers and sellers are unresponsive to price inducements to trade with unfamiliar partners. This stickiness, and the result that adjustments must then be made in quantities, so the market is not cleared, is important not only in tribal and peasant settings; macroeconomist Arthur Okun (1981) argued for a similar impact in modern markets, where most trades are carried out not in auction markets but in what he called "customer markets" with continuing relationships.

Another example of the impact of embeddedness on prices comes from labor markets, and involves the "skill differential" in pay between skilled and unskilled blue-collar workers. Economist Melvin Reder wanted to explain why it typically diminishes in times of economic boom. Standard theory suggests that a surge in aggregate demand should increase the demand for skilled and unskilled workers alike, bidding up wages for both. Reder (1955) suggested that rather than raise skilled workers' wages, employers promote workers from the next to highest skill level. Pursued vigorously, this strategy leaves a shortage in this next-to-highest level that is met by substitution from the group below that, and so on. When finally a shortage appears in the lowest skill category, and no new labor is available from outside the workforce, the wages there must be bid up in relation to higher grades, reducing the skill differential.

I suggest a generalization: any set of jobs in which such substitution chains are possible may have its wage differentials compressed. How do we identify such sets? Reder suggests a simple progression from skilled down to unskilled. But I argue that in practice, which workers *appear* available to employers for upgrading into a particular job actually depends on the history and structure of employers' and workers' communications networks. Purely technical considerations are unlikely to be primary since the question is not whether workers can perform work previously done, but how adaptable they would be to a different, more complex set of tasks. We know that when making hiring decisions, employers rely on personal contacts even to assess a worker's previous productivity (Granovetter 1974); it seems all the more likely that they would do so where the productivity question is inherently more ambiguous.

Thus, where networks of contacts cross firm boundaries rather than being contained within firms, wage differentials might be especially widely affected. Whether such interfirm links exist depends in part on the previous mobility history of current workers, since one's pool of work contacts results directly from these histories. This in turn determines how widespread such effects will be. Thus, the embeddedness of economic action may be structured in such a way as to blunt and contain individual actions, so they never do accumulate into larger outcomes—as, for example, when all networks are contained within firms—or may amplify and concatenate such actions, as where networks cross the boundaries of individual firms. Patterns of network coupling and decoupling are again central here, and substantial outcomes such as economy-wide skill differentials may be, in effect, the trace of these patterns, rather than the effect of some larger functional or macroeconomic logic.

Embeddedness and Economic Institutions

I focus on institutions that account for the production of goods and services: firms, industries, and professions. The question of why firms exist— why all economic activity is not simply coordinated by autonomous agents through a market—was introduced to the economic literature by Ronald Coase in 1937, and revived by Oliver Williamson (1975, 1985). Their answer was that firms arise when their existence economizes on transaction costs.

I have argued (1985) that firms are often not more efficient than markets in reducing such costs. But even if they were, it would remain problematic how they could be constructed. There is a question logically dual to that of "why firms?" that Coase and Williamson do not ask: "how firms?" Like most functionalist accounts, theirs implicitly assumes that whatever problem presents itself will be solved, and does not specify the mechanisms that make this possible, alluding instead to some vague process of "natural selection" (as in Williamson 1981:573–574).

But the development literature often notes situations in which firms are economically desirable but can be constructed only with difficulty. What are the barriers? One traditional candidate in this literature was precisely the embeddedness of economic action in diffuse obligations of kinship and friendship, which was alleged to discourage businesslike operations.

Studies from, among others, Indonesia (Geertz 1963; Dewey 1962), the Philippines (Davis 1973; D. Szanton 1971; M. Szanton 1972; Omohundro 1981) and Morocco (Geertz 1979) show, however, that where this embeddedness is lacking, and traders and producers are overwhelmingly individual profit-maximizers—where, in other words, the undersocialized model of human action is not far off—this cultural pattern presents an enormous obstacle to the construction of firms: viz. the absence of trust, which results in the inability to delegate authority or resources to others—exactly the Hobbesian problem that I have argued (1985) is logically implied by the undersocialized model.

Is a high level of social solidarity what is needed then? This also leads to problems: Geertz and others report, just as traditional development theory predicts, that, as the abdicated king of Tabanan in Bali told Geertz, firms "turn into relief organizations rather than businesses" (Geertz 1963:123). They start easily because trust is not problematic; but they expand beyond the efficient level because all sorts of friends and relatives make claims on the businesses' resources that cannot easily be denied. The welfare of the local community is put ahead of that of the business as such. Similar reports can be found about Filipino, Malaysian, and Thai firms (Omohundro 1981; Lim and Gosling 1983).

But there are a few groups that successfully construct efficient firms. In Southeast Asia, it is especially overseas Chinese who do so. Why? I argue that the two problems I have cited are overcome by the Chinese because of their particular social structure. Chinese businesses experience dramatically lower costs because their close-knit community promotes a high level of trust: credit is extended, capital pooled, and authority delegated without fear of default or deceit. The social structure makes malfeasance not only difficult to conceal and costly to engage in, but even hard to imagine.

Why then are Chinese firms not drained by the claims of friends and relatives? Part of the answer is that overseas Chinese are typically a small minority, and there are simply not enough of them for such claims to cause trouble. But the organization of social networks also limits claims, because people belong to nonoverlapping groups. Patrilineal kinship groups are so clearly defined that the number of relatives with credible claims on a business is small. People also divide into groups based on recency of immigration and on home area in China. Particular businesses are organized along such kinship and organizational lines, and which individuals can make claims is thus sharply defined. By contrast, most non-Chinese Southeast Asian kinship patterns are more diffuse, so it is hard to limit the number of relatives who will make claims; and people typically belong to many other overlapping groups, so that if one is the core of a business, its members may still be subject to claims from fellow members of others (see Geertz 1963:Chapter 4). Briefly put, overseas Chinese social structure has a pattern of coupling and decoupling that produces highly cohesive groups that are sharply delimited from one another in everyday practice; thus, trust is available but noneconomic claims are illegitimate beyond these group boundaries.

More generally, in any historical or cultural setting where firms have successfully emerged, this success requires the dual problems of trust and of noneconomic claims to have been addressed. The analytic task implied by my argument is to investigate how the social structure of successful entrepreneurial groups allowed this to occur. The Chinese solution need not be the only viable one, nor should one always expect to find a particular group with ethnic or communal identity that is entrepreneurially successful. Rather, this identity is one strategy by which the trust required to do business may be constructed. Other strategies, such as those of guild-like organizations, may prevail depending on the circumstances, or no strategy may be successful. Much more empirical and historical work is required to flesh out this argument. My claim is simply that any successful strategy can be most usefully analyzed by studying the distinctive pattern of interpersonal relations that it entails.

My last two examples concern the evolution of industries and of professions. We take for granted the existing way industries and professions are defined, as if they could not be other than they are. But like firms, these are social constructions that often might have been otherwise. Their existing form is not simply the automatic response to the technical requirements imposed by market demand and supply, factor costs, and available technology.

I use the case of the electrical utility industry in the United States from its inception in the 1880s to about 1930, relying especially on the account of McGuire (1986). He wanted to explain why certain alternatives that seemed quite likely to occur rather than the present form of the industry did not: for example, public ownership of all electrical utilities, or private generation of electric power by each large industrial company, which would have consigned utility companies to a minor role.

McGuire finds a series of stages. When there was no standard way to meet the demand for electricity, the personal networks of a few major individuals were crucial. Samuel Insull arrived in Chicago in 1894 to take over a small, new company, Chicago Edison, and brought with him a unique set of personal ties: to financiers in both Chicago and London, to local political leaders, and to inventors in both the United States and Britain. Many of these had been forged as the result of his 10 years of association with Thomas Edison. His combination of financial and technical expertise and political connections allowed him to assemble capital, political favors, and ways of operating that other utility companies had found impossible to implement, even though some were well aware of their potential.[9] What made Insull unique was that his network of contacts reached into a variety of usually separated institutional spheres; had he been narrowly ensconced in a tightly knit network of close associates, it is unlikely that he could have constructed the outcomes he did. This exemplifies what I have called the "strength of weak ties" (1973, 1983).[10]

Later, Insull and others encouraged regulation by states and developed the holding company form, that led to regular relations with local industry and with regulators. Soon, this network of firms, holding companies and regulators congealed. Personal networks still mattered, but only those of people central in the holding companies. By the 1920s the institutional forms were in place, and the outcome that we now see in the industry was already recognizable.[11]

What has happened here, as with Chinese firms in Southeast Asia, is that institutions that arise and stabilize begin as accretions of activity patterns around personal networks. Their structure reflects that of the networks, and even when those networks are no longer in place, the institutions take on a life of their own that limits the forms future institutional development can take—a "lock-in" phenomenon of the sort studied by economists Paul David (1986) and Brian Arthur (1985) for technology.

One reason that it has always been difficult to think about firms or industries as social constructions is that with the exception of Knight and Schumpeter, the entrepreneur as an actor and the nature of entrepreneurial activity have been almost completely ignored in classical and neoclassical economic theory, in favor of an implicit assumption that entrepreneurial activity is somehow automatically called forth by economic circumstances.

But a social constructionist account does not imply that the economic situation of an industry is irrelevant to how it is constructed. The possibility of a highly centralized outcome is greater for products that lend themselves to the establishment of market power. Highly competitive industries would be more decentralized geographically and less structured institutionally. Something like this is true as well for the professions: knowledge that is difficult to monopolize does not lend itself to the development of a profession. Thus, auto repair, despite the similarity of its conceptual problems to those of medicine, has never acquired the status of a profession.

We have a few detailed accounts of how particular professions were constructed out of networks of collective action—as in Randall Collins's (1979) account of the successful implementation of monopolies in medicine and law and its failure in engineering. The development of professions can be traced through stages similar to those in the electric utility industry. The case of psychiatry is laid out by Andrew Abbott (1988), beginning with a collection of nineteenth-century individuals connected by personal, informal ties who built an organization around those ties—the Association of Medical Superintendents of American Institutions for the Insane—which eventually became institutionalized as the American Psychiatric Association. This is then another case of an institution arising as the congealed form of previous social networks.

Our image of what the proper role of various industries and professions is becomes fixed by the outcomes of these processes, and other possibilities fade from awareness. Thus, we now suppose that people who are unable to cope with everyday life should logically seek psychiatric treatment. But not long ago we would have assumed they should visit their clergyman. Abbott traces the sometimes violent competition between psychiatry and competitors such as the clergy, lawyers, and social workers for the right to treat peoples' troubles.

In many ways the arguments appropriate for these analyses of how industries, professions, and firms are constructed resemble those that are useful in theories of resource dependency and mobilization in the construction of social movements and political action. This is no accident: if we are doing anything right, there should be one general theory of social institutions, not a separate one for each kind of institution.

Conclusions

I have laid out a general argument about the embeddedness of economic action in social structure, and some more specific arguments about how this embeddedness has its effects at three different levels of economic life.

Now I want to stand back and make some observations about my argument. Though critical of neoclassical economic theory, I share with its proponents the positivist quest for general, universal explanations. In this respect, my position is close to Hempel's (1965) whose student I was. But then I find my own argument frustrating because it relies so heavily on contingencies. I deny that a given set of economic problems or a given technology calls forth individual, organizational, or institutional outcomes in some unconditional way. In less contingent arguments, including most neoclassical economic work, many versions of Marxism or population ecology, and functionalism of all varieties, outcomes are predicted without the necessity of looking closely at the historical background of particular settings, the preexisting economic institutions, or the social structure and collective action of individuals.

I argue instead that outcomes can vary dramatically even for the *same* economic problems and technologies, if the social structure, institutional history, and collective action are different, and that these crucially limit and shape future possibilities. Less contingent arguments are cleaner, simpler, and more elegant. But they fail to identify causal mechanisms; they do not make an adequate connection between micro and macro levels, and so explain poorly when historical circumstances vary from the ones under which they were formulated.

Many economists would agree that dynamics is the weakest part of modern economics. I believe that an account of the social construction of economic institutions can be useful in making more sophisticated dynamic models. Existing ones are frustrating because they are often underdetermined, with multiple stable equilibria. As in similar physical models, it is possible to understand which state the system reaches only by looking at its history. But the contingencies involved in that history are outside the economic framework, and thus seem ad hoc and unsatisfying to economists; within a sociological framework, however, they can be given systematic treatment.

Such multiple equilibrium models, even if underdetermined, are far from the historicist argument that every case is unique and anything is possible. In the case of electric utilities, for example, McGuire, in effect, identified three possible system equilibria—public ownership, private decentralized generation of power, or privately held utilities. I argue that even given the constraints of the particular set of political, technical, and economic parameters in place in late nineteenth-century America, any of these three might have occurred. Historical contingencies embedded in the structure of social networks, of resource mobilization, and of relations between key actors and government determined which of them did occur. An important part of the general arguments about such matters is the identification of those circumstances under which there indeed are multiple equilibria, and networks of collective action may determine outcomes. Part of my argument about the utilities was that later, once the industry form was locked in, the other possibilities were foreclosed; it follows that in those periods, less contingent theoretical accounts might have sufficed.

Thus, the agenda that follows from my conception of economic sociology is one that aims to produce a theoretical argument consistent with the high level of contingency I see operating in the actual construction of economic institutions, but to do so without sliding down the slippery slope into historicism. This is not the only possible agenda for economic sociology, but it is a broad and challenging one that I claim has great potential to add a new dimension to our understanding of economic life.

ACKNOWLEDGMENTS

An earlier draft of this paper was presented at the first annual seminar of the Center for Economy and Society, University of California, Santa Barbara: May 20–21, 1988. I am greatly indebted to seminar participants for their many useful suggestions.

NOTES

1. For a fuller account of this attitude see Swedberg (1987:14–17). I rely heavily on this excellent source for the nineteenth and early twentieth century background.

2. Camic (1987) gives a detailed account of Parsons's 1930s work on the division of labor in the social sciences.

3. Parsons's attacks were consistent and uncharacteristically *ad hominem*. He refers, for example, to Veblen as a "highly unsophisticated person. . . . Weber . . . was on a totally different level of scientific and cultural sophistication. The fact that a Veblen rather than a Weber gathers a school of ardent disciples around him bears witness to the great importance of factors other than the sheer weight of evidence and analysis in the formation of 'schools' of social thought" (1947:40n).

4. As in the rest of this paper I make no claim to present a detailed history of relevant developments, but only select a few highlights that illuminate the failure of sociological and economic ideas to connect. An excellent account of the history of industrial sociology, industrial relations and organizational research in general can be found in Perrow (1986).

5. The brief comments here on the "new economic sociology" are not meant as a full or adequate summary of the large volume of interesting new work, but only as a quick sketch. For a fuller account see Swedberg (1987:63–134).

6. I avoid examples I have elaborated elsewhere, such as my critique of the "transactions-cost" theory of industrial organization (1985), my comparison of economic and sociological approaches to the labor market (1988a), and my work (with Charles Tilly) on inequality and labor processes (1988). The examples I offer in the present paper are highly condensed, and will be treated in much more detail in my forthcoming book (see available draft chapters, Granovetter 1990).

7. This definition is substantially identical to that of Lionel Robbins (1932), which has become economists' standard definition of their field, and is repeated at the beginning of most textbooks.

8. Richard Posner (1980) gives these relations a neoclassical interpretation by attributing them to information and trust difficulties inherent in all primitive societies. For an extended critique of this effort see Granovetter (1990:Chapter 3).

9. This last point is crucial to combat technological determinist arguments; much more is required to implement a new technology than simply a technical understanding of how it will work.

10. Insull's ability to pull together resources from a variety of institutional spheres is reminiscent of Barth's (1967) definition of entrepreneurs, in a tribal setting, as those who are able to breach traditionally decoupled spheres of exchange.

11. This very truncated version of the social construction of the electrical utility industry will be amplified in a paper I am writing in collaboration with McGuire and my colleague Michael Schwartz.

REFERENCES

Abbott, Andrew. 1988. *The System of Professions*. Chicago: University of Chicago Press.

Arthur, W. Brian. 1985. "Competing Technologies and Lock-In by Historical Small Events: The Dynamics of Allocation Under Increasing Returns." Publication #43, Center for Economic Policy Research, Stanford University.

Baker, Wayne. 1984. "The Social Structure of a National Securities Market." *American Journal of Sociology* 89(4):775–811.

Barth, Fredric. 1967. "Economic Spheres in Darfur." In *Themes in Economic Anthropology*, edited by R. Firth. London: Tavistock.

Becker, Gary. 1976. *The Economic Approach to Human Behavior*. Chicago: University of Chicago Press.

———. 1981. *Treatise on the Family*. Cambridge: Harvard University Press.

Berg, Ivar, ed. 1981. *Sociological Perspectives on Labor Markets.* New York: Academic Press.

Berger, Peter and Thomas Luckmann. 1966. *The Social Construction of Reality.* New York: Doubleday.

Bowles, Samuel and Herbert Gintis. 1976. *Schooling in Capitalist America.* New York: Basic.

Braverman, Harry. 1974. *Labor and Monopoly Capital.* New York: Monthly Review Press.

Burawoy, Michael. 1979. *Manufacturing Consent: Changes in the Labor Process Under Monopoly Capitalism.* Chicago: University of Chicago Press.

———. 1985. *The Politics of Production.* London: Verso.

Burt, Ronald. 1983. *Corporate Profits and Cooptation: Networks of Market Constraints and Directorate Ties in the American Economy.* New York: Academic Press.

Camic, Charles. 1987. "The Making of a Method: A Historical Reinterpretation of the Early Parsons." *American Sociological Review* 52 (August):421–439.

Chrisman, Lawrence. 1967. "The Segmentary Structure of Urban Overseas Chinese Communities." *Man (New Series)* 2(2):185–204.

Clawson, Dan. 1980. *Bureaucracy and the Labor Process.* New York: Monthly Review Press.

Coase, Ronald. 1937. "The Nature of the Firm." *Economica N.S.* 4:386–405.

Collins, Randall. 1979. *The Credential Society: An Historical Sociology of Education and Stratification.* New York: Academic Press.

Crozier, Michel. 1964. *The Bureaucratic Phenomenon.* Chicago: University of Chicago Press.

Dalton, Melville, 1959. *Men Who Manage.* New York: Wiley.

David, Paul. 1986. "Understanding the Necessity of QWERTY: The Necessity of History." Pp. 30–49 in *Economic History and the Modern Economist,* edited by William N. Parker. London: Blackwell.

Davis, William G. 1973. *Social Relations in a Philippine Market: Self-Interest and Subjectivity.* Berkeley, CA: University of California Press.

Dewey, Alice. 1962. *Peasant Marketing in Java.* Glencoe, IL: Free Press.

Duesenberry, James. 1960. Comment on "An Economic Analysis of Fertility." In *Demographic and Economic Change in Developed Countries,* edited by the Universities-National Bureau Committee for Economic Research. Princeton: Princeton University Press.

Dunlop, John. 1957. "The Task of Contemporary Wage Theory." In *New Concepts in Wage Determination,* edited by G. Taylor and F. Pierson. New York: McGraw-Hill.

Durkheim, Emile. 1893 (1984). *The Division of Labor in Society.* Translated by W. D. Halls. New York: The Free Press.

Farkas, George and Paula England (eds.) 1988. *Industries, Firms, and Jobs: Sociological and Economic Approaches.* New York: Plenum.

Festinger, Leon, Stanley Schachter, and Kurt Back. 1948. *Social Pressures in Informal Groups.* Cambridge: MIT Press.

Form, William. 1985. Verbal presentation to a session on industrial sociology, American Sociological Association meetings, Washington, D.C.

Friedman, Milton. 1953. *Essays in Positive Economics*. Chicago: University of Chicago Press.

Gandossy, Robert. 1985. *Bad Business: The OPM Scandal and the Seduction of the Establishment*. New York: Basic Books.

Geertz, Clifford. 1963. *Peddlers and Princes*. Chicago: University of Chicago Press.

———. 1979. "Suq: The Bazaar Economy in Sefrou." Pp. 123–224 in *Meaning and Order in Moroccan Society*, edited by C. Geertz, H. Geertz, and L. Rosen. New York: Cambridge University Press.

Granovetter, Mark. 1974. *Getting a Job: A Study of Contacts and Careers*. Cambridge: Harvard University Press.

———. 1985. "Economic Action and Social Structure: The Problem of Embeddedness." *American Journal of Sociology* 91(3):481–510.

———. 1988. "The Sociological and Economic Approach to Labor Markets: A Social Structural View." Pp. 187–216 in *Industries, Firms and Job: Sociological and Economic Approaches*, edited by George Farkas and Paula England. New York: Plenum.

———. 1990. Draft Chapters from *Society and Economy: The Social Construction of Economic Institutions*.

Granovetter, Mark and Charles Tilly. 1988. "Inequality and Labor Processes." In *Handbook of Sociology*, edited by Neil Smelser. Newbury Park, CA: Sage Publications.

Hempel, Carl. 1965. *Aspects of Scientific Explanation*. New York: Free Press.

Hicks, John. 1939. *Value and Capital*. Oxford: Oxford University Press.

Hirsch, Paul. 1986. "From Ambushes to Golden Parachutes: Corporate Takeovers as an Instance of Cultural Framing and Institutional Integration." *American Journal of Sociology* 91(4):800–837.

Hirschman, Albert. 1982. "Rival Interpretations of Market Society: Civilizing, Destructive or Feeble?" *Journal of Economic Literature* 20(4):1463–1484.

Hirshleifer, Jack. 1985. "The Expanding Domain of Economics." *American Economic Review* 85(6):53–68.

Homans, George. 1950. *The Human Group*. New York: Harcourt Brace.

———. 1961. *Social Behavior: Its Elementary Forms*. New York: Harcourt, Brace Jovanovich.

Leibenstein, Harvey. 1976. *Beyond Economic Man*. Cambridge: Harvard University Press.

Lim, Linda Y. C. and L. A. Peter Gosling (eds.) 1983. *The Chinese in Southeast Asia, Volume I: Ethnicity and Economic Activity*. Singapore: Maruzen Asia.

McGuire, Patrick. 1986. *The Control of Power: The Political Economy of Electric Utility Development in the United States, 1870–1930*. Ph.D. Dissertation, Department of Sociology, State University of New York at Stony Brook.

Mintz, Beth and Michael Schwartz. 1985. *The Power Structure of American Business*. Chicago: University of Chicago Press.

Mizruchi, Mark and Michael Schwartz (eds.) 1988. *Intercorporate Relations: The Structural Analysis of Business*. Cambridge: Cambridge University Press.

Moore, Wilbert. 1955. *Economy and Society*. New York: Doubleday.

Okun, Arthur. 1981. *Prices and Quantities*. Washington, D.C.: Brookings Institution.

Omohundro, John T. 1981. *Chinese Merchant Families in Iloilo: Commerce and Kin in a Central Phillipine City.* Athens, OH: Ohio University Press.

Parsons, Talcott. 1935. "Sociological Elements in Economic Thought. II. The Analytical Factor View." *Quarterly Journal of Economics* 49 (August):646–667.

———. 1937. *The Structure of Social Action.* New York: McGraw-Hill.

———. 1947. Pp. 3–86 in Introduction to *Max Weber: The Theory of Social and Economic Organization,* translated by A. M. Henderson and Talcott Parsons, New York: Oxford University Press.

———. 1953. The Marshall Lectures: On the Integration of Economics and Sociology. Cambridge: University of Cambridge.

———. 1968. Introduction to paperback edition, *Structure of Social Action.* New York: Free Press.

———. 1970. "On Building Social System Theory: A Personal History." *Daedalus* 99:826–881.

Parsons, Talcott and Neil Smelser. 1956. *Economy and Society: A Study in the Integration of Economic and Social Theory.* Glencoe, IL: The Free Press.

Perrow, Charles. 1986. *Complex Organizations: A Critical Essay,* 3rd ed. New York: Random House.

Phelps Brown, Ernest Henry. 1977. *The Inequality of Pay.* Berkeley: University of California Press.

Piore, Michael. 1975. "Notes for a Theory of Labor Market Stratification." Pp. 125–150 in *Labor Market Segmentation,* edited by R. Edwards, M. Reich, and D. Gordon. Lexington, MA: D.C. Heath.

Posner, Richard. 1980. "A Theory of Primitive Society, with Special Reference to Law." *Journal of Law and Economics* 23:1–56.

Reder, Melvin. 1955. "The Theory of Occupational Wage Differentials." *American Economic Review* 45:883–852.

Robbins, Lionel. 1932 (1984). *An Essay on the Nature and Significance of Economic Science.* New York: New York University Press.

Samuelson, Paul. 1947. *Foundations of Economic Analysis.* Cambridge: Harvard University Press.

Seashore, Stanley. 1954. *Group Cohesiveness in the Industrial Work Group.* Ann Arbor: Survey Research Center, Institute for Social Research.

Smelser, Neil. 1963. *The Sociology of Economic Life.* Englewood Cliffs, NJ: Prentice-Hall.

Stark, David. 1986. "Rethinking Internal Labor Markets: New Insights from a Comparative Perspective." *American Sociological Review* 51(August):492–504.

Stearns, Linda. 1986. "Capital Market Effects on External Control of Corporations." *Theory and Society* 15:47–75.

Swedberg, Richard. 1987. "Economic Sociology: Past and Present." *Current Sociology* 35(1):1–221.

Sykes, Gresham and David Matza. 1957. "Techniques of Neutralization: A Theory of Delinquency." *American Sociological Review* 22(December):667–669.

Szanton, David L. 1971. *Estancia in Transition: Economic Growth in a Rural Philippine Community.* Quezon City, Philippines: Ateneo de Manila University Press.

Szanton, Maria C. B. 1972. *A Right to Survive: Subsistence Marketing in a Lowland Philippine Town*. University Park PA: Penn State University Press.

Weber, Max. 1921 (1968). *Economy and Society,* edited and translated by Guenther Roth and Claus Wittich. New York: Bedminster Press.

White, Harrison. 1981. "Where Do Markets Come From?" *American Journal of Sociology* 87 (November):517–547.

Whyte, William F. 1955. *Money and Motivation: An Analysis of Incentives in Industry.* New York: Harper and Bros.

———. 1961. *Men at Work.* Homewood IL: Dorsey.

Williamson, Oliver. 1975. *Markets and Hierarchies.* New York: Free Press.

Williamson, Oliver. 1981. "The Economics of Organization: The Transaction Cost Approach." *American Journal of Sociology* 87 (November):548–577.

———. 1985. *The Economic Institutions of Capitalism.* New York: Free Press.

Cultural Aspects of Economic Action and Organization   4

Paul DiMaggio

In this chapter, I suggest that economic behavior is embedded not only in social structure, as Mark Granovetter has argued so compellingly in the previous chapter, but also in culture. I develop this argument with reference to three economic problems: contingent aspects of economic rationality, the efficiency of firms, and the origins of preferences.

WHAT IS CULTURE?

The analytic distinction between culture and social structure that Parsons presented in *The Structure of Social Action* (1949; see Camic 1987) is in many ways artificial. Patterns of social relations drive and channel the acquisition and expression of culture, and patterns of cognition are deeply implicated in the constitution of social structure. On the other hand, the isolation of "culture" as an object of inquiry is useful in so far as it calls attention to matters we might otherwise overlook.

I use "culture" to refer to social cognition, the content and categories of conscious thought and the taken-for-granted. Culture consists of shared cognitions that vary within some theoretically relevant population. It follows that understanding culture requires the study of boundaries, the pervasiveness of cultural understandings within human populations, and patterned cultural variation.[1]

The Architecture of Culture

Culture is *multileveled*, that is, it comprises a variety of analytically distinct shared cognitive phenomena among which no necessary coherence may be assumed. (To take a trivial example, one's *norms* may tell one that smoking is stupid at the same time one's *script* for starting to work involves lighting a cigarette.) To do research, one must be clear about the particular types of culture in which one is interested; the relationship among these types is always an empirical question.

One level of culture consists of those cognitive phenomena—beliefs, attitudes, norms, evaluations—that constitute the conventional concerns of social psychology. The relevance of these to economic decisions is palpable and well known. Weber's (1958) Protestant Ethic thesis is about precisely this level of culture: Calvinist religious beliefs produced agonizing uncertainty that impelled believers to lives of this-worldly asceticism. Adam Smith in his *Theory of Moral Sentiments* [1976 (1790)] and Talcott Parsons in *The Structure of Social Action* (1949) called attention to the role of sentiments and behavioral norms in regulating economic conduct.[2] Contemporary economists tell us that people with buoyant attitudes invest more freely than equally resourceful pessimists. The most fundamental attitudes from the standpoint of modern economics are preferences, which, when ordered, fuel microeconomics' analytic engine.[3]

At a deeper level of cognition, we find what sociologists call strategies, logics, or the *habitus* (Swidler 1986; Friedland and Alford 1991; Bourdieu 1977), and psychologists refer to as scripts or production systems (Schank and Abelson 1977; Klahr et al. 1987).[4] Despite differences among these concepts, all refer to habitual, often preconscious, behavioral or problem-solving routines, complex combinations of simpler cognitive elements that work like macros in computer programs to provide menus for action that shape people's interpretations of the world and responses to it. Swidler (1986) views culture in this sense as a toolkit of strategies of action that men and women use in defining and pursuing self-interest. Bourdieu (1974) describes struggle within the French peasantry over conceptions of life trajectories attendant on the industrialization of the French economy. The existence and power of scripted orientations to economic exchange were most vividly illustrated when Garfinkel (1967) sent students into retail establishments to "breach" the social order by haggling over small purchases.

At a still more basic level of social cognition are rules of relevance that guide the invocation of scripts and strategies. As Garfinkel illustrated, script-shifting (e.g., from behaviors associated with family roles to the role of guest) can throw social exchanges into disarray. With respect to the economy, Friedland and Alford (1991) argue persuasively that political debates often become contests over the salience of competing "logics" to particular situations, as when feminists seek to economize family relations by placing a dollar value on domestic labor.[5]

Finally, at the foundation of social cognition are systems of classification, category schemes that define the objects of thought and evaluation, grounds of comparison, and contents of material and social groups (Schwartz 1981; Zerubavel 1985). As Polanyi (1957; and see Gudeman 1986) illustrated so well, the market itself is a cultural construct in terms of which people orient their behavior, as well as a system of social relations in which they participate.[6]

The foregoing will seem hopelessly reductionist to many sociologists and most anthropologists. With respect to my view of culture, I plead guilty; I think it is imperative that "culture" be disaggregated into simpler elements if we are to make any progress. With respect to people, the "culture-bearers," the matter is more complex. I have referred to the elements of social cognition at the individual level, which is, I think, a proper unit of observation. It is not necessarily the right unit of analysis, however. Only when we consider social cognitions as patterned phenomena within collectivities do they become properly cultural. For example, the willingness of one or a few members of a traditional society to sell land is of little economic consequence; but when the notion that land is a commodity is widespread, a market in real estate becomes possible. I will say more about patterning below; for now, the point is that the distribution of cultural elements is as important as their content.[7]

Culture in Economics

Culture, in the sense the word is used here, is strangely absent from most economic theory. When social cognitions exhibit consequential variation, as do tastes, economists treat them as exogenous matters better left to sociologists. When variation in cognitions can be ignored, economists are content to receive wisdom from cognitive psychologists.

Sociologists worry about statistical variation and its explanation almost to the exclusion of anything else. Cognitive psychologists are the opposite. If sociologists are obsessed with variance, they love the intercept and are happiest when they find evidence that some cognitive process is universal. (Psychologists acknowledge individual variation primarily in terms of adeptness of cognitive function.) It is convenient for economists to listen to cognitive psychologists, both because cognitivists have well-developed paradigms and robust findings and because accepting the notion that cognitive processes are invariant removes what might otherwise be embarrassing sources of heterogeneity from economic models.[8]

Sociologists who study culture have much to learn from cognitive psychologists, because they are clearer in conceiving and better at measuring their analytic objects than we are. But they ask different questions and consequently get different answers. Whereas cognitive psychologists are interested in *how* people think, sociologists are concerned with the *content* of thought and the preconscious. I shall argue that the latter concern is more germane to understanding economic phenomena than many economists have realized.

CULTURAL ISSUES IN ECONOMIC ANALYSIS

In the remainder of this paper, three illustrations of the interpenetration of culture and economy are explored. The first concerns systems of classification and rules of relevance as they influence the propensity of persons to act with intended economic rationality (i.e., in a calculating and self-interested manner) and the definition of situations in which (or exchange partners with whom) such an orientation is inappropriate. It is possible, of course, that such variation is not culturally patterned, but subject only to personal idiosyncrasies or traits of personality (e.g., risk averseness, ability to delay gratification) that may prove largely independent of social determinants. If so, however, this is worth establishing empirically, all the more so because it would be surprising.

The second cluster of issues involves what we might call the "scriptedness" of economic institutions and the possibility that the symbolic construction of such objects as firms and markets creates a divergence between the putative functions and actual consequences of intended rational economic behavior [as when employees manipulate time-and-motion studies to establish quotas well below their capacity to perform (Noble 1977)]. What role do rituals play in enacting markets and bureaucracies, what are their consequences, and under what conditions and with what effects do such rituals fail?

The third problem—"tastes" and their social origin—lies close to both the surface of culture and the base of economics. Beginning with Weber's observations about the opposition of status groups and markets as means of organizing social life, I suggest that a cultural understanding of commodities requires a different conception of demand than that present in most economic accounts, that taste formation is a heterogeneous and contingent process, and that this has implications for economic models of demand.

Rules of Relevance, Classification, and Exchange

The course of economic history can be viewed as a gradual loosening of restrictions on exchange, and a broadening of the classes of objects that may be exchanged and of persons among whom exchanges may be conducted. With respect to the rise of capitalism, this story has been told many times (Weber 1968; Marx 1971:106–118; Polanyi 1957). Under capitalism the market has extended its reach to include more and more commodities (see Titmuss 1971; Zelizer 1979, 1985; Barber 1983).

As Polanyi taught us, the expansion of markets was a cultural as well as an economic phenomenon, all the more so because the absolutist rhetoric of self-regulating markets was superimposed on the craggy contours of actual exchange systems. The denizen of the self-regulating market is *homo economicus,* whose dispassionate and methodical regard for his own material well-being drives economics' most powerful models.

Many critics have observed that *homo economicus* is seemingly asocial, a "social moron" (Sen 1977:336). One line of criticism focuses on structural embeddedness, perduring relationships that limit persons' choices of exchange partners, create long time horizons, and facilitate social control (Granovetter 1985, and this volume). An older tradition in sociology and anthropology emphasizes what might be called the *cultural* embeddedness of economic exchange: the tendency of persons to view exchanges in terms of role relationships, normative scripts defining what one can exchange with whom and how one should go about it (Parsons 1949; Swedberg and Himmelstrand 1987; Appadurai 1986; Etzioni 1988). Both approaches draw on the sociological notion of "role," the first in its structural version (as a distinct position in a relational network), the second in its cultural guise (as a set of rights and obligations attached to a status).[9] The remarkable thing about *homines economici* in this light is that they are quite literally *roleless,* free to exchange anything with anybody in much the same way or, in Weber's telling phrase, "without regard to persons."

Homo economicus, however socially vacuous, is a useful idiot for many kinds of economic models, particularly if structural assumptions are included. Moreover, role expectations may be built into otherwise conventional economic models as utilities attached to the welfare of role-partners or disutilities associated with the violation of moral injunctions.[10] Orientations toward exchange are important, however, in their own right, and not simply as a source of heterogeneity in economic models. Plotting the social coordinates of *homo economicus* is of intrinsic interest and relevant to the closely related problem of altruism and to policy issues bearing on workplace democracy, surrogate motherhood, and sales of body organs (Hansmann 1988).

Variation in Orientations towards Exchange. Four axes of variation in economic orientation are salient. The first is global variation among persons: some people are more likely than others to approach exchanges with scripts drawn from market ideology [what Friedland and Alford (1989) call "market logic"] as opposed to other available cultural resources. Other things being equal, I would expect to find such an orientation to be stronger among men than among women, among employees of corporations than among people who work for nonprofit organizations, among owners of capital and managers than among workers, among people who work with things than among people who work with people, and among economics majors than among majors in social work or art history.

The second kind of variation is with respect to the role relations that evoke impersonally self-interested economic orientations. Holding global variation constant, we expect people to be more willing to deal impersonally with strangers than with acquaintances, with those who are dissimilar from themselves than with those who are similar, with non-kin than with family members, and so on. This issue is related to, but different in two ways from, economic and social-structural arguments about exploitation—for example, that one is less likely to exploit an exchange partner who is associated with other exchange partners lest one ruin one's reputation or incur reprisals from allies of the exploited party. First, as Weber and Parsons pointed out, the impersonal orientation of the market is not strictly exploitative; in its purest form, market behavior is governed by well-institutionalized norms of honest dealing and fair price. Second, cultural injunctions should operate in the absence of credible threats of disclosure.

A third form of variation is among goods or services. Holding constant global orientations and exchange partners, we expect exchanges involving soybeans, screwdrivers, or saran wrap to more readily evoke the orientation typical of *homo economicus* than exchanges involving land and labor, which in turn may more broadly trigger market scripts than those in which babies, body organs, or emotional or physical intimacy are exchanged. Trade in even minor forms of intimacy, the smiles of a stewardess for example, may be deeply stressful to the vendor (Hochschild 1983). Firms trading in quasi-sacred commodities often symbolically disguise the nature of the transaction: art galleries keep prices hidden within binders, away from artworks. Commercial blood banks adopt the decor and atmosphere of doctors' offices and emphasize social benefit rather than financial gain in recruiting clients (Espeland and Clemens 1988).[11]

A fourth and final form of variation is among situations. Other things being equal, people's readiness to treat an exchange as impersonal, or to engage in exchange at all, is influenced by the setting in which it takes place: high, for example, in retail establishments and low, perhaps, in churches or at family reunions.

Why might we expect orientations to exchange to differ? Here I can do no more than suggest several directions of investigation with respect to global variation among persons.[12]

First, certain patterns of social relations are more likely than others to engender individualistic rather than collectivist notions of interest and its attainment. Persons whose social networks are dense and multiplex (e.g., who interact with the same people in many ways and whose interaction partners also interact with one another) are less likely to find individualistic models of action attractive than are people whose social relations are more diffuse. The reasons for this are both positive (collective rationality is easier to achieve under such circumstances) and negative (egoistic action is more likely to call forth sanctions). Systems of collective rationality are usually embedded in explicitly collectivist value systems, such that even individualistic striving is justified in terms of common interest or tradition (see Bourdieu 1977). This dynamic is consistent with the often observed non-market ethos of solidary working-class communities and ethnic enterprises (Waldinger 1989). Similarly, the relatively kin-centered or neighborhood-based nature of many women's relational networks may explain why individualistic calculative rationality is said to be less pervasive among women than among men. [13]

Second, people vary in the extent to which they are exposed to cultural environments that celebrate the value of individualistic, calculating orientations toward exchange. In some cases, such celebration reflects the material imperatives of a social position (e.g., that of business proprietors in a competitive market environment). In other cases (e.g., managers of oligopolistic firms or economists), it may be largely ideological. The findings that those in the market sector are more likely to support economistic values than equally well-to-do professionals employed by the state or nonprofit organizations (Macy 1988) or that economics majors are more likely than other college students to behave exploitatively in experimental settings (Marwell and Ames 1981) are consistent with this expectation. [14]

There are likely to be numerous interactions among individual disposition, relationship, commodity, and situation. Indeed, if *homines economici* exist, we may know them by the immunity of their economic orientations to ordinary influences of social ties, exchange types, and context.

Classification and Exchange.   Thus far, I have viewed orientations toward exchange in terms of relatively superficial levels of social cognition, especially scripts. It is with respect to relations, objects of exchange, and situations that social classification becomes important. Anthropologists have argued, and cognitive psychologists have confirmed, that people tend to conceive of their worlds in terms of binary oppositions. Among the most important of these is that of sacred vs. profane (Douglas 1966). There is an inescapable antagonism between impersonal exchange and the sacred, in so far as sacredness entails both the notion of irreducibility—that the sacred object has value that cannot be expressed in monetary terms—and rituals regulating access to the sacred and prescribing appropriate behavior in its presence (Zelizer 1985). There is striking boundary dissensus in modern societies about what is sacred and, consequently, about what things should not be commodified. Comprehending variation in people's economic orientations toward different goods and services requires that we explore the bases of variation in the classification sacred versus profane.

A second kind of classification, between "inside" and "outside," underlies social restrictions to impersonal exchange. A scoundrel is often described as someone who "would sell his grandmother"; for many, someone who would sell *to* his grandmother is only slightly better. Sales of goods within kin or friendship circles are often accompanied by such symbols of co-membership as obligatory small-talk, token price reductions, or informal warranty arrangements. It seems likely that different people draw we/other boundaries differently and that the distribution of inside/outside classifications influences the probability of exchange among classes of persons, orientations toward exchanges that do take place, and terms of trade.

Markets and Firms as Cultural Constructs

Culture influences economy at the organizational as well as the individual level of action. Just as Polanyi showed that the self-regulating market is a cultural construct, so organizational researchers have demonstrated that bureaucracies are cultural, as well as material, artifacts. Indeed, as Meyer has argued, our notions of both firm and market can be viewed as emanating from a "Western cultural account."

Although Selznick is usually considered the progenitor of "institutional theory," as this line of argument is called, some key ideas were anticipated by New Dealer Thurman Arnold in his essay "The Social Psychology of Institutions," published in 1937. "Smaller social organizations functioning within the general national structure," he wrote, "resemble, in so far as their purpose permits, the larger organizations. They must do so to maintain a logical place within it." The reason for this is that national cultures are dominated by "institutional creeds," organizational models and behavioral scripts that people value so highly that they permit them to obscure their perception of concrete organization. Arnold found

> the transition from the life of a trial lawyer to that of a professor at the Yale School of Law a most interesting one. The academic life was different from practice in that the scholarly heroes were men who dug up little sections of truth for the love of it—a purely monastic ideal. Yet this mythology was tempered and molded by the great overshadowing divinity, the American Businessman. Yale was doing what it could to search for truth in the same organized efficient way in which the United States Steel Corporation made steel. There was much about Yale in 1930 in common with the Rotary Club of Laramie, Wyoming, from which the writer hailed. "Service" was the watchword and the organized "project" was the crusade. (p. 39)

Once certain organizational structures become so widespread as to serve as signals of legitimacy, formal organizing represents "a sort of manic outburst of rationality created under considerable competitive urgency, and, for the same reason, unlikely to work as chartered" (Jepperson and Meyer 1991). Managers of business firms become so enthralled by popular models of organization as to misperceive the principles by which they operate. If, as Powell (1990), White and Eccles (1986), and Sabel (1982) contend, actual firms resemble not just hierarchies but also markets and status systems, how is firm behavior influenced by the tendency of managers to conceive of and talk about them as if they were typical Weberian bureaucracies? Moreover, if images of firms are changing in the face of assaults by management consultants and organization theorists, how will new cognitive models change the behavior of managers?

Rituals of Rationality. With respect to the first question, recall Roy's classic study (1954) of a Chicago machine shop. Roy found the shop's bosses committed to the hierarchical model of bureaucracy, convinced that knowledge should reside at the top, and insistent upon controlling the labor process. Management's interventions into the workplace uniformly impeded efficiency and required workers to develop ingenious stratagems to keep production moving.

Why did management persist in behavior that seems from Roy's description decidedly unfruitful? We have no reason to believe that they were threatened by comparable inefficiencies deriving from a lack of workplace control. Nor does it seem reasonable to attribute their behavior to an Adlerian drive to power, for such an urge could have been expressed in ways less harmful to the firm's efficiency. Rather the managers appear to have been blinded by strongly held cultural conceptions of organization, doggedly enacting bureaucracy in the face of evidence that their actions were ineffective. As Roy put it (with a jibe at the Hawthorne researchers' counterposition of management's "logic of rationality" to the workers' "logic of sentiment"), the managers were driven by "sentiments of rationality" to fix a production process that was not broken.

The objection might be that managerial ideologies change, however glacially, and that the vices depicted by Roy would not afflict modern firms, devoted as their managers are to "soft" control, internal labor markets, a self-actualizing professional work force, and "strong company cultures." Yet Kunda's (1987) revealing ethnography of one such company, a high-tech participant in the "Massachusetts miracle," suggests that if cultural conceptions of the firm have in some instances changed, they have become no less seductive. This company's professional work force is introduced to "the culture" on arrival by "culture specialists" whom management employs to socialize recruits, most of whom are well-educated engineers not noted for their "people skills." From the author's account, the firm seems to be a Barnardian nightmare of symbolic leadership, a matrix structure gone wild, in which task groups are cast adrift with ambiguous mandates and instructed to "do the right thing."

Kunda quite rightly emphasizes the use of "the culture" as an instrument of domination. Yet from a purely economic view, management's obsessive concern with "culture" seems no more rational than the hierarchical tinkering of Roy's bosses. Both firms were scenes of frenzied enactments of cultural prescriptions of organization, albeit quite different ones, that seem at best orthogonal to the achievement of an efficient production process, and quite possibly counterproductive.

The notion of rationality as ritual has been most extensively developed by John Meyer, who introduced it to contemporary organization theory in his research on public schools, which highlighted such paradoxes as the routine collection of reams of performance data that are never used for evaluation (Meyer and Rowan 1977; Thomas et al. 1987). Most of the work has focused on nonmarket organizations and on matters such as organizational structure, control, and environmental relations. What is less clear from work in this tradition is the *economic* impact of cultural enactments.

A few recent studies have inspected institutional processes in for-profit firms, and have found behavior influenced by factors apparently unrelated to efficiency. Galaskiewicz and Wasserman's Minneapolis corporations (1988) imitated the donative patterns of philanthropic elites in their grants to non-profit organizations. Mezias (1988) reports that institutional factors were related to firms' adoption of the flow-through accounting method of treating capital investment tax credits. Fligstein's research (1985) revealed that once the diffusion process was underway, firms were more likely to adopt multi-divisional structures if such structures were in fashion in their industries. It might be concluded from such studies that large companies can get away with far more than rational stories about organizational structure suggest— that much company behavior is irrational because it responds not to market incentives but to executive whim or corporate fashion. As usual, however, still other rational stories can be spun. To the extent, as Meyer, Hannan and Freeman (1984), Zucker (1983), DiMaggio and Powell (1983), and others have suggested, that organizations must be legitimate to survive, and that cultural enactments of bureaucracy are requisite warrants of legitimacy, adoption of unproductive but conventional structures may be entirely ra-tional, even if not technically efficient. It is also possible that "rituals of rationality" have only trivial effects on economic performance, or that they are so constitutive of firms as to require new ways of modeling their ac-tivities. At this point, the jury is out and research is required to establish the implications of such recent work in organization theory to the concerns of economics.[15]

Production Systems, Economic and Cognitive.   The foregoing line of ar-gument views systems of economic production as shaped by what cognitive psychologists call "production systems"—behavioral routines that contain rules for, and thus permit while at the same time constraining, adaptive innovation (Klahr et al. 1987). "Production systems" are cognitivists' answer to the behavioral version of the old linguistic question of why people are able to emit novel utterances. They are supplanting the notion of "script," with its implication of static routines that persons are relatively powerless to change. Sociologists have faced a version of this problem in the debate about the "oversocialized" concept of "role" inherited from Parsons (Wrong 1961). Thus, it is no coincidence that contemporary solutions to the "role" problem—such as Bourdieu's (1977) definition of the *habitus* as "structuring structure," Giddens' (1985) "structuration," or Burns and Flam's (1987) "rule systems"—resonate with the imagery of "production system" in positing a structured capacity for improvisation and change.

Such concepts are solutions only if they are accompanied by sophisticated and detailed accounts of mechanisms of change. Otherwise, they simply deny oversocialization without offering a real alternative. Bourdieu (1977) provides little guidance as to the plasticity of the *habitus* and Giddens (1985) hedges the question with even-handed references to "agent knowledgeability." How free are humans to escape "production systems" to engage in rational pursuit of their interests? The answer appears to be "somewhat, but not too much." Under such circumstances, the economist's solution—assume rationality and press ahead—is comforting indeed.

If culturally mandated "production systems" and classifications are sufficiently plastic—if managers can go off auto-pilot and create new routines as soon as something goes awry—then social cognition is epiphenomenal and need not concern us. If, as seems likely, the grip of culture is stronger, is it simply a drag on adaptation, an element of friction in the expression of rationality, or does it fundamentally shape the direction of strategic behavior? And, if the latter, does it do this by providing metaphors for problem-solving, strategies for search, or blinders making certain solutions literally unthinkable? Answering such questions will require fundamental research on the relationship between managerial assumptions, organizational change, and performance outcomes.

Culture, Status, and Demand

If there is any field of study that economists are willing to relegate to sociology, it is the issue of tastes and their formation. The problem of taste and its transformation into demand is worth considering in some detail as a natural ground for a rather direct contribution of sociology to economic models.

Economists are limited in their ability to deal with taste formation by their discomfort with interdependence. Taste does not lend itself to atomistic thinking; indeed, it can hardly be considered except in relation to systems of stratification. The usage of "taste" to refer to qualitative evaluation is itself a product of the rise of the commercial middle class in the seventeenth century, closely associated with the emergence of antiquarianism and connoisseurship (Abrams 1985).

Weber (1968) called attention to the intimate relationship between markets and taste in his discussions of the antagonism of dynamic markets to elite status cultures. By making insignia of membership in dominant groups available to anyone with sufficient funds to pay for them, markets break down status cultures and engender inflationary competition for prestige. Veblen (1899) developed a similar line of argument in his discussions of pecuniary emulation and the symbolic uses of goods and pastimes for "rating and grading" persons with respect to an ideal cultivated style of life. Bourdieu (1984) uses the notion of "cultural capital" to describe socially valued symbolic goods over which people compete, and develops both a rational model of the conditions under which "cultural capital" will be more or less valuable and an explanation, linked to group membership and socialization, of the mechanisms generating actors' behavior.

Other sociological and anthropological approaches to consumption place less emphasis on the competitive and more on the constitutive functions of goods. According to Mary Douglas (Douglas and Isherwood 1982), consumption is an expression of social membership, a way of locating oneself in the world: things, she writes, "are good to think with." Czikszentmihalyi and Rochberg-Halton (1981) report that people instill their possessions with meanings extrinsic to their actual form and content, often having to do with social relationships in which the objects played a role. Wallendorf and Arnould (1988) found that 60% of their Americans respondents said their attachments to "favorite" objects were based on social rather than technical criteria and that Nigerians responded similarly, although the form of social content—status-based in Nigeria, biographically centered in the United States—differed cross-culturally.[16]

All these arguments suggest that persons' tastes for particular goods and services are shaped by qualities extrinsic to the good. This is not true, of course, of any good or service; nor, as we will see, does each argument imply the same behavioral consequences. But what the sociological accounts *do* share is significant: a view of consumption as producing utilities derived not simply from the technical or aesthetic qualities of goods, per se, but also from the capacity of goods to locate the self and others in the social world. In other words, the formation of tastes is an intensely social process.

Economic approaches to taste are markedly different (Etzioni 1985): In considering taste, as Bourdieu (1984:12) puts it, we enter "into the area par excellence of the denial of the social." In traditional demand theory, tastes are regarded as exogenous preferences, not theorized but revealed in behavior (Sen 1977).[17] Economists who have written about tastes for symbolic goods (e.g., art objects or aesthetic experiences) view them as deriving from individual capacities. Thus the "cultivation" hypothesis (Scitovsky 1976) suggests that in consuming art one develops skills that increase the utility of subsequent consumption, avoiding satiation and increasing demand. Similarly, addiction models (McCain 1981) suggest that demand for certain goods—controlled substances and aesthetic experience—increases with consumption rather than reaching satiation.

Stigler and Becker (1977) dispute such contentions by simply denying that tastes vary, either among people or over time. To do this, they must redefine commodities to make them unobservable, treating them as utilities produced by households from a combination of inputs, including consumer goods (the objects of "taste" in conventional analyses) and various kinds of human capital. This enables them to tell clever rational stories without reference to taste. But the price of this accomplishment is high because it renders unmeasurable the key variables of economic analysis—prices, incomes, and quantities of commodities consumed. Moreover, their characterization of ultimate commodities is so vague as to make predictions from their framework unfalsifiable.

A related but more realistic class of economic models derives from the work of Kelvin Lancaster (1971, 1979). Like Stigler and Becker, Lancaster views goods not as discrete things but as bundles of characteristics to which consumers attach varying values (according to their utility in achieving desired ends). This step makes it possible to treat commodities (goods, in the conventional sense) as comparable and to predict demand for new or varied commodities from knowledge of past consumer decisions and of the technical qualities of the products themselves. In contrast to Stigler and Becker, Lancaster and similar authors (e.g., Rosen 1974) pay explicit attention to heterogeneity among consumers with respect to tastes, defined as the weightings assigned to various characteristics.

Exogeneity assumes that tastes can come from anywhere, but that preference orderings are stable over time. Cultivation and addiction models suggest that marked shifts may occur within preferences for specific goods, but attribute these to changes internal to individuals. Lancaster's approach focuses on variations among goods of a similar class and heterogeneity among consumers, but reduces goods to clusters of utility-bearing characteristics with no holistic character. Tastes, he writes, "have some inherent stability" and "are not preferences over collections of specific goods but deeper preferences over objectives which are to be achieved by the consumption of goods" (1979:7).

Note how these perspectives clash with the findings of research by sociologists and cultural anthropologists, who stress that tastes reflect relationships among people and symbolic attributes of discrete objects, which may be unrelated to the technical characteristics of the objects themselves. For one thing, research in this tradition suggests that tastes are *not* exogenous, but rather are to some extent socially determined: that is, consumption decisions are interdependent, such that ego's preference for a certain good is a function of the probability that certain others have purchased or are likely to acquire it. For another, some goods possess holistic symbolic significance and thus cannot be treated as bundles of technical characteristics. It follows that we may not assume stability in tastes for specific goods, for the very interdependence of tastes may produce substantial volatility in persons' preference orderings.[18]

The domain within which these assertions hold is no doubt finite and its scope is an empirical issue. But this domain presumably includes any goods with substantial symbolic content, especially those in which style plays an important role (e.g., decorative objects, works of art and aesthetic experience, dress, cuisine, places of residence, other consumer goods), such that they can serve as symbols of membership and definers of the self. Different sociological accounts provide different suggestions as to the structure of taste interdependence. Take, for example, Veblen's model of status competition. Persons compete for status by purchasing prestigious items, and the prestige of an object is a function of the social status of those who are known to consume it. (Call this *vertical interdependence*.) Under such conditions, consumers' "taste" for a good (e.g., gold shoes) is a positive function of the number of persons hierarchically superior and a negative function of the number of persons hierarchically inferior to themselves who are believed to possess it.[19]

Given constant or falling prices, such premises yield the familiar trickle-down model of fashion, or, for one-time purchases, a conventional logarithmic diffusion curve (Simmel 1957). As more mid-status persons buy and wear gold shoes, fewer high-status persons will buy them, making them less appealing to people of middle rank but still attractive to those on the rung below that. Eventually, the cycle plays itself out and old gold shoes clutter the back closets of the rich and middle class.[20]

The limitations of such a model are evident: although we can all think of people whose behavior it describes, in fact competitive consumption is less typical than the model implies. (If it were not, overconsumption on status goods would be so rampant as to drive savings and other forms of consumption to points well below those observed.) What is missing from this "Veblen" model is social structure. As Frank (1985:140) and DiMaggio (1987) have observed, people embedded in durable and close-knit social networks need fewer status cues than those whose interactions are characteristically more fleeting, and therefore are likely to invest less in status commodities or cultural capital.

By contrast, then, consider a society that is segmented into several groups, each with its own status culture. The elements of the status cultures include styles of dress, forms of food preparation, or aesthetic preferences that the groups have succeeded in monopolizing, through sumptuary laws, control of ancillaries to consumption (e.g., concert halls or cooking classes), or choices of elements that others find unattractive. (Note that this means we are speaking about imperfect markets.) Here ego's taste for such goods is a positive

function of how others in the same status group evaluate them and is unaffected by the evaluations of other groups. (Call this *horizontal interdependence.*) The more salient others consume it, the more effective a symbol is the
good of group membership and thus the more attractive to its members.
Within a status culture preferences are typically stable, but once a new item
reaches a take-off threshold it spreads by contagion within the group.

Finally, imagine a two-class system wherein one group (e.g., a solidary
upper class) plays by the rules of status groups (horizontal interdependence),
whereas another (the *arrivistes*) engages in individualistic status competition
(vertical interdependence). Assume, further, that the cultural economy is a
market system so that the *arrivistes* are not prohibited by law or custom from
purchasing symbols of upper-class membership. Under these conditions, we
would expect conventional elite insignia to diffuse quickly to *arrivistes*, who
will drop them once they extend downward to the middle class; being
indifferent to the tastes of persons outside their group, the upper class will
retain these insignia.

Taste for stylistic *innovations* will follow a separate course. Innovations
first adopted by members of the upper class will be especially attractive to
arrivistes, and through the latter will spread to those groups within the
middle class who engage in status competition. By contrast, such innovations may or may not spread within the upper class; at any rate, few of them
will reach the threshold necessary to become elements of the status culture.

This is not the place to develop such models, or rather notes toward
models, quantitatively.[21] But some qualitative implications are arresting. For
one thing, following Weber's emphasis on tendencies toward monopoliza-
tion of status cultures (for reasons both of internal solidarity and external
prestige), we would not expect our upper class to sit still as the *arrivistes*
adopt their insignia. They cannot innovate too rapidly, however, for to fulfill
their ritual functions, status cultures must be relatively consistent and slow to
change. What is the solution?

There are several, each of which involves symbolic product differentiation—by intensifying consumption of symbolic goods that require esoteric
skills or knowledge or huge time investments as prerequisites to enjoyment,
by emphasizing clusters of tastes rather than consumption of single items,
and by the adumbration of rituals and ideologies of appropriation that render
acts of consumption qualitatively different even if what is consumed is the
same. As Bourdieu (1977) has argued, such rituals attempt to sacralize the
items consumed by severing their connection to the market; when this
cannot be done through a process of monopolistic closure, it is attempted
through symbolic means. Thus wealthy patrons of U.S. museums supported
an ethos of connoisseurship that justified removing educational aids from
exhibits in the early nineteenth century; and certain restaurants fail to translate their menus into English.

Second, we might expect that clever entrepreneurs will engage small but visible upper-class clienteles to attract larger middle-class markets, thus exerting a steady corrosive pressure on the integrity of the elite status culture. Under such circumstances, a steady diversification of elite taste and a tendency for status cultures to break down into multiple competing styles and genres may result. Just such a process can be observed in the contemporary erosion of the once sacrosanct boundary between "high" and "popular" culture (see DiMaggio 1987).

The perspective I have outlined presents a variety of challenges to economic approaches to taste and consumption. First, it suggests that tastes are highly interdependent, from which it follows both that goods cannot be treated as stable bundles of utilities and that individual consumption decisions cannot be modeled in isolation from one another. Second, a model of status competition is inadequate unless one specifies the ways in which social networks pattern such competition: the same motives will lead to different outcomes given different social structures. Third, even models that entail sophisticated views of social structure in specifying forms of interdependence will lack realism, because many tastes are culturally embedded [see, e.g., Bourdieu's discussions of the underlying dimensions of different tastes in *Distinction* (1984, Chap. 5)] and thus slower to change than a strategic model would predict, and because status groups pursue distinctive life styles not simply through consumption but also by limiting the access of others to them through the market. Nonetheless, I suspect that formal models meeting the first and second of these challenges may enhance substantially our understanding of markets for symbolically laden goods and services.

CONCLUSIONS

My goal has been to describe several sets of intriguing problems at the intersection of culture and economy and a few ideas that may bear on their solution. Such a treatment is not an end in itself but an invitation to empirical research and mathematical modeling. As economics' modeling capacity has expanded, the discipline's empirical talents have atrophied. We know remarkably little about the three topics I have raised—variability in calculative, self-interested behavior, the relationship between ritual and efficiency in firms, and the social interdependence of tastes—because they have fallen between disciplinary cracks. Once we focalize culture as a variable affecting economic behavior, we must systematically measure it to liberate ourselves from what Sen (1977:399) has called "the informational shackles of the traditional approach." Because the study of culture has been perhaps the least systematically propositional and empirical province of sociology, such a view has methodological consequences for the latter discipline, which must draw on the conceptual and methodological advances of social and cognitive psychology.

Economics and sociology (which, with anthropology, carries the flag of culture) are not easily merged, nor is it necessary to do so. There is much work in this area that sociologists, or for that matter historians or anthropologists, can do without engaging the tribal antagonisms that separate economics from its sister disciplines (see Hirsch et al. 1989). Many of the most interesting questions have to do with the evolution of cultural understandings of such economic categories as "careers," "trust," "value," or "capital" (Bledstein 1976; Jepperson and Meyer 1989; Zelizer 1979, 1985; Zucker 1986). Such research is intrinsically illuminating and at the same time serves to relativize economic concepts and call attention to the scope conditions of economic models. The other social sciences can assist economics by developing explanatory accounts of exogenous features of these models—for example, taste (although, as we have seen, such an account may force a reworking of the models themselves) or risk (Douglas 1986). And at times it will be necessary to engage economics directly by demanding greater realism in models based on unsound assumptions. In particular, cultural analysis points to heterogeneity in areas in which economists have often assumed uniformity (e.g., in the formation of tastes or in the degree to which persons orient themselves to material gain) and to points at which social rituals and economic rationality stand in decided tension.

ACKNOWLEDGMENT

Revision of paper prepared for the first annual spring seminar of the Center for Economy and Society, University of California, Santa Barbara, May 19-21, 1988. I am grateful to Amitai Etzioni, Roger Friedland, George Farkas, Henry Hansmann, Kevin Lang, A. F. Robertson, and participants at the Santa Barbara conference for useful criticism and suggestions for revision.

NOTES

1.   I use the adjective "cognitive" broadly to apply to the full range of conscious and preconscious phenomena that constitute men and women's mental lives. Etzioni (1988) distinguishes values from other cognitive elements; Frank (this volume) pays special attention to emotions or "passions." I blur the distinction, which others take as fundamental, between the "normative" (referring to attitudes, norms, values, or moral sentiments governing or regulating behavior; see Etzioni 1988) and the "constitutive" (the taken-for-granted scriptedness of behavior of which ethnomethodologists have written; see Giddens 1985; Molotch 1988). Ultimately, I suspect that some distinction of this sort is necessary, that is, that the moral salience and taken-for-grantedness of particular actions vary independently and have different behavioral consequences. Because the relationship between the normative and the constitutive is complex, poorly understood, and empirically underdeveloped, I bracket the issue here.

2. Contemporary economists often acknowledge this as well (e.g., Frank, this volume). As Arrow (1975:15) states, "the process of exchange requires or at least is greatly facilitated by the presence of . . . truth, . . . trust, loyalty, and justice in future dealings. . . . In short, the supply of a commodity [virtue] in many respects complementary to those usually thought of as economic goods is not itself accomplished in the marketplace but rather comes as an unrequited transfer." Note that Arrow here reduces constitutive rules to commodities: trust becomes a "complementary good," not unlike the batteries that might accompany a portable radio. On the constitutive nature of trust, see Barber (1983), Zucker (1986), and Etzioni (1988).

3. To be sure, as Sen (1977) and Etzioni (1988) point out, preferences are peculiarly stylized in economic neoorthodoxy. A cultural approach necessarily requires a broader view that rejects the notion of "revealed preferences" to make problematic the connection between preference and behavior.

4. I use vertical imagery in describing these different forms of social cognition for two reasons. First, each level to some extent constrains the ones above it. The attitudes toward what an employer may legitimately expect from an employee, for example, will be shaped by cultural definitions of work/nonwork, by rules discriminating between work relationships and other relationships, and by scripts defining anticipated role behavior in employment relations. Second, lower levels are less easily beckoned to consciousness in ordinary action than the higher, or, to put it another way, lower levels are associated with practical and higher levels with discursive reason. This point is tentative, however; the nature and degree of coupling among levels are empirical issues.

5. Sen (1977) argues that people have multiple ranked preference orderings (themselves ranked by "metapreferences") and Etzioni (1988, Chapts. 2–4) suggests that they possess separate moral and material utility functions. Where moral preferences do not simply act as imperatives, the notion of relevance rules is useful for understanding the conditions under which different utility functions are to be invoked.

6. Many readers will ask, "what of ideology?" Ideologies are arrays of cultural elements (from all levels) with the special properties of interdependence (a strain toward internal coherence) and convenience (they serve to justify the material interests of those who espouse them). Because of these properties, elements of ideologies may be especially resistant to change. Ideologies are important but they are also extremely complex and most economic action proceeds without recourse to them. (Socialists and free-marketers proceed in much the same way at the supermarket checkout line or in negotiating book contracts.) Therefore, I suspect that research on the simpler forms of cognition I have mentioned will be more productive, at least provisionally, than further efforts to fathom the problem of ideology.

7. The observation is unsurprising, but sociology of culture has paid relatively little detailed, empirical attention to the distribution, as opposed to the content, of social cognitions (but see Rossi and Berk 1985).

8. Of course, economists and cognitive psychologists find ample scope for disagreement [see, e.g., the essays in Hogarth and Reder's useful volume (1987)]. And economists do not attend to cognitive psychology only when it supports orthodoxy; some of the best recent work in economics takes account of Tversky and Kahnemann's work on decision heuristics, for example, in building models of bounded rationality (see, e.g., Frank, this volume; Earl 1983). But note that such models concern uniform processes of cognition rather than diverse contents of thought.

9. Structural and cultural approaches are analytically distinct in so far as the former emphasizes the impact of external constraint on behavior (e.g., the way in which ego's misconduct toward another person may contaminate his or her other relationships) and the latter stresses the internalization or taken-for-grantedness of role-related norms or scripts. If only structural embeddedness counted, individuals might transgress whenever they felt they could avoid detection. If only cultural embeddedness mattered, they might be indifferent to the likelihood of retribution. In practice, supportive social relations are necessary, in the long run, to reproduce

norms and scripts, and people who adhere to the norms and scripts of their groups are more likely to maintain stable social relations.

10.   See Etzioni (1988) for a challenging criticism of this view; and Frank (1987) for a related argument that "conscience" pays off in the long run.

11.   Frank (1985, Chapt. 10) argues that ethical systems that seek to keep certain goods outside of the market represent a collectively rational impulse to prevent what could otherwise be costly competition that, in the end, would fail to change people's relative positions materially. Legal and moral injunctions against trade in morally privileged items (e.g., body organs and children) serve to protect people from such competition. "Just as it may make sense to demand restrictions that keep us from selling our safety and our labor too cheaply, in the workplace, so it may also make sense to limit the extent to which we are able to market other important aspects of ourselves." Although this argument offers a brilliant basis for a normative defense of such moral injunctions, it does not explain why different people define "important aspects of ourselves" differently—an essentially cultural difference that is basically at the root of why people differ in the extent to which they support categorical exclusions of certain goods from markets. In other words, Frank provides a good case for why we *should* consider such exclusions, but not an explanation of why we *do*.

12.   For a probing discussion of factors encouraging self-interested behavior within organizations, see Perrow (1990). For an insightful review of factors conducive to rationality more broadly defined, see Etzioni (1988, Chap. 9).

13.   An alternative explanation for gender differences is psychoanalytic. As Chodorow (1978; described in England 1988) has argued, where women do most of the parenting, the process of achieving gender identity causes males to individuate more markedly than women. Because my impression is that much of the variance in dispositions toward economic action falls within, rather than between, genders, I find the more general explanation provided by a social-network framework preferable to Chodorow's. But the matter is susceptible to empirical adjudication.

14.   An important essay by Jepperson and Meyer (1991) suggests a third axis of variation in calculative rationality, this one at the societal level. In their view, with attenuation of solidary, informal groups and the emergence of mass publics, modern polities constitute "individuals" as legitimate actors with "portfolios of legitimated economic interests." Although all modern polities rationalize action in terms of collective goals, they vary in the extent to which they "incorporate persons as what American theorists call individual actors, by linking them tightly to the collectivity as a project, and then validating them as carriers of sovereign capacity and commitment" and in the extent to which public functions are institutionalized as "epiphenomenal outcomes . . . of the ongoing operation of society as a natural community." Liberal/individualist polities, high on both these dimensions, seem likely to entail more calculative rationality on the part of individuals within them than do, for example, statist polities.

15.   The notion of ritual is related to that of "routine" in the work of "Carnegie School" decision theorists like Herbert Simon, James March, and Richard Cyert. The most sophisticated development of this work with reference to economic theory is Nelson and Winter's *An Evolutionary Theory of Economic Change* (1982). We cannot maintain that firms fail to *optimize* without some notion of routine, that is, standardized, scripted ways of dealing with repetitive tasks and problems as an alternative to repeated choices based on full-information analyses of alternative courses of action. The existence of routines is not in itself inconsistent with optimization, however: good routines may serve to economize on information and search costs. Routines are good (as long as an organization's task environment is stable) when they result from some combination of analysis and experiential learning. By contrast, rituals consist of routines based on external cultural prescriptions rather than learning. Whether they are also "rational" depends on the extent to which they serve as signals on the basis of which the environment selects firms for survival.

16.   See also, Mukerji (1983) and Miller (1987, Chapt. 10).

17. There is an underground stream within economics, stemming from the work of Duesen-berry (1949) and developed impressively by Frank (1985), that does regard consumption deci-sions as interdependent. (For an excellent discussion of this earlier work, see Smelser 1963:92–98.) This position has not, however, been accorded the prominence it deserves.

18. One could imagine attempting to encompass nontechnical characteristics of goods—for example, prestige or contributions to a sense of social membership or to certain kinds of personal identities—within a Lancastrian framework. But because the "characteristics" of the same good vary depending on the social location of the consumer (what I regard as an amusing or precious antique, another may code as a second-rate hand-me-down), such an elaboration is likely to be impractically complex. Moreover, because the utility of the same good for such purposes will change over time as a function of the social locations of those who possess it, such a procedure would not permit us to assume stability of tastes for goods over time even if we assumed (as seems reasonable) that taste for prestige and social membership are constant.

19. Potential realistic refinements, for example, weighting others by status distance from ego, or positing information loss over wide status distances, are numerous but go beyond the illustrative purpose of this example.

20. Stigler and Becker (1977) treat fashionable goods as inputs with which consumers produce distinction, an ultimate commodity that is a function of goods and a "social environ-ment" constituted by the "distinction" of an unspecified set of others, which raises the cost of distinction by lowering the productivity of one's own goods. Although the imagery is similar to the Veblen model, the empirical utility of such an approach—which treats all fashionable goods as fungible, which cannot generate predictions about the "careers" of fashionable goods, and which treats the "social environment" as an undifferentiated argument in a production function (rather than a specific and changeable set of others)—is limited.

21. There are hints, however, in Hansmann's (1986) development of economic "club theory" to deal with interdependent consumption decisions that occur when ego's taste for membership in an association is contingent upon the status of its other members. There are hints, as well, in the literature on "demonstration effects" (Frank 1985, and this volume) that links individuals' propensities to save to the consumption behavior of those around them; and in models of change in political preferences that include effects of the perceived opinion of others (e.g., Kuran 1987). Granovetter and Soong's model (1986) of bandwagon and snob effects illustrates the powerful consequences of quite simple assumptions about behavioral in-terdependence.

REFERENCES

Abrams, M. I. (1985. "Art-as-Such: The Sociology of Modern Aesthetics." *Bulletin of the American Academy of Arts and Sciences* 38:8–33.

Appadurai, Arjun (ed.) 1986. *The Social Life of Things.* Cambridge: Cambridge University Press.

Arnold, Thurman. 1937. "The Psychology of Social Institutions." Chapter 2 in *The Folklore of Capitalism.* New Haven: Yale University Press.

Arrow, Kenneth. 1975. "Gifts and Exchanges." Pp. 13–28 in *Altruism, Morality, and Economic Theory,* edited by Edmund S. Phelps. New York: Russell Sage Foundation.

Barber, Bernard. 1983. *The Logic and Limits of Trust.* New Brunswick: Rutgers University Press.

Berk, Richard A. and Peter Rossi. 1985. "Varieties of Normative Consensus." *American Sociological Review* (1985):333–347.

Bledstein, Burton. 1976. "Careers." Chapt. 5 in *The Culture of Professionalism*. New York: Norton, 1976.

Bourdieu, Pierre. 1974. "Avenir de classe et causalité du probable." *Revue Française du Sociologie* 15:3–42.

———. 1977. *Outline of a Theory of Practice*. New York: Cambridge University Press.

———. 1984. *Distinction: A Social Critique of the Judgement of Taste*. Translated by Richard Nice. Cambridge: Harvard University Press.

Burns, Tom R. and Helena Flam. 1987. *The Shaping of Social Organization: Social Rule Theory with Applications*. Newbury Park: Sage Publications.

Camic, Charles. 1987. "Historical Reinterpretation of the Early Parsons." *American Sociological Review* 52:421–39.

Chodorow, Nancy. 1978. *The Reproduction of Mothering*. Berkeley: University of California Press.

Czikszentmihalyi, Mihalyi and Eugene Rochberg-Halton. 1981. *The Nature of Things: Symbols and the Development of the Self*. Cambridge: Cambridge University Press.

Duesenberry, James. 1949. *Income, Savings, and the Theory of Consumer Behavior*. Cambridge: Harvard University Press.

DiMaggio, Paul. 1987. "Classification in Art." *American Sociological Review* 52:440–455.

——— and Walter W. Powell. 1983. "The Iron Cage Revisited: Institutional Isomorphism and Collective Rationality in Organizational Fields." *American Sociological Review* 48:147–160.

Douglas, Mary. 1966. *Purity and Danger: An Analysis of the Concepts of Pollution and Taboo*. London: Routledge & Kegan Paul.

———. 1986. *Risk Acceptability According to the Social Sciences*. New York: Russell Sage Foundation.

Douglas, Mary and Baron Isherwood. 1982. *The World of Goods: Towards an Anthropology of Consumption*. New York: Norton.

Earl, Peter E. 1983. *The Economic Imagination: Towards a Behavioural Analysis of Choice*. Armonk, NY: M. E. Sharpe.

England, Paula. 1988. "Assessing Rational Choice Models: Lessons from Economic, Sociological, and Feminist Views." Paper presented at the August meetings of the American Sociological Association.

Espeland, Wendy and Elisabeth S. Clemens. 1988. "Buying Blood and Selling Truth: The Cultural Constitution of Boundaries by Emerging Organizations." Paper presented at the annual meeting of the American Sociological Association.

Etzioni, Amitai. 1985. "Opening the Preferences: A Socio-Economic Research Agenda." *The Journal of Behavioral Economics* 14:183–205.

———. 1988. *The Moral Dimension: Toward a New Economics*. New York: Free Press.

Fligstein, Neil. 1985. "The Spread of the Multidivisional Form, 1919–1979." *American Sociological Review* 50:377–391.

Frank, Robert H. 1985. *Choosing the Right Pond: Human Behavior and the Quest for Status*. New York: Oxford University Press.

———. 1987. "If *Homo Economicus* Could Choose His Own Utility Function

Would He Want One with a Conscience?" *American Economic Review* 77:593–604.

Friedland, Roger and Robert Alford. Forthcoming. "Bringing Society Back in: Symbols, Practices, and Institutional Contradictions." In *The New Institutionalism in Organizational Studies*, edited by Walter Powell and Paul DiMaggio. Chicago: University of Chicago Press.

Galaskiewicz, Joseph and Stanley Wasserman. 1988. "Mimetic and Normative Processes within an Interorganizational Field: An Empirical Test." Manuscript, University of Minnesota.

Garfinkel, Harold. 1967. *Studies in Ethnomethodology*. Englewood Cliffs, NJ: Prentice-Hall.

Giddens, Anthony. 1985. *The Constitution of Society*. Berkeley: University of California Press.

Granovetter, Mark. 1985. "Economic Action and Social Structure: The Problem of Embeddedness." *American Journal of Sociology* 91:481–510.

Granovetter, Mark and Roland Soong. 1986. "Threshold Models of Interpersonal Effects in Consumer Demand." *Journal of Economic Behavior and Organization* 7:83–89.

Gudeman, Stephen. 1986. *Economics as Culture: Models and Metaphors of Livelihood*. Boston: Routledge & Kegan Paul.

Hannan, Michael T. and John Freeman. 1984. "Structural Inertia and Organizational Change." *American Sociological Review* 49:149–164.

Hansmann, Henry. 1986. "Status Organizations." *Journal of Law, Economics and Organization* 2:119–130.

———. 1988. "The Economics and Ethics of Markets for Human Organs." Working Paper #91, Civil Liability Program, Center for Studies in Law, Economics, and Public Policy, Yale Law School.

Hirsch, Paul M., Stuart Michaels, and Ray Friedman. 1990. "'Dirty Hands' vs. 'Clean Models': Is Sociology in Danger of Being Seduced by Economics?" Pp. 39–56 in *Structures of Capital: The Social Organization of Economic Life*, edited by Sharon Zukin and Paul DiMaggio. New York: Cambridge University Press.

Hochschild, Arlie. 1983. *The Managed Heart: Commercialization of Human Feeling*. Berkeley: University of California Press.

Hogarth, Robin M. and Melvin W. Reder (eds.) 1987. *Rational Choice: The Contrast between Economics and Psychology*. Chicago: University of Chicago Press.

Jepperson, Ronald L. and John W. Meyer. Forthcoming. "The Public Order and the Construction of Formal Organizations." In *The New Institutionalism in Organizational Studies*, edited by Walter W. Powell and Paul DiMaggio. Chicago: University of Chicago Press.

Klahr, David, Pat Langley, and Robert Neches (eds.) 1987. *Production System Models of Learning and Development*. Cambridge: MIT Press.

Kunda, Gideon. 1987. *Engineering Culture*. Ph.D. dissertation. Cambridge: Massachusetts Institute of Technology.

Kuran, Timur. 1987. "Preference Falsification, Policy Continuity, and Collective Conservatism." *The Economic Journal* 97:642–665.

Lancaster, Kelvin. 1971. *Consumer Demand: A New Approach*. New York: Columbia University Press.

————. 1979. *Variety, Equity, and Efficiency.* New York: Columbia University Press.

Macy, Michael W. 1988. "New-Class Dissent among Social-Cultural Specialists." *Sociological Forum* 3:325–356.

Marwell, Gerald and Ruth Ames. 1981. "Economists Free Ride. Does Anyone Else?" *Journal of Public Economics* 15:295–310.

Marx, Karl. 1971 [1857–58]. *The Grundrisse,* edited and translated by David McLellan. New York: Harper Torchbooks.

McCain, Roger. 1981. "Reflections on the Cultivation of Taste." *Journal of Cultural Economics* 3:30–52.

Meyer, John and Brian Rowan. 1977. "Institutionalized Organizations: Formal Structure as Myth and Ceremony." *American Journal of Sociology* 83:66–94.

Mezias, Stephen J. 1988. "Institutional Sources of Organizational Practice: Financial Reporting at the Fortune 200." Manuscript, Yale University, School of Organization and Management.

Miller, Daniel. 1987. *Material Culture and Mass Production.* New York: Basil Blackwell.

Molotch, Harvey. 1988. "Sociology and the Economy." Manuscript, University of California, Santa Barbara, Sociology Department.

Mukerji, Chandra. 1983. *From Graven Images: Patterns of Modern Materialism.* Berkeley: University of California Press.

Noble, David. 1977. *America by Design: Science, Technology, and the Rise of Corporate Capitalism.* New York: Oxford University Press.

Parsons, Talcott. 1949. *The Structure of Social Action,* Vol. 1. New York: The Free Press.

Perrow, Charles. 1990. "Economic Theories of Organization." Pp. 121–52 in *Structures of Capital: The Social Organization of Economic Life,* edited by Sharon Zukin and Paul DiMaggio. New York: Cambridge University Press.

Polanyi, Karl. 1957 [1944]. *The Great Transformation.* Boston: Beacon Press.

Powell, Walter. 1990. "Neither Market nor Hierarchy: Network Forms of Social Organization." Pp. 295–336 in *Research in Organizational Behavior,* Vol. 12, edited by Barry Staw and L. L. Cummings. Greenwich, CT: JAI Press.

Rosen, Sherwin. 1974. "Hedonic Prices and Implicit Markets: Product Differentiation in Pure Competition." *Journal of Political Economy* 82:34–55.

Roy, Donald. 1954. "Efficiency and 'the Fix.'" *American Journal of Sociology* 60:155–166.

Sabel, Charles. 1982. *Work and Politics: The Division of Labor in Industry.* Cambridge: Cambridge University Press.

Schank, Roger and Robert Abelson. 1977. *Scripts, Plans, Goals and Understanding: An Inquiry into Human Knowledge Structures.* Hillsdale, NY: Lawrence Erlbaum.

Schwartz, Barry. 1981. *Vertical Classification: A Study in Structuralism and the Sociology of Knowledge.* Chicago: University of Chicago Press.

Scitovsky, Tibor. 1976. *The Joyless Economy.* New York: Oxford University Press.

Sen, Amartya K. 1977. "Rational Fools: A Critique of the Behavioral Foundations of Economic Theory." *Philosophy and Public Affairs* 6:317–344.

Simmel, Georg. 1957 [1904]. "Fashion." *American Journal of Sociology* 62:541–558.

Smelser, Neil J. 1963. *The Sociology of Economic Life.* Englewood Cliffs, NJ: Prentice-Hall.

Smith, Adam. 1976 [6th ed., 1790]. *Theory of Moral Sentiment.* New York: Oxford University Press.

Stigler, George and Gary Becker. 1977. "De Gustibus non est Disputandum." *American Economic Review* 67:67–90.

Swedberg, Richard and Ulf Himmelstrand. 1987. "The Paradigm of Economic Sociology: Premises and Promises." *Theory and Society* 16:169–214.

Swidler, Ann. 1986. "Culture in Action." *American Sociological Review* 51:273–286.

Thomas, Robert, John Meyer, Francisco Ramirez, and John Boli. 1987. *Institutional Structure.* Newbury Park: Sage Publications.

Titmuss, Richard. 1971. *The Gift Relationship: From Human Blood to Social Policy.* New York: Pantheon.

Veblen, Thorstein. 1967 [1899]. *Theory of the Leisure Class.* New York: Viking Press.

Waldinger, Roger. 1990. "Immigrant Enterprise: A Critique and Reformulation." Pp. 395–424 in *Structures of Capital: The Social Organization of Economic Life,* edited by Sharon Zukin and Paul DiMaggio. New York: Cambridge University Press.

Wallendorf, Melanie and Eric J. Arnould. 1988. "'My Favorite Things': A Cross-Cultural Inquiry into Object Attachment, Possessiveness, and Social Linkage." *Journal of Consumer Research* 14:531–547.

Weber, Max. 1958 [1904–5]. *The Protestant Ethic and the Spirit of Capitalism.* New York: Scribner's.

———. 1968. *Economy and Society,* edited by Guenther Roth and Claus Wittich. New York: Bedminster.

White, Harrison C. and Robert Eccles. 1986. "Agency as Control." Manuscript, Columbia University, Department of Sociology.

Wrong, Dennis. 1961. "The Over-Socialized Conception of Man in Modern Sociology." *American Sociological Review* 26:183–193.

Zelizer, Viviana. 1979. *Morals and Markets: The Development of Life Insurance in the United States.* New York: Columbia University Press.

———. 1985. *Pricing the Priceless Child: The Changing Social Value of Children.* New York: Basic Books.

Zerubavel, Eviatar. 1985. *Hidden Rhythms: Schedules and Calendars in Social Life.* Berkeley: University of California Press.

Zucker, Lynne G. 1983. "Organizations as Institutions." Pp. 1–48 in *Research in the Sociology of Organizations,* Vol. 2, edited by S. Bacharach. Greenwich, CT: JAI Press.

———. 1986. "The Production of Trust: Institutionalized Sources of Economic Structure, 1840–1920." Pp. 87–138 in *Research in Organizational Behavior,* Vol. 8, edited by Barry M. Staw and L. L. Cummings. Greenwich, CT: JAI Press.

The Idea of Economy: Six Modern Dissenters 5

Keith Hart

THE IDEA OF ECONOMY

The reason for this volume, and the conference on which it is based, is that orthodox economics has carved out an impressive intellectual space for itself that leaves the rest of us feeling marginal and frustrated. Marginal because it is hard for us to match the formal intellectualism and public recognition that economists of the postwar period have arrogated to themselves. Frustrated because the monopoly exercised by the economics profession leaves out most of the interesting questions about the movement of economies at our time in history.

In this paper I will make a partial report on an attempt at synthesis on which I have recently embarked, and introduce six classical texts from the early twentieth century that, taken separately and together, may help us to clarify the intellectual task ahead of us. All of these texts were written on modern economic subjects in more or less self-conscious defiance of orthodox economics; all were prophetic in their dissent from dogma; and several helped to shape our world. They can help us build forms of understanding appropriate to our present and future societies, as conventional economics cannot.

The world we live in is substantially the result of western economic history. It was Europe that first broke decisively with agrarian civilization, began the process of global economic integration, and initiated the industrial revolution that determines the progress and survival of modern societies. The West thus made a bridge in the last half-millennium between mankind's fragmented agricultural past and an emergent world society driven by industrialization. This period has been marked by a degree of western dominance, both political (imperialism) and intellectual (scientific rationality), that appeared to be underwritten by its superior economic efficiency. If this observation is indisputable, it is equally clear to our generation, if not to any previous one, that the epicenter of human society is rapidly shifting back to where most of the people and the oldest civilizations are to be found—namely, Asia. It is no longer appropriate to assume that modern progress requires backward nations to westernize themselves. Rather the West must now ask whether its cultural patterns will survive competition with new syntheses arising in the East. The future of the world order is moot, more than at any time since World War II.

Anthropology has grown out of western civilization's aspiration to be universal. In the eighteenth century, the task was to discover what is general in human nature and reasoning. In the nineteenth century, it was to arrange the variety of human societies within an evolutionary order that explained western dominance. In the twentieth century anthropologists have been content to occupy a niche in the academic division of labor where they collect comparative exotic materials with which to test the pretension of western science and culture to universality. I would suggest that the anthropology of the twenty-first century will have to address the question of what is generally valid in the historic achievements of western civilization and what is so much parochial baggage, to be discarded by the cultures that arise to satisfy the wants and needs of that majority of mankind that is nonwestern. Such an anthropology will explore the tension between universal reason and specific culture history that must inform any systematic attempt to evaluate the human significance of the West's 500 years in the driving seat of world history.

Science is an expression of the desire to generate replicable knowledge whose application in the world is reliable within an acceptable range of error. Its distinguishing characteristic is formalism, the search for regular means of intellectual reproduction. The limits of established scientific forms are normally revealed in practice, so that new questions and the need for new solutions command the attention of specialists in the production and reproduction of knowledge. Of all the social sciences, economics has gone furthest in the direction of scientific formalism and it has flourished as a discipline in those societies whose institutions have enabled them to take the lead in global industrialization—Britain in the nineteenth century and the United States in this one. For 150 years other nations have had to ask how they intend to emulate the achievements of these English-speaking societies. Moreover, within the advanced economies, there has been a debate throughout this period over the adequacy of existing intellectual procedures to solve their current policy dilemmas. It is to this discourse that we must turn for precedents in our quest for economic forms suited to the predicaments of the world we expect to live in before long.

The idea of economy is an invention of western civilization. Economics is more narrowly the product of Anglo-American social history since the seventeenth century. How generalizable are the methods and findings of this science? Does the fact of its culturally specific origin preclude any legitimate claim that it is a form of universal reason? Everything has to begin somewhere; but some human discoveries have general application. Does the inescapably Victorian cultural framework of Darwin's thought mean that evolutionary biology is only a western myth, that nonwestern cultures will have to start from scratch if they want to comprehend the chain of life on this planet? Ever since Einstein and quantum mechanics, physicists have recognized that knowledge is relative to its location in time and space. But that has not prevented them from attempting to systematize our understanding of nature and the universe as a whole, with some impressive technical results. Economics is based on a claim to place human public and private affairs on a more rational footing. The task of economic anthropology is to discover the limits of such a claim, by standing outside the western civilization that produced it and asking how suited its intellectual forms are to the sort of world society that is emerging in our time.

The idea of economy was revived by medieval scholastics one and a half millennia after Aristotle made it a central concept of his politics. Its aim was to justify and protect the institutional core of agrarian civilization, the Great House, land ownership linked to military domination of a servile people. Trade and finance were seen in this theory to be the anarchic antithesis of natural order; urban capitalism and international commerce undermined the self-sufficiency of the rural ruling classes and had to be kept within acceptable bounds. The process whereby European capitalism broke out of this straitjacket has become well-known, not least because of the efforts of Max Weber. A combination of civic independence, new forms of state and a more rationalist Christian ethos enabled some parts of Europe to place their economies on a more calculable footing. This eventually was translated into the means of western global dominance—colonial empires, commercial and financial networks, and military and industrial efficiency. In the process, Aristotle's idea of economy was turned on its head: social order was now seen to be most reliably vested in institutions guaranteeing a substantial measure of individual freedom to make rational decisions aimed at pecuniary advantage.

The only way to make sense of historical movements in the idea of economy is to adopt a dialectical method. Once an idea has been identified by a nominal category, it creates a residue, whatever it is not, which in turn may be categorized as its explicit antithesis. This paired negation can for a time capture fluctuating realities as a frozen state of polarized oscillation, much as Hegel characterized the antinomies of Kantian understanding. But, in times of historical transformation, the dialectical pair may come to be seen as a contradiction that can be resolved only by the invention of a new idea, a new synthesis incorporating both sides of the previous negation. This process is often obscured by the propensity of words to retain successive layers of historical meaning, allowing for further poetic manipulation of intended emphasis in specific usage.

"Economy" is one such word that has been formed by several dialectical

oppositions in its history. Relevant pairs include countryside and city, agriculture and trade, domestic budgeting and profit-making business, private
and public domains, individual and social organization, subjective and
objective value, market and state, and economics and politics. Most of these
oppositions remain concretely embedded in different aspects of its modern
meaning, just as new oppositions emerge to strain the definition of economy, such as those between industry and services or production and finance.
Positivist incantations purporting to fix this meaning unequivocally cannot
abolish either the porous boundaries of the concept or the continuing evolution of the English language.

The original idea of economy—self-sufficient estate management—had
as its negation a complex consisting of the city, commerce, and central
government. This notion of natural economy survived in Europe until the
nineteenth century. Jane Austen's "economist" is an efficient female manager of a large rural household. It is retained in the modern sense of "economizing" as the efficient allocation of scarce resources by individuals, private
or domestic budgeting. In agrarian civilization, the state, conceived of as a
monarch's household writ large (as palace economy or, in Weber's expression, patrimonial bureaucracy), could be included in this sense without
serious discontinuity. But large centralized states are addicted to money (to
pay soldiers and officials), and taxation is symbiotic with trade. So increases
in the powers of government were usually associated with the rise of a class
of merchants and bankers differentiated from military land owners and religious specialists. Moreover, in early modern Europe, cities began to assert
their political independence from overrule by the military–agrarian complex
and to develop that style of government by impersonal laws and of economy
based on rational profit making that we now think of as "bourgeois."

At the time of Europe's explosion into the world as a number of competing
mercantile colonial powers, new nation-states emerged on the foundation of
an alliance between absolutist monarchs and their respective national bour-
geoisies. In the pivotal Hapsburg case, both the state and the bourgeoisie
were multinational. For these states, economy was essentially a political
process involving international competition between rival powers (mercan-
tilism) and the pursuit of profit as both a private and a public enterprise. In
the seventeenth and eighteenth centuries, the opposition between public
and private economy became entrenched in two ways: (1) by the articulation of a separation of interests between the state and bourgeois or "civil"
society, that is by a differentiation of political and economic interests, manifested most clearly in England by the emergence of the market or commerce
as a distinct institutional sphere (see Hobbes, Locke etc.); and (2) by the
identification of public management of economic affairs as "political economy" (a French term introduced into English by the Scottish Enlightenment
thinker, Sir James Steuart) in contrast with its domestic counterpart.

The tension between the state (top down administration) and the market (bottom up decision-making by calculating individuals) as institutional foci of economy has remained throughout the early phases of industrialization (the last 200 years). The economics profession, on the other hand, has, since the late nineteenth century, largely settled on a concept of its field of study that is individual, private, subjective, and grounded in the idea of market competition. England and the United States have, at different times, pushed the institutional autonomy of the market further than any other societies; and it is here that economics was born and still flourishes. (Most Nobel prize winners in economics are English speakers.)

The Cold War after 1945 crystallized the opposition between capitalism and communism as a death struggle between the free market and state socialism. Even so, observers of America and Russia have, for several decades, been pointing to the similarities between their economic systems, giving rise to a new vocabulary of intellectual confusion—state capitalism and market socialism, for example. At the same time, a new level of economic management has emerged, the international, embodied in the multilateral institutions of the postwar United Nations order, transnational corporations, and the shrinking sovereignty of national governments faced with rapid economic and technological evolution on a global scale. The possibility arises in all this that a new idea of economy could be emerging, harbinger of a new phase of world history.

There is thus no longer just one western economic idea, either the medieval church's version or the Victorian liberal synthesis that gained currency a century ago under the label of "economic man." It is not my intention to represent western economic science as monolithic. Indeed there is far more fundamental variation of economic thought within western culture as a whole than there is outside it. Moreover, there is an increasingly sophisticated discourse concerning the history and philosophy of science that I cannot attempt to summarize here. My contention is that the epistemology of economics was more or less fixed when it originated in the English revolutions of the seventeenth century—those revolutions in politics, religion, commerce, finance, agriculture, colonialism, and science that culminated in the institutional synthesis of the Glorious Revolution of 1688. I refer to constitutional monarchy, the two-party system, the merger between the City of London and the landed aristocracy, the extension of Puritanism to America and Ireland, the Bank of England, the East India company, Caribbean sugar, the Royal Society, Newton's physics, Locke's philosophy, and the birth of scientific economics.

If the King's divinely authorized word is no longer good enough, how does anyone persuade others to adopt his ideas? The answer, pioneered in England and subsequently adopted by secular elites throughout the modern world, is to make an appeal to scientific authority. Positivism is the attempt to lay down social rules arrived at by methods analogous to those thought to be responsible for the intellectual and practical achievements of natural science. Like its religious predecessors, positivism appeals to universal reason, which is presumptively absolute. It had two foundations in the seventeenth century, positions as old as pre-Socratic philosophy, the ideas of Pythagoras and Heraclitus. The first of these insists on the intrinsic harmony of axiomatic logic. It finds its best expression in mathematical deduction. It is Descartes' rationalism, inspired by the properties of mind contemplating itself. The second is based on practical knowledge of the material world. Its method is inference from systematic observation, measurement, and experiment, the empiricism of Gallileo and Bacon. Its focus is nature itself, the object of all human experience. As William Letwin (1963) has shown, the early economists (North, Petty, Locke etc.) drew on one or both of these scientific models. Their successors today still base claims to intellectual authority on an appeal to analytical logic (microeconomic theory) or to quantification (econometrics).

This means that mainstream economic orthodoxy remains trapped in an epistemological mold that, as Veblen pointed out, has not moved beyond the world of Newtonian mechanics, a world of handicrafts and agriculture that is essentially preindustrial. Even the natural scientists have long recognized that all knowledge is relative to our location and purposes, that scientists alter everything they measure, that we are lost in a universe of infinite scale and movement, with no fixed central point, no absolute a priori basis for knowing. Appreciation of this point has arrived more easily in those societies whose task it was to adapt to the dominance of English speakers, notably the Germans. Kant discovered cultural relativism and Hegel's dialectical method was intended to link knowledge of the way the world is and has been (the empirical past and present) to an ideal vision of what it may become (the future), to create a way of seeing and believing that conceives of our existence as a movement of communities, not just individuals, in history.

Positivism is conservative and pessimistic: in a positivist worldview, there is nothing we can do beyond adapt to what is and always has been, to make the best of what we've got. The Germans refused to accept that message and we may be sure that most Asians, following in the footsteps of the Japanese, will not do so either. Economics is "the dismal science" (Carlyle) because it is still locked into an inversion of Aristotelian theology, into a static model of causal laws that fails to take account of the fact that history is moving on.

SIX MODERN DISSENTERS

My second aim in this paper is to draw attention to a handful of major works by specialists in economic subjects whose example may serve us well in our attempts to grapple with the epistemology of formal economic science, with the task of devising more effective approaches to the historical problems we face. Their authors all flourished in the first half of this century; they saw deeply enough into their own times to create ideas that are relevant to our own. Each work, a creative synthesis, inspired a distinctive analytical approach to understanding economy. If we familiarize ourselves with this intellectual history in a more than superficial way, we may have more secure grounds for making claims on universities and governments to support our own synthetic efforts. My list is personal and it is as follows:

1. Max Weber: *General Economic History*—(published after his death in 1920 as *Wirtschaftsgeschichte*)—400 pages;
2. Thorstein Veblen: *The Theory of Business Enterprise* (1904)—200 pages;
3. V. I. Lenin: *The Development of Capitalism in Russia* (1899)—700 pages;
4. Talcott Parsons: *The Structure of Social Action* (1937)—800 pages;
5. J. M. Keynes: *The General Theory of Employment, Interest and Money* (1936)—400 pages;
6. Karl Polanyi: *The Great Transformation* (1944)—300 pages.

From these original works (less than 3,000 pages in total, but still a hefty chunk of reading by modern standards) we can trace a number of possible alternatives to mainstream economic science: the economic and cultural history of western civilization, institutional economics, modern Marxism, economic sociology, macroeconomics and philosophical relativism, and economic anthropology. It is from such a history of organized dissent that we may take our inspiration as we challenge the prevailing academic division of labor in social science and the humanities.

Weber

The critique of formal economics was carried out nowhere with greater vigor than in the German-speaking world at the end of the nineteenth century, when Britain's industrial hegemony was being challenged for the first time. The "Battle over Methods" (Methodenstreit) was waged principally between Schmoller in Berlin, the dean of historical economists, and Menger in Vienna, one of the founders (with the Englishman Jevons and the Swiss Walras) of marginalist economics in the 1870s. This was the clearest manifestation of the conflict between recognizing the cultural specificity and historical limitations of economic knowledge and the new orthodoxy's claim to be a species of universal reason, no longer even limited in application to the operations of the market (as had been political economy, "the science of trade").

The logical argument was conducted in terms of Kant's dialectic of form (also known as idea, rule, category, mental preconception) and substance (also known as content, material, stuff, sensual experience).[1] As often happens in heated arguments, the dialectic was fractured into its separate poles, with one side emphasizing the essential sameness of economic phenomena and the other their essential difference. The voice of reason and mediation in this instance was Max Weber, whose sympathy for liberal economics was tempered by extensive familiarity with western history. He pointed out that all knowledge depends on the dialectical contradiction between sameness and difference (Hegel's original thesis). Any two things can be shown to be alike or different. Unless we can postulate what phenomena have in common, we have no way of identifying their differences and vice versa. We need to be able to discriminate within a putatively universalizing approach to human affairs. This version of neo-Kantian philosophy sought to combine German romanticism with Anglo-French positivism, rather than maintain the paired negation in immobile opposition.

Weber's dense masterwork of political and economic sociology, *Wirtschaft und Gesellschaft,* is variously translated as *Economy and Society* and *The Theory of Social and Economic Organisation.* Neither translation is adequate since the root contrast is between housekeeping and fellowship. His *General Economic History* is more accessible, having been compiled posthumously from notes made of a lecture course he gave in Munich during 1919–1920. Part IV deals with "The origin of modern capitalism." Its admirably balanced account stresses the conditions allowing for reliable calculation, touching also on speculative crises, free trade, colonialism and slavery, industrial technique, citizenship, and the rational state. The final chapter is a more comprehensive and succinct version of his famous thesis concerning the protestant ethic and the spirit of capitalism, pointing to the Reformation's secularization in the Enlightenment and the socially disastrous death of religion in the "Age of Iron," the nineteenth century.

Although Weber's field is European history as a whole, his focus is mainly on England from the seventeenth century, without ever making this contrast explicit. Moreover, he does not seek to weight the influence of the successive phases of western economy—medieval cities, the Renaissance and Reformation, mercantilist colonialism, and the industrial revolution. This is a methodological weakness that we must rectify. He does, however, emphasize the novelty of industrialization as distinct from the earlier period of mercantile colonialism and refuses to follow Marx (*Capital* Volume 1, Part VIII on "Primitive accumulation") in assigning causal significance to wealth accumulated during that period. This remains one of the great points of division in the reconstruction of what is essential and what is peripheral to the evolution of modern economy.

Weber's contribution to social thought is supposed to be well-known in the English-speaking world. Unfortunately, the Parsonian version with which we are familiar is almost unrecognizable to most German scholars and is perpetuated by American commentators who flourish at the expense of original texts that are readable only with great difficulty. I wish to stress here that my own enterprise depends entirely on his massive precedent. He saw clearly the need to explore the dialectic between universal reason and the cultural history of western civilization. He rejected the Victorian assumption that human society can be understood in exclusively rational terms. He insisted that all knowledge is relative to time, place, and the investigator's purpose. He sought to unify the study of power and economic analysis. His subjective sociology of understanding (Verstehendesoziologie) was always situated in an objective structuralist history of the widest comparative scope. No one struggled harder to reconcile the contradiction between science and politics. He was a pessimist and a depressive; but then early twentieth-century Germany was not an easy place in which to live.

Veblen

America's place in the evolution of western economy, its distinctiveness and centrality, is poorly understood. European synthesizers after Tocqueville have known little about the United States, and Americans, having escaped from the old regime and in a sense from history itself, prefer to think of themselves as rational individual agents making life anew. The American century, our own, has produced few great works of historical synthesis, and, in consequence, we are poorly placed to assess the period of U.S. hegemony since 1945, which may or may not now be drawing to a close. Karl Marx always believed that the Yankee version of industrial capitalism was a purer and more progressive form than Britain's, and he justly celebrated the American civil war as a decisive phase of the global bourgeois revolution. Moreover, not only was Locke's philosophy given its most systematic application in the American political experiment, but American economists, ever since Irving Fisher turned the old (verbal) quantity theory of money into an equation ($MV = PT$), have far transcended their English and European counterparts in the use of mathematical techniques. Just as the relationship between England and the rest of Europe needs to be clarified, so too does America's contribution to the idea and practice of economy.

The decades leading up to World War I saw a fundamental shift in the social organization and technology of industrial economies. We will never make sense of our own revolutionary times unless we grasp fully what happened then, with all the benefits of hindsight. Fortunately we have a wonderful analysis of the making of the twentieth century in Thorstein Veblen's *The Theory of Business Enterprise* (1904), a work that is less well-known than his notorious satire, *The Theory of the Leisure Class* (1899), but better known than another masterpiece, *Imperial Germany and the Industrial Revolution* (1915). The value of *The Theory of Business Enterprise* to us is that its focus is modern America. Marx first drew attention to the importance of machines in modern economic development. A Scandinavian Midwesterner, Veblen, half a century later and with the robber barons operating right under his nose, saw how machine production could be hijacked by financial speculators. He recognized the extraordinary implications of the recent legal fiction that would treat huge corporations as if they were individual persons with the natural rights of ordinary citizens. At the same time he revealed how "captains of industry" were able to pile up personal fortunes at the expense of society's real interests while hiding behind this fiction. He was scornfully derisive of the intellectually backward and self-serving platitudes of the economics profession, proposing instead to remake economics as the study of institutions. No doubt he would have his own interpretation of the rise of formal economics to the virtual standing of a world religion since World War II.

Veblen saw a fundamental contradiction between the social discipline imposed by machine production and the motives of businessmen who controlled the industrial system through their ability to make money by selling. Businessmen will promote any useless activity as long as it brings a profit; they do not care about production or livelihood as such. In consequence, power in industry had passed from the factory floor to the financial managers at the head office. The cultural system of business enterprise originated in seventeenth-century England, which he described as "an isolation hospital for technology, science and civil rights." Its foundation is the institution of private ownership—the idea that free labor should own the product of its workmanship or "natural rights." The system of market competition laid down in the eighteenth century (see Adam Smith) was based on handicrafts and its philosophy is preindustrial. Machine production transformed the nineteenth-century economy and developments in the legal forms of corporate capitalism were rapidly reorganizing the logic of business enterprise in Veblen's day.

Yet economists still persevered with a preindustrial myth of economy ("a conventional anthropomorphic fact") that was as relevant to modern understanding as Newtonian mechanics or the artisan's notion of God as a creator. The organization of machine industry removed de facto natural rights long ago; its culture is skeptical, matter of fact, and relativistic and modern science reflects this attitude. The spirit of pecuniary gain that motivated the speculative operations of modern businessmen (and that the economics profession slavishly endorses) cannot be reconciled with the material and social needs of machine industry. Veblen predicts that the idea of economy as free market competition is a transitory halfway house on the road either to socialism based on machine production or to a new barbarism, dynastic politics conducted along medieval lines, with war and games the principal occupations of the ruling class.

This was not the message that twentieth-century Americans wanted to hear and Veblen's institutional economics was swiftly sidelined into the margins of academia. (He got his own back on the universities in his brilliant 1918 work, *The Higher Learning in America: A Memorandum on the Conduct of Universities by Businessmen.*) The field he sought to establish scored some notable subsequent successes, such as John Commons' *Institutional Economics* (1934) and Clarence Ayres' *The Theory of Economic Progress* (1944). It remains a significant, if marginal undercurrent of American social science. But its fundamental critique of orthodox economics as a mathematical mystification of an outmoded preindustrial ideology still falls largely on deaf ears—for now.

Lenin

Marx's critique of political economy (as economics was known before the 1890s) lies beyond the scope of this paper. The best short example of his economic philosophy is the Introduction to *Grundrisse* (1857–1858) particularly the section called "The method of political economy" (Marx 1974:100–108). Here he argues that we must start with the concrete whole, our moment in history; discover a few abstract, general relations; then retrace our journey back to the concrete starting point, this time with the aid of analysis. In Marx's view capitalism reveals for the first time the economic logic of society and it is this that makes economic analysis possible. Such an analysis can inform our understanding of precapitalist economic phenomena, but it is truly suited only to the capitalist epoch that gave it birth. He outlines his intellectual task as follows: (1) to arrive at some general abstractions such as the commodity; (2) to determine the categories that make up the inner structure of bourgeois society, knowing that their analytical order is the opposite of the historical sequence of their evolution. These two aims he achieved in *Capital*. He never reached the rest, which together would have brought him back to the starting point, present world history—(3) the state; (4) international relations; and (5) the world market and its crises.

In *Capital Volume I* (1867), Marx shows that the accumulation of capital can take one of two forms: absolute surplus value is squeezing profit out of workers by making them work harder (the feudal method) or relative surplus value is profit derived from making their labor more efficient. His judgment is that the latter path, depending as it does on substituting machines for human labor, is the progressive way. And he bases his assessment of the prospects for a communist alternative on the contradictions arising from the centralization of production entailed in capitalist industrial development. Marx never made clear the relationship between the specific economic history of mid-nineteenth-century Britain and the "laws of motion of the capitalist mode of production" in general. Oscar Lange (1935) is one commentator who, while finding Marx's prediction concerning the centralization of industry more impressive than any comparable achievement of orthodox economics, attributes this not to the theory of surplus value (which he considers to be so much metaphysical junk), but to the ethnographic insight gained firsthand by Marx and Engels into the empirical workings of Victorian capitalism.

This problem became crucial when, after Marx's death in the 1880s, the movement he founded sought to apply his analysis to conditions outside England. In particular, the German and Russian Social Democrats had to work out a socialist strategy appropriate to countries with large surviving peasantries. Kautsky's *Die Agrarfrage* (*The Agrarian Question,* 1899) has unaccountably never been translated into English. In it he argues that the persistence of small farmers in Germany is a systematic feature of that country's capitalist economy, so that any mass movement cannot simply expect them to wither away, but rather has to decide whether to leave them out or to seek to forge an alliance between them and the urban proletariat. Lenin devoted three years of his life (1896–1899) to a similar theoretical and empirical examination of the applicability of Marx's ideas to conditions in an even more agrarian economy, Russia's.

Lenin's *The Development of Capitalism in Russia* (1899) is, in my view, the best book on economic development ever written. It anticipates all the central issues confronted by Third World economies in the twentieth century and pursues its analysis with a rigor that has never been matched since. He was aided in this by the accumulation of an amazing record of rural conditions after the Alexandrine reforms of 1861, the so-called "zemstvo statistics." Lenin is the only marxist after Marx to take dialectical method seriously enough to alter the master's concepts when faced with an intransigent historical reality for which there was no precedent in Marx's writings. Indeed, his opponents, the Narodniks (populists), could claim support from Marx himself for their view that Russia could make a direct transition to communism without an intervening capitalist stage.

The subtitle of the work is *The Formation of a Home Market for Large-Scale Industry.* Lenin's thesis is that capitalism was already well entrenched in the Russian economy. This is obscured by the survival of a large number of "peasants" in the countryside whom he regards as a sort of agroproletariat, by virtue of their dependence on wage labor for part of their income. Moreover, a lot of manufacturing, although fundamentally capitalist in its organization, is carried out in rural areas. This means reformulating Marx's notion of the proletariat as a class lacking all forms of property except in their own labor power. Lenin concludes in an extraordinarily interesting final chapter (pp. 557–607) that the Russian home market stands ready to support an evolution to the level of large-scale industry that would make a strategy of proletarian revolution feasible under Russian conditions.

George Lichtheim (1961) and others have suggested that Lenin converted Marxism in this way from an Enlightenment philosophy of world history into a political recipe for the forced industrialisation of backward areas, its historical role as a twentieth-century ideology. Lenin himself admits that he may have overstressed the intensification of industrial and agrarian capitalism in the Russian heartlands at the expense of considering the geographical extension of the national economy into its various hinterlands, notably Siberia. But there is an intellectual honesty about this work that transcends any political teleology. It deserves to stand as a model of analytical enquiry into the continuing contradictions of western capitalist expansion into a precapitalist periphery.

In the past 20 years or so, Marxist political economy has become academically respectable in the West. This is partly due to the failure of orthodox economics to throw significant light on the development problems of the Third World, and partly to the recognition that academic marxism is just as harmlessly mystifying of contemporary realities as its conventional twin. The problem of the empirical limits to formalism is endemic to marxism. So is the tension between an appeal to universal reason ("scientific socialism") and dialectical method. Lenin tackled this problem as forthrightly as any of our intellectual predecessors and he should be read in that light, not merely as the apical ancestor of twentieth-century Stalinism.

Parsons

It should not be necessary to remind Americans interested in "Economy and Society" of the importance of Talcott Parsons. But, given the faddish dismissal of "functionalism" since the 1960s and the weakly developed historical awareness of most American social scientists, even this is not certain. Parsons set out self-consciously to discover the intellectual foundations of the revolution in European social science at the turn of this century and to synthesize its results for the purpose of creating a new American sociology. The result of his labors was *The Structure of Social Action* (1937). The merit of this work is that it represents an earlier attempt to do exactly what we need to do—use intellectual history to synthesize a new approach to economy and society and then devise an analytical strategy suitable for its reproduction.

The first paragraph of Parsons' book concludes "Spencer is dead. But who killed him and how? This is the problem." Herbert Spencer's synthesis of Mill's political economy and Darwin's evolutionary biology was the source of prevailing right-wing orthodoxy in Britain and America at the beginning of our century.[2] It still survives in vulgar neoliberalism of the sort sometimes known today as "Reagonomics" or "Thatcherism." Its catchphrase was "survival of the fittest," drawing on the obvious parallels between natural selection and market competition. Yet, by the 1930s, this naive apologia for capitalism could find no respectable takers in the western academy. Why?

Parsons' answer to this question was that Victorian utilitarian evolutionism had been killed off by European social democracy (with marginalist economics mending the bridge between England and the continent). His four leading assassins were Alfred Marshall (who popularized the new label, "economics"—rhymes with mathematics and physics for the correct musical effect), Vilfredo Pareto (a Swiss eclectic and author of a famous theory in welfare economics), Emile Durkheim (the founding father of French sociology), and, of course, Max Weber. All of these men were motivated by the desire to humanize capitalism, to mediate its social contradictions, and to reconcile scientific method (positivism) with the romantic ideal of free individual action (voluntarism). This involved attacking the pseudoscientific pretension to have rational answers to all the world's problems and specifically refuting the vulgar economism of the day (which certainly persists in our own). In the process they invented the social science disciplines that dominate the universities of the 1980s (just as Freud invented psychology, de Saussure linguistics, and so on). Parsons succeeded in inventing modern American sociology, for which benefaction he is now roundly vilified by his epigones. It is not likely that current academic divisions will survive the coming epoch of world history, and this is a good reason for seeking to emulate Parsons, by turning him into an element of some future synthesis.

The argument hinges on three issues: (1) the nature of the marginalist revolution in economics and the sacrifice of political economy to a new functional division of academic labor in which state, economy (market), and society were studied by different groups of specialists who were thereby prohibited from grasping their interaction and who, moreover, claimed to know nothing of mind, nature, or history; (2) the attempt of the professional middle classes to establish social democracy in the face of what looked like building up into a death struggle between intransigent capitalists and the newly organized working class (now endowed with a revolutionary theory, Marxism); and (3) the ability of what Parsons called "action theory" to solve the age-old dialectic between freedom and necessity, represented here as the relationship between individual will and social structure. Parsons took 800 pages and Anthony Giddens has filled a library shelf trying to tackle these questions. I balk at attempting a summary in a couple of paragraphs, especially since the relevant ideas are still in current academic circulation. I will merely cite the following guides that have influenced me: J. Schumpeter *History of Economic Analysis* (1954), T. W. Hutchinson *On Revolutions and Progress in Economic Knowledge* (1978), A. Giddens *Capitalism and Modern Social Theory* (1971), and A. Gouldner *The Coming Crisis of Western Sociology* (1970).

Parsons shifted after World War II to a systems approach that was much more explicitly positivist, functionalist, and evolutionary, that is to a version of sociological theory not unlike Herbert Spencer's (see *The Social System,* 1951). He also combined with Neil Smelser to develop a fully-fledged analytical framework for economic sociology (*Economy and Society: A Study in the Integration of Economic and Social Theory,* 1956). By personal example, writing, and social influence, Parsons almost single-handed made the postwar academic division of labor in American social science. His prose is sometimes said to be turgid and obscure. That is a matter of taste: it is a massive improvement over Max Weber's writing and it is in English. As mentioned above, his incorporation of Weber into the American mainstream if as far from German intellectual culture as Emerson's transcendentalism was from Kant. But Parsons, like Emerson and unlike Veblen, knew his audience and he succeeded as a builder of institutions. Others may comment on the lasting relevance of the subdiscipline he created in the 1950s.

Keynes

It is a commonplace that Keynes invented macroeconomics, that branch of the modern subject that deals with the influence of the state on economic affairs in market economies, that the book that effectively launched this project is *The General Theory of Employment, Interest and Money,* that the postwar welfare state is the expression of Keynesian ideas, and that, since the inflation scare of the 1970s, orthodox opinion has retrenched once again onto the old market liberalism that for a while enjoyed the revivalist label of "monetarism."[3] Here I wish only to stress Keynes' role as a critic of scientific economics. I contend that, because of the incorporation of Keynes' thought into mainstream twentieth-century economics, his radical philosophical critique of the discipline has been buried from view.

All western philosophy reflects a deeply felt need for certainty, determinacy, conceptual closure, proof, and rigor, in other words the need to escape from the limitations of everyday language. The urge to transcend the linguistic practices of one's time, to find something necessary to cling to as truth, is a basic element of western culture. The polarization of science and mere opinion may have some justification in the evolution of the natural sciences. But twentieth-century philosophy has been casting serious doubt on the applicability of such a rigid opposition to social thought. The contributions of the late Wittgenstein, Derrida, Rorty etc. have firmed-up a shift to philosophical relativism that was well aired in the German sociology of Weber and Simmel. Economics has remained immune to such intellectual trends, but Keynes, an active member of the "Bloomsbury Set," was not.

Keynes regretted that Ricardo's "machine of blind manipulation" was victorious over Malthus' "vaguer intuitions." He judged this victory to have set economics back 100 years: "The mix of logic and intuition and a wide knowledge of facts (mostly imprecise) required for the highest economic interpretation is too difficult for people who can only imagine the implications of simple facts known with a high degree of precision" (Keynes 1930). The key to Keynes' thought on these matters is the Wittgenstein of "Philosophical Investigations" who argued that, between mathematics and poetry, there exists a wide spectrum of linguistic practices ("language games"), each with its own logic, truth, and standards of rigor. The sorting of rival theories in social science is best conducted by means of argument ("rhetoric") rather than by deduction. There is no ideal universal language beyond our common ability to grasp our own times. If the subject matter of economics is inherently vague, as Keynes suggests, then seemingly precise languages turn out to be paradoxically inefficient compared with everyday language. As the pragmatists say, nothing useful can be said of the properties common to all true statements; we gain nothing by reducing discourse to some primary level of abstraction. Eclecticism pays. We can be serious in our arguments without aping natural science.

Keynes rebelled against the analytical philosophy of Russell and Whitehead, which lent authority to his economist predecessors. He preferred vague and rhetorical relevance to rigorous irrelevance. Words in natural language are inherently vague, suggesting relations, correspondences, and analogies between phenomena. A priori dedication to precision in communication makes our language bulky and complex, an obstacle to communication. Keynes aired these views in the *Treatise on Probability,* but he drove the point home in *The General Theory,* in which he inveighs against "symbolic pseudo-mathematical methods" as "mere concoctions which allow the author to lose sight of the complications and interdependencies of the real world in a maze of pretentious and unhelpful symbols" (Keynes 1936). He inverts the scientific notion of clarity by showing that for a class of statements, including economic theory, apparent vagueness aids precision. Menger (1981) made a similar point when he insisted that "the principle of marginal utility," expressed in words, says more than any mathematical derivation from it.

Keynes was concerned with making contact with his audience, something that most ordinary economists never attempt, beyond the narrow circle of fellow professionals. In this respect, modern economists are a priestly caste, speaking a sort of Latin in a world of demotic languages. Keynes knew that "a theorist requires much good will and intelligence and a large measure of cooperation from his readers"; that he must "take up the tale much closer to the conclusion" than is normal for social scientists; that economists, to be effective, have to learn to speak and write precisely in everyday language.

His methodology is matched by his policy conclusions. The old rules of monetary policy were thought to have a timeless, universal validity, and this led the British Treasury in the Great Depression into blind incompetence. Keynes offered discretionary standards of judgement which were relative to a specific problem, time and place, the now of the short run. Keynes beat the policy makers of his day in argument and had more influence over the shape of modern institutions than any other 20th century social theorist. He knew that the task is not so much to invent new ideas as to escape the old ones which "ramify into every corner of our minds". Hence his belief in the receptivity of the young, as the very last words of his great book attest: "In the field of economic and political philosophy there are not many who are influenced by new theories after they are 25 or 30 years of age, so that the ideas which civil servants and politicians and even agitators apply to current events are not likely to be the newest. But, soon or late, it is ideas, not vested interests, which are dangerous for good or evil" (Keynes 1936). One wonders what would have been the result if Keynes had known German as well as his mentor, Alfred Marshall, did.

Polanyi

All the authors I have highlighted were, in a fundamental sense, right, and, with the exception of Veblen, this is reflected in their historical influence on society and intellectual life. Karl Polanyi was wrong; but he failed gloriously. *The Great Transformation* (1944) was written toward the end of World War II by a Hungarian exile in Vermont who had spent much of the 1930s in England teaching and writing about the need for socialist planning. His tone in the book is that of an Old Testament prophet. Victorian industrial civilization, after 100 years of peace (1815–1914), had broken down in a series of unmitigated catastrophes—two world wars, the depression, fascism, Stalinism, and the flight from the Gold Standard. This was because England had sponsored a false premise for the organization of society according to the rules of the self-regulating market, but had held the world together for a time by means of the Gold Standard and the balance of power, underwritten by its own industrial and maritime hegemony. The liberal state was a hollow sham and its creed a lie. Inevitably the market mechanism collapsed and the illusion of freedom was replaced by the brutality of the twentieth century. Polanyi's recipe for a better world was what Marx called "utopian socialism" and his view of Marxism was equally uncomplimentary.

Judaism, according to Polanyi, gave us knowledge of death and Christianity knowledge of individual freedom. Nineteenth-century liberalism denied the knowledge of society that had been given us by the Enlightenment. Robert Owen (of all people) had penetrated to the truth of the necessity of society for our survival and recognized that man can be free only when he is resigned to his limitations, that is, to death and society. This means that we have to exchange an illusory freedom of the individual for real freedom based on acknowledgment of necessary evils. This curious neo-Aristotelian message reflects the mental torture of a Central European whose country was trapped between Hitler and Stalin, the excesses of fascism and communism. He took refuge in England and the United States, but was passionately convinced of the necessity for a planned alternative to their markets.

No would-be prophet was more cruelly treated by history than Polanyi. After the war he was forced to sit in American academia as witness to the greatest economic boom in world history, a market revival under U.S. leadership. Yet his book is a marvelous inspiration to all those who know intuitively that there is something fishy about economics. His vision is broad and well informed. He correctly focuses on the specific cultural history of England's industrial revolution as the crucible of the modern world. His critique of liberal market orthodoxy is brilliant. His institutional analysis is accurate and original. He even attempts an anthropological framework for his argument, suggesting that human societies have always relied on reciprocity, redistribution, and householding as alternatives to the antisocial market mechanism. It is salutary to consider how someone who got so much right could be so wrong.

Polanyi has been the single most influential figure in postwar economic anthropology. This is more because of his role in a 1957 symposium called *Trade and Market in the Early Empires* than for his masterpiece, *The Great Transformation*. Here, apart from paying homage to Aristotle ("Aristotle discovers the economy"—there's nothing new in the world), he attempted grand theory in "The economy as instituted process." Without acknowledging Kant, Weber, and the whole history of Central European thought (he was, after all, living in a society that has escaped from history), he claimed to have identified two analytical constructs of economy, one formal (rational calculation) and the other substantive (material provisioning). The former is appropriate to industrial market economies and the latter to nonindustrial economies, where markets may have a peripheral existence, but do not constitute The Market, taking a back seat to principles of reciprocity (symmetrical exchange) and redistribution (asymmetrical pooling). Weber made exactly the same distinction, but retained the dialectic as two sides of capitalist economy that he found to be in contradiction.

To their eternal shame, anthropologists grabbed Polanyi's vulgar rupture of the Kantian dialectic and spent the best part of the 1960s and 1970s in a so-called "formalist-substantivist debate" that, far from adding to the German argument, seriously detracted from its level of insight.[4] Polanyi's followers, known as "substantivists", opposed the application of formal economic analysis to non-western societies; but their own implicit formalism was never examined and their craven acceptance of the economics profession's monopoly in the advanced economies meant that they had no epistemological foundation for a thoroughgoing critique of the discipline.

The intellectual backwardness and general confusion of economic anthropology is revealed by its best product so far—Marshall Sahlins' justly
renowned *Stone-age Economics* (1972). Sahlins, a self-styled "substantivist"
and advocate of an "anthropological economics," here presents a new theory of what he calls "the domestic mode of production," the underlying
feature of all tribal and peasant economies. This marxist concept is in essence a reworking of A. V. Chayanov's *The Theory of Peasant Economy*
(1924, English translation 1966) with the support of ethnographic materials
from Zambia and Highland New Guinea. The fact that Chayanov drew on
Austrian marginalist economics to oppose Lenin's marxism and explicitly
restricted his analysis to one of seven historical types of precaptitalist agrarian economy did not detain Sahlins. Nor did it prevent the widespread
uncritical adoption of his ideas as conventional knowledge by a generation
of anthropologists and others outside the discipline. Whatever the value of
their exotic fact gathering, modern anthropologists have been too ignorant of
the history of economic ideas to make a serious contribution to the revision
of economic orthodoxy.

THE PRESENT TASK

As Keynes says, we must "take up the tale closer to the conclusion," if we
are to engage our readers. Western civilization represents itself as an economy these days. The TV news bombards us with the ephemeral movements of
stock prices, exchange rates, and the latest unemployment figures. Elections
are fought and lost on a government's economic record. International diplo-
macy is mainly about trade and banking. The dependent societies of the
Third World are compelled to give an economic account of themselves to
the agents of global order, the IMF and the World Bank. All of this is supervised by the high priests, the economists, who can be relied on to issue
incomprehensible statements purporting to show that they know what is
wrong or that everything is alright. It is almost impossible to discuss public
affairs in any terms other than economic. Even the revolutionaries are as
fixated on the economy as their opponents.

It was not always so. When the western bourgeoisie was struggling to
make the modern world, politics and religion figured prominently on their
agenda. They knew they had to create a whole new culture to break away
from the dead hand of the military—agrarian complex. It follows from this
that economics has become the religion of our secular scientific civilization.
Our predecessors as social theorists have left numerous analytical guides to
any investigation into such a proposition. Durkheim would see the economists as the upholders of what is sacred in capitalist society (following his
mentor, Auguste Comte, who had sociology in mind for the job). Weber
would stress their legitimation of a coercive social order running out of

control. Marx would talk about alienation and "the opiate of the masses." And Hegel anticipated all of them in *The Philosophy of Right* (1821). There is a lot to be said for going back closer to the source, to the original philosophers of our modern age.

It is tempting to portray our epoch as a war of world religions. Western civilization contributes five layers of its development, all still active—Judaism, Catholicism, and Protestantism, and the twin rival Scientisms, Economism and Marxism, which America and Russia have pushed via the cold war to the brink of nuclear holocaust. To these we should perhaps add Nationalism, a German invention now strikingly manifested as Europeanism, the most dynamic political force in the world today, but hardly yet elevated to the standing of a religion. Against these protagonists of an ancient and ongoing civil war within the West, there are arrayed Islam (increasingly its Iranian Shiite branch), Confucian Economism (the Southeast Asian NICs), Confucian Marxism (China), Japan Inc. (Nationalist Buddhism?), whatever pluralistic synthesis is slowly emerging from India's fusion of English culture and Asia's oldest religions, and Black Nationalism (the unification of the world's peoples of African descent as a result of western racist domination over a period of 500 years). Weber's massive comparative enquiry into world religions means that half of this work is already done. Our perspective on history makes it less easy to assume that the outcome of this cultural competition will be favorable to the West.

Human societies will continue to struggle for the economic forms that can reliably underpin their material existence in the modern world. It is because of its success as a religion that economics has been frozen in a seventeenth-century English world view. This should not lead us to imitate Veblen and Polanyi in scorning the efforts of the economics profession. Indeed they failed to influence society because, unlike my four other dissenters, they did not respect bourgeois cultural forms enough. Reproduction of viable forms is intrinsic to life. Formalism, whether of the state or the market, is crucial to any lasting solution to the problem of rational social organization. It is worth remembering (Marx and Lenin never forgot it) that western capitalism and science are the winning team—so far. Even so, it may be that an institutional approach to economic life would be valuable at this stage—not at the expense of formal theory, but as the excluded middle that modern social science has neglected to its cost.

There are three levels of social organization: (1) organization from the top down (states), (2) organization from the bottom up (typically individuals brought together by markets), and (3) intermediate organization between the two extremes (associations, especially durable social units or corporate groups). Modern social theory conceives of society as the interaction between the first two levels (frequently as one of them operating in isolation), refusing often to recognize the continuing importance of intermediate forms of association.[5]

Historically, nation-states and their industrial market economies are sup-posed to have broken down the ties linking individual citizens to the particu-laristic identities and structures typical of agrarian civilization. At least this is the prevailing intellectual orthodoxy. Ideological struggle focuses on the appropriate balance between coordinated public action and individual free-dom. Socialists emphasize the former, liberals emphasize the latter, and social democrats argue for some sort of enlightened mixture. I would suggest that the intermediate level of social organization, invisible as it may be to modern social theory, is essential to the functioning of viable institutions at all stages of economic development. Whereas the behavior of states and of individuals may often plausibly be described in terms of abstract general principles, membership in social bodies located between the two extremes is always specific and concrete. This is one reason for the reluctance of social scientists to take corporate associations seriously (it is too much em-pirical work to find out what they are), even though they have long been a preoccupation of anthropologists, historians, and lawyers.

The state is a conception of society as a unified whole, often embodied in one person—the monarch or, today, the president. Its members are repre-sented as individual citizens whose aggregate patterns of behavior are gener-ated on the ground by a mass of independent decisions of the sort that are given fullest expression in markets. A statistical logic postulates quantitative variation within a population of isomorphic units. At one extreme, there is centralized administration of policy; at the other there is a decentralized, democratic, anonymous mass. But ordinary people seek some measure of protection from the power of the state and from their isolation as individuals, and they find it in associations where they can identify with others like themselves, whether in corporate groups, political parties, informal networks of interpersonal relations or classes (cultural categories based on presumed shared interests within a system of ranked inequality). They form business corporations, labor unions, municipalities, churches, families, sports clubs, criminal fraternities, pressure groups—a vast variety of social movements and semistable reference points in a chaotic, frightening world. If provision for such groups is not made in planned developments, they will emerge spon-taneously, since social life is impossible without them. One of their main tasks is education for participation in societies whose systems of formal training are grossly inadequate.

British social anthropology announced its aim to concentrate on the inter-mediate level of institutions in a collection of essays published 50 years ago (M. Fortes and E. Evans-Pritchard, eds. *African Political Systems,* 1940). Here the customary political organization of African societies was used to highlight the exclusion of this practical level of human life forms from the abstract political philosophy then current in the West. To this critique we may now add the limitations of formal economics and the need to investi-gate both institutions and the interaction of state and market mechanisms.

Unfortunately, these erudite founders of modern anthropology covered up their intellectual tracks, preferring to represent their findings as the result of scientific fieldwork observations than as part of a sophisticated and long-standing debate within western social theory. This ensured that their students and successors were cut adrift from mainstream intellectual culture and never internalized that healthy respect for literate scholarship that is indispensable to lasting academic progress.

Nevertheless, ethnography for its own sake has a value, and the anthropology profession has in this century piled up a remarkable record of exotic firsthand investigations that will be of permanent value to mankind. It was as a fledgling ethnographer of this kind that I carried out a study of a city slum in Accra, Ghana more than two decades ago. The gap between my experience there and anything my English education had taught me before then was so vast that I have spent all of the intervening period, in one way or another, trying to bridge it. My struggle to connect the empirical world I discovered in West Africa to western discourse on economic development led me to articulate the notion of an "informal economy" or sector of economic life (Hart 1973).

Since then the concept has been used widely to discuss the failure of formal economics to understand contemporary Third World and even industrial countries' economic realities.[6] I have lately come to see this intellectual development, which at first was a mystery to me, as a response to the failure of state capitalism on a global scale, as people taking back into their own hands some of the economic power that centralized agents sought to deny them, as a response of "the untamed market." The rampant informalization of the world economy (off-shore banking, barter, drugs trafficking, "grey" markets, corrupt arms sales, etc.) is simply another manifestation of a world-wide phenomenon.

We may or may not be in a world crisis at this time. But it is increasingly obvious that we need a new idea of economy to help us grasp what is going on in the world. The economics profession, having opted for parasitism on the existing social order, is powerless to help. Apart from the desperate situation of Africa and much of Latin America, the West now has to come to terms with the rise of the East, not this time its Russian Marxist twin, but the oldest and largest civilizations on the planet, who have absorbed what we threw at them and are now poised to define the world in their own terms. California, where the enterprise of this book originated, is well placed to lead one wave of western rethinking of the problem of economy.

NOTES

1. I have addressed this issue at greater length in my Malinowski lecture (Hart 1986).
2. See Hofstadter (1944).

3. See Hart (1986). I am indebted in what follows to an unpublished paper by John Coates ("Tropophobia"), which he showed me some years ago. Donald McCloskey's *The Rhetoric of Economics* (1985) is also obviously relevant.

4. See Leclair and Schneider (1968). A more up-to-date and diverse collection is Ortiz (1983), the proceedings of the first conference of the Society for Economic Anthropology.

5. Heroic exceptions to this would have to begin with Hegel and Tocqueville. A more recent iconoclast is the West Indian writer C. L. R. James (1948).

6. See my article on "the informal economy" in the *New Palgrave Dictionary of Economic Theory and Doctrine* (1988).

REFERENCES

Ayres, C. 1944. *The Theory of Economic Progress.* Chapel Hill: University of North Carolina Press.

Chayanov, A. V. 1966 (1924). *The Theory of Peasant Economy.* Homewood, IL: Irwin.

Commons, J. 1934. *Institutional Economics.* New York: Macmillan.

Fortes, M. and E. Evans-Pritchard, (eds.) 1940. *African Political Systems.* London: Oxford University Press.

Giddens, A. 1971. *Capitalism and Modern Social Theory.* Cambridge: Cambridge University Press.

Gouldner, A. 1970. *The Coming Crisis of Western Sociology.* New York: Avon Books.

Hart, K. 1973. "Informal Income Opportunities and Urban Employment in Ghana." *Journal of Modern African Studies* 11(3):61–89.

———. 1986. "Heads or Tails? Two Sides of the Coin." *Man (N.S.)* 21:637–656.

———. 1988. "The Informal Economy." *New Palgrave Dictionary of Economic Theory and Doctrine.* London: Macmillan.

Hegel, G. W. F. 1952 (1821). *The Philosophy of Right.* London: Oxford University Press.

Hofstadter, R. 1944. *Social Darwinism in American Thought.* Philadelphia: University of Pennsylvania Press.

Hutchison, T. W. 1978. *On Revolutions and Progress in Economic Knowledge.* Cambridge: Cambridge University Press.

James, C. L. R. 1980 (1948). *Notes on Dialectics.* London: Allison and Busby.

Kautsky, K. 1899. *Die Agrarfrage* Stuttgart: Dietz.

Keynes, J. M. 1930. *A Treatise on Money.* London: Macmillan.

———. 1936. *The General Theory of Employment, Interest and Money.* London: Macmillan.

Lange, O. 1935. "Marxian Economics and Modern Economic Theory." *The Review of Economic Studies* 2 (June):189–201.

Leclair, E. and H. Schneider. (eds.) 1968. *Economic Anthropology.* New York: Holt, Rinehart & Winston.

Lenin, V. I. 1974 (1899). *The Development of Capitalism in Russia.* Moscow: Progress Publishers.

Letwin, W. 1963. *The Origin of Scientific Economics.* London: Methuen.

Lichtheim, G. 1961. *Marxism* London: Routledge & Kegan Paul.

McCloskey, D. 1985. *The Rhetoric of Economics*. Madison: University of Wisconsin Press.

Marx, K. 1970 (1887). *Capital Volume 1*. London: Lawrence and Wishart.

———. 1974. *Grundrisse*. New York: Vintage.

Menger, C. 1981 (1871). *Principles of Economics*. New York: New York University Press.

Ortiz, S. (ed.) 1983. *Economic Anthropology: Topics and Theories*. Lanham, MD: University Press of America.

Parsons, T. 1937. *The Structure of Social Action*. New York: McGraw-Hill.

———. 1951. *The Social System*. New York: Free Press.

Parsons, T. and N. Smelser. 1956. *Economy and Society*. New York: Free Press.

Polanyi, K. 1944. *The Great Transformation*. Boston: Beacon.

Polanyi, K., C. Arensberg, and H. Pearson. (eds.) 1957. *Trade and Market in the Early Empires*. New York: Free Press.

Sahlins, M. 1972. *Stone-age Economics*. Chicago: Aldine.

Schumpeter, J. 1954. *History of Economic Analysis*. London: Oxford University Press.

Veblen, T. 1899. *The Theory of the Leisure Class*. New York: Modern Library.

———. 1904. *The Theory of Business Enterprise*. New York: Charles Scribner.

———. 1915. *Imperial Germany and the Industrial Revolution*. New York: Mentor.

———. 1918. *The Higher Learning in America*. New York: Kelley.

Weber, M. 1981 (1927). *General Economic History*. New Brunswick, NJ: Transaction Inc.

SOCIETY AS MARKET   **III**

Markets, Marriages, and Other Mates: The Problem of Power

6

Paula England and Barbara Stanek Kilbourne

INTRODUCTION

What is the distribution of power between husbands and wives or other heterosexual cohabitants, and what explains this distribution? This is as central a question to the study of the family as the distribution of authority is to the study of bureaucracies. After offering a definition of power and reviewing empirical research on marital power, we criticize past theorizing about power among mates. Writing by many sociologists, Marxists, and feminists has taken the link between men's higher earnings and their greater marital power to be so obvious that little theoretical explanation is needed. By contrast, neoclassical economists have ignored power differentials within the family. We suggest that neither approach is satisfactory, and seek to problematize power among mates rather than to assume it as an obvious consequence of earnings or to ignore it.

We propose an understanding of power among mates that is presented in four propositions. They explain why men generally have more power than women, and why power flows from earnings more than from domestic work. We draw on ideas from structuralist sociology, radical/cultural feminist theory, neoclassical economics, game theory, and sociological exchange theory. Yet we argue that writers using these perspectives in past work have inadequately theorized marital power. Specifically, we suggest that domestic contributions are less effective in producing marital power than earnings because of (1) cultural forces that devalue traditionally female work and encourage women to be altruistic, (2) the fact that the beneficiaries of much domestic work are children rather than men, (3) the fact that some domestic work involves making investments that are specific to a particular relationship rather than "general," and (4) the fact that even "general" investments in domestic skills are less "liquid" than earnings because they do not ensure survival until one finds another partner. We conclude with a discussion of the consequences of the increases in women's marital power that have presumably resulted from increased employment. This discussion draws on Hirschman's (1970) distinction between exit, voice, and loyalty as possible responses to dissatisfaction. Because of resistance to changing the male gender role, increased female power is moving women from 1950s-style "loyalty" to the "exit" of divorce more often than to the "voice" of greater power vis-à-vis their male mates.

DEFINING POWER

We begin with a definition of social power. "Social" denotes that the power has effects on at least one other person. One has more social power to the extent that one's objective situation allows the advance of one's own wishes even when this is detrimental to another person's wishes.[1] The other we are concerned with is the spouse or cohabitant. Defining power in terms of an objective situation that allows one to advance one's own interest against another's interest permits us to distinguish between having power and exercising that power. That is, the definition admits the possibility that individuals will sometimes fail to fully exercise the power made possible by their objective position because of altruism, an egalitarian or patriarchal ideology, or a choice to leave the relationship rather than exercise power within it.

EMPIRICAL EVIDENCE ON POWER IN MARRIAGES

Sociologists have used several approaches to measuring marital power. One approach begins by identifying a number of decision-making areas. Within each of these, the respondent is asked to report who usually makes the final decision governing this matter, with possible responses such as "husband always," "husband usually," "half and half," "wife usually," and "wife always." An early study of this genre was Blood and Wolfe's (1960) exploration of decision-making areas that included what job the husband should take, which automobile to purchase, whether or not to purchase life insurance, where to go on vacation, what house or apartment to choose, and whether or not the wife should begin or quit work outside the home. There are several problems with this method of measuring power. First, since husbands and wives typically specialize in different areas, any global measure of marital power (summed over all decision-making areas) is sensitive to which areas are chosen for study. Further, the researcher may mistake the importance of different areas to spouses' utilities, and spouses may themselves differ in this, so that it is not clear how to weight the topical areas to compute an overall measure of power. Finally, the fact that one party makes more decisions does not necessarily mean that the other has less power. Indeed, the party with more power may relegate many minor decisions to the less powerful party because of a preference to avoid menial decisions. These problems have contributed to a second strategy to measure marital power. Here respondents identify areas of conflict in the marriage, and then report who usually "wins" in these areas (Heer 1963; Scanzoni 1970; Bahr 1974; Scanzoni and Scanzoni 1981:441).

Whatever their method of measurement, sociological studies generally find that, on average, husbands have more power than wives, that male power is stronger when the wife is exclusively a homemaker than when she is employed outside the home, and that male power is less extreme when women have higher earnings (Glueck and Glueck 1957; Heer 1958, 1963; Blood and Wolfe 1960; Blood 1963; Scanzoni 1970, 1979; Bahr 1972; Duncan and Duncan 1978:205; McDonald 1980; Blumstein and Schwartz 1983). We accept this empirical generalization, but believe that it requires more theoretical interpretation than past writers have offered.

LIMITATIONS OF PAST THEORIZING ABOUT MARITAL POWER

We find the theoretical treatment of marital power in prior writings to be inadequate. Sociologists using exchange theory often write as if it were obvious that the partner bringing in money is contributing more to the exchange and hence will have more power (e.g., Scanzoni 1972, 1979). But this conclusion implicitly assumes that women's fertility, child rearing, emotional work, and housework are somehow less of a contribution than men's earnings. The reason for this is seldom discussed.

A similar bias is seen in Marxist discussions of sexism, particularly in the work of orthodox Marxists, and to a lesser extent in the writings of socialist-feminists. (For an overview of these positions, see Agger 1989b.) The classic Marxist doctrine on the family is Engels' (1884) *The Origin of the Family, Private Property, and the State.* He argued that women's subordination came about with a shift to a system of production that could produce a surplus, and, thus, made land, animals, humans, or machines valuable as "capital." The first such system, agriculture using domesticated animals, made private property consequential and made men the owners of such property. The essence of the argument is that class societies are stratified on the basis of property, disadvantaging women because they do not own property, and giving male property owners a motivation to control female sexuality to ensure legitimate heirs. In this formulation, sexism is an epiphenomenon of capitalism. Women's domestic work scarcely entered the discussion, and a discussion of why wives of working class men were subordinate to their husbands who were not property owners was never made clear.

A step toward acknowledging the importance of household work within the Marxist tradition was provided by James and Dalla Costa (1973) who argued that housework is an economic contribution to capital in that it reproduces the labor power of the next generation and of current male workers. Other socialist-feminists go even farther toward acknowledging that patriarchy—male power—subordinates women and that sexism is not merely an epiphenomenon of capitalism (Hartmann 1979, 1981; Eisenstein 1981; Delphy 1984; Walby 1986). The socialist-feminist position recognizes that women's domestic role involves women's exploitation by their own male partners as well as by capitalists. Although we applaud this recognition, we are, nonetheless, critical of these authors for writing as if male power in the family were an obvious consequence of men's earnings without explaining the inference (e.g., Hartmann 1981). Some socialist-feminists continue to use a vocabulary that distinguishes between production (waged labor) and reproduction (nonwaged domestic labor). This vocabulary obscures the fact that homemakers do *produce* goods and services. Why, for example, is the socialization of one's own children at home not as much a part of production as working in a day care center or writing advertisements? And why is "production" the determinant of marital power? As Agger (1989b) puts it, these authors are subtly under the sway of an "economism" that regards whatever has traditionally been considered part of the economy more significant and valuable than women's domestic work. (See also Agger 1989a, and forthcoming.)

Sociologists proposing macrostructural theories that explain variations in gender inequality across societies and historical periods have been guilty of this same "economism" that leads them to fail to see the need for theorizing about why earnings translate into marital power more readily than domestic work. Chafetz (1984, 1988) argues that women's access to all types of rewards (which presumably includes marital power) is greater when women are less involved in childrearing and homemaking and more involved in work outside the home. Chafetz implicitly defines the terms "work," "productive activity," and "economic" to exclude the childrearing and other domestic labor women perform in many societies. But not calling women's work "work" only obfuscates the issue. It does not tell us why work done at home does not yield the rewards of other work. Similarly, Huber summarizes one of the three propositions of her cross-cultural theory this way: "Those who produce goods tend to have more power and prestige than those who consume them. It is better to be able to give than to have to receive" (Huber 1988:13). But by whose count are homemakers giving less than they receive? Huber seems to accept the devaluation of women's domestic work without comment or explanation.

Why would exchange theorists, Marxists, and macrostructural theorists all discount domestic contributions to marriage? Although authors are seldom explicit about it, we can speculate about their implicit logic. Perhaps domestic contributions are thought to be discounted because women produce services rather than goods whereas men produce goods. But this makes no sense since some homemakers do produce goods (e.g., sewing clothes), and many men are employed in service industries. Indeed, many very highly paid predominantly male occupations such as doctor, lawyer, and advertising executive involve no production of goods. Perhaps, then, the distinction is that men bring cash into the family whereas women who are homemakers do not. To use Marxist categories, men produce for exchange value, and women produce for use value. But this, too, is misleading for two related reasons. First, if exchange theorists are right that marriage is (at least in part and implicitly) an exchange of domestic services for financial support, then women's work *is* for exchange. Second, domestic work saves the family cash since it provides goods or services that would otherwise have to be purchased with cash. Thus, it hardly escapes the cash/exchange nexus.

There are some unexamined assumptions buried in the reasoning of these authors. All these views present themselves as theories in which outcomes are contingent on "objective," "structural," or "material" conditions rather than values. But the unacknowledged assumption in all of them is that domestic work is either inherently less valuable than other work, or, at least, that it is seen as less valuable by the members of any society to which the theory purports to apply. This added assumption would allow the perspectives to yield the prediction of women's lesser power. But if this assumption that domestic work is seen to be worth less than other work is made explicit, each of these views is seen to rely in part on a proposition about cultural values, not entirely on material, structural, or objective matters. Indeed, if there is anything about the structural position of earner that yields greater power *without* the assumption of a cultural value devaluing domestic work, these theories have not made clear what it is.

We try to remedy these problems of prior theorizing on two fronts. First, we are explicit about the fact that culture *is a part* of the source of the lesser marital power of women. In asserting this, we are arguing both that the realm of ideas matters, and that culture cannot be separated too sharply from the material. When the cultural devaluation of traditionally female tasks is a hidden rather than explicit tenet of theorizing, we believe it contributes to making sexist values seem inevitable and universal rather than as contingent social facts. Second, we suggest several "noncultural" reasons why the structural role of earner yields greater power than does the structural role of homemaker. In sum, we believe that past theorizing about marital power by sociologists, feminists, and Marxists has been unwittingly antifeminist in its devaluation of women's contributions, and inadequately scientific in its failure to provide an adequate explanation of women's lesser power in the family.

Ironically, our criticism of neoclassical economists is *not* centered on their narrow "economism" as we have used the term above. Although it is true that economists have been somewhat guilty of this in their failure to include the value of household work in the gross national product, this failure is not seen in recent theoretical work on the household such as the "New Home Economics" of Gary Becker (1981). (For a nontechnical overview, seen England and Farkas 1986, Chapter 4.) Our criticism of neoclassical economists is that they ignore the existence of *unequal power* in the household and elsewhere. Economists define power in terms of lack of competition. A market lacks competition when it has only one or a few buyers (a monopsonist or oligopsonist) or only one or a few sellers (a monopolist or oligopolist). (In rough terms, we can call all four phenomena "monopoly.") To economists, power means that the monopolist gets more than would be obtained in perfect competition. Since our definition of power does not require a deviation from competition, it differs from the neoclassical definition. Below we will apply the concept of monopoly to marriage, arguing that after certain relationship-specific investments at the beginning of a marriage, each partner is in a position of monopoly vis-à-vis the other. This is because there are no alternative partners who have been similarly "trained in." But the monopoly is bilateral. Thus, economists do not see one party as necessarily having *more* power than the other.

What if there is an asymmetry in amount of relationship-specific investments such that more of women's investments are specific to a particular marriage and more of men's investments are "portable" if one leaves the relationship? We will argue below that this contributes to men's power. But economists have not recognized this power disparity. We suggest that this is because what we and other noneconomists mean by unequal power implies (as a consequence if not as part of the definition) that the party with more power receives more utility from the relationship than the party with less power. But economists will eschew a conceptualization of power that implies differences in the utility parties receive because neoclassical theory assumes that interpersonal utility comparisons are impossible. Although we concede that utility comparisons are very difficult to measure, we suggest that this be seen as a practical measurement problem rather than an "in principle" nod to radical subjectivism. As a result of ignoring power differences between men and women in marriage or elsewhere, economists have missed the fundamental insight that women are subordinated to men.

A further problem with the neoclassical approach is the assumption that tastes (preferences, values) are always exogenous to economic models. This implies that economic models being used to describe the division of labor by sex do not recognize that adults can have their tastes modified by the roles they take on within the family. We prefer the structural view in sociology that sees roles as molding the preferences and habits of their incumbents (e.g., Kohn and Schooler 1983). Thus, although some values may be exogenous to the structural roles women and men hold, others flow from them.

DETERMINANTS OF POWER AMONG MATES: FOUR EXPLANATIONS

Our goal is to explain why earnings provide power more readily than domestic work (in which we include fertility, child rearing, the work of making emotional or sexual accommodations to a partner, and housework), and, hence, why men have more marital power than women.

Our argument here takes the typical division of labor by sex as given, though a few words on its explanation seem warranted. One way to categorize writings that purport to explain sex differentiation is in terms of whether they see roles in the family or in employment as having greater causal priority. Many neoclassical economists have seen women's household role (which they believe to be determined by exogenous social or biological forces) as explaining the intermittent employment and low pay of women within the labor force. Another view of the life cycle also begins the causal arrow within the household, seeing early life decisions about both employment and household behavior as the determinants of adult roles within both arenas. Some sociological work emphasizing socialization agrees with this view that social forces are exogenous to employment outcomes. Other economists and sociologists have reversed the causal arrow, pointing to discrimination against women in labor markets as affecting career plans and the division of labor at home. We would stress that the position of men and women in households and in employment has reciprocal effects. (An overview of these dynamics is presented in England and Farkas 1986.) Such reciprocal links do not completely rule out change; indeed, they mean that change in either arena will be the precursor of change in the other.

Our discussion focuses on the way in which the typical division of labor by sex across both household and employment sectors affects marital power. Yet we do not deny the possibility that marital power may affect sex differentiation as well. Some sex differentiation may *result* from men's power to avoid a more equal sharing of household and career roles, though this causal direction is not our focus.

The sexual division of labor puts men and women in different structural positions. By "structural positions" we refer to roles whose characteristics transcend those of any particular incumbents. Examples of structural positions are "homemaker," "earner," or more specific job or occupational categories. The typical marriage features men contributing the bulk of earnings and women contributing either exclusively domestic work or some combination of such work and a relatively small paycheck. Why does this arrangement yield more power to men than women?

We propose an answer that draws on a neoclassical model of implicit contracts, sociological exchange theory (Cook 1987), game theory (Schotter and Schwodiauer 1980; Binmore et al. 1986), a sociological view in which habits and preferences flow from one's structural roles (Kohn and Schooler 1983), and a view of culture taken from interdisciplinary radical/cultural feminist theory (England 1990, Chapter 6). Although we have criticized theorizing about marital power offered by writers working in some of these traditions, we think that they have much to offer the study of marital power. Let us preview the argument we present below: One's power depends on how much one contributes to a relationship, the ease with which one could leave the relationship and take the fruits of such contributions, the extent to which one is inclined toward self-interested bargaining, how much one's contributions are valued by the partner, how this compares to the value the partner places on what could be had outside this relationship, and how one compares what is had within the current relationship to what could be had outside it. The four propositions are discussed in turn below.

The Role of Culture: Devaluation of the Traditionally Feminine
Sphere and Differences between "Male" and "Female" Values

We argued above that a devaluation of tasks traditionally done by women is an unacknowledged assumption of much writing on marital power, and suggested that writers contribute to such a devaluation by making it invisible. We think it important to acknowledge that Western culture has privileged the traditionally male sphere, and that these values limit women's power through limiting the value men place on what women offer in relationships. Western thought features a series of dichotomies such as rational/emotional, mind/body, active/passive, good/evil, and superordinate/subordinate. In each of these dichotomies, the first category has been valued more highly and assigned to males. Thus, men may benefit from and enjoy what women provide but have been socialized to take such benefits for granted or to find them not deserving of any credit. It is striking, for example, how classical liberal thought saw the nurturance of men and children by women as outside the sphere deserving of moral status but rather as something women "naturally" supplied (Benhabib 1987). It is the low valuation of their roles as well as the assignment to these roles that disadvantages women. This is overlooked when economists focus on "barriers to entry" and functionalist sociologists focus on social mobility as if they were the only possible mechanisms of group subordination. Since this cultural devaluation of everything associated with females has a long history, it is in part exogenous to, or at least jointly endogenous with, the structural and market realities we emphasize below.

In response to our cultural argument, one might ask how men get away with rewarding what women provide at less than is commensurate with the utility they themselves experience from receipt of these services. Couldn't women get their due by threatening to withdraw their services? Below we consider structural reasons why it is difficult for women to do this. But here we answer this query with another cultural argument: women seem disinclined to act in such a self-interested manner. Women hold a subcultural value system emphasizing connection and mutual altruism. Holding such a value system is not inherently subordinating, except if one's partner is more narrowly selfish. We believe that women do not bargain as far toward the margins of their power as men do because of a greater valuation of altruism, a value women wish that men would reciprocate. This cultural difference between men and women may itself be explained in part by women's experience in the structural role of nurturer. It may also, in part, be an act of resistance of women against the prevailing masculinist model of separative self that dominates our culture, and that radical/cultural feminists criticize (Chodorow 1978; Gilligan 1982; E. F. Keller 1983, 1985; Hartsock 1983, 1985; C. Keller 1986; Benhabib 1987; England 1989, 1990, Chapter 6). If there is, in some sense, a male and a female culture, an important question about power in intimate male–female relationships is what happens when these two styles are paired.

To explore this, suppose that there are two kinds of dispositions toward self and other coexisting in the social world: (1) Model "S" (for separative) deemphasizes empathy, sees self-interested behavior as natural, and takes advantage of being in a powerful bargaining position when it occurs. (2) Model "C" (for connective) emphasizes the rewards of emotional connection, and takes both one's own and a connected other's utility as roughly of equal importance, regardless of who is in a stronger bargaining position. One way to put this is that those who practice model S fit economic and exchange theories better than those who practice model C. Suppose further that existing social structures and socialization practices produce more males practicing S and more females practicing C. To oversimplify, suppose that all men practice S and all women practice C.

Under these assumptions, marriage would feature men pressing their bargaining harder and getting more of what they wanted as a function of the amount of their earnings relative to their wives' earnings. The extent to which wives pushed for their own way at the expense of a partner's would be uncorrelated with their earnings. Overall, the fit of men's behavior with exchange theory would be sufficient to produce the correlation between earnings and power observed in the literature, though the correlation would be less than if women, too, practiced S. In such a situation, there are two ways for women to rectify the power imbalance. The first way is through increasing their earnings and using them for bargaining power, but this requires that they abandon model C, which they do not want to do. Their second option is to persuade men to adopt model C with them, but this is a "hard sell" to men already thinking in S terms. We might think of this as the altruistic self's version of the prisoner's dilemma. That is, Model C is disadvantageous only when you cannot get your partner to collude with you and practice it too.

A recent study by Blumstein and Schwartz (1983) produced findings consistent with this view. They interviewed four types of cohabiting couples: married, unmarried heterosexuals, gay men, and lesbians. They found that the magnitude of the relationship between relative earnings and power varied across the four types of couples. Disparities in earnings produced the greatest disparities in power among gay male couples and moderate disparities among heterosexual couples (married or not). There was no correlation between earnings and power among lesbian couples (Blumstein and Schwartz 1983:53–63). We might interpret the numerical presence of males versus females in each type of couple as indicative of the numerical preponderance of practitioners of models S and C. On that assumption, it is striking that the strongest correlation of earnings to power is in the couples containing two practicing S, the intermediate correlation is in the group where couples have one S and one C, and there is no relationship between relative earnings and power in the group with both partners practicing C. In short, a cultural system in which women value altruism and connection disadvantages women when men do not share this value system. If men shared these values, they would be less a source of disadvantage to women.

Women's Contributions to Children's Well-Being

If we think of marriage as an exchange in which men offer earnings and women offer household work, the language suggests that men receive the benefits of women's domestic work (e.g., Hartmann 1981). However, in the case of child rearing, the direct recipients of the work are children, not men. This work seems less something that women offer their husbands as part of reciprocal exchange, and more something they freely offer their children.

Yet several factors mitigate against work for children translating into marital power for women. First, an exchange or game-theoretic perspective implies that something one offers one's partner creates power on the assumption that offering it implies the ability to retract it. But since women usually retain custody of children in divorces, any benefits men perceive from what women do for their children will not be lost even if the marriage ends. Women cannot derive power from a credible threat to stop taking care of the children when men know that the woman's bond to and commitment to the children transcends the relationship to the men. Indeed, historian Gerda Lerner (1986) speculates that the origins of patriarchy may lie in the fact that women made better slaves than men precisely because they were likely to cooperate with their masters for the sake of their children.

Second, several factors militate against men placing a high value on the well-being that comes from the care of their children. Men will place value on women's child-rearing services to the extent that they are altruistic and empathic toward their children. The evidence suggests that men are much less altruistic toward children than are women. For example, Blumberg (1988) provides cross-cultural evidence that when women control family income they allocate more of it to children than do men. We suggest that the very fact that women not men do the nurturing of children creates sex differences in felt bonds of empathy and altruism with children. This explanation of women's limited marital power is an example of seeing values endogenous to one's structural role. It contrasts with the neoclassical assumption that preferences are exogenous to economic roles, and is more consistent with the view in sociology that sees one's psychology to be influenced by one's structural role (Kohn and Schooler 1983).

The Asymmetry of Relationship-Specific vs. Portable Investments

One reason for women's lesser power in marriage is that more of the fruits of men's investments are portable outside this particular marriage whereas more of women's than men's investments after marriage are "relationship-specific." We use the term "investment" here as economists do, to indicate incurring a cost at an earlier time that yields a benefit at a later time. Costs may be pecuniary or nonpecuniary, and they may be either directly paid or opportunity costs. By "relationship-specific" we refer to investments that not only require one to be in some relationship to pay off, but that require that one stay *in the specific relationship in which the investment was made.* Thus a relationship-specific investment will not pay off in a new marriage or in a single state.

This explanation of marital power follows England and Farkas' (1986, Chapter 3) conceptualization of marriage as an implicit contract rather than either a "spot market exchange" or an explicit contract. The explanation draws on new conceptual developments in economics alternatively called implicit contract theory (England and Farkas 1986, Chapters 3 and 6), the "new institutionalism" (Farkas and England 1988), or the transaction–cost approach (Williamson 1988). These new ideas have generally been used to analyze labor markets and other business transactions (Williamson 1988), but apply to the family as well. Although these new concepts have developed from within the neoclassical paradigm to explain anomalies, in true Kuhnian fashion, they may ultimately create significant change in the paradigm. Although we use these neoclassical concepts to help explain unequal marital power, the reader should recall that most economists do not admit *unequal* power as we have defined it to be a meaningful concept because of its link to interpersonal utility comparisons.

A fundamental insight of these new ideas is that parties often make investments that will continue to benefit them only if this particular exchange relationship is continued. In labor markets, workers sometimes receive on-the-job training. This training has present costs and future benefits, and thus may be seen as an investment. The training may entail directly paid expenses for materials or teachers. Even when the training is informal, it has the opportunity-cost of foregone productivity while an experienced worker teaches a new worker. These costs are the investment the employer has made in the human capital of the workers. Neoclassical theory also suggests that employees share some of these costs by accepting lower wages at first. While some on-the-job training may provide skills that one could transfer to another company, what is central in the new theories is the training that produces knowledge and skills that are useful only in this particular firm. This is called firm-specific training; in the terms we use here it is "relationship-specific" in that it is specific to the relationship between this particular employer and employee. This training makes it more likely that the worker is more productive to the employer than workers that might be newly hired (since new workers would not have this firm-specific training), and that the worker is more productive here than at other firms (since the worker has not received the specific training of other firms). Thus, both employer and employee have invested in an asset (firm-specific human capital) that pays off to either party only if the employee continues to work there. Williamson (1988) calls this a situation of "asset specificity." Because there are no workers outside the firm who have received such training and no other firms for which the present workers have received specific training, economists see a situation of bilateral monopoly to develop after the firm-specific training has occurred. Williamson (1988) calls this passage from before to after firm-specific investment the "fundamental transformation." It is the transformation into a situation in which a competitive market model is no longer fully appropriate because each side has a sort of monopoly power over the other. Thus, the situation becomes suitable for analysis by game theory (Crawford 1985; Crawford and Rochford 1986; Binmore et al. 1986).

Several authors have applied insights from implicit contract theory and game theory to marriage (Manser and Brown 1980; McElroy and Horney 1981; Pollak 1985; Sen 1985; England and Farkas 1986; Brown 1988). In this section we follow the formulation of England and Farkas (1986). We can think of a market for spouses or cohabitants in which an individual searches for the optimal partner (given one's preferences) and in which the partner one can "land" is limited by the attributes one has to offer (given the preferences of those on the other side of the market). Once a couple begins a relationship, is each party still "in the market" such that the moment a better deal comes along she/he will leave the relationship? If so, we would consider marriage markets "spot markets." The fact that about half of currently contracted marriages are projected to end in divorce (Cherlin 1981) might suggest a spot market. Yet, if we compare marital "turnover" with what it would be if there were no relationship-specific investments, marriages and even nonmarital cohabitation look quite stable. One reason for this is the psychic and pecuniary "search costs" of finding a new partner (England and Farkas 1986:36–42). But even ignoring the costs of constant search, a personal relationship is highly valued over the relative impersonality of being continuously in the rating–dating game. Surprisingly, the new economics can illuminate this via the distinction between general and relationship-specific investments that is their key innovation.

Many of the things people value in marriage are a result of relationship-specific rather than general investment. To call an investment relationship-specific means that it has value only within the current relationship, and would be of no benefit outside a relationship or in a different one. Firm-specific training is the analog in labor markets. In marriage or cohabitation, once such investments have been undertaken, both partners are likely to be better off within this relationship than they would be were they to start over with someone else. Marital investments that transfer poorly to a new relationship involve learning to deal with the idiosyncrasies of one particular partner, such as learning his or her preferences and personal history, forming attachments with in-laws, learning this partner's sexual preferences, learning how to resolve disagreements with this partner, or contributing to the felt solidarity of the marriage by investments in children. To the extent that such learning takes time and/or resources that could be profitably or enjoyably spent doing other things it has costs and can thus be viewed as an investment. Such relationship-specific investments mitigate against rapid turnover among partners just as firm-specific training mitigates against employee turnover. As with employer and employee, both parties in a marriage have an incentive to make some long-term "contract" to protect their relationship-specific investments.

What is the nature of such contracts? One might think that partners would agree on a formal contract indicating each side's rights and responsibilities under various contingencies, what economists call a "perfect contingent-claims" contract. Yet despite their seeming usefulness, formal prenuptial contracts are rare. One reason is the transaction costs of negotiating and enforcing such contracts, such as lawyers' fees to write a contract and the divisiveness caused by the negotiations. Enforcement costs continue indefinitely. For example, consider a couple that had a contract specifying that if either party failed to do half the housework, the other party could keep a higher share of pooled earnings. What if the parties disagree about who is doing less than half the housework? If an arbitrator/observer is to be hired, this is a transaction cost. If the couple simply haggles, this haggling is a nonpecuniary transaction cost. To avoid future haggling, the contract may have to be ludicrously specific, and this increases the initial negotiation costs. A second reason that explicit contracts are rare is that they undermine trust (Shapiro 1987). A third reason is legal restrictions on the "specific services" to which parties can bind themselves and still have the contracts enforceable.

Given the benefits of some long-term arrangement over the spot market, and the aforementioned problems of formal contracts, marriages can be seen as implicit contracts. This refers to the informal understandings grounded in each party's incentive to remain in and conscientiously contribute to the marriage by virtue of past relationship-specific investments. An interesting feature of relationship-specific investments (whether in employment or marriage) is that they provide incentives that "bind" *both* partners, regardless of which partner has made the investment. For example, once an employee has learned to use equipment that is idiosyncratic to one firm, this gives the firm a motivation to pay this employee more than they would a new person, thus also providing the employee with an incentive to stay with this firm. Both parties are more "bound" the more relationship-specific investments have been made, *regardless of which side paid for the investment*. Thus, in a marriage, relationship-specific investments by either partner increase the durability of the marriage.

Investments are called "general" rather than "relationship-specific" if they produce benefits outside this particular relationship. The analog in the analysis of paid employment is "general human capital," which refers to education or vocational training that provides skills of use in many different firms. When looking at marriage, there are two kinds of investments in human capital that will benefit the marriage but that are not specific to this marital relationship. The first is one's development of skills at aspects of child rearing, emotional work, and household work that could just as easily transfer to exchange in another marital relationship because they do not entail learning anything idiosyncratic to this partner. *Note, then, that although we argue below that more of the homemaker's than earner's role entails relationship-specific investments, this does not mean that all aspects of domestic work are relationship-specific.* The skills learned at housecleaning are as portable to another marriage as typing skills are to another job. A second type of investment that is portable back into the marriage market is the investment in earning power that is represented by job search, schooling, or the on-the-job training of career building. Whether or not such investments are firm-specific, their fruits are not specific to *this* marriage. Except for the typically small and badly enforced amounts of child support one may pay, earning power is entirely portable out of relationships.

Although in marriages, both partners make general and relationship-specific investments, in general, women make proportionately more of the latter. For example, women concern themselves more with the emotional work of learning this partners' idiosyncrasies. Of what use is this if the relationship terminates? Women typically invest more time forming emotional attachments to in-laws than do men. These do little for the solidarity of a future marriage. Women invest much more in the socialization of children. If one is divorced, having well-adjusted children may be appreciated by both oneself and a new partner, but not having had children might make one more valued on the marriage market and in a new marriage. Whereas women focus on these relationship-specific investments, men's general investments build portable earning power. Investments in earnings (such as schooling, on-the-job training, job search) lack specificity to this particular marriage and benefit the man whether he stays in this marriage or not.

This asymmetry in which women make proportionally less general or portable investments contributes to men's power in marriages. Both sociological exchange theory and game theory suggest that the better one's alternatives outside the relationship, and the worse one's partner's alternatives, the more one can afford to risk the other partner leaving by bargaining harder within the marriage. Game theorists express this in terms of "threat points." (See note 1.) The threat points of a bargaining situation determine what each person would "walk away with" (and without) if the bargaining over how to allocate the surplus from the relationship-specific investment breaks down and the parties walk away from the relationship. Thus, one's threat points are more advantageous the more one's investments have been portable. Relationship-specific investments increase the "surplus" over which bargaining is occurring and thus the motivation of both parties to stay in the relationship. Having made relationship-specific investments does not directly reduce the favorableness of one's threat points. However, it does so indirectly to the extent that the time and effort put into relationship-specific investments have taken one away from making portable investments that do improve one's threat points. Thus, making fewer portable investments disadvantages one's potential bargaining power in comparison to making more portable investments. Since making relationship-specific investments (especially child-rearing) takes time that would otherwise go into portable investments such as one's career, being the one to make relationship-specific investments indirectly disadvantages one by lessening one's portable resources. If we extend this to an interpersonal utility comparison, we can say that the person making less portable investments has less power, as we have defined it. Neoclassical economists would eschew this last step, though the rest of what has been said in this section is consistent with implicit contract theory and game theory.

Our theorizing about investments is consistent with the empirical finding that men generally have more power than their wives since men's employment entails investments that are general rather than relationship-specific. It is also consistent with the finding that employed women have more power than homemakers, since in employment women are making general investments. In this interpretation, what is disadvantageous about women's homemaking role is the fact that the relationship-specific nature of some of the investments entailed keeps women from accumulating portable resources, and what is advantageous about being an earner is that it entails investments portable out of this relationship.

Imperfect Capital Markets and the Limited Liquidity of Women's General Domestic Investments

Women's domestic role lessens their power, not only because it entails relationship-specific investments not portable to a new relationship, but also because even *general* (rather than relationship-specific) investments in domestic skills are less "liquid" than investments in earning power. As we noted, learning domestic skills is not all a relationship-specific investment. The "on-the-job training" of being a homemaker may teach one to keep an attractive house, budget money well, develop the best in children, be a good listener and lover, and be a gracious entertainer. These skills enhance one's desirability on the "marriage market" because they are transferable to a new relationship. Yet even if there were no inequality between men and women in amount of relationship-specific investment, homemakers would still be disadvantaged in power because general investments in being a good marital partner are less "liquid" than general investments in earning power. If one leaves a marriage having made general investments in earnings, one can survive without another marriage. But if one has made general investments in skills as a marital partner, one needs to find a new partner on the marriage market to "cash in" these investments. This requires a period of search. One of the costs of marital search is the foregone income from a partner during the period of singleness. (The analog in labor markets is the foregone earnings while one is unemployed looking for a job.) This particular search cost is less important to someone who has their own earnings while reentering the marriage market. Underlying this argument is an assumed hierarchy of needs: one can go without emotional benefits of marriage for a while during search, but one cannot meet even the most basic needs of food and shelter without earnings. This factor makes leaving a marriage more detrimental for women than for men, owing to women's absent or lower earnings. Women's "threat points" and ability to bargain within the marriage are adversely affected.

One factor contributing to this limited liquidity in marriage markets is what economists would call imperfect capital markets. Capital markets are those in which one borrows money for future investments. When money is borrowed for investment in firms, neoclassical theories of "perfect capital markets" suggest that capital should be available at interest rates that reflect the expected value of the return. Although there are debates within economics about whether any capital markets work according to the theory, there is a consensus that markets for investment in *human* capital are imperfect. For example, outside of federally guaranteed programs, it is difficult for college students to get loans for their investment in human capital, even at high enough interest rates that reflect the risk of a loan without collateral. The nonavailability of such loans in the private sector, even at high interest rates, is counter to economic theory, though widely acknowledged. Economists view the process of search for a better job as an investment, so the nonavailability of loans to workers with much general human capital to finance a search period of unemployment is another example of imperfect markets for human capital.

There is a parallel between this imperfection in markets for loans to finance investments in human capital and the inability of homemakers to divorce and then borrow living money while they search for a new husband. The theory of perfect capital markets suggests that such loans for marital search should be available at interest rates that reflect the probability of a woman finding a husband and being able to repay the loan. This probability, in turn, would be assessed according to how much the woman's attributes (some reflecting past general investments during marriage) are viewed as desirable in marriage markets. As we all know, such loans are unheard of. This imperfection in capital markets makes the prospect of marital search prohibitive for many women with investments in domestic skills, even when their investments are general rather than relationship-specific. Thus, general investments in earning power yield more marital power than general domestic investments.

There is another way in which imperfect capital markets disadvantage women's bargaining power in marriage. Much of the argument in this and the previous section was that, in game theoretic terms, women's "threat points" are harmed because not making more portable investments was the opportunity-cost of the time and energy they put instead into relationship-specific investments. But marital bargaining after the "fundamental transformation" of relationship-specific investments can be seen as the second stage of a two-stage bargaining sequence. The first stage, before the "fundamental transformation," is the bargaining that leads to the decision of who is to make more relationship-specific, portable domestic, and portable earnings-related investments. This stage may occur before cohabitation, during co-habitation but before marriage, or after marriage. One might think that if women know that a division of labor that damages their later bargaining power is what they are agreeing to in stage-one bargaining, they would require some kind of insurance or payment to compensate for their later power loss. The tradition of giving women engagement rings might be view-ed this way. But even if women did press from some "up-front" insurance payment, imperfect capital markets make sizable payments unlikely since men typically marry early in their career trajectories and would need loans against their future earning to make such payments. One way around imper-fect capital markets for such loans would be for women to require explicit prenuptial contracts guaranteeing later payments in the case of divorce—an alimony of sorts. But the transaction costs and other barriers to explicit contracts have been discussed above.

In sum, women's domestic investments often require *some* marriage even though not *this* marriage to yield their benefits in exchange. This disadvan-tages women's marital power, though less so than if their domestic work entailed only relationship-specific investments. Either kind of domestic in-vestments limits women's ability to leave marriages, and hence reduces their bargaining power within.

OUTCOMES OF CHANGES IN WOMEN'S POWER: EXIT, VOICE, OR LOYALTY?

The link between earnings and power implies that recent dramatic in-creases in married women's employment should have increased women's average marital power. Since, compared to men, women's earnings are still less and their domestic contributions still greater, we would expect women's power to be less than men's but to be more than previously. At present this is a conjecture since data using a similar instrument to measure power at two points in time are not available. One thing that might make us doubt the increase in women's power is the fact that as women have increased their employment and earnings, men have increased the time they spend in do-mestic work only marginally, and, as a result, women generally enjoy less leisure than men (Miller and Garrison 1982; Shelton forthcoming). If house-work is seen as onerous and leisure as enjoyable, one would expect women to use some of their new power to persuade men to do more housework. But the adjustment to female employment is generally a decrease in total house-work done, rather than a substantial increase in husbands' participation (Farkas 1976; Berk and Berk 1979; Robinson 1980; Geerken and Gove 1983). There is some evidence that husbands of employed women do more housework than comparable men whose wives are homemakers (Blood and

Wolfe 1960:65; Gecas 1976; Slocum and Nye 1976:92; Duncan and Duncan 1978:207; Weingarten 1978; Berk and Berk 1979; Ericksen et al. 1979; Beer 1983; Huber and Spitze 1981:1980; Geerken and Gove 1983; Coverman 1985) and that men do more when wives earnings are higher relative to husbands (Ross 1987). But this link between male housework and women's employment or earnings is not found by all studies (Vanek 1974; Farkas 1976; Walker and Woods 1976; Szinovacz 1977; Ferber 1982). And even those that do find the link find the male adjustment to be very small.

The double burden of household and paid work of many women makes one wonder if women's well-being has really increased with the presumed increase in female power in marriage. The possibility that women's well-being in marriage could fail to increase while their marital power increased reminds us of the usefulness of defining power as the structural *ability* to act in one's own interest even against the interest of another rather than as the *outcome* of having advanced one's own interest at the expense of another's. That is, various factors such as an altruistic ideology or an acceptance of patriarchal values may prevent one from exercising one's power within the relationship and make it more likely that one will leave the relationship rather than pushing one's power within the marriage as far as it can go. Our discussion of women's versus men's culture suggests that women may leave relationships with men who practice a separative model of self hoping to find a man who will join them in jointly practicing the model of an altruistic connective self.

Our understanding of this anomaly is aided by the insights of Albert Hirschman's (1970) classic book, *Exit, Voice, and Loyalty.* He pointed out three options people have when they are dissatisfied with a relationship: They may exit (leave the relationship), voice their disagreement through some bargaining process, or remain stoically loyal. For example, if parents are unhappy with the public schools in their city, their options are passive loyalty, an exit from the school district (either through moving their home or using private schools), or voicing their concerns through activism in things such as School Board elections and the PTA. Freeman and Medoff (1984) apply this distinction to their study of unions, arguing that neoclassical theory has overemphasized the efficiency of "exit," workers leaving one firm for a more desirable job to equilibrate supply and demand, while failing to realize the efficiencies in reducing turnover (and hence in guarding firm-specific investments) that unions provide through an institutional mechanism for "voice."

This distinction between exit, voice, and loyalty can be usefully applied to marriage.[2] During the 1950s, women's limited marital power meant that even those deeply dissatisfied with their marriages generally chose loyalty because their only option was destitution. Men's greater power allowed them to respond to dissatisfaction either through "exit" (divorce or separation) or a bargaining "voice" in which their greater power usually brought them concessions. The low divorce rate of the period suggests that men generally chose "voice."

If women's power has increased due to their increased employment, women could choose either to leave unsatisfactory marriages (exit) or to utilize their new power by bargaining harder for what they want in marriage. That the two options of voice and exit go hand in hand is implied in our discussion above. We highlighted the fact that portable resources allowing one to lose less if a relationship is left also increase one's bargaining power in the relationship. The anomaly of women's continued responsibility for most household work has cast doubt on whether women are using "voice" to bargain for a more equitable distribution of work. The steep increase in divorce, correlated as it is temporally with increases in women's employment (Preston and McDonald 1979; Cherlin 1981), suggests that women may be using their new power to exit more than to change their current marriages. This view is buttressed by evidence that, at least in the last decade, women predominate over men as the partner who suggests divorces and separations (Wallerstein and Kelly 1980; Spanier and Thompson 1984; Kelly 1986:309). Casual observation suggests that this female predominance is greater among younger couples. This would be expected from our discussion above, since younger cohorts of women have more continuous employment and higher earning prospects, and hence have more marital power to be used in either exit or voice.

Why are women using their increased power more often for exit rather than voice within marriages? To guide our answer, we might first ask what women would most like to change about their marriages if they were to use voice. We believe they would most like to change the degree to which men provide the emotional intimacy of talking about and listening to feelings (Rubin 1983; Hite 1987; Kelly 1986:312–317) and the degree of men's participation in domestic work. Both of these things would require a significant change in the men's roles. One result of women using exit rather than voice is to protect men's roles from having to change, leading to a profound asymmetry in gender role change such that men's roles are being redefined much less than women's (England and Swoboda 1988). Thus, the question of why exit is used rather than voice may reduce to the question of why men's roles are so much harder to change than women's even in the face of changes in some of the objective, structural arrangements of power.

Nancy Chodorow's (1978) feminist revision of psychoanalytic theory provides one possible explanation. She argues that gender identity is tied to gender roles much more for men than for women. This is because males but not females generally have a caretaker of the other sex. This encourages males to achieve gender identity by rejecting their first attachment and by filling the resultant hurt with a role. As a result, she suggests that boys at first define their gender role in a negative rather than positive way—as whatever females are not. This may contribute to a fierce resistance on men's part to changing their gender role—a resistance much deeper than their resistance to women changing their roles by entering "male spheres."

The deprecation of traditionally feminine roles discussed by radical/cultural feminists may contribute to men's resistance to enter these roles as well. Whatever the explanation, if women find it extremely difficult to change their partners' roles, and this is what it would take to make marriage more satisfactory to them, women may respond to their increased marital power through divorce. Of course, if lack of change in the male role is an important cause of women's discontent, it is illusory to think that they can be happy with marriage to a new man who has not made the changes they feel hopeless about persuading their current partner to make! But such may be the confusions of a period of transition during which women see male resistance to change as unique to this partner rather than as a generalized phenomenon. And some women may prefer life without a marital relationship to staying in a marriage in which men's role does not change.

This trend of large changes in women's roles, few changes in men's roles, and a high divorce rate has two important consequences. One is a reduction in the economic well-being of children who are increasingly disconnected from the earnings of men. After divorces, the per capita income of the household containing the mother and children generally goes down substantially, while that of the father goes up (Preston 1984). This flows from the facts that women usually have child custody, men's earnings are usually much higher, and the amounts of child support awarded are small and the amounts paid even smaller. The economic effects on children are very adverse.

A second consequence of the asymmetric nature of gender role is the demise of traditionally female values of nurturing and connection. Without men joining women in a connective, altruistic notion of self, women are able to gain power only through entering traditionally male roles. Women are unable or unwilling to use their new power to bring men into traditionally female activities. The march of rationalization (to use Weberian terms), commodification (to use Marxist terms), extension of market relations (to use neoclassical terms), or masculinist values (to use feminist terms) is thus advanced rather than altered by women's changing roles. This follows from the fact that labor markets are even less organized around principles of altruism and reciprocity than are families. This consequence reminds us of the tension between liberal feminism, that would open all roles formerly monopolized by men to women, and radical/cultural feminism that would do this as well as elevate the traditionally female principles of connection, altruism, and mutual nurturance to a higher place in our priorities and reward system. Under current conditions, women's increased power results from and enhances the liberal feminist program but not the radical/cultural feminist program. If women are to live with men, the latter would require a profound change in men's roles and a redefinition of power even as women increase their relative power.

CONCLUSION

To summarize, we have argued that women's lower earnings and greater involvement in domestic work disadvantage them in marital power because (1) our culture devalues traditionally female activities and encourages men but not women to bargain self-interestedly, (2) much of women's work contributes to the well-being of children rather than men, (3) fewer investments of women than men are general rather than relationship-specific, and (4) even women's general investments lack liquidity when they can transfer to a new marriage but not provide support outside of a marriage. Given the continuing division of labor in which women do more domestic work and men have larger earnings, these factors explain why men have more marital power than women, while employed women have more marital power than homemakers. However, power implies a potential to either leave a relationship or bargain for change within it. As women's employment has brought them more power, it appears they are using this power more to leave relationships than to change them. This may be because women have thus far been unable to change the male gender role to involve more traditionally female tasks of child rearing, housework, and emotional work.

NOTES

1. Although we draw on game theory below, the reader should note that our definition of power is somewhat different from that used by game theorists. Game theorists often define power as the ability to win a larger share of the "surplus" defined by each party's "threat points." In contrast, as we define power, more favorable threat points (for example, having earnings one can keep if the marriage dissolves) increase one's power.
2. Violence is a fourth option, a variation on "voice" that occurs in many marriages (Straus et al. 1980). Although family violence is often reciprocal, women are much more likely than men to be seriously hurt in the process (Berk et al. 1983).

REFERENCES

Agger, Ben. 1989a. *Fast Capitalism*. Champaign: University of Illinois Press.
———. 1989b. "Shot-gun Wedding, Unhappy Marriage, No-fault Divorce: Rethinking Sexism in Capitalism." Paper presented at the annual meeting of the American Sociological Association.

————. 1990. "Marxism, Feminism, Deconstruction." In *Dialectical Anthropology: Essays in Honor of Stanley Diamond*, edited by Christine Gailey and Steven Gregory. Tallahassee: Florida State University Press.

Bahr, S. J. 1972. "A Methodological Study of Conjugal Power: A Replication and Extension of Blood and Wolfe." Unpublished doctoral dissertation, Washington State University.

————. 1974. "Effects on Power and Division of Labor in the Family." Pp. 167–185 in *Working Mothers*, edited by L. W. Hoffman and F. E. Nye. San Francisco: Jossey-Bass.

Becker, Gary. 1981. *A Treatise on the Family*. Cambridge: Harvard University Press.

Beer, William R. 1983. *Househusbands: Men and Housework in American Families*. New York: Praeger.

Benhabib, Seyla. 1987. "The Generalized and the Concrete Other: The Kohlberg-Gilligan Controversy and Moral Theory." Pp. 154–178 in *Women and Moral Theory*, edited by Eva Feder Kittay and Diana T. Meyers. Totowa, NJ: Rowman & Littlefield.

Berk, Richard A., Sarah Fenstermaker Berk, Donileen R. Loseke, and David Rauma. 1983. "Mutual Combat and Other Family Violence Myths." Pp. 197–221 in *The Dark Side of Families*, edited by David Finkelhor, Richard J. Gelles, Gerald T. Hotaling, and Murray J. Straus. Beverly Hills: Sage Publications.

Berk, Sarah Fenstermaker and Richard A. Berk. 1979. *Labor and Leisure at Home: Content and Organization of the Household Day*. Beverly Hills: Sage.

Binmore, Ken, Ariel Rubinstein, and Asher Wolinsky. 1986. "The Nash Bargaining Solution in Economic Modelling." *Rand Journal of Economics* 17:176–188.

Blood, R. O., Jr. 1963. "Rejoinder to 'Measurement and Bases of Family Power'." *Journal of Marriage and Family* 25:475–478.

Blood, R. O., Jr. and D. M. Wolfe. 1960. *Husbands and Wives: The Dynamics of Family Living*. New York: Free Press.

Blumberg, Rae Lesser. 1988. "Income under Female versus Male Control: Hypotheses from a Theory of Gender Stratification and Data from the Third World." *Journal of Family Issues* 9:51–84.

Blumstein, P. and P. Schwartz. 1983. *American Couples*. New York: William Morrow.

Brown, Murray. 1988. "Optimal Family Contracts." Unpublished, Economics Department, State University of New York at Buffalo.

Chafetz, Janet S. 1984. *Sex and Advantage: A Comparative, Macro-Structural Theory of Sex Stratification*. Totowa, NJ: Rowman and Allanheld.

————. 1988. "The Gender Division of Labor and the Reproduction of Female Disadvantage: Toward an Integrated Theory. *Journal of Family Issues* 9:108–131.

Cherlin, Andrew J. 1981. *Marriage, Divorce, Remarriage: Social Trends in the United States*. Cambridge: Harvard University Press.

Chodorow, Nancy. 1978. *The Reproduction of Mothering: Psychoanalysis and the Sociology of Gender*. Berkeley: University of California Press.

Cook, Karen. (ed.) 1987. *Social Exchange Theory*. Beverly Hills: Sage.

Coverman, Shelley. 1985. "Explaining Husbands' Participation in Domestic Labor." *Sociological Quarterly* 26:81–97.

Crawford, Vincent P. 1985. "Dynamic Games and Dynamic Contract Theory." *Journal of Conflict Resolution* 29:195–224.

Crawford, Vincent P. and Sharon C. Rochford. 1986. "Bargaining and Competition in Matching Markets." *International Economic Review* 27:329–348.

Delphy, Christine. 1984. *Close to Home: A Materialist Analysis of Women's Oppression.* London: Hutchinson.

Duncan, Beverly and Otis Dudley Duncan. 1978. *Sex Typing and Social Roles: A Research Report.* New York: Academic Press.

Eisenstein, Zillah R. 1981. *The Radical Future of Liberal Feminism.* New York: Longman.

Engels, Friedrich. 1884. *The Origin of the Family, Private Property, and the State,* 1902 edition. Chicago: Charles Kerr.

England, Paula. 1989. "A Feminist Critique of Rational-Choice Theories: Implications for Sociology." *American Sociologist* 20:14–18.

———. Forthcoming. *Comparable Worth: Theories and Evidence.* New York: Aldine de Gruyter.

England, Paula and George Farkas. 1986. *Households, Employment, and Gender: A Social, Economic, and Demographic View.* New York: Aldine de Gruyter.

England, Paula and Diane Swoboda. 1988. "The Asymmetry of Contemporary Gender Role Change." *Free Inquiry in Creative Sociology* 16:157–161.

Ericksen, J. A., W. L. Yancey, and E. P. Ericksen. 1979. The Division of Family Roles." *Journal of Marriage and the Family* 38:301–313.

Farkas, George. 1976. "Education, Wage Rates, and the Division of Labor between Husband and Wife." *Journal of Marriage and the Family* 41:473–483.

Farkas, George and Paula England. (eds.) 1988. *Industries, Firms and Jobs: Sociological and Economic Approaches.* New York: Plenum.

Ferber, Marianne. 1982. "Labor Market Participation of Young Married Women: Causes and Effects." *Journal of Marriage and the Family* 44:457–468.

Freeman, Richard B. and James L. Medoff. 1984. *What Do Unions Do?* New York: Basic.

Gecas, V. 1976. "The Socialization and Child Care Roles." Pp. 35–59 in *Role Structure and Analysis of the Family,* edited by F. I. Nye. Beverly Hills: Sage Publications.

Geerken, Michael and Walter R. Gove. 1983. *At Home and at Work: The Family's Allocation of Labor.* Beverly Hills: Sage Publications.

Gilligan, Carol. 1982. *In a Different Voice: Psychological Theory and Women's Development.* Cambridge: Harvard University Press.

Glueck, S. and E. Glueck. 1957. "Working Mothers and Delinquency." *Mental Hygiene* 41:327–352.

Hartmann, Heidi. 1979. "Capitalism, Patriarchy, and Job Segregation by Sex." Pp. 206–247 in *Capitalist Patriarchy and the Case for Socialist Feminism,* edited by Zillah Eisenstein. New York: Monthly Review Press.

———. 1981. "The Unhappy Marriage of Marxism and Feminism: Toward a More Progressive Union." Pp. 1–41 in *Women and Revolution,* edited by Lydia Sargent. Boston: South End Press.

Hartsock, Nancy C. M. 1983. "The Feminist Standpoint: Developing the Ground for a Specifically Feminist Historical Materialism." Pp. 283–310 in *Discovering Reality: Feminist Perspectives on Epistemology, Methaphysics, Methodology and Philosophy of Science,* edited by Sandra Harding and Merrill B. Hintikka. Dordrecht, Holland: D. Reidel.

———. 1985. "Exchange Theory: Critique from a Feminist Standpoint." *Current Perspectives in Social Theory* 6:57–70.

Heer, David. 1958. "Dominance and the Working Wife." *Social Forces* 36:341–347.

———. 1963. "The Measurement and Bases of Family Power: An Overview." *Journal of Marriage and the Family* 25:133–139.

Hirschman, Albert O. 1970. *Exit, Voice, and Loyalty.* Cambridge: Harvard University Press.

Hite, Shere. 1987. *Women and Love: A Cultural Revolution in Progress.* New York: Knopf.

Huber, Joan. 1988. "A Theory of Family, Economy, and Gender." *Journal of Family Issues* 9:9–26.

———. 1981. "Wife's Employment, Household Behaviors, and Sex-Role Attitudes." *Social Forces* 60:150–169.

James, Selma and Mariarosa Dalla Costa. 1973. *The Power of Women and the Subversion of the Community.* Bristol: Falling Wall Press.

Keller, Catherine. 1986. *From a Broken Web: Separation, Sexism, and Self.* Boston: Beacon Press.

Keller, Evelyn Fox. 1983. *A Feeling for the Organism: The Life and Work of Barbara McClintock.* New York: Freeman.

———. 1985. *Reflections on Gender and Science.* New Haven: Yale University Press.

Kelly, Joan Berlin. 1986. "Divorce: The Adult Perspective." Pp. 304–337 in *Family in Transition,* 5th ed., edited by Arlene S. Skolnik and Jerome H. Skolnik. Boston: Little, Brown.

Kohn, Melvin and Carmi Schooler (with J. Miller, K. Miller, and R. Schoenberg). 1983. *Work and Personality: An Inquiry into the Impact of Social Stratification.* Norwood, NJ: Ablex.

Lerner, Gerda. 1986. *The Creation of Patriarchy.* New York: Oxford University Press.

———. 1980. "Marriage and Household Decision-Making: A Bargaining Analysis." *International Economic Review* 21:31–44.

McDonald, Gerald W. 1980. "Family Power: The Assessment of a Decade of Theory and Research, 1970–1979." *Journal of Marriage and the Family* 42 (2, November):841–851.

McElroy, Marjorie B. and Mary Jean Horney. 1981. "Nash-Bargained Household Decisions: Toward a Generalization of the Theory of Demand." *International Economic Review* 22:333–349.

Miller, Joanne and Howard H. Garrison. 1982. "Sex Roles: The Division of Labor at Home and in the Workplace." *Annual Review of Sociology* 8:237–262.

Pollak, Robert A. 1985. "A Transaction Cost Approach to Families and Households." *Journal of Economic Literature* 23:581–608.

Preston, Samuel H. 1984. "Children and the Elderly: Divergent paths for America's Dependents." *Demography* 21:436–458.

Preston, Samuel H. and John McDonald. 1979. "The Incidence of Divorce within Cohorts of American Marriages Contracted Since the Civil War." *Demography* 16:1–25.

Robinson, John P. 1980. "Housework Technology and Household Work." Pp. 53–68 in *Women and Household Labor*, edited by S. F. Berk. Beverly Hills: Sage Publications.

Ross, Catherine E. 1987. "The Division of Labor at Home." *Social Forces* 65:816–833.

Rubin, Lillian B. 1983. *Intimate Strangers: Men and Women Together*. New York: Harper & Row.

Scanzoni, John. 1970. *Opportunity and the Family*. New York: Macmillan.

———. 1972. *Sexual Bargaining*. Englewood Cliffs, NJ: Prentice-Hall.

———. 1979. "A Historical Perspective on Husband-Wife Bargaining Power and Marital Dissolution." Pp. 10–36 in *Divorce and Separation*, edited by G. Levinger and O. Moles. New York: Basic Books.

Scanzoni, L. D. and J. Scanzoni. 1981. *Men, Women, and Change*, 2nd ed. New York: McGraw-Hill.

Schotter, Andrew and Gerhard Schwodiauer. 1980. "Economics and the Theory of Games: A Survey." *Journal of Economic Literature* 18:479–527.

Sen, Amartya K. 1985. "Women, Technology and Sexual Divisions." *Trade and Development: An UNCTAD Review* 6:195–223.

Shapiro, Susan. 1987. "The Social Control of Impersonal Trust." *American Journal of Sociology* 93:623–658.

Shelton, Beth Anne. Forthcoming. *Women, Men and Time: Gender Differences in Paid Work, House Work and Leisure*. Westport, CT: Greenwood Press.

Slocum, W. L. and F. I. Nye. 1976. "Provider and Housekeeper Roles." Pp. 81–99 in *Role, Structure and Analysis of the Family*, edited by F. I. Nye. Beverly Hills: Sage Publications.

Spanier, Graham and Linda Thompson. 1984. *Parting: The Aftermath of Separation and Divorce*. Beverly Hills: Sage Publications.

Straus, M. A., R. J. Gelles, and S. Steinmetz. 1980. *Behind Closed Doors: Violence in the American Home*. Garden City, NY: Doubleday.

Szinovacz, M. E. 1977. "Role Allocation, Family Structure and Female Employment." *Journal of Marriage and the Family* 39:781–791.

Vanek, Joann. 1974. "Time Spent in Housework." *Scientific American* 231:116–120.

Walby, Sylvia. 1986. *Patriarchy at Work: Patriarchal and Capitalist Relations in Employment*. Minneapolis, MN: University of Minnesota Press.

Walker, K. E. and M. Woods. 1976. *Time Use: A Measure of Household Production of Family Goods and Services*. Washington, DC: American Home Economics Association.

Wallerstein, Judith S. and Joan Berlin Kelly. 1980. *Surviving the Breakup: How Children and Parents Cope with Divorce*. New York: Basic Books.

Weingarten, Kathy. 1978. "The Employment Pattern of Professional Couples and Their Distribution of Involvement in the Family." *Psychology of Women Quarterly* 3:43–52.

Williamson, Oliver. 1988. "The Economics and Sociology of Organization: Promoting a Dialogue." Pp. 159–186 in *Industries, Firms, and Jobs: Sociological and Economic Approaches*, edited by G. Farkas and P. England. New York: Plenum.

Class Conflict as a Dynamic Game   7

Michael Wallerstein

INTRODUCTION

Capitalism is a market system in which the suppliers of labor are paid by the hour (or by the piece) while the suppliers of capital receive the residual after the costs of production have been paid. Since both labor and capital are essential for production, both workers and investors stand to gain from combining their assets. But there is no commonality of interest over how to distribute their joint gains. And since the consequences of the agreements or conflicts between wage-earners and capital owners affect the material well-being of the entire society, governments frequently seek to influence the bargains that are struck.

The purpose of this essay is to review work in economics and political science that has modeled the interaction of unions and firms in capitalist democracies as a dynamic game. The dynamic game approach is distinguished by two features. First, workers are assumed to be organized in unions strong enough to control wages, but not the level of investment. This is a conventional assumption in models of trade union behavior (Oswald 1985; Malcomson 1987). Nevertheless, unions rarely have the power to set wages as they choose. To endow unions with such powers in a formal model is to study the limiting case in which unions' control over wages reaches its logical maximum. An enormous amount of work has been premised on the opposite limiting case of perfect competition in the labor market. Since reality often lies somewhere in between, both extremes merit attention.

The second distinctive feature of the dynamic game approach is its focus on the intertemporal trade-offs inherent in the strategies adopted by unions and firms. Unlike most models of union behavior that emphasize the impact of union wages on unemployment, the work reviewed here highlights the effect of wages on investment and growth (as well as the influence of investment and growth on wages). All societies contain some mechanism for determining how resources are to be allocated between consumption and investment and how consumption is to be distributed among social groups. The central concern of this literature is how these two allocative decisions intertwine in a society in which one group determines how much it will consume and another group determines how much of the remaining output will be invested.

The dynamic game framework thus combines a microeconomic mode of analysis with social democratic institutional assumptions. The approach is neoclassical in the sense that all agents are assumed to be rational actors. At the same time the approach is social democratic in that wages and investment are determined in the strategic interaction of unions and owners of firms rather than in competitive markets for labor and capital. If the general equilibrium model is a theory of a competitive economy, the dynamic game model is a theory of a capitalist economy with strong trade unions.

Although unions and firms are generally the only explicit actors in the models that follow, the questions being asked have important political implications regarding workers, unions, and governments. If relations between organized workers and firms are inherently unstable, as Marx believed, then the evident stability of capitalist countries with strong unions indicates either that workers do not pursue their material interests with full rationality or that workers are continually betrayed by the leaders they choose. If workers always want more, as Samuel Gompers asserted, then unions that voluntarily participate in policies of wage restraint cannot be internally democratic. The question of workers' limited militancy in capitalist democracies is addressed in the next section.

A second set of questions centers on corporatist systems of interest representation. The corporatist countries in Western Europe have experienced relatively low strike rates throughout the postwar period and comparatively low growth rates of real and nominal wages since the 1960s. In turn, corporatism and wage restraint are related to successful economic performance: lower rates of both inflation and unemployment, less pronounced slowdown of growth following the oil crises, and higher rates of investment. Yet, as many have noted (Shalev 1983; Cameron 1984), the criteria used to define a corporatist pattern of interest representation for workers—a centralized, united, and encompassing union movement accepted as a legitimate and powerful player by both business and the government—are indistinguishable from the criteria used to assess union strength. The impact of corporatist or centralized bargaining on wage demands is discussed in the third section.

A third set of questions concern the economic constraints on government policies. Can governments alter the distribution of income between wage earners and owners of capital through taxes and welfare expenditures? The answer is obviously positive only if the behavior of workers and owners of firms is not altered by taxes and transfers. But the choices of workers and capital owners generally depend on the tax and transfer schedule. Thus, government attempts to modify the distribution of income in favor of their constituents may be completely ineffective when anticipated by unions and firms. Whether political outcomes matter for the distribution of income between workers and owners of firms is addressed in the fourth section.

The paper concludes with a discussion of the feasibility of extending the model to encompass direct investment by workers and the addition of the government as a third type of actor.

CAPITALISM AS A DYNAMIC GAME

Lancaster (1973) was the first to formulate class conflict as a dynamic game. He observed that workers may, through trade unions or political parties, achieve a large say in the distribution of income but the owners of capital continue to be the primary source of investment. In Lancaster's words, this places workers in the following dilemma:

> Should they forego present consumption by handing over part of total income to the capitalists? If they do not, they will obtain no higher consumption in the future. If they do, they have no guarantee that the capitalists will actually invest sufficient of this income to bring about the desired level of increase. (1973:1095)

Capitalists, on the other hand, have no assurance that future wage demands will not confiscate the increased output that new investment makes possible. Thus, owners of capital face a dilemma that mirrors that of workers:

> Should [capitalists] spend now, or accumulate in order to spend more later? If they spend now, they know what they have available. If they accumulate, they may fail to obtain their expected share of the increased output when they come to spend. (1973:1096)

Lancaster proceeded to model the choices of workers and capitalists by dividing output at time t, $Y(t)$, into wages, $W(t) = m(t)Y(t)$, and profits, $P(t) = [1 - m(t)]Y(t)$, where $m(t)$ is the share of output that workers receive as wages.[1] Workers consume all of their income. All investment $I(t)$, therefore, comes from savings out of profits, $I(t) = s(t)[1 - m(t)]Y(t)$, where $s(t)$ denotes the rate of savings by firms or their owners. Lancaster assumed that the productivity of capital v (the amount of output that can be produced with each unit of capital) is constant. This implies that economic growth $Y'(t)$ equals the product of investment and the productivity of capital, or $Y'(t) = vI(t) = vs(t)[1 - m(t)]Y(t)$. Employment is also implicitly assumed to be a fixed multiple of the capital stock.[2] The supply of labor is never binding. The output produced, or, equivalently, the total income received by firms and workers, depends entirely on the supply of capital.

In Lancaster's model, workers unilaterally control the wage share $m(t)$.

Since there is no substitution of labor for capital, choosing the share of wages in output is equivalent to choosing the wage rate. Capitalists, in turn, unilaterally choose the rate of saving out of profits, $s(t)$. Private ownership of capital implies that capitalists are free to allocate profits as they choose.

Lancaster assumed that both classes sought to maximize their consumption over a fixed time horizon. These assumptions permitted, in Lancasters' words, "that rarest of all prizes in differential game models—a full explicit solution" (1973:1098).[3] Nevertheless, the cost was high in terms of plausibility. The combination of linear production and utility functions and a fixed time horizon produced a bang-bang solution: Both classes consume at their minimal level during an initial phase and then switch to maximal consumption in a second and final phase. Note that a fixed time horizon is not the same thing as a finite time horizon. Lancaster's results depend on the assumption that the time horizon of the actors actually shrinks over time, as if unions and firms behaved like individuals with no heirs approaching the end of their life. As the terminal date comes near, both classes consume what they can in the present and growth comes to a halt.

Lancaster conjectured in a footnote that "it ought to be possible to build a smooth-trajectory, infinite-time version of the basic model" by assuming a utility function with diminishing marginal utility of consumption (1973: 1109). This was approach taken by Pohjola (1985b), Wallerstein and Prze-worski (1988), and Przeworski and Wallerstein (1988).[4] In the formulation of Przeworski and Wallerstein, both classes are assumed to maximize their utility of present and future consumption. Let the intertemporal preferences of both classes be written as the present value of utility at each moment in time where $U(\cdot)$ is the instantaneous utility function and ρ, $\rho > 0$, is the rate at which workers and owners of firms discount the future. Then, in mathematical notation, workers choose $m(t)$ to maximize

$$W^* = \int_0^\infty e^{-\rho t} U\{m(t)Y(t)\}\, dt \tag{1}$$

and owners of capital choose $s(t)$ to maximize

$$P^* = \int_0^\infty e^{-\rho t} U\{[1 - s(t)][1 - m(t)]Y(t)\}\, dt \tag{2}$$

such that

$$Y'(t) = vI(t) = vs(t)[1 - m(t)]Y(t). \tag{3}$$

If the instantaneous utility functions happen to have the property that a measure of risk aversion, the coefficient of relative risk aversion, $\gamma = -xU''(x)/U'(x)$, is independent of consumption, the optimal strategies of workers and capitalists do not depend on time (Wallerstein 1988a,b). Moreover, the case where γ does not depend on consumption is substantively important, as empirical tests of household asset holdings have found γ to be roughly constant (Friend and Blume 1975). To ensure convergence of the integrals in (1) and (2) for all feasible strategies, it is necessary to assume that $\gamma > 1 - (\rho/v)$. In fact, empirical estimates of γ range from one (Hansen and Singleton 1983) to two (Friend and Blume 1975).

There are two fundamental similarities between wage-earners and owners of capital in this model. The first is the assumption that capitalists do not maximize profits but, like workers, maximize their utility of present and future consumption. Mehrling (1986) argues that dynamic models of class conflict should have capitalists maximizing accumulation to stay within the Marxian spirit. It can be argued that the assumption of intrinsic psychological differences between owners of capital and wage-earners is even farther from the spirit of Marx's analysis. More importantly, if capitalists maximize accumulation, there is no source of conflict once workers control wages. Accumulation is maximized by investing all income from capital. If everything that workers did not consume was invested, and if workers controlled the wage rate, capitalism would be the best of all possible worlds for workers.[5]

In fact, there is no conflict between the assumption that firms invest to maximize the utility of consumption out of profits and profit maximization in the neoclassical tradition. Profit is the appropriate maximand in models where the cost of capital to the firm is exogenous. The utility of consumption out of profit is the appropriate maximand when the quantity of capital available for investment is endogenous. We may distinguish between owners and firms and assume that owners save to maximize utility whereas firms invest the savings to maximize profits. Or we may simply assume that firms invest to maximize their owners' utility. The two formulations are equivalent (Hirshleifer 1970).

The second and more unusual similarity consists of the treatment of organized workers as implicit investors. If owners of capital expect workers to choose a constant wage share, their best response is to save at the rate[6]

$$s(m) = \frac{1}{\gamma} \left[1 - \frac{\rho/v}{1 - m} \right]. \tag{4}$$

At the same time, if workers expect firms to save at a constant rate, their best response is to allow firms to receive a profit share equal to

$$1 - m(s) = \frac{1}{\gamma} \left[1 - \frac{\rho/v}{s} \right]. \tag{5}$$

Workers balance present and future consumption in the same manner as owners of firms. A higher wage share means greater consumption now but less investment and lower consumption in the future. When workers choose a wage share less than one, they are investing indirectly. The catch is that the return on workers' investment depends on capitalists' frugality. The social rate of return on investment is v, the productivity of capital. The rate of return workers receive, however, is only vs since $v(1 - s)$ is consumed by owners of firms. As far as workers are concerned, the proportion of profits that owners consume is lost. In parallel fashion, the return owners of firms receive on their investment is $v(1 - m)$ since vm goes to workers as higher wages. In fact, Eqs. (4) and (5) reveal that the rate of saving for both classes depends in the same way on their respective rates of return. Greater (relative) risk aversion, γ, or a higher discount rate, ρ, reduces investment by both classes. A rise in the productivity of capital, v, and a higher rate of invest-ment by the other class increase the investment of both.

The best responses of workers and capitalists [Eqs. (4) and (5)] are illus-trated in Figure 1. The Cournot–Nash equilibria are all pairs of strategies where both classes are simultaneously doing the best they can given the choice of the other. In the picture the Cournot–Nash equilibria are the points at which the two best response curves intersect. There is a third Cournot–Nash equilibrium: the point of maximal consumption by both classes. If workers demand wages that eliminate profits, capitalists will disin-vest as rapidly as possible and, if investment approaches zero or becomes negative, workers will demand the entire product and more. Thus, open conflict with both sides attempting to consume as much as possible is also an equilibrium.[7]

The Cournot–Nash equilibria are analogous to the solutions originally obtained by Lancaster (1973) and explored by Hoel (1978), Pohjola (1983a, 1984a,b), Schott (1984a,b), and Mehrling (1986). The Cournot–Nash equi-librium concept, however, is subject to well-known objections in models with few players. Why would workers, for example, assume a fixed rate of investment when choosing their wages? If the rate of investment depends on wages in a predictable way, wage-earners should take that into account when deciding what to demand in collective bargaining. In duopoly mod-els, the name given to asymmetric solutions where one actor anticipates the best response of the other is Stackelberg equilibria. Przeworski and Wallers-tein (1982), Pohjola (1983b), and Basar et al. (1985) introduced Stackelberg solutions as alternatives to the Cournot–Nash equilibria in the dynamic game framework.

Workers as Stackelberg leaders will seek the point on capitalists' best response curve that maximizes their welfare. Mathematically, instead of choosing m to maximize $W^*[m,s]$ for a fixed s, workers choose m to max-imize $W^*[m,s(m)]$. Again writing the solution in terms of the profit share, workers' optimal choice given $s = s(m)$ from Eq. (4) is

$$1 - m = (1/\gamma)[1 - (\rho/v)]. \tag{6}$$

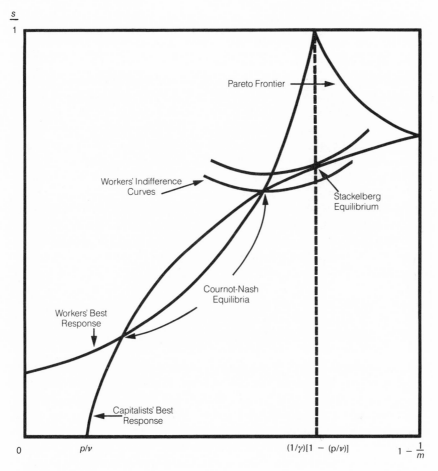

Figure 1.

As can be seen by comparing Eq. (6) with Eq. (5), workers as Stackelberg leader act as if all profits were invested, or $s = 1$, even though capitalists' best response is always to invest at a rate less than one.

In Figure 1, the Stackelberg solution with workers as the leader can be found by drawing workers' indifference curves and finding the point of tangency with capitalists' best response curve.[8] Workers' indifference curves are flat where they cross workers' best response curve (since by definition the best response curve is optimal for a fixed savings rate). Thus, workers at any Cournot–Nash equilibrium can reach a higher indifference curve, or attain a higher level of welfare, by reducing their wage demands in exchange for a higher rate of investment along capitalists' best response curve.

Workers are induced to moderate their wage demands by their anticipation of capitalists' reaction. Moreover, as Pohjola (1983b) emphasized, the Stackelberg solution is Pareto superior to the Cournot–Nash solutions: both workers and owners of firms are better off. Workers' welfare increases since as Stackelberg leader they choose their optimal point on capitalists' best response curve. Capitalists are better off because workers' choice as Stackelberg leader is at a lower level of wage militancy.

In theory, there is another Stackelberg equilibrium with firms as the leader (Przeworski and Wallerstein 1982; Pohjola 1983b; Basar et al. 1985). But there is an asymmetry between wages, on the one hand, and savings and investment on the other. In labor negotiations, wages are determined collectively. Thus, workers can coordinate wage demands to take into account the impact of aggregate wages on investment. The rate of saving, in contrast, is not determined collectively. To act the part of Stackelberg leader, owners of firms would have to collectively save more than is individually optimal. Although workers as followers would reduce wage demands in response to an increase in the aggregate rate of savings, wages would not respond to the saving decision of any individual shareholder. There is, therefore, a collective action problem inherent in owners of firms assuming the role of Stackelberg leader. Without coordinated saving decisions, capitalists cannot deliver a higher rate of investment than is individually optimal.

Maximal militancy is not a dominant strategy for workers. Workers, as Stackelberg leaders who can set wages as they choose, will not confiscate profits as long as the rate of discount is less than the productivity of investment, or $\rho < v$. This is not a stringent condition since the cessation of investment is socially optimal if the discount rate equals or exceeds the productivity of investment. Allowing the owners of firms to consume some of the output is the price that union members must pay for future increases in wages and employment. Even when no longer constrained by competition in the labor market, workers whose future depends on investment will limit their wage demands.

The political issues at stake concern the relationship of organized workers to their unions and the government. Ross (1948), in an early and influential study of unions as political institutions, argued that the simple demand of the rank and file was always "more." Democratic unions, according to Ross, are militant unions. More recently, Panitch (1977, 1981) has argued that union cooperation with incomes policies and other forms of wage moderation is possible only where union leaders are no longer accountable to their members (see, also, Sabel 1981). In contrast, if some measure of wage restraint is in workers' interest, then unions that cooperate with incomes policies are not necessarily betraying the rank and file (Lange 1984a). Indeed, the evidence gathered by Lange (1984b) indicates little relationship between the ability of the rank and file to influence union policy and the adoption of policies of wage restraint.

There are similar implications for the relationship between workers and governments, particularly labor governments. A central thesis in much of the Marxist literature on the state is that capitalism is always threatened by the potential power of organized workers. The state is to be understood by the function if fulfills as "the first and last defender of the old order" in Miliband's phrase (1977:65). Yet workers in capitalist economies, no matter how strongly organized in the labor market, are disciplined by their dependence on private investment.[9] Active intervention by the government to coopt, disorganize, or repress unions is not essential for the stability of capitalism (Przeworski and Wallerstein 1982).[10] Whether working class parties are similarly disciplined when they win elections is discussed below.

Note the difference with the arguments of Burawoy (1979, 1988). Burawoy explains the general absence of revolutionary demands among workers in capitalist societies by the ideological and political effects of social relations on the shop floor. Przeworski and Wallerstein, in contrast, locate the source of the restraint shown by organized workers in workers' concern for their future.

EFFICIENCY AND CENTRALIZATION

Lancaster was not concerned with the issue of the stability of capitalism. He, along with most others who have extended his model, simply assumed that workers' wage demands are bounded by exogenous upper and lower limits. The primary question for economists who have studied dynamic game models of capitalism concerns efficiency.

Lancaster's central conclusion was given in his title: capitalism is dynamically inefficient. The outcome of the strategic interaction between workers and capitalists in Lancaster's model is a consumption path that is inferior for both classes than other feasible paths. In the model represented in Figure 1, neither the Nash nor the Stackelberg solutions are Pareto optimal. Both workers and capitalists would be better off if they could move in a northeasterly direction, trading a higher rate of investment for a lower wage share.

The set of efficient points, or the Pareto frontier, is found by maximizing workers' welfare [W^* in Eq. (1)] with respect to the wage share m and the rate of saving out of profits s such that capital owners' welfare does not fall below an arbitrary threshold [$P^* \geq P_0$ in Eq. (2) where P_0 is a positive constant]. Written in terms of the profit share, the first-order condition for an efficient solution is

$$1 - m = (1/\gamma s)[1 - (\rho/\nu)]. \qquad (7)$$

By comparing Equation (7) with Eq. (5), it can immediately be seen that the efficient profit share is greater than workers' best response unless $s = 1$. Similarly, Eq. (7) can be rewritten in terms of s to show that, given some wage share, the efficient rate of saving exceeds capitalists' best response except where $(1 - m) = 1$. In fact, the Pareto frontier slopes downward from workers' ideal point where $s = 1$ to capitalists' ideal point where $m = 0$ as illustrated in Figure 1.

Trade unions enable workers to obtain a share of the future gains in income that investment makes possible. At either the Stackelberg or Cournot–Nash equilibria, neither class receives the full return on its savings: workers lose $(1 - s)$ of profits; owners of firms lose m of their investment. As is generally the case when the private rate of return is below the social rate of return, the resulting level of investment is less than socially optimal. Market equilibria are not necessarily Pareto optimal in the dynamic game framework.[11]

The large literature on corporatism in political science suggests that the inefficiency of collective bargaining is affected by the centralization of union and employers' federations. Numerous studies have found an empirical association between indicators of centralized bargaining and real and nominal wage restraint (Heady 1970; Blyth 1979; Cameron 1984; Bruno and Sachs 1985; McCallum 1985; Marks 1986). Pohjola (1984b) sought to capture the impact of centralization by considering Lancaster's model with multiple unions.[12] Pohjola's idea can be easily put in the framework of this paper (Wallerstein 1988a). Suppose there are n unions, each of which receives the wage share m_i where $i = 1,2,...,n$, bargaining independently with the same employers' association. The total wage share is then Σm_i and the share received by firms is $1 - \Sigma m_i$. Each union, acting independently as a Stackelberg leader vis-à-vis its employer, would optimally set its share such that

$$1 - m_i = \frac{1 - \rho/\nu + (n - 1)(\gamma - 1)}{1 + n(\gamma - 1)} \qquad (8)$$

Note that Equation (8) reduces to Equation (6) when $n = 1$. In the case where $\gamma > 1$, each union will demand a lower wage share as the number of unions, n, increases.

The aggregate wage share, however, increases as the number of independent unions rises. With multiple unions, the profit share becomes

$$1 - \Sigma m_i = \frac{1 - n\rho/\nu}{1 + n(\gamma - 1)} . \qquad (9)$$

As the number of unions increases, the profit share declines. Since capitalists' best response is a positive function of the profit share, the rate of investment falls as n rises. Workers are collectively worse off than before; otherwise the aggregate wage share in Eq. (9) would have been chosen by one big union. Since the total wage share is higher, owners of firms are also worse off. The larger the number of independent unions, the larger the aggregate wage share demanded, the lower the level of investment, and the greater the inefficiency. When multiple unions set wages simultaneously, bargaining has the logical structure of an *n*-person prisoners' dilemma among unions. Both unions and owners of firms do better when bargaining is centralized, but separate bargaining is the dominant noncooperative strategy for individual unions.

Wallerstein (1988a) extends the model with multiple unions to consider wage leadership where one union sets its wages before the others. If the coefficient of relative risk aversion, γ, is greater than one, wage leadership transfers income shares from the wage followers to the wage leader and from profits to wages. (If $\gamma = 1$, wage leadership has no effect on the outcome.) The wage leader is better off but the other unions and the owners of firms are worse off than when all wages are set concurrently. Moreover, with wage leadership, it no longer follows that centralized bargaining is necessarily Pareto superior to decentralized bargaining. Centralized bargaining is better for all parties other than the wage leader, but the wage leader may prefer decentralization. Every union would always prefer to be the only union to opt out of centralized bargaining. A wage leader may prefer to opt out of centralized bargaining even when the consequence is decentralized bargaining by all.

Centralized bargaining has been attacked by both the right and the left. Liberals in the European sense reject centralized bargaining as being the greatest distance from the ideal of competitive labor markets. Militants on the left condemn centralization as a means of coopting union bureaucrats and containing the working class. Yet the models of Pohjola (1984b), Wallerstein (1988a), and Rubin (1988) indicate that centralization of bargaining can increase the welfare of most union members and owners of firms. This does not mean that centralized bargaining is stable. At best the situation is a prisoners' dilemma among unions. At worst there are unions that prefer mutual defection to mutual cooperation in bargaining. In practice, centralized bargaining often depends on the willingness of employers or the government to help unions solve their collective action problem.[13]

Much of the empirical work on incomes polices or relative growth rates finds that the interaction of union centralization and Social Democratic control of government is more significant than either variable alone in explaining wage moderation (Heady 1970; Marks 1986; Lange and Garrett 1985; Garrett and Lange 1986; Hicks 1988). Przeworski and Wallerstein (1982) and Lange (1984a) suggest that prolabor governments reduce the rate at which workers discount the future. Workers' future benefits from current wage restraint depend on multiple unknown factors such as the future demand for the industry's output and workers' future bargaining power. If left governments provide unions with greater insurance against unfavorable surprises, unions would be more willing to accept sacrifices for future and uncertain benefits when the left is in power.

Another interpretation of the evidence is that unions reduce wage demands in response to increases in welfare expenditures championed by social democratic governments. But this explanation demands an investigation of wages and investment in the presence of taxes and expenditures on welfare policies.

REDISTRIBUTIVE POLICIES

Many have contended that the dependence of all on the willingness of firms to invest places severe restraints on redistributive policies. Whatever the political forces supporting the government, it is asserted, governments are compelled to maintain the income of owners of firms. Thus, all reforms end up as redistributions among wage and salary earners. The wealth of the owners of capital remains sacrosanct.

In the Marxist literature, this claim has been named the structural dependence of the state on capital. Miliband presented the argument as follows:

> Given the degree of economic power which rests in the 'business community' and the decisive importance of its actions (or its nonactions) for major aspects of economic policy, any government with serious pretensions to radical reform must either seek to appropriate that power or find its room for radical action rigidly circumscribed by the requirements of 'business confidence.' (1969:152)

Claus Offe articulated the basic dilemma facing governments in capitalist economies as follows:

> The political system can only make offers to external, autonomous bodies responsible for decisions: either these offers are not accepted, thus making the attempts at direction in vain, or the offers are so attractive in order to be accepted that the political direction for its part loses its autonomy because it has to internalize the aims of the system to be directed. (1975:234)

Or, in the non-Marxist language of Charles Lindblom:

> because pubic functions in the market system rest in the hands of businessmen, it follows that jobs, prices, production, growth, the standard of living, and the economic security of everyone else all rest in their hands. . . . In the eyes of government officials, therefore, businessmen do not appear simply as representatives of a special interest. . . . They appear as functionaries performing functions that government officials regard as indispensable. (1977:172 175)

Nor are these claims heard only from scholars on the left. The Chicago School argues that support-maximizing politicians are tempered in their zeal for redistribution by the response of owners of assets who increasingly with-draw their endowments from productive uses as taxes rise (Peltzman 1976; Becker 1983) (see, also, Bates and Lien 1985).

Wallerstein and Przeworski (1988) and Przeworski and Wallerstein (1988) analyze the argument of structural dependence by introducing taxes and transfers in the game between firms and unions. Government policies are assumed to be purely redistributive. The government neither consumes nor invests any of the tax revenues itself. In addition, it is assumed that the government moves first. Wage-earners and owners of firms choose their strategies in each period knowing the tax and transfer schedule. All groups in society seek to maximize their utility of consumption after taxes have been paid and transfers received.

The first tax Przeworski and Wallerstein considered was a simple flat income tax on profits: $T = t_i(1 - m)Y$. Workers thus consume wages plus transfer payments: $W + T = [m + t_i(1 - m)]Y$. Owners of firms consume what is left out of profits after investment and taxes have been subtracted: $P - I - T = (1 - m)(1 - s - t_i)Y$. Note that if $t_i < 0$, it is wage-earners who are being taxed and firms that receive the transfer payments. The tax should be interpreted as the net tax paid by owners of capital after transfers are sub-tracted from tax payments.

The question is whether the imposition of taxes and transfers can alter the post tax and transfer distribution of income between wage-earners and owners of firms. With a flat tax on profits, the answer is no. To start with owners of firms, the optimal rate of investment is now given by

$$s(m,t_i) = \frac{1}{\gamma}\left[1 - t_i - \frac{\rho/\nu}{1 - m}\right]. \tag{10}$$

Thus, the rate of investment falls as the tax on profits increases provided workers' wage share m remains constant. A profit tax reduces both aggregate posttax profits and the fraction of posttax profits that is reinvested. If workers do not adjust their wage demands, the share of income going to investment falls as the share of income going to workers in wages and transfer payments increases.

But taxes and transfers affect the choices of workers as well. As Stackelberg leaders, unions would adopt wage demands such that the share of income left for profits equals

$$1 - m(t_i) = \frac{1}{\gamma}\left[\frac{1 - (\rho/\nu)}{1 - t_i}\right]. \tag{11}$$

The pretax profit share increases as the tax on profits rises. Workers respond to the increase in transfer payments and the decline in investment by reduc-ing private wage demands. In fact, workers' choice of profit share in (11) implies that workers' posttax and transfer income share is unchanged. In terms of the share of income workers do not receive, it is quickly calculated from (11) that

$$1 - \left(\frac{W + T}{Y}\right) = (1 - t_i)(1 - m) = (1/\gamma)[1 - (\rho/\nu)] \tag{12}$$

which is the same as the profit share without taxes and transfers [Equation (6)].

After both owners of firms and unions have adjusted to the tax on profits, workers' share of income is unaltered. Since workers' preferred point on capitalists' best response curve has not changed, unions as Stackelberg leaders would modify their wage demands to return to the same income share as before. It is easily verified that the income shares of investment and consumption out of profits are also unchanged. With a tax on profits, the government faces the same trade-off as workers. The cost of increased tax revenues in terms of lower investment is identical to the cost of an equal increase in the wage bill. As long as workers and firms anticipate the tax when choosing their strategies, fiscal policy changes nothing except the share of income passing through the government's coffers.[14]

But this striking confirmation of the claims of structural dependence is very sensitive to the form of the tax schedule. In fact, governments in all advanced industrial societies tax profits which are reinvested at a different rate than profits that are consumed. Depreciation allowances that differ from actual depreciation, investment tax credits, investment grants, special treatment capital gains, and double taxation of distributed profits are only some of the common deviations from a straight profit tax (Bracewell-Milnes and Huiskamp 1977; King and Fullerton 1984). Suppose the tax was levied instead on consumption out of profits: $T = t_c(1 - s)(1 - m)Y$. Administratively, this tax could be imposed by allowing an immediate deduction of the full value of investment from taxable profits.

Unlike the profit tax, a tax on consumption out of profits does not directly alter capital owners' preferred level of investment:

$$s(m,t_c) = \frac{1}{\gamma}\left[1 - \frac{\rho/\nu}{1 - m}\right] \tag{13}$$

which is identical to (4). A tax on consumption out of profits does not change firm owners' intertemporal trade-off since it taxes present and future consumption at the same rate. Thus, if unions do not alter their wage demands, governments can raise or lower the posttax profit share without affecting investment. With a tax on consumption out of profits, it is only firm owners' consumption that declines as tax revenues and transfers increase.

Unions, however, will not maintain their wage demands unchanged if they are acting as Stackelberg leader. With a tax on consumption out of profits, workers would set wages such that

$$1 - m(t_c) = \frac{1}{\gamma}\left[\frac{1 - (\rho/\nu)}{1 - t_c(1 - s)}\right]. \tag{14}$$

Again the pretax profit share increases as the tax goes up. With a tax on consumption out of profits, as with a tax on profits, workers' optimal posttax and transfer income share remains the same. Equation (14) implies

$$1 - \left(\frac{W + T}{Y}\right) = [1 - t_c(1 - s)](1 - m) = (1/\gamma)[1 - (\rho/\nu)] \tag{15}$$

which is identical to the posttax profit share with an income tax [Eq. (12)] or the profit share without taxes and transfers [Eq. (6)].

Unions, in this model, engage in the political exchange described by Pizzorno (1978), Hibbs (1978), and Korpi and Shalev (1980) and verified empirically by Friedland and Sanders (1986): Private wage demands are reduced as welfare expenditures increase. Moreover, since the consumption tax is neutral with respect to investment, lower wage demands lead to greater investment when transfer payments are financed by a tax on consumption out of profits. In fact, if t_c is increased from zero until it approaches one, the outcome will move up the vertical line in Figure 1 from the Stackelberg solution with no taxes to just below workers' ideal point where workers' best response curve intersects the top of the box. These are not Pareto improvements: firm owners' welfare declines as the tax on consumption out of profits rises. A proworker government, however, could bring workers' welfare arbitrarily close to the welfare workers would enjoy if they owned the capital stock without disturbing private investment. With taxes on consumption out of profits, private ownership of capital does not by itself limit the distribution of consumption among classes.

The model with transfer payments to workers financed by a tax on consumption out of profits can also be interpreted as a model of a union that receives a wage share of m and a bonus equal to t_c of the firms' net income after wages and investment have been subtracted. Increases in wages reduce investment, but increases in the bonus leave investment unaffected. Thus, the greater share of income workers receive as a bonus rather than a wage, the more favorable the trade-off between workers' consumption and investment.

This conclusion is subject to a number of caveats. Both workers and owners of firms are assumed to care only about the utility of present and future consumption. Workers are assumed to value private wages and transfer payments equally. Finally, it is assumed that the quality of investment is independent of the tax on consumption out of profits. This last assumption would not hold to the extent that owners of firms could escape the tax by disguising consumption as investment.

A common objection concerns the absence of international mobility of capital in the model. Suppose, for example, that firms can either invest at home and receive the return of $v(1 - m)$ or invest abroad and receive the return of r where r is exogenous. Without taxes, the intuition that firms will invest at home if and only if the domestic rate of return equals or exceeds the rate of return abroad, or $v(1 - m) \geq r$, is correct. Therefore, the wage demands of workers who care about investment are bounded by $m \leq 1 - (r/v)$. But does the existence of foreign opportunities for investment put additional constraints on redistributive policies? The answer, as shown in Wallerstein (1988b), is negative. If the government imposes a tax on consumption out of profits, firms will still invest at home as long as $m \leq 1 - (r/v)$. Firms' willingness to invest at home is not directly affected by the tax on consumption out of profits. Profits are reduced by the tax but so is the cost of investment by an equal amount. Moreover, if unions lower wage demands in response to increases in the tax on consumption out of profits, as described in Eq. (14), a tax on consumption will increase domestic investment. A reformist government can reduce the consumption of owners of firms and increase either investment or workers' consumption without controls on capital mobility. All that is necessary is a tax system that taxes foreign investment and consumption out of profits equivalently.

A different objection concerns the static nature of the formulation. The analysis of the imposition of taxes described above implicitly assumes that the current tax schedule is seen by all groups as lasting forever. If, however, owners of firms anticipate that the tax on consumption out of profits will increase in the future, would they not consume more in the present while the tax is still low? The answer given by Abel and Blanchard (1983) is no as long as the coefficient of proportional risk aversion γ is greater than or equal to one.[15] If $\gamma > 1$, owners of firms who anticipate a reduction in consumption when the tax increase goes into effect will seek to smooth their consumption path by raising their rate of saving in the period before the tax increase. Thus, the prospect of a future tax on consumption out of profits will increase current investment. [If $\gamma = 1$, Eq. (13) remains valid before and after the anticipated increase in the tax on consumption out of profits.] Faced with a future sudden drop in their consumption, owners of firms will reduce their consumption prior to the tax increase thereby accumulating greater wealth and mitigating the drop in their consumption after the tax increase.

Thus, the conclusions of Przeworski and Wallerstein remain valid when the model is expanded to include international capital mobility or the transitional period between the time a tax increase is anticipated and the time the tax is implemented. However, the conclusions may not be valid when both extensions are considered simultaneously. My conjecture is that owners of firms will invest abroad, not at home, in response to an anticipated tax on consumption out of profits. But the question is not yet settled.

CONCLUSION

The model used here to illustrate the results of dynamic game models of capitalist economies with strong trade unions relies on the restrictive assumptions of a linear production function and utility functions with a constant coefficient of relative risk aversion to achieve explicit solutions. If these particular specifications are replaced by general production and utility functions, as in Hoel (1978) or Rubin (1988), the ability to solve the model explicitly is lost but many of the general conclusions remain.

More critical is the arbitrariness of the limits that must be imposed on the feasible strategies of the actors. In the Przeworski and Wallerstein framework, no exogenous upper and lower bounds on workers' wage demands are imposed. However, workers are limited to demanding wages. In particular, workers are assumed to be unable to save and invest directly. If workers could invest directly and receive the rate of return v, workers would never save through wage restraint where their return is only sv. Thus, workers with control over wages would eliminate profits and replace the current owners as the investors.

The *Histadrut*, Israel's major union confederation, is unique among unions in advanced capitalist economies in owning a large number of enterprises. In the 1970s, however, proposals for investment funds whereby union members would collectively receive shares of stock partially in lieu of wage increases were advanced in several Western European countries, the most notable example being the Swedish Meidner Plan (Martin 1984). Pohjola (1983a) studies workers' investment funds in the context of Lancaster's model, where the wage share is assumed to have some upper bound less than one. The outcome has workers immediately setting their wages at the upper bound. Thus wages are higher, but so is aggregate investment, since workers save more when they can save directly than when they must save indirectly through wage moderation. In practice, the idea of wage-earner funds antagonized business more than it mobilized union members. After bitter conflict, the Meidner Plan was eventually adopted by the Swedish government in 1982, but in a form so diluted as to be of little importance to either unions or firms.

The same issue arises when workers are allowed to bargain for a share of profits net of investment expenditures. Union demands for a share of net profits are not constrained in the same manner as wage demands: The unions' share of profits net of investment does not affect the firms' optimal level of investment. Yet the movement toward profit-sharing in North America and Western Europe, like the movement toward wage-earner funds, has been glacial. The explanation suggested by the literature on implicit contracts (reviewed by Rosen 1985), is that current arrangements optimally allocate a large share of the variance in income to owners of firms who can diversify their portfolios. Another explanation is that profit-sharing conflicts with unions' universal desire to reduce wage differentials among members (Freeman and Medoff 1984; Hirsch and Addison 1986). The question of why union demands take the form they do is far from resolved.

A different possible extension is to introduce the government as a third actor. The government has been present all along as part of the environment. Left governments may reduce workers' uncertainty. Taxes and transfer payments affect the strategies adopted by unions and firms. But governments also play an active role in public and private sector bargaining, whether directly participating in labor negotiations or indirectly affecting the outcome of bargaining by threatening to intervene in strikes and lockouts.

There are enough models of strategic interaction between unions and governments that focus on macroeconomic policy to warrant a separate survey (Calmfors and Horn 1985; Hersoug 1985; Driffill 1985; Soederstroem 1985; Scharpf 1988). These macroeconomic models are not easily reconciled with the dynamic games reviewed here, however. The dynamic game approach assumes fully rational behavior including, implicitly, rational expectations. But rational expectations generally render policies of demand management ineffective in Keynesian models. If anticipated expansionary policies cannot reduce unemployment without lowering real wages, the logic of the macroeconomic games collapses.

There are two difficulties that introducing the government as a third actor presents in the dynamic game. The first is inherent in the analysis of games with three actors. It is no accident that the macroeconomic models that bring the government in take firms out. The complexity of the game increases by an order of magnitude when the number of actors goes from two to three. Assuming that owners of firms always move last because of their collective action problem, there are six possible orderings of moves between workers, firms, and the government, counting simultaneous moves. Case studies seem to indicate that the order of moves varies from country to country and even from bargaining round to bargaining round within the same country.

The second difficulty is the problem of specifying the government's objectives. There are two conventional practices. The first, common in the macroeconomic models, is to assume the government maximizes some social welfare function over outcomes, typically employment and inflation. The second is to assume the government maximizes some function of the welfare of various social groups, for example, a weighted geometric average (Winden 1983; Przeworski and Wallerstein 1988). Both choices are generally justified in terms of governments' underlying objectives of securing reelection and helping their constituents, but the connection is loose.[16]

Yet the difficulty raised by the government is deeper than the question of appropriately defining the government's objective function. The government is not an actor but a set of institutions with prescribed powers. How those powers are to be used is the object of political struggles among political parties, interest groups such as unions and firms, and, perhaps, government bureaucrats. The state, like the market, is an arena of conflict and compromise. In a particular round of wage negotiations, the government may well enter as an actor with fixed preferences. But from a longer term perspective, the government's goals are an outcome off political conflict. Ultimately, models of conflict over private wages and investment must be integrated with models of conflict over public policy to capture the full range of strategies and outcomes in capitalist economies with strong trade unions.

ACKNOWLEDGMENTS

This draft has benefited from the comments of Jeff Frieden, John Wooley, and Roger Friedland. Financial support was provided by a grant from the National Science Foundation (SES 87 12222) and the Institute for Industrial Relations, UCLA.

NOTES

1.   I have replaced Lancaster's notation with that used in Wallerstein and Przeworski (1988) and Przeworski and Wallerstein (1988).

2.   A constant output–capital ratio implies a constant capital–labor ratio. In other words, Lancaster implicitly assumed the fixed coefficient production function: $Y(t) = \min[\nu K(t), \lambda L(t)]$, where 'lamba' represents the constant productivity of labor. Firms will always set employment such that $L(t) = (\nu/\lambda)K(t)$.

3.   For many years, Lancaster's model received more attention as an early application of dynamic game theory in economics than for its substantive argument. See Pohjola (1985a) for a review of dynamic games in macroeconomics.

4.   Przeworski and Wallerstein (1982) assumed that both classes maximized their discounted consumption over a finite (but not fixed) time horizon. Both classes were assumed to always look, say, 30 years into the future. With a finite horizon, simulations had to be employed to obtain solutions.

5.   Mehrling escapes this result by introducing an upper bound on workers' wage demands that is a function of the rate of unemployment. This gives capitalists who maximize accumulation an incentive not to invest at the maximal level, since investment decreases unemployment and allows maximally militant workers to increase their wages. In this way, Mehrling's argument is similar to Kalecki's (1943) famous analysis. But Mehrling's reasoning depends on a dubious assumption that capitalists invest collectively. If capitalists invest individually, profit maximization implies $s(m) = 1$ for any m as long as the productivity of capital ν exceeds the discount rate ρ.

6.   See the appendix in Wallerstein and Przeworski (1988) or Przeworski and Wallerstein (1988) for the derivation of these results for the particular case with $\gamma = 1$. Wallerstein (1988a,b) presents the general case.

7.   The location of the curves depends on the parameters γ, ρ, and ν. Specifically, as $(\gamma\rho/\nu)$

increases, the curves move away from each other. When $\gamma\rho/\nu$) exceeds ¼, the curves no longer intersect, and the only Nash equilibrium is maximal consumption.

8. Workers' indifference curves are defined to be all combinations of s and m that produce the same value of W*. The higher curve in Figure 1, the higher workers' welfare.

9. In the models discussed in this paper, employment is strictly determined by investment. In more conventional static models with substitution between labor and capital, unions may be constrained by the threat of unemployment (Oswald 1982a,b). It is necessary to say "may be" because efficient collective agreements would set employment independently of wages (McDonald and Solow 1981; Malcomson 1987). Note that workers' wage demands are constrained by the effect of wages on investment as long as savings or the cost of capital is endogenous, whether or not contracts cover employment.

10. This does not imply that government intervention to reduce wages would never occur. Owners of capital benefit from lower wages as long as firms can attract sufficient labor.

11. See Grout (1984) or van der Ploeg (1987) for cooperative bargaining models of labor negotiations that yield the same conclusion. Not all equilibria of the dynamic game are inefficient. Benhabib and Radner (1988) demonstrate that Pareto-optimal outcomes of the games discussed in this survey can be Nash equilibria of trigger strategies. (Trigger strategies are strategies in which player one plays x as long as the player two plays y, for some feasible x and y. If player two deviates in any way from y, player one adopts the policy of maximal militancy forever. As long player two's payoff from the pair of strategies (x,y) is superior to player two's payoff from maximal militancy on both sides, player two's best response is to choose y.)

12. See Rubin (1988) for an alternative model of centralized and decentralized bargaining within the Lancaster framework.

13. One example: In the 1987/1988 bargaining round in Norway, the main union federation agreed to a wage freeze on the condition that Parliament pass a law freezing wages and salaries throughout the economy.

14. This result is similar to a common result in macroeconomic models with rational expectations that only unanticipated changes in the money supply or budget deficits influence employment (Lucas 1981; Barro 1981).

15. Przeworski and Wallerstein (1988) incorrectly give an affirmative answer to this question.

16. There are important questions about the objectives of trade unions as well. One is the principal-agent problem, also present in the firm, of the divergence of the interests of the leadership from their constituents. Another is the general nonexistence of well-defined objectives for majority-rule institutions when the issue space consists of two or more dimensions, say employment and wages in the union context (Blair and Crawford 1984). A third is the extent to which workers care about wages as opposed to unemployment (Oswald 1985; Pencavel 1985).

REFERENCES

Abel, Andrew B. and Olivier J. Blanchard. 1983. "An Intertemporal Model of Saving and Investment." *Econometrica* 51:675–692.

Barro, Robert J. 1981. *Money, Expectations and Business Cycles.* New York: Academic Press.

Basar, Tamer, Alain Haurie, and Gianni Ricci. 1985. "On the Dominance of Capitalist Leadership in a 'Feedback-Stackelberg' Solution of a Differential Game Model of Capitalism." *Journal of Economic Dynamics and Control* 9:101–125.

Bates, Robert H. and D. D. Lien. 1985. "A Note on Taxation, Development and Representative Government." *Politics and Society* 14:53–70.

Becker, Gary S. 1983. "A Theory of Competition among Interest Groups for Political Influence." *Quarterly Journal of Economics* 48:371–400.

Benhabib, Jess and Roy Radner. 1988. "Joint Exploitation of a Productive Asset: A Game-Theoretic Approach." New York University and AT&T Bell Laboratories: Unpublished manuscript.

Blair, Douglas H. and David L. Crawford. 1984. "Labor Union Objectives and Collective Bargaining." *Quarterly Journal of Economics* 547–566.

Blyth, Conrad. 1979. "The Interaction between Collective Bargaining and Government Policies in Selected Member Countries." In OECD, *Collective Bargaining and Government Policies in Ten OECD Countries*. Paris: OECD.

Bracewell-Milnes, Barry and J. C. L. Huiskamp. 1977. *Investment Incentives: A Comparative Analysis of the Systems in the EEC, the US and Sweden*. Deventer: Kluwer.

Bruno, Michael and Jeffrey Sachs. 1985. *The Economics of Worldwide Stagflation*. Cambridge: Harvard University Press.

Burawoy, Michael. 1979. *Manufacturing Consent*. Chicago: University of Chicago Press.

———. 1988. "Marxism without Micro-Foundations: Przeworski's Critique of Social Democracy." University of California, Berkeley: Unpublished manuscript.

Calmfors, Lars and Henrik Horn. 1985. "Classical Unemployment, Accommodation Policies and the Adjustment of Real Wages." *Scandinavian Journal of Economics* 87:234–261.

Cameron, David R. 1984. Social Democracy, Corporatism and Labor Quiescence: The Representation of Economic Interest in Advanced Capitalist Society. P. 143–178 in *Order and Conflict in Contemporary Capitalism*, edited by J. H. Goldthorpe. Oxford: Oxford University Press.

Driffill, John. 1985. "Macroeconomic Stabilization Policy and Trade Union Behavior as a Repeated Game." *Scandinavian Journal of Economics* 87:300–326.

Freeman, Richard B. and James L. Medoff. 1984. *What Do Unions Do?* New York: Basic Books.

Friedland, Roger and Jimy Sanders. 1986. "Private and Social Wage Expansion in the Advanced Market Economies." *Theory and Society* 15:193–222.

Friend, Irwin and Marshall E. Blume. 1975. "The Demand for Risky Assets." *American Economic Review* 65:900–22.

Garrett, Geoffrey and Peter Lange. 1986. "Economic Growth in Capitalist Democracies, 1974–1982." *World Politics* 38:517–545.

Grout, Paul A. 1984. "Investment and Wages in the Absence of Legally Binding Labour Contracts." *Econometrica* 52:449–460.

Hansen, Lars P. and Kenneth J. Singleton. 1983. "Stochastic Consumption, Risk Aversion, and the Temporal Behavior of Asset Return." *Journal of Political Economy* 91:249–265.

Heady, Bruce W. 1970. "Trade Unions and National Wages Policies." *Journal of Politics* 32:407–439.

Hersoug, Tor. 1985. "Workers versus Government: Who Adjusts to Whom?" *Scandinavian Journal of Economics* 87:270–292.

Hibbs, Douglas A., Jr. 1978. "On the Political Economy of Long-Run Trends in Strike Activity." *British Journal of Political Science* 8:153–175.

Hicks, Alexander. 1988. "Social Democratic Corporatism and Economic Growth."
     Journal of Politics 50:677–704.
Hirsch, Barry T. and John T. Addison. 1986. *The Economic Analysis of Unions: New
     Approaches and Evidence.* London: Allen & Unwin.
Hirshleifer, Jack. 1970. *Investment, Interest and Capital.* Englewood Cliffs, NJ: Pren-
     tice-Hall.
Hoel, Michael. 1978. "Distribution and Growth as a Differential Game between
     Workers and Capitalists." *International Economic Review* 19:335–350.
Kalecki, Michal. 1943. "Political Aspects of Full Employment." *Political Quarterly*
     October/December:322–331.
King, Mervyn A. and Don Fullerton. 1984. *The Taxation of Income from Capital: A
     Comparative Study of the United States, the United Kingdom, Sweden and West
     Germany.* Chicago: University of Chicago Press.
Korpi, Walter and Michael Shalev. 1980. "Strikes, Power and Politics in Western
     Nations, 1900–1976." *Political Power and Social Theory* 1:301–334.
Lancaster, Kelvin. 1973. "The Dynamic Inefficiency of Capitalism." *Journal of Politi-
     cal Economy* 81:1092–1109.
Lange, Peter. 1984a. "Unions, Workers and Wage Regulation: The Rational Bases of
     Consent." Pp. 98–123 in *Order and Conflict in Contemporary Capitalism,* edit-
     ed by John H. Goldthorpe. Oxford: Clarendon Press.
———. 1984b. *Union Democracy and Liberal Corporatism.* Ithaca: Cornell Univer-
     sity, Center for International Studies.
Lange, Peter and Geoffrey Garrett. 1985. "The Politics of Growth." *Journal of Politics*
     47:792–827.
Lindblom, Charles E. 1977. *Politics and Markets: The World's Political-Economic
     Systems.* New York: Basic Books.
Lucas, Robert E., Jr. 1981. *Studies in Business-Cycle Theory.* Cambridge: MIT
     Press.
Malcomson, James M. 1987. "Trade Union Labour Contracts: An Introduction."
     European Economic Review 31:139–148.
Marks, Gary. 1986. "Neocorporatism and Incomes Policy in Western Europe and
     North America." *Comparative Politics* 18:253–277.
Martin, Andrew. 1984. "Trade Unions in Sweden: Strategic Responses to Change
     and Crisis." Pp. 190–359 in *Unions an Economic Crisis: Britain, West Germany
     and Sweden,* edited by Peter Gourevitch, Andrew Martin, George Ross,
     Christopher Allen, Stephen Bornstein, and Andrei Markovits. London: Allen &
     Unwin.
McCallum, John. 1985. "Wage Gaps, Factor Shares and Real Wages." *Scandinavian
     Journal of Economics* 87:436–459.
McDonald, Ian M. and Robert W. Solow. 1981. "Wage Bargaining and Em-
     ployment." *American Economic Review* 71:896–908.
Mehrling, Perry G. 1986. "A Classical Model of Class Struggle: A Game-Theoretic
     Approach." *Journal of Political Economy* 94:1280–1303.
Miliband, Ralph. 1969. *The State in Capitalist Society.* New York: Basic Books.
———. 1977. *Marxism and Politics.* Oxford: Oxford University Press.
Offe, Claus. 1975. "The Theory of the Capitalist State and the Problem of Policy
     Formulation." Pp. 125–144 in *Stress and Contradiction in Contemporary Cap-
     italism,* edited by L. Lindberg. Lexington: Lexington Books.

Oswald, Andrew J. 1982a. "The Microeconomic Theory of the Trade Union." *Economic Journal* 92:576–595.

―――. 1982b. "Trade Unions, Wages, and Employment: What Can Simple Models Tell Us?" *Oxford Economic Papers* 34:526–545.

―――. 1985. "The Economic Theory of Trade Unions: An Introductory Survey." *Scandinavian Journal of Economics* 87:160–193.

Panitch, Leo. 1977. "The Development of Corporatism in Liberal Democracies." *Comparative Political Studies* 10:61–90.

―――. 1981. "Trade Unions and the Capitalist State." *New Left Review* 125.

Peltzman, Sam. 1976. "Toward a More General Theory of Regulation." *Journal of Law and Economics* 19:211–240.

Pencavel, John. 1985. "Wages and Employment under Trade Unionism: Microeconomic Models and Macroeconomic Applications." *Scandinavian Journal of Economics* 87:197–225.

Pizzorno, Alessandro. 1978. "Political Exchange and Collective Identity in Industrial Conflict." In *The Resurgence of Class Conflict in Western Europe Since 1968*, Vol. 2, edited by C. Crouch and A. Pizzorno. London: Macmillan.

Ploeg, Frederick van der. 1987. "Trade Unions, Investment, and Employment." *European Economic Review* 31:1465–1492.

Pohjola, Matti. 1983a. "Workers' Investment Funds and the Dynamic Inefficiency of Capitalism." *Journal of Public Economics* 20:271–279.

―――. 1983b. "Nash and Stackelberg Solutions in a Differential Game Model of Capitalism." *Journal of Economic Dynamics and Control* 6:173–186.

―――. 1984a. "Threats and Bargaining in Capitalism: A Differential Game View." *Journal of Economic Dynamics and Control* 8:291–302.

―――. 1984b. "Union Rivalry and Economic Growth: A Differential Game Approach." *Scandinavian Journal of Economics* 86:365–370.

―――. 1985a. "Applications of Dynamic Game Theory to Macroeconomics." Pp. 103–133 in *Dynamic Games and Applications in Economics*, edited by T. Basar. Berlin: Springer-Verlag.

―――. 1985b. "Growth, Distribution and Employment Modelled as a Differential Game." Pp. 581–592 in *Optimal Control Theory and Economic Analysis*, Vol. 2, edited by G. Feichtinger. Amsterdam: North-Holland.

Przeworski, Adam and Michael Wallerstein. 1982. "The Structure of Class Conflict in Democratic Capitalist Societies." *The American Political Science Review* 76:215–236.

―――. 1988. "The Structural Dependence of the State on Capital." *American Political Science Review* 82:11–29.

Rosen, Sherwin. 1985. "Implicit Contracts: A Survey." *Journal of Economic Literature* 23:1144–1475.

Ross, Arthur. 1948. *Trade Union Wage Policy.* Berkeley: University of California Press.

Rubin, Barnett R. 1988. "The Political Economy of Capital Formation: Some Models of Collective Action, Class Struggle, Class Formation, and the State under Capitalism and Socialism." Yale University: Unpublished manuscript.

Sabel, Charles F. 1981. "The Internal Dynamics of Trade Unions." Pp. 209–248 in *Organizing Interests in Western Europe*, edited by S. Berger. Cambridge: Camstbridge University Press.

Scharpf, Fritz W. 1988. "The Political Calculus of Inflation and Unemployment in Western Europe: A Game-Theoretical Interpretation." Presented at the Conference on the Micro-Foundations of Democracy, University of Chicago.

Schott, Kerry. 1984a. *Policy, Power and Order: The Persistence of Economic Problems in Capitalist States.* New Haven: Yale University Press.

———. 1984b. "Investment, Order and Conflict in a Simply Dynamic Model of Capitalism." Pp. 81–97 in *Order and Conflict in Contemporary Capitalism,* edited by John Goldthorpe. Oxford: Clarendon Press.

Shalev, Michael. 1983. "The Social Democratic Model and Beyond: Two Generations of Comparative Research on the Welfare State." Pp. 315–352 in *Comparative Social Research,* Vol. 6, edited by R. T. Tomasson. Greenwich, CT: JAI Press.

Soederstroem, Hans Tson. 1985. "Union Militancy, External Shocks and the Accommodation Dilemma." *Scandinavian Journal of Economics* 1985:335–351.

Wallerstein, Michael. 1988a. "The Centralization of Bargaining and Union Wage Demands." Presented at the Annual Meetings of the American Political Science Association, Washington DC.

———. 1988b. "The Structural Dependence of the State on Internationally Mobile Capital." University of California, Los Angeles: Unpublished manuscript.

Wallerstein, Michael and Adam Przeworski. 1988. "Workers' Welfare and the Socialization of Capital." Pp. 179–205 in *Rationality and Revolution,* edited by Michael Taylor. Cambridge: Cambridge University Press.

Winden, Frans van. 1983. *On the Interaction between State and Private Sector: A Study in Political Economics.* Gravenhage: Drukkerij J. H. Pasmans B. V.

MARKETS IN SOCIETY ————————————— IV

A Complex Relationship: Family Strategies and the Processes of Economic and Social Change   8

Tamara K. Hareven

INTRODUCTION

The historical study of the family has provided important linkages between individual lives and larger social and economic processes such as industrialization, technological change, urbanization, and business cycles. An examination of the family's interaction with markets and the grand processes of economic change enables us to understand more precisely how such change was accomplished: how industrial production processes evolved, how labor markets functioned, and how consumption patterns changed. The nature of the family's response to these processes, namely, how it both initiates change and adjusts to change and how it translates the impact of larger structural changes and demands to its own sphere, is best unraveled through the study of family strategies.

Until recently, sociological and economic literature has portrayed the family primarily as responding passively to the impact of institutions and external economic and social developments. Over the past decade and a half, historical studies of the family have reversed the economists' and sociologists' views of the family as a passive unit to that of an active agent. Standard questions, such as "What was the impact of . . . on the family," have been rephrased to: How did families plan their lives under conditions of adversity and rapid social change? What kinds of strategies did they follow in their adaptation to changing economic conditions? How did family members juggle multiple roles and obligations as husbands and wives, parents, and children and as members of a kinship network over their life course, and in relation to changing external economic conditions? And how were individual careers synchronized with collective family goals? (Hareven 1982). Current historical research has redirected attention to the ways in which families took charge of their lives, allocated their resources, and charted their strategies in reaction to institutions and larger processes of social and economic change. Such strategies can be best described as a set of interrelated family decisions and plans governing the family or household membership, migration, demographic behavior, labor force participation, and consumption patterns.

Family strategies involve explicit or implicit choices families make for the present, for the immediate future, or for long-term needs (Goldin 1981). Formed in response to opportunities and constraints, strategies are also aimed at generating new opportunities. They cover various aspects of family life, ranging from inheritance to the decision to migrate and the organization of one's relatives' migration, from decisions on the membership of one's household to family limitation and child rearing, and from labor force participation to family income and expenditure patterns. Strategies involve not only the decisions individuals or families make, but the actual *timing* of such decisions in response to opportunities or needs: for example, decisions about when to send a son or daughter to another community, when to join kin, and when to change residence. Strategies involve calculated trade-offs in order to achieve solvency: to buy a house, to facilitate children's education or their occupational advancement, to save for the future, and to provide for times of illness, old age, and death.

By examining family strategies we can reconstruct the ways in which family decisions were made in response to external economic opportunities and constraints, and the ways in which the family's internal values, which guided these choices, interacted with external, societal values. As W. I. Thomas put it, "A family's behavior is influenced by what it brings to new situations, the demands and options or constraints of the situation, and situational interpretations. . . . The family is both the product and the producer of its career" (quoted in Elder 1981:500).

Central to this perspective is an emphasis on family action as a dynamic process, which involves a constantly changing interaction of personalities within it, rather than as a monolithic organization or institution. This approach is strongly linked to a life course perspective, because it assumes change and a redefinition of strategies over the life course as well as in relation to external historical conditions (Elder 1981). The stage at which the family finds itself at different points in its life course affects its interactions with economic processes and the market place (such as marriage markets, job markets, and housing markets). This interaction also influences family members' timing of life transitions, as their roles, needs, and obligations change over their life course.

A crucial contribution of historical research on the family has been to shift attention from viewing the interaction of individuals with changing economic conditions as being a strictly *individual* process, to its being tied to a *collective* family one (Anderson 1971; Tilly and Scott 1978; Hareven 1982). Individuals did not enter the market as completely free agents, considering only their own utilities. They operated, instead, within a system in which family responses played a significant role. In the past, the family made decisions as a collective, corporate unit, rather than as the sum of its individual members. For that very reason, family strategies often determine the timing of individual life transitions. Using family strategy, individuals and families weigh benefits of acting "now" rather than later, by a comparison of the value of the present state to the value of the future state, discounted for the uncertainties of attaining the desired state in the future. For example, an additional year of school may be undertaken when either the school itself or its consequences are desirable, or when leaving school immediately would not lead one into a new job, a new family status, or some other utility. Leaving school will not be deferred, however beneficial further schooling might be, if waiting involves a serious chance of losing the job or the intended spouse.

Thus, the timing of present transitions depends on the intended timing of subsequent (or simultaneous) ones and on the certainty with which subsequent conditions can be predicted. But it also depends on the needs and priorities of the family of orientation. A synchronization of individual members' careers and priorities with family ones is at the base of most family strategies. The collective familial character of decisions pertaining to individuals' interactions with the economy (not only that of families) distinguishes many historical patterns from contemporary ones.

Historical research has examined family strategies, particularly in relation to the process of industrialization, along the dimensions of the roles of kinship and internal family strategies, on labor force participation, household membership, allocation of resources, and consumption patterns. This paper addresses the role of family strategies in relation to external economic and social forces in a historical context, in the four areas outlined above. It focuses primarily on American society but draws comparisons from European cases as well.

Since the family is a dynamic, complex organization, economists may have exaggerated the degree to which families plot strategies rationally and calculate the respective economic values of their members' services to one another (Becker 1960). By contrast, historians are much more inclined to examine the interrelationship between economic and cultural variables in the strategies that families use. As Engerman has observed in his commentary on late nineteenth-century family strategies in American urban communities:

> Family decision-making has peculiar aspects of jointness, since it affects and is meant to affect, the entire family group. The family is in essence a group of individuals of varying ages with rather unequal decision-making power, and with a bond of "love" and "altruism" not generally thought to be found in other groups in our society. The family unit operates as a primary income redistribution unit, pooling the income (those funds actually received being only a part of its potential income since some of the potential is

foregone for current or future family good) of one or more of its members, and allocating it among its members whether or not they earned it. Moreover, the "altruism" felt for offspring, and their futures, by parents requires considering the integrational impact of certain key decisions. This involves determining the magnitude of intergenerational transfers and their specific form, such as the choice between physical assets and educational expenditures that increase the value of human capital. (Engerman 1978:275)

Without necessarily assuming rational calculation as the major mode of action in family decision-making, historians have, nevertheless, identified purposeful planning and the weighing of options as the basis of the family's interaction with the economy. Strategies that were often implicit in people's actions in the past were not always consciously defined. Since very few ordinary people left behind diaries and correspondence, it has often been necessary to detect implicit strategies in demographic or other types of family behavior. For example, Smith (1974) has inferred women's strategies of family limitation in early nineteenth-century New England from the gender of the last-born child, and strategies of parental control over the timing of marriage through an analysis of marriage records and wills in the same period. Similarly, many of the strategies of children's and women's labor force participation that will be discussed here are inferred from the census manuscript household schedules in the late nineteenth century. Recently, historical research has begun to reconstruct consciously articulated strategies from interviews and other types of verbal testimony (Tilly and Scott 1978; Hareven 1982).

The conscious strategies most frequently uncovered by historians have been those underlying inheritance contracts in rural society, where sons agreed to support aging parents in exchange for inheriting the family farm or other property (Demos 1970; Berkner 1972; Gaunt 1987; Segalen 1987; Plakans 1987), or in the planning of marriages intended to serve the preservation or consolidation of family estates or lineages (Stone 1977). The use of oral history and ethnographic methods has also enabled historians to reconstruct conscious strategies for the late nineteenth and twentieth centuries, in areas such as the use of kin to organize migration to industrial communities and to support their members' adaptation to industrial conditions; the selection of relatives or godparents to act as custodians of children in times of crisis; and prudential planning for the future, such as education, savings, and insurance (Hareven 1982).

Strategies were part of a larger life plan, or what William Thomas called "life organization" (Thomas and Znaniecki 1918–1920), defined as "the individual's conception of his aims and the codes and rules by which the individual seeks to maintain this conception and this project in a changing world." Life organization constantly changes over the life course in relation to other family members and in response to new challenges, crises, and historical circumstances. People adapt their life plans in response to the "continually increasing sphere of social reality." As people encounter new circumstances, they modify and reshape their life plans and strategies in the context of their own culture and traditions.

The use of the term "strategies" presupposes that individuals and families make choices and exercise priorities when responding to external constraints or opportunities, and at times they generate new opportunities. The most important contribution of historical research has been to emphasize that these choices were not guided exclusively by economic needs, but rather by the interaction of economic and cultural factors. Individuals and families in the past did not always respond to economic conditions strictly in economic terms. In issues such as children's or wives' labor, or expenditure patterns, even economically marginal families did not always make the most "prudent" choices from a strictly economic point of view, if such choices were inconsistent with their family history and their own cultural values (Modell and Hareven 1978; Hareven and Modell 1980).

THE FAMILY IN THE PROCESS OF INDUSTRIALIZATION

The family's relationship to the process of industrialization provides a grand example of the interaction between internal family strategies and external economic processes. It also reveals the extent to which the family not only responded to the process of industrialization, but actually facilitated its advancement.

Over the past two decades, some of the most important contributions of historical studies of the family have revised the stereotypic assumptions that the family was passive in the process of industrialization. This significant reversal of a long-standing stereotype in sociological and economic theory was initially proposed by Goode (1963) on the basis of the experience of industrialization in the Third World. Indeed, historical research proved Goode's hypothesis to be correct. However, historians have gone beyond Goode to reconstruct a more complex pattern of interaction between the family and the process of industrialization in the past.

Instead of simply reversing the stereotype of the family from a "passive" agent to an "active" agent, historians have addressed the questions: Under what historical conditions and at what points in its own development was the family able to control its environment? And conversely, under what circumstances did the family's control diminish? How did the family reorder its priorities to respond to new conditions, and how did this reordering affect internal family relations?

A view of the family as an "active agent" does not imply that the family was in full control of its destiny; nor does it mean that factory workers and their families were successful in changing the structures of industrial capitalism. It suggests that families were actively responding to the new opportunities presented by industrial capitalism, and were organizing their members' migration and employment patterns to take advantage of these opportunities. Conversely, when the system "let them down" by imposing insecurities through unemployment, the shutdown of factories, or depressions, families charted alternative strategies, rather than passively succumbing to adversity.

Families did not merely formulate their strategies in response to the structures, constraints, and opportunities that were dictated by external processes. Family strategies encompassed both the family's interaction with the industrial system externally and the marshalling of its members' labor force and resources internally. When following its own priorities, the family also facilitated the advance of industrialization by releasing the labor force needed for the newly developing factories and by organizing its migration to industrial centers.

The case of protoindustrialization provides an especially poignant example of this point: protoindustrialization, a stage of industrial development that preceded the industrial revolution, emerged in the late eighteenth century in the countryside in Western Europe. It involved the introduction of new technology into the household production of goods for an external market. This new "cottage" industry could not be carried out without family initiative. The entire system rested on household production, and rural families and manufacturers entered into arrangements that, at least initially, were mutually beneficial (Medick 1976). The development of spinning and weaving, knitting, lace-making, hat-making, and other such crafts in the countryside enabled families under this system to introduce new modes of production and new sources of income into their households while supplementing their agricultural production.

In England, for example, the opportunities presented by the introduction of machinery and new production systems for outside markets into rural households enabled farmers to maximize their family income by engaging their entire household in protoindustrial production. In Leicestershire, the families of frame knitters employed one or both of the following strategies to increase production and income: hire additional workers from the outside and/or establish independent households earlier (Levine 1983). The frame knitters embarked, therefore, on earlier marriage, increased the number of children born, and concentrated child-bearing in the years immediately following their marriage. Thus, the economic opportunities presented by the protoindustrial system led families to revise their priorities and to increase family size at a time when the overall population in these countries had begun to experience a fertility decline (Wrigley 1977).

Family involvement in protoindustrial production set the stage for the subsequent recruitment of entire family groups into factories as a new system gradually began to replace the cottage industry from the early nineteenth century on. Family members who had gained experience in their joint production effort and who had learned the use of machinery in the household industry were better equipped to enter factories. Once protoindustrial production began to decline, rural families that had invested in cottage industries became vulnerable to unemployment. Recruitment to the factories provided them with a viable alternative; workers who had already gained experience in protoindustrial production were more attractive to the manufacturers.

With the introduction of the factory system, families revised their labor force strategies and either entered factory work as family units or sent individual members to work. Rural as well as urban working class families participated actively in the initial stage of the industrial revolution. The family was, indeed, the main labor recruiter of its own members for factory work. Entire family groups entered the textile factories as work units during the early stages of the industrial revolution in Britain (Smelser 1959). Fathers contracted for their children, collected their wages, and often supervised and disciplined them in the factory. Families depended on the factory as their employer; the factory, in turn, depended on the workers' families to recruit their members and to help maintain a steady labor supply. Smelser argued that this pattern of family work units in the factory was limited to the first phase of the industrial revolution. By the early 1830s, the development of new machinery had introduced specialization, so that families no longer worked together in the factory. As Anderson (1971) has shown, however, in Lancashire, laborers' recruitment in family units into the textile factories continued into the middle of the nineteenth century. Both in Britain and in the United States, the family survived as a work unit in different forms throughout the nineteenth century.

Even after families ceased to work as units in the factory (from the middle of the nineteenth century on), they continued to function as collective units in the family wage economy. The continuation of the practice of recruitment of workers along kinship lines led to the clustering of several members of a kin group in the same factory. The nuclear family and the larger kin group functioned as important intermediaries between individual members and the factory system in recruiting workers from rural areas, not only during the initial phases of industrialization, but throughout the nineteenth and twentieth centuries (Hareven 1982).

The continuity of vital kinship ties and kin assistance was central to rural laborers' migration to industrial centers and their adaptation to the pressures of the industrial system. Workers' kinship ties with their communities of origin were reinforced by the back-and-forth migration of individual members and the transfer of resources from premigration communities to communities of settlement (Anderson 1971; Hareven 1982; Schwarzweller et al. 1971).

The very success of the industrial system depended on a continuous flow of labor from the countryside to the newly emerging factories. Most of the migration of workers to factory towns was carried out under the auspices of kin. Families who were prepared to leave their rural communities and enter industrial employment or to send some members (usually daughters) to the factory were indispensable to the early development of industry. The declining fortunes of rural families led to the release of the necessary labor force required for industrialization. The conscious use of kinship ties for labor recruitment and migration to industrial centers became a widespread practice as the factory system emerged as a major force in New England in the early nineteenth century. This pattern can be seen in both styles of recruitment of rural laborers for the emerging textile mills in New England—the "family system" and the "mill girl" system.

The family employment model, which was imported from England in the late eighteenth century, was most prevalent in, but not restricted to, small, company-owned industrial villages in Rhode Island and southern Massachusetts. In the early nineteenth century, rural New England families often sent one or more members to work in nearby textile mills. Factory wages were low, and survival often depended on the employment of all family members. The laboring families did retain, however, some choice and control over their economic endeavors by maintaining subsistence farming as a backup if the factory failed. Even when entire families moved to industrial centers, they did not completely abandon their rural bases. Much to the frustration of industrial employers, some rural families worked in factories for a time, then returned to their villages, and at a later point returned to the factory, often following the rhythms of the agricultural seasons, hunting, and fishing.

The second system employed "mill girls"—young women from rural New England, who were the dominant labor base of the planned, large-scale textile towns such as Lowell, Massachusetts, and its sister communities, including Manchester, New Hampshire. This system depended heavily on the strategies of rural families in New England. For most young women, factory work represented a transitional phase—usually 1 or 2 years—between work in their parents' farm homes and marriage. The young women sent part of their earnings from their factory labor back to their families on the farm and also saved some for their dowry (Dublin 1979). In the United States as well as in Europe, this work by single women was part of a family labor force strategy governing who should be sent to work where. It was the common expectation that these single women workers would send their wages back home (Tilly and Scott 1978).

The back-and-forth migration of kin linked the countryside and the factory into an interdependent system. The need for young women's labor in the new factory system corresponded with the strategies of rural families, whose economy was declining, and who were trying to find a source of income for their daughters. The factory provided more attractive temporary employment for girls in the transitional stage prior to marriage than the earlier outlet of domestic service.

From the middle of the nineteenth century on, however, as New England "mill girls" gradually left factory work because they refused to accept lower wages, they were replaced by a cheaper immigrant labor force. Family employment emerged once again as the dominant pattern—but with a difference. New immigrant workers, first Irish, and later French, Canadian, Portuguese, and East European, were recruited in family units, replicating, in some respects, the experiences of the earlier family employment system. Unlike the New England and French Canadian factory workers, however, European immigrants could not maintain their access to a rural hinterland in their home communities while working in American factories (Hareven 1982).

STRATEGIES OF KIN ASSISTANCE

Among the transatlantic immigrants, despite the long-distance migration, kin in the communities of origin and in the communities of settlement continued to function as part of the same social system. Relatives on both sides of the Atlantic continued to engage in various exchanges, and kin assistance flowed back and forth.

Maintaining a backup system in the community of origin was a crucial strategy because various immigrants to the United States during the early part of the century did not consider their migration final. To migrate, individuals needed not only assistance on arrival, but also psychological and economic support in preparation for departure. The care for aging parents who were left behind, and for the family farm necessitated planning and mutual exchanges among kin. Those who went to the United States to work in factories spearheaded the migration for other relatives by locating housing and jobs; and those who remained in the community of origin often took care of the farm and dependent kin (Hareven 1982). The assurance that the property and kin would be taken care of provided migrants with a much needed sense of security.

Kin were central, not only in organizing migration from rural areas to industrial cities, but also in facilitating settlement and adaptation to new working and living conditions. Relying on one's kin to find a job was an important strategy among immigrants to industrial communities. Finding employment for newly arrived immigrants or young relatives later developed into more complex patterns of assistance, such as placing relatives in preferred jobs or departments. Kin were especially instrumental in finding jobs for young relatives in situations in which the bosses were known to be more considerate and flexible, and in which parents did not need to be concerned about their children's exposure to bad habits (Hareven 1982).

Workers often used their good relations with the overseers to hire their kin or to provide them with better jobs. For example, in the Amoskeag Mills in Manchester, New Hampshire, workers wrote to the bosses letters such as these:

June 22, 1904

Please mister if possible you get job to give it that man because he is my cousin and he is family man for family holder.

no signature

Dear Sir (Mr. Foreman)

I am sure that you know that my Brother is working here quite long while now all most six months since, and I hope you be kinde if you Please, and give him another one which with little more Pay to satisfying his own Poor self and he will be very much obliged to you.

Very truely yours,
E. Piter (in Hareven 1982)

Workers' kinship networks effectively interacted with the modern, industrial system and cushioned the adaptation of their members to new settings without excessively restricting their mobility. Relatives often acted as major brokers between the workers and the industrial corporations. They initiated the young and the new immigrants into the work process, handling machinery, and industrial discipline. Through their watchfulness, they provided young workers with protection on the job (Hareven 1978a, 1982).

At the same time, relatives socialized newly arrived immigrant workers to collective working-class behavior, for example, to cooperate with fellow workers in resisting the management's pressures to speed up the pace of work. Such responses were expressed in the workers' collective slowdown of machinery, in exercising job controls, and in setting quota on piece rates. The workers' kinship networks were thus instrumental in serving the strategies of the industrial employer as well as their own, individually and collectively.

Kinship strategies were, however, not uniformly effective. Workers were not always successful in placing their relatives and in influencing the industrial work processes. Kin were most instrumental during periods of labor shortage when the factory system depended on workers to recruit their relatives. They were less successful during periods of labor surplus and during curtailment of industrial production. On the latter occasions, the strategies of kin were directed toward helping their members find work in other places, renewing contact with kin in other industrial communities, assisting members' temporary migration there, and helping the ones remaining in the home community to cope with the consequences of unemployment and loss of income.

Conscious family strategies governed the active intervention of kin in recruiting their members to the industrial workplace, organizing their migration, placing them in desirable jobs in the factory, helping them adjust to work pressures, and socializing them to being disciplined in their work and cooperative with their fellow workers. Immigrant laborers intentionally organized their migration to the factory along kinship lines to secure these various supports for newly arrived workers in what would otherwise have been alienating conditions, conceivably causing social breakdown.

Chain migration—the organizing principle in this movement of workers to factory cities—was itself the product of carefully calculated family strategies. First the family would send a son or a daughter, or a married couple without children to the factory. After they found work and housing, they would send for other relatives. Aging parents, aunts, and uncles often remained behind. Sometimes even young children were left behind, until the migrants decided whether they would settle in the new community.

Even when people migrated as individuals, they represented a family strategy. As Antonia Bergeron recalled her own migration from Quebec to Manchester, New Hampshire, at the turn of this century:

> So when my neighbors went to the U.S., I decided to go with them. It cost [my parents] a little to let me go (not money cost, but feeling cost) but they knew the people well and they had faith in me. . . . I didn't know anyone when we arrived. . . . Then I met a woman who had taught me school in Canada when I was small. She worked in the mills here. She helped me, found me a job in the mills. . . . My mother came up later with my little brother and my little sister. . . . As time went on, we'd have another person come up, and another, and finally the whole family was here. (Hareven 1982:86).

Living in proximity to one's kin in the community of settlement was a critical housing strategy. Despite the pervasiveness of residence in nuclear households, working class populations in industrial cities lived near each other—whenever possible, in the same neighborhood—often on the same street, and at times even in the same building. The main goal was to live in separate households, but to be available in times of need.

Strategies in the use of kin also extended beyond the immediate community to encompass long-distance functions. To be sure, kinship ties were most effective in interaction with local institutions and in meeting immediate crises in the local community. Yet kinship networks typically stretched over a region wider than the industrial city. They were most instrumental during crises in the community of settlement, when it was necessary to obtain help from relatives in other communities. For example, during strikes or layoffs workers in the affected community relied on the assistance of kin in other communities in providing access to jobs and temporary housing. The strength of locally based kinship networks lay in their stability; the strength of long-distance kinship networks was in their fluidity and continuous reorganization to meet new needs (Schwarzweller et al. 1971; Hareven 1978a, 1982).

Assuring the availability of kin over one's life course and during critical life situations necessitated dual strategies: demographic strategies entailed efforts to secure an available pool of kin, especially during periods of high infant mortality and risk; geographic strategies entailed assuring the presence and proximity of kin, especially for those who emigrated from their communities of origin. Having kin engaged in mutual assistance required careful planning and negotiation of exchanges with kin at different points in the life course and the socialization of the young to subordinate personal preferences to obligations toward kin.

The role of kin was thus central in the lives of immigrants and urban working classes because kin were the main, if not the only, source of assistance and survival. In the absence of public welfare agencies and social security, kin were the exclusive source of social insurance. Kin assistance was crucial in handling personal and family crises (such as child-bearing, illness, and death), and in coping with the insecurities imposed by the industrial system (such as unemployment, accidents, and strikes). In an environment of insecurity, where kin assistance was the only continuing source of support, collective family considerations and needs guided or controlled most individual decisions.

Strategies for kin assistance required both short-term and long-term investments over the life course. Short-term investments entailed assistance in the workplace, in housing, in loaning money or tools, and trading skills, goods, or services. Long-term investments were more demanding and less certain in their future returns. Among the long-term investments, the most pervasive exchange was that between parents and children—old-age support in return for child-rearing (Anderson 1971; Hareven 1982; Smith 1979). Under conditions of frequent migration, exchanges along the life course also occurred between aunts and uncles, and nieces and nephews, with the older relatives frequently acting as surrogate parents for their young immigrant relatives.

The opportunities and pressures presented by the industrial system led immigrant laborers to revise their original strategies for kin. Traditional functions of kin in rural society were modified to fit the needs and requirements of urban, industrial life. Immigrants from rural backgrounds transferred to the industrial city the principles and practice of kin solidarity, and the practice of exchanging resources and assistance along the life course. These principles in the use of kin were put, however, to new uses and developed new functions in response to new industrial conditions: Functioning in an industrial environment required familiarity with bureaucratic structures and organizations, adherence to modern work schedules, planning in relation to the rhythms of industrial employment (rather than agriculture), and specialization in tasks and technological skills.

Immigrants to industrial cities thus revised their strategies for the use of kin in their interaction with complex industrial processes and urban housing markets. A premium was now put not on a relative who was instrumental in planting, harvesting, or acquiring new agricultural machinery, but rather on a relative who was skillful in manipulating industrial personnel and production schedules and negotiating urban real estate and markets; strategies of kin interaction thus changed at different points in the life course, and also over historical time.

FAMILY LABOR FORCE STRATEGIES AND THE HOUSEHOLD ECONOMY

The various aspects of the family's interaction with external economic processes necessitated a careful marshalling of the family's internal resources, the management of the family members' labor force participation, consumption patterns, and household resources. This section examines the family's internal strategies in these areas.

Women's and Children's Work

The gainful employment of children and married women outside the home posed a critical dilemma for working-class families. Economic constraints and aspirations for mobility necessitated contributions from women's and children's labor. The participation of women and children in a collective family effort was sanctioned by the cultural values that immigrant workers brought with them from their rural preimmigration communities. Nevertheless, mothers' gainful employment outside the home was not always consistent with premigration values governing married women's work and was in conflict with middle-class norms in American society.

In these areas, family strategies had to accommodate economic constraints and ethnic or class traditions, as well as the values of the dominant culture. The dilemma of juggling wives' work outside the home vis-à-vis economic need in the family and the attraction of employment opportunities frequently recurred among urban working-class and immigrant families. The conflict between family needs and the values of the American native-born middle class, which censored the employment of married women and mothers, necessitated major adjustments by immigrant and working-class families.

The nineteenth-century American ideal that the fathers' incomes were to support their entire families was at odds with the realities of life for working and peasant classes in the communities of origin. It was uncharacteristic of native-born rural and working-class families in the United States. Many immigrants came from a setting in which both agricultural tasks and some household manufacturing were carried out cooperatively, with a division of labor among family members. Working-class families in Europe, too, had learned that multiple incomes were required to meet the high cost of urban living. Consequently, immigrant families frequently brought to the United States a view of the family as a collective work unit. The American ideal that men were to work, women to tend the home, and children to attend school was new to them.

This discrepancy in values did not pose great problems of adjustment until the late nineteenth century, when the American ideal was fully developed and to some extent mandated by law. At that point, compulsory school-attendance laws and legal limitations on child labor challenged the complex family economy that had been characteristic of both European and American industrial settings. These restraints were particularly disturbing to newcomers because of the economic insecurity caused by frequent fluctuations of the economy and by the absence of social insurance. Even under relatively stable economic conditions, families were vulnerable, especially during the early phase in the life course when they had many young children to feed but few earners (Rowntree 1901).

The ethnic culture in which families developed guided the way they managed their children's transitions into the labor force, their marriage patterns, and their labor force strategies for wives and daughters. Even under conditions of economic marginality, the strategies of immigrant families were guided by their cultural values: Foremost was their commitment to survival, and that usually meant autonomy—maintaining their own family unit, heading their own household, and raising their children at home. Despite pressures of poverty and insecurity, most immigrant husbands, like their native United States counterparts, tried to keep their wives out of the labor force, especially if they had children. The degree of immigrant workers' commitment to this goal varies in accordance with the families' economic needs and employment opportunities for women in various communities (Hareven and Modell 1980; Goldin 1986).

Throughout the nineteenth and early twentieth centuries, women's labor-force participation followed a life course pattern. Working-class women commenced work in their teens and dropped out after marriage or the birth of their first child. Unlike what occurred in the 1950s and 1960s, they rarely returned to the labor force after the completion of child rearing. Those mothers who engaged in outside employment did so intermittently throughout their child-bearing years. Even if married immigrant women did not work regularly on a full-time basis outside the home, many spent at least some portion of their time working for pay, often by taking in laundry and sewing or by housing a boarder (Byington 1910). Whenever possible, immigrant women followed their traditional premigration patterns—trying to select those occupations that were least in conflict with traditional practices, and viewing necessary outside work as inseparable from their duties at home.

Although working class families viewed children's work as a basic source of income, they viewed wives' work outside the home merely as a supplement to the family budget. Despite the reluctance to send wives to work, women's labor-force participation in certain urban areas was much more widespread than would be believed from a "snapshot" gleaned from the census. [The underenumeration of women's labor force participation in the census has been a recurring problem in the historical analysis of women's work patterns (Mason et al. 1978).] Even when married women pursued regular and continuous careers, they considered their work outside the home as an extension of their domestic roles and as a supplement to the family economy, rather than as a primary occupation (Hareven 1982; Scott and Tilly 1975).

Women tended to move in and out of the labor force in accordance with childbearing, familial needs, and the availability of employment (Hareven 1982; Mason et al 1978). Thus, the occupational structure of cities, in terms of the availability of jobs for women, also had an impact on the families' labor force strategies. The tendency of married women to work in industries such as textiles and food processing reflects both the greater availability of opportunities for women in such female-intensive occupations and a cultural preference for sending wives and daughters to jobs related to what had been traditional "home" production (Yans-McLaughlin 1977). When employment alternatives were available, wives and daughters tended to work, preferably in industries in which several other members of their family were employed. This provided a continuity between the family and the workplace, as well as an opportunity for the supervision and protection of young workers, especially females, by their older relatives.

The recurring pattern to the family's response to economic conditions in the nineteenth and early twentieth centuries was shaped by the dictates of the family's subculture. In this pattern, families relied first on the labor of their children to supplement their heads of household's income or to substitute for a missing, unemployed, or sick father. The widespread preference was first to send the children to work, next take boarders into the household, and for the wife to do other paid work at home or a combination of these strategies. Sending the wife to work was the last resort. But families on the margin of subsistence followed all three routes: they sent children and wives into the labor force and took boarders into the household.

Although taking in a boarder or lodger eased economic pressures somewhat, most immigrant families depended on the wages of their children, either simply to survive or to lay aside savings to buy a house. As Thernstrom (1964) has shown for nineteenth-century Newburyport, Irish immigrant families chose to defer or forego entirely their children's education to buy a house. Reformers concerned with the child-labor issue viewed immigrant families' dependence on the labor of their children as a form of exploitation by employers and parents and as a product of indifference or even hostility to formal education. In their view, child labor was not a solution to poverty, but instead a cause of future poverty. From the perspective of immigrant parents' strategies, on the other hand, child labor was a means of family survival and an investment in future security. The definition of "future security" initially also had a different meaning for native-born families than for immigrants. For native-born families it meant education and occupational mobility for their children; for immigrants it meant property ownership first.

The economic contribution to the family's income from children's work, especially from that of older children, was the steadiest crucial supplement or substitute for the family head's earnings (Goldin 1981; Hareven 1978a, 1982; Mason et al. 1978; Modell 1978). Child labor was a common recourse in cases of need, which varied greatly according to time, place, and stage in the life course. Employment opportunities for children varied by the occupational structures of the communities. Manufacturing, especially low-capitalization, low-wage, large-shop industry, offered fewer economic rewards to skilled operatives, but extensive work opportunities for young children. The availability of employment opportunities for children was thus a major incentive for families with numerous children to migrate to certain areas.

Despite its critical importance to the family's economy, child labor in itself was not a uniform practice. Family strategies caused differentials within child labor patterns among various groups in the population and depending on need. Whether a child worked depended on the family income, the child's gender and age, the labor force participation of other siblings, the presence of a father in the household, and, of course, the family's ethnic background. The stage in the life course in which the family found itself was one of the most crucial determinants of the labor force participation of children. The older the head of household, the greater the family's reliance on the children's work (Haines 1981). As Rowntree and subsequent generations of analysts of poverty pointed out, children's contribution to the family economy was crucial in the parents' later years of life, as the head of the household's earning power was declining. Child labor was typically the only source of support for widowed mothers, since widows rarely reentered the labor force.

In Philadelphia in the late nineteenth century a younger child's labor force participation often depended on whether older siblings worked or not. Daughters were less likely to work if they had older brothers working—a clear expression of cultural preferences (Goldin 1981). Among the textile workers in Manchester, New Hampshire, on the other hand, parents sent sons and daughters to work in the factory from a young age. They gave priority to keeping sons in high school, while they expected the daughters to keep the family solvent through their labor (Hareven 1982).

At the peak of immigration, the extent to which families were dependent on the work of several members is apparent from Modell's reconstruction of the labor-force participation rates of children 10 to 15 years of age in 1900 (Hareven and Modell 1980). In a great majority of cases such children were living at home and contributing to a complex family income. Wage and occupational structures encouraged child labor more in some cities than in others. In all cities, foreign-born children formed a larger percentage of the child-labor force than did native-born or blacks. This tendency was less pronounced but still visible in immigrant families whose children had been born in the United States. Black children were not as likely to work as immigrant children; on the other hand, black married women had a very high employment rate, including those who had husbands present. The black family economy was distinctive.

The differences in employment patterns of white and black women and children confirm the interactions of cultural values with economic constraints in guiding family strategies. The fact that both married and widowed black women were more likely than white women to be gainfully employed could be interpreted as a result of the greater poverty of black families. But the lower tendency for black than for white children to be employed may reflect a trade-off within black families—a strategy of keeping children in school longer as well as a greater acceptance of married women's work among blacks. Or it might reflect the absence of employment opportunities for black children, which increased the family's dependence on the work of wives (Goldin 1981).

Household consumption patterns, another area governed by family's work strategies, again reflect the centrality of children's work to the family's economic strategies. The allocation of family resources to realms such as necessities, luxuries, leisure, and investments in the mobility of the next generation depended on active planning within the constraints of the family's income. Similar to labor force strategies, family consumption patterns thus reflect strategies based on the interaction between the family's cultural values and economic opportunities.

An examination of family consumption and expenditure patterns over the late nineteenth century reflects changes in family strategies. By comparing expenditure patterns of Irish and native-born workers from the family budgets that had been collected by the Massachusetts-Bureau of Labor Statistics, Modell (1978) found that by the end of the nineteenth century, Irish workers' consumption patterns were moving in the same direction as those of American native-born workers. Changing values among Irish immigrants led them increasingly to approximate American values on child labor as well as "tastes" in expenditure priorities. By 1889 the Irish had developed essentially the same consumption patterns as had Yankee working class families, although the income of Irish working fathers still constituted only 85% of the income of native-born working fathers.

To approximate the expenditure patterns of the American native-born, Irish families had to rely on the labor of at least one child to supplement their fathers' lower income. "The Irish, kept in a tight position by the lower earning capacity of fathers, found children's earnings essential to consume in an American Way" (Modell 1978:221). Thus, although the Irish had become "Americanized" in their tastes, they had not yet become Americanized in their values concerning child labor. By the late nineteenth century, however, Irish families gradually further approximated the Yankees: they replaced child labor by taking in boarders.

Both Irish and American-born families were discriminating in their expenditure patterns: Neither spent money earned by children on labor union dues or on vacations and amusements. On the whole, even Irish families avoided using income from children as a source of expenditure when alternatives (other than the wife's gainful employment) were available. Modell concludes, therefore, that "for working-class people in the American Northeast in 1889, it was father's income more than any other income category that determined the style of life to which a family would direct its expenditures. All dollars were not equal" (Modell 1978:225). Even though the Irish relied more heavily on child-labor than native-born families, they did not use that income indiscriminately. In their family strategies, the Irish were "embryonic Yankees." By 1889–1901, Irish family incomes from fathers' jobs were converging with those of Yankees, and their labor force strategies were converging accordingly; eventually Irish fertility patterns also converged with those of native-born.

Use of the Household as a Resource

Strategies concerning membership and composition of the household were closely related to labor force strategies and consumption patterns. Among immigrant and working-class families in the past, the determination of who, besides nuclear family members, resided in the household was guided by the family's internal economic strategies, and depended on migration patterns and housing markets. Unlike today, when the household—"home"—serves primarily as a private retreat for the family and is, therefore, primarily a locus of consumption, in the past the household was an important resource for exchanges over the life course. Housing space could be shared with boarders and lodgers in exchange for services or rent, or it could be shared with children who had already left home and married, but who, during periods of economic crisis or housing shortages, returned with their spouses to coreside with their parents in exchange for services or support.

The flexible responsiveness of the household to changing economic needs was negotiated and achieved within a fairly rigid framework of an overall commitment to nuclear residence in American society, which was practiced by ethnics and native-born Americans alike. In the United States, as in Western Europe, there has been a continuity in the predominance of a nuclear household structure since the seventeenth century. Despite this general tendency, households did expand to include kin in times of need or at the later stages of the family cycle (Laslett and Wall 1971; Hareven 1977). Households expanded and contracted like accordions, as family members moved over their life course, either by choice or under the pressure of external social or economic conditions. This flexibility, rarely seen today, due to a strong commitment to privacy, provided households and families in the past with their special resilience.

Since the household was considered, to a large extent, an economic resource, household arrangements changed in relation to the family's changing economic needs over the life course, or in response to new opportunities. Households were like a revolving stage on which different family members appeared, disappeared, and reappeared at their own initiative or under the impact of external conditions such as migration, labor markets, or housing markets. Households engaged in direct exchanges across neighborhoods and wide geographic regions. As some members went out into the world, newcomers moved in. Those whose families were disrupted by migration or death were often absorbed into other people's households. Young people could move to new communities, confident that they would board or lodge with relatives or strangers. Similarly, working mothers were able to place young children in the homes of relatives or strangers, and dependent elders, at times, moved into their children's or other people's households. Such exchanges among relatives, neighbors, or complete strangers were laced through the entire society.

The most widespread reliance on the household in family strategies was in the taking of boarders and lodgers into the household. Throughout the nineteenth century and the early part of the twentieth century, between one-half and one-third of all households took in boarders or lodgers at some point over their life course. In the later years of the life course, boarding and lodging represented "the social equalization of the family," a strategy by which young men or women who left their own home communities moved into the households of people whose own children had left home (Modell and Hareven 1973). It provided young migrants to the city with surrogate family arrangements, middle-aged or older couples with supplemental income, and families with young children with alternative sources of income and child-care. The income from boarders and lodgers enabled new homeowners to pay mortgages, and wives to stay out of the labor force. The taking in of boarders and lodgers thus made it easier for families to adhere to their traditional values without slipping below the margin of poverty.

In a regime in which nuclear family residence predominated, taking boarders into the household was a more widespread family strategy than admitting extended kin. Why families preferred to take unrelated individuals into their household, rather than kin, is still an open question. Possibly arrangements with boarders could be negotiated on a more strictly economic basis than with kin; time limits for residence and boundaries within the households could also be set more firmly, and arrangements could be negotiated more "rationally" than with kin.

Despite these preferences, families also took kin into the household, though usually for limited time periods and at specific stages in the life course. [Only about 12 to 18% of all urban households in the late nineteenth and early twentieth centuries took in extended kin (Hareven 1977).] The proportion of households taking in kin increased to 25% over the twentieth century, and declined to 7% by 1950 (Ruggles 1988). Sharing one's household with kin was nevertheless an important migration and life course strategy. In industrial communities, which attracted large numbers of migrants from the countryside or immigrants from abroad, there was a visible increase in household extension over the nineteenth century. Newly arrived migrants usually stayed with their relatives, albeit for a limited time period— until they found jobs and housing (Glasco 1978; Hareven 1982).

Sharing household space with kin was a most effective strategy in the later years of life, when aging parents traded much-coveted household space with their newlywed children, who delayed establishment of an independent household because of housing shortages. Holding on to the space and headship of their household in exchange for future assistance in old age was a prudential life course strategy for urban elders—one reminiscent of the contracts between inheriting sons and rural elders in preindustrial Europe and Colonial New England.

Finally, the least common but nonetheless important use of the household as a resource was in taking in elderly parents, especially widowed mothers, when they had become too infirm or poor to live alone. In these cases, the child taking in the parent headed the household while in the case of the newlywed couples, discussed above, the parents retained the headship of their own household (Chudacoff and Hareven 1978, 1979; Chudacoff 1978). Continuing to head one's own household was an almost sacred goal in American society among native as well as foreign-born. It was a guiding principle in family strategies. Older people, especially widowed mothers, avoided at all cost moving into their children's household. They usually expected the youngest daughter to postpone her marriage and stay with them; if that was not possible, they took in boarders and lodgers. If all these failed, they moved in with a child or another relative.

Wives and children's labor force participation, family consumption patterns, and the sharing of the household with boarders or kin were all interrelated strategies and were used as needs arose at different stages in the life course and in response to external conditions.

WHOSE STRATEGIES WERE FAMILY STRATEGIES?

Since the historical study of family strategies is still in its beginning stages, historians have not yet sufficiently examined the process of decision-making *within* the family. The emphasis on the family as charting its own strategies and making its own choices raises the questions: Whose strategies within the family were "family" strategies? To what extent and in what ways did various family members participate in the collective decisions impinging on their lives? The paucity of historical sources containing conscious articulations of strategies has made it difficult to differentiate attributes within the family and to identify the respective roles and positions of various members in the charting of collective strategies. It has been impossible to reconstruct perceptions and priorities from census and family budget schedules, except by inference from behavioral patterns reconstructed from quantitative demographic data and the census.

The use of oral history has enabled social historians, however, to reconstruct some of the internal dynamics of the family's collective decision-making process. Family collectivity did not necessarily imply mutual deliberation or "democratic" participation in the process. It is possible that major decisions were imposed by the male head of the family on the other members, although there is significant evidence that consultation and bargaining took place between husbands and wives, and occasionally between parents and children.

Even within a "patriarchal" family system, where husbands had officially the dominant role in charting strategies pertaining to migration and their own as well as their family members' work careers, wives bore the major responsibility for decisions that were close to their roles and areas of concern. For example, strategies of family limitation were commonly left to the initiative of women, especially during time periods when such matters were not discussed openly (Smith 1974). This is particularly true in nineteenth-century society where roles of husbands and wives were separated within their respective spheres. Wives also had a major role in deciding whether and when their children, especially their daughters, should go to work. Since it was largely mothers who made the decisions governing their daughters' entry into the labor force, mothers also usually prepared their daughters for their new tasks, introduced them personally to the employer, or attached them to a relative or neighbor who would escort them to the new workplace and introduce them.

When walking the tight rope between keeping the family solvent and violating some of the traditional sanctions about women's roles, wives often attempted compromises such as working outside the home, but, at the same time, reassured their husbands and other kin that this work was only "temporary." Women were also resourceful in finding supplemental sources of income by taking various jobs into the household, taking in boarders, and producing various goods for informal sale (sandwiches or candy, for example). Maria Lacasse, the wife of a textile worker in the Amoskeag Mills, worked in the mills intermittently during the 1920s while raising nine children and carrying out a variety of other household jobs:

> My husband never stopped me going to work when we needed the money. I had to make all the clothes, even the pants for the little boys. I used to sell sandwiches to the girls in the mill if they didn't bring their lunch. (Hareven 1982:205)

Maria's daughter remembered, however, the domestic conflict provoked by the multiplicity of her mother's work roles:

> My father didn't really want her to work. That was a big issue because she always wanted to go in and earn a little money. But the minute she said she wanted to work, there would be a big fight. He'd say, "No, you're not going to work. You're going to stay home." And that's why she did other things. She'd make clothes for him, take in boarders, rent rooms. . . . Sometimes she'd also work little stretches at night in the mills, from six to nine because we lived right in front of the mills. When there were big orders, the mills were always looking for people to work. But my father didn't want to keep the children. That was women's work; his work was outside. (Alice Olivier, in Hareven 1982:205)

Although men were considered to be the main breadwinners and were, therefore, expected to make the major economic decisions for the family, women were much closer to the routine management of household resources. Women made the daily decisions regarding the family budget, the allocation of household space, and family consumption. Since the responsibility of feeding and clothing family members was primarily theirs, women were more sensitive to shortages in food and supplies, and pursued independent strategies to fulfill these basic tasks.

Wives also took the leadership in family decision-making, especially in times of depressions, unemployment, or strikes. They were more inclined to make compromises to secure food for the family, a tactic that men, due to their pride and standing among peers, would have considered demeaning. For example, during strikes, wives went into work while their husbands (forced by peer pressure more than by conscience) were striking. Maria Lacasse describes her decision to cross the picket line during the 1919 strike at the Amoskeag Mills:

> It was the men who didn't want to go back during the strike, because there were pickets. They were afraid they were going to get killed. There was another woman on the block who said, "How about us women going to work? If we go to work, they're not going to attack us because we're women." So I decided I was going to go back because fall was coming, and we didn't have any money. We didn't know how we were going to live. That's what the strike was all about: they didn't give the workers enough money. But I knew they were not going to win; so when that woman asked me, I had the children kept, and I went in to work. I told my husband to stay home; I was afraid he would be hurt by the pickets. (Hareven and Langenbach 1978:260–261)

Similarly, during the Great Depression it was the women who surreptitiously went to welfare agencies to receive food staples for the family, while their husbands pretended that the family continued to be self-sufficient.

Women also took initiatives and had a central role in strategies governing the care of kin during critical life situations—in handling childbirth, illness, infirmity, or death. Since women usually had nurturing responsibilities in all these areas, they had the main initiative in charting strategies of exchanges with kin. In this way, women were the "kin keepers," the family members who maintained ties with kin over the life course and who held kinship networks together across geographic distances.

Some kin keepers remained single or married unusually late because they started to care for older relatives or younger siblings in early adulthood, and had to postpone or give up marriage altogether. Their responsibilities as kin keepers extended and escalated as they grew older. Maintaining a "kinship communication center," they kept track of different family members who migrated, or who married, and left town; they scheduled family reunions and celebrations. They monitored conflict among relatives, and tried to resolve feuds by acting as intermediaries. Kin keepers did everything to maintain vital kinship ties over the life course, so that relatives would be available to each other in times of need.

The extent to which children had an active role in charting family strategies is yet to be explored. The decision to send a child into the labor force was primarily, if not entirely, a parental one. Collective family values dictated that children follow their parents' decisions; however, the very dependency of the family on the earnings of children gave the latter considerable maneuverability in implementing these decisions. Children working and living at home had less latitude or bargaining power with their parents than children who left home to work in other communities. To continue to exercise control over these far-away children and to keep them more closely tied to the collective family economy, parents had to exercise greater flexibility in bargaining with them, and in tolerating these children's preferences, to the extent that they differed from their own (Anderson 1971; Tilly and Scott 1978).

Within the dictates of "collective" family strategies individual members did not always succumb blindly to family demands. Interviews used to supplement quantitative behavioral data have suggested areas of tension surrounding the trade-offs and sacrifices that individuals were expected to make for the collective good of their families. Whenever possible, individuals tried to resist having to pay the high price expected of them for maintaining family solidarity. Strain and conflict revolved around such issues of family timing as when to leave home, when to marry, how to allocate responsibilities among siblings for parental support, and how to divide resources and inheritance.

Under certain situations individuals pursued their own strategies to protect themselves from excessive family control over their own opportunities to live individual lives. This was particularly true for young daughters, who tried to avoid the predicament of being the last child at home and having to carry the burden of support for aging parents. Anna Fregau Douville, for example, was the last child of working age in her family. She left school and started working at age 14 and postponed her own marriage. When Anna finally announced she was going to get married, her sisters pressured her to cancel her engagement, claiming that her fiancé was a "drunkard." Actually, "they were scheming to get me to support my folks until they died. . . . But my mother told me, 'Anna, don't wait too long. What if I die or your father dies? Then you'd insist on staying with me, and you'll lose your boyfriend.' " She got married and lived two houses away from her parents. Although Anna had been determined to live her life independently of her family, she was never quite free of guilt:

> They [her parents] were on the city welfare . . . even with the hard times I had during
> my life, I never stopped for sympathy for myself, because I knew about my mother's
> life. . . . A lot of things go through your head when your folks are gone. . . . You don't
> realize it when they are living. You want to live your own life; but when folks are gone
> and you think of all the good things that you have today, you wish they could share them.
> (Hareven 1982:110)

Having grown up in a large family where she experienced firsthand the pressures imposed by kin, Anna subsequently set strict boundaries with her husband's family immediately after marriage: She refused to pay her mother-in-law's debts and made it clear to her husband and her in-laws that they could not rely on her to compensate for their extravagances:

> I put my foot down the first year that I got married. . . . When his parents used to come
> and visit me and ask to borrow money . . . I said, "Listen, I don't go down to your house
> to bother you. I'm happy with my husband and get the hell out. Don't ever come here
> and try to borrow anything from him or from me." . . . My husband agreed with me. He
> said, "I'm glad that you can open up with them. I couldn't talk that way to my own
> family." (Hareven 1982:110)

Collective family strategies, although uniform on the surface, were never simple and streamlined in reality. Most individuals and families living under conditions of economic insecurity found themselves in a double bind: on the one hand, the family's collective requirements imposed enormous pressures and burdens on individuals; on the other, individuals were dependent on family collectivity for assistance in time of need. Thus, a rebellion against familial requirements, however onerous, would deprive individual members of access to the only source of support under conditions of insecurity.

CONCLUSION: LONG-TERM HISTORICAL CHANGES

This excursion into nineteenth-century and early twentieth-century family migration, work, and household economic strategies has highlighted the continuous interaction between the family and the process of economic change. It has provided various examples of the family's role as an active agent, where the family followed its own strategies and priorities. It has shown that under certain historical and market conditions, the family had greater latitude to exercise its own initiatives, while under other conditions it had to respond to the adversities imposed by business cycles and depressions.

The family was more able to be in control of its own destiny under conditions of labor shortage, and less able during periods of labor surplus. When particular skills or experience that the family commanded were in demand, the family was more in control over the economy; when such skills or resources became obsolete, the family's control diminished. At times when the family had less control over the economic system, it exercised adaptive strategies to cushion its members from the adverse impact of these conditions and to devise alternative means of survival.

In interacting with the larger processes of social change and with the institutions of industrial capitalism, the family exercised a considerable degree of flexibility in organizing migration, placing its members in various labor force configurations, allocating resources, and using land or the household as trade-offs during periods of need. The family modified its strategies in response to its changing needs over the life course as well as to external conditions.

The family developed these flexible strategies within the constraints imposed by markets and historical circumstances, and within the context of the cultural prescriptions guiding its behavior. Such prescriptions were especially powerful in the context of a collective family economy where the choices and preferences of individual members were subordinate to the dictates of the family unit. As shown above, individual choices were not always uniformly streamlined within the family collectivity. Families experienced internal tensions and, at times, conflict when individual members pulled in various independent directions. But the collective goals usually won out.

Historical changes since the early part of this century, especially since the 1920s, have gradually modified the models of the family's interaction with the economy discussed above. Changing values have led to an increasing separation of individual careers from collective family ones. The erosion of values of interdependence among kin has frequently led individuals to place priority on their own careers, independently of the dictates of the family. Consequently, the timing of life transitions has become more individualized and subject to personal choice, rather than to collective family needs.

This type of individualization has weakened the family's impact on the economy as a labor recruiter and as an active agent in the workplace. Family needs, such as child care for working mothers, have continued to influence the workplace, and to have an impact on mothers' labor force participation. But the family as a unit does not interact with the workplace in the same manner as it had in the past, nor does it influence styles of production or work schedules.

As part of an ongoing historical process, the family's economic behavior has come to focus predominately, if not exclusively, on consumption. The household has ceased to be the main unit of production following industrialization in the nineteenth century. Urban working class families, however, continued to behave as collective work units in the wage economy, even when their members were individually employed in separate establishments. Family members working as individuals, often living away from home, still viewed their wage labor as an integral part of a collective family economy, and continued to send remittances home.

Institutional and legislative changes have further fragmented the family's functioning as a collective work unit, primarily since the 1920s. The implementation of child labor laws and compulsory school attendance laws, especially since the 1930s, has led to the exclusion of children from the family's collective work process. The regulation of child labor was finally achieved because technological changes rendered industrial child labor obsolete from the employer's point of view. Parents also changed their attitudes toward child labor, when new values and aspirations among second generation immigrants led to an increasing acceptance of the middle class white native-born standard that children stay out of the labor force (Bremner et al. 1971). The increase in married women's labor force participation since the 1950s, especially in married women entering into continuous careers, rather than returning after the completion of child rearing, has rendered the typical contemporary family a dual earner family (or single earner family where only one parent is present). This pattern is significantly different from that of the multiple-income family of the past that had rested so heavily on the labor of children.

Since the middle of the nineteenth century the family itself has undergone dramatic changes that have impinged on the family's economic role and on its interaction with economy and society. Following the processes of urbanization and industrialization, functions that had previously been concentrated within the family were gradually transferred to other institutions (Smelser 1959). The preindustrial family embraced a variety of functions: It was a workshop, church, reformatory, school, and asylum (Demos 1970). Over the past century and a half, these various familial functions have become the responsibility of other institutions. The surrender of these functions also reversed the family's relationship to the market and to the state. The market now provides the goods families once produced; it also provides insurance, vocational training, and many financial transactions that had once been carried out mainly within families. Similarly, the state now provides education, social insurance, and health care in old age. The family has become a specialized, private consumption unit.

The role of the household has changed from that of being an economic resource to being merely a site of consumption. An increasing commitment to the privacy has led to the segregation of the family from the larger community. Rather than producing goods and generating income, the household has become mainly a unit of consumption. The family as a unit has withdrawn from the world of work, insisting on the privacy of the home and its separation from the outside world. The workplace has generally become impersonal and bureaucratic. Once considered an asset, familial involvement in the workplace is now denigrated as nepotism. The home is viewed increasingly as a retreat from the outside world. The family has turned inward and has assumed domesticity, intimacy, and privacy as its major characteristics. As a consequence, the family has lost some of its earlier flexibility in relying on the household as an economic resource.

This historical transition of the family from a collective production unit to primarily a consumption unit, in which members follow individual careers, has not occurred uniformly across American society. Although these patterns predominate overall, they are more typical of the urban middle classes. Among working-class and newer ethnic families, however, some of the historical characteristics of family behavior have persisted, although in modified form. Similarly, the survival of viable functions of kin in relation to economic change suggests that the privatization and individualization of family life has not been consummated across the entire society.

The family's interaction with the economy has followed a complex, uneven pattern. The family has been both a custodian of tradition and an agent of change. As a guardian of traditional culture, the family provided its members with a sense of continuity and with resources on which to draw when confronting change. As an innovator, the family charted new strategies in response to social and economic change. An understanding of how the process of economic change takes place can be enhanced, therefore, through an understanding of the complexity of family behavior.

ACKNOWLEDGMENTS

I am indebted to Kathleen Adams and to Nancy Wilson for their valuable comments and editorial assistance, and to Claudia Goldin for her constructive critique.

REFERENCES

Anderson, M. 1971. *Family Structure in Nineteenth Century Lancashire.* Cambridge, England: Cambridge University Press.

Becker, G. 1960. An Economic Analysis of Fertility. *Demographic Change in Developed Countries.* Universities-National Bureau Conference Series No. 11. Princeton, NJ: Princeton University Press.

Berkner, L. K. 1972. "The Stem Family and the Developmental Cycle of the Peasant Household: An 18th-Century Austrian Example." *American Historical Review* 77:398–418.

Bremner, R. H. et al. 1971. *Children and Youth in America,* Vol. II. Cambridge, MA: Harvard University Press.

Byington, M. F. 1910. *Homestead: The Households of a Mill Town* Vol. 5. *The Pittsburgh Survey.* New York: Russell Sage Foundation, Charities Publication Committee.

Chudacoff, H. P. 1978. "Newlyweds and Family Extension: First Stages of the Family Cycle in Providence, Rhode Island. Pp. 179–205 in *Family and Population in Nineteenth-Century America,* edited by T. K. Hareven and M. A. Vinovskis. Princeton, NJ: Princeton University Press.

Chudacoff, H. and T. K. Hareven. 1978. "Family Transitions and Household Structure in the Late Years of Life. Pp. 217–244 in *Transitions: The Family Life and the Life Course in Historical Perspective,* edited by T. K. Hareven. New York: Academic Press.

———. 1979. "From the Empty Nest to Family Dissolution. *Journal of Family History* 4:59–63.

Demos, J. 1970. *A Little Commonwealth: Family Life in Plymouth Colony.* New York: Oxford University Press.

Dublin, T. 1979. *Women at Work: The Transformation of Work and Community in Lowell, Massachusetts, 1826–1860.* New York: Columbia University Press.

Elder, Glen H., Jr. 1981. "History and the Family: The Discovery of Complexity." *Journal of Marriage and the Family* 43 (August):489–519.

Engerman, S. 1978. "Economic Perspectives on the Life Course." Pp. 271–286 in *Transitions: The Family and the Life Course in Historical Perspective,* edited by T. K. Hareven. New York: Academic Press.

Gaunt, D. 1987. "Rural Household Organization and Inheritance in Northern Europe." *Journal of Family History* 12:1–3, 121–41.

Glasco, L. 1978. "Migration and Adjustment in the Nineteenth-Century City: Occupation, Properties and Household Structure of Native-Born Whites, Buffalo, New York. Pp. 154–178 in *Family and Population in Nineteenth-Century America,* edited by T. K. Hareven and M. A. Vinovskis. Princeton: Princeton University Press.

Goldin, C. 1981. Family Strategies and the Family Economy in the Late Nineteenth-Century: The Role of Secondary Workers. Pp. 277–310 in *Philadelphia,* edited by T. Hershberg. New York: Oxford University Press.

Goldin, C. 1986. The Female Labor Force and American Economic Growth, 1890–1980. In *Long-Term Factors in American Economic Growth,* edited by S. L. Engerman and R. E. Gallman. Chicago: University of Chicago Press.

Goode, W. J. 1963. *World Revolution and Family Patterns.* New York: The Free Press.

Haines, M. 1981. "Poverty, Economic Stress, and the Family in a Late-Nineteenth-Century American City: Whites in Philadelphia, 1880. Pp. 240–276 in *Philadelphia,* edited by T. Hershberg. New York: Oxford University Press.

Hareven, T. K. (ed.). 1977. *Family and Kin in American Urban Communities, 1780–1940.* New York: Franklin Watts.

———. 1978. *Transitions: The Family and the Life Course in Historical Perspective.* New York: Academic Press.

———. 1978a. "The Dynamics of Kin in an Industrial Community." *American Journal of Sociology* (Supplement).

———. 1982. *Family Time and Industrial Time.* New York: Cambridge University Press.

Hareven, T. K., and R. Langenbach. 1978. *Amoskeag: Life and Work in an American Factory-City.* New York: Pantheon.

Hareven, T. K. and J. Modell. 1980. "Family Patterns." Pp. 345–354 in *Harvard Encyclopedia of American Ethnic Groups,* edited by S. Thernstrom. Cambridge: Harvard University Press, Belknap Press.

Laslett, P. and R. Wall. (eds). 1971. *Household and Family in Past Time.* Cambridge: Cambridge University Press.

Levine, D. 1983. Proto-industrialization and demographic upheaval. Pp. 9–34 in *Essays on the Family and Historical Change,* edited by L. Moch and G. Stark. College Station, Texas: Texas A&M University Press.

Mason, K. O., M. A. Vinovskis, and T. Hareven. 1978. "Women's Work and the Life Course in Essex County, Massachusetts, 1880. Pp. 187–216 in *Transitions: The Family and the Life Course in Historical Perspective,* edited by T. K. Hareven. New York: Academic Press.

Medick, H. 1976. "The Proto-industrial Family Economy. *Social History* 3:291–315.

Modell, J. 1978. Patterns of Consumption, Acculturation, and Family Income Strategies in Late Nineteenth-Century America. Pp. 206–250 in *Family and Population in Nineteenth-Century America,* edited by T. K. Hareven and M. Vinovskis. Princeton: Princeton University Press.

Modell, J. and T. K. Hareven. 1973. "Urbanization and the Malleable Household: An Examination of Boarding and Lodging in American Families. *Journal of Marriage and the Family* 35:467–479.

Modell, J. and T. K. Hareven. 1978. "Transitions: Patterns of Timing." Pp. 245–269 in *Transitions: The Family and the Life Course in Historical Perspective*, edited by T. K. Hareven. New York: Academic Press.

Plakans, A. 1987. "Interaction between the Household and the Kin Group in the Eastern European Past: Posing the Problem." *Journal of Family History* 12:1–3, 163–175.

Rowntree, E. S. 1901. *Poverty: A Study of Town Life*. London: Longmans, Green.

Ruggles, S. 1988. "The Demography of the Unrelated Individual, 1900–1950." *Demography* 25:4.

Schwarzweller, H. K., J. S. Brown, and J. J. Mangalam. 1971. *Mountain Families in Transition: A Case Study of Appalachian Migration*. University Park: Pennsylvania State University Press.

Scott, J. W. and L. A. Tilly. 1975. "Women's Work and Family in Nineteenth-Century Europe. Pp. 145–178 in *The Family in History*, edited by C. E. Rosenberg. Philadelphia: University of Pennsylvania Press.

Segalen, M. 1987. "Life-Course Patterns and Peasant Culture in France: A Critical Assessment." *Journal of Family History* 12:1–3, 213–24.

Smelser, N. J. 1959. *Social Change in the Industrial Revolution*. Chicago: University of Chicago Press.

Smith, D. S. 1973. Parental Power and Marriage Patterns: An Analysis of Historical Trends in Hingham, Mass." *Journal of Marriage and the Family* 35:419–28.

Smith, D. S. 1974. "Family Limitation, Sexual Control, and Domestic Feminism in Victorian America. Pp. 119–137 in *Clio's Consciousness Raised: New Perspectives on the History of Women*, edited by M. S. Hartman and L. Banner. New York: Harper & Row.

Smith, D. S. 1979. "Life Course, Norms, and the Family System of Older Americans in 1900." *Journal of Family History* 4:285–98.

Stone, L. 1977. *The Family, Sex, and Marriage in England 1500–1800*. New York: Harper and Row.

Thernstrom, S. 1964. *Poverty and Progress: Social Mobility in a Nineteenth-Century City*. Cambridge: Harvard University Press.

Thomas, W. and F. Znaniecki. 1918–1920. *The Polish Peasant in Europe and America*, 3 volumes. Chicago: University of Chicago Press.

Tilly, L. and J. Scott. 1978. *Women, Work and the Family*. New York: Holt, Rinehart & Winston.

Wrigley, E. A. 1977. "Reflections on the History of the Family." *Daedalus* 106:71–85.

Yans-McLaughlin, V. 1977. *Family and Community: Italian Immigrants in Buffalo, 1880–1930*. Ithaca, NY: Cornell University Press.

Explaining the Politics of the Welfare State or Marching Back Toward Pluralism?

9

Frances Fox Piven and Richard A. Cloward

As welfare state programs expanded over the past quarter of a century, so, naturally enough, did academic efforts to explain the political dynamics underlying this growth. The emergence in some countries of intense political controversy over welfare state programs added to the intellectual ferment, and to the proliferation of explanations. The result is that a variety of institutional contexts—mainly the market, parliamentary democracy, state bureaucracies, and the patriarchal family—have been identified as the key sites that generate and pattern the political orientations and capacities ultimately expressed in welfare state politics. In effect, we have produced a theoretical profusion of substructures. Laid end to end, these intellectual developments suggest either a retreat from theory, or the resurgence of an essentially pluralistic perspective on the politics of the welfare state, and inevitably on politics in general.

Although welfare state programs have a long historical lineage, interpretations of the welfare state by social scientists are much more recent. Indeed, until a few decades ago, explanations of the political history of programs that provided income and services to population groups at risk were largely left to professionals in the field of social welfare. And, like professionals in other fields, they tended to develop explanations that gave a large role to the ideas and activities of professionals themselves, as well as to their philanthropic forebears, in the development of welfare state programs. These interpretations tended toward insularity and self-promotion, in the sense that the dynamics of welfare state growth were located not in society or economy, but in the welfare state itself, and in the professionals who stood guard over it. [Heclo's work (1974) on the initiation of welfare state programs in Britain and Sweden gave a belated boost to this mode of interpretation, although the professionals whom he identifies as the innovative actors are top civil servants, and not merely social welfare reformers.]

In the wake of the enormous postwar expansion of welfare state programs, the politics of the welfare state attracted much broader attention in the academy. Professional interpretations were soon overshadowed by a series of studies that located the political dynamics of welfare state programs in larger institutional contexts. The most influential of these studies explained the growth and elaboration of the welfare state in relation to the institutional dynamics of industrial capitalism. One large body of work, strongly influenced by structural–functionalist perspectives, saw welfare state programs as adaptations to the needs generated by industrial dislocation, urbanization, and an aging population. And, of course, the economic growth that created new needs simultaneously created the capacity to pay for programs to respond to those needs (see, for example Wilensky and Lebeaux 1965; Wilensky 1975; Flora and Heidenheimer 1981).

Another set of interpretations also traced welfare state programs to the dynamics of industrial capitalism, but with an emphasis on capitalism rather than industrialization. Thus, one familiar stream of argument rooted the development of the welfare state in the dual requirements of capitalist accumulation and legitimation (see, for example Offe 1972; O'Connor 1973; Gough 1979). Another traced welfare state programs not to the systemic requirements of capitalism, but to the classes and class conflicts formed by capitalist economies. Workers, organized and educated into class collectivities by their role in capitalist industries, sought protection from the vicissitudes of labor markets and human biology. Employers resisted, unwilling to pay the costs of such protections, or to allow workers any shield from market sanctions. Welfare state programs were presumably forged in the vortex of these conflicting forces (see, for example Piven and Cloward 1971, 1985, 1987; Gough 1979).

Whatever their other disagreements, all of these interpretations shared the underlying assumption that welfare state politics were fundamentally formed by the dynamics of the capitalist economy. It was in the institutional domain of industrial capitalism that the systemic requirements said to shape welfare state policies were generated, or that the class-based political interests and capacities were shaped that were ultimately reflected in welfare state programs. More recently, however, new interpretations have emerged—stimulated partly by reversals in the politics of the welfare state itself, and partly by the emergence of new academic schools. They challenge the older economistic perspectives and give pride of place in explaining the politics of welfare states to entirely different institutional domains, namely liberal democracy, state bureaucracies, and the patriarchal family. And there are also the theorists of the "new social movements" who reject the assumption that any single institutional domain is preeminent in shaping politics, including the politics of the welfare state.

SOCIAL DEMOCRACY AND THE POLITICS OF THE WELFARE STATE

One influential stream of contemporary interpretation assumes the existence of classes and class conflict, but focuses on electoral representative arrangements as the formative institutional context in explaining the politics of the welfare state. In contrast to perspectives that root the political dynamics of the welfare state mainly in the market economy, state bureaucracies, or the family, this is a hybrid model. The fundamental interests reflected in welfare state policies are class interests, formed in a capitalist system of production. But the subordination of the working class in the sphere of production is overcome not by workplace struggles but by the entrance of the working class into electoral politics. The class interests that originate in economic spheres take form and are expressed in political spheres where class-based political parties compete for state power using resources and strategies distinctive to electoral-representative institutions. The welfare state thus results from a developmental sequence that begins with industrialization and the growth of an industrial working class, leading in turn to the growth of trade unions. The roughly simultaneous development of electoral representative arrangements facilitates the formation of political parties based on this unionized working class. These labor-based parties, together with the union infrastructure that undergirds them, are the instrument through which the working class wins the welfare state policies that modify the distributional inequalities of the market (Hibbs 1977; Korpi 1983; Shalev 1983; Esping-Anderson 1985; Castles 1982; Myles 1984).

In its basic outlines, this "new political economy" reaches back to Eduard Bernstein's early advocacy of an electoral road to socialism that had a pervasive influence on European social democratic parties, and perhaps especially on the Swedish Social Democratic Party.[1] Social democratic theorists also point to T. H. Marshall's influential argument that democratic ideas themselves have developed according to an evolutionary dynamic that makes the struggle for social rights a virtually inevitable corollary of political democracy.

The contemporary work in this tradition is, however, infinitely more empirically complex and methodologically sophisticated than these historical precedents. On the one hand, analysts have pondered the predictive significance of a variety of measures of class-based political power on welfare state development, including the numerical strength and degree of centralization of trade unions, labor party strength in the electorate, variable partisan alignments and cleavages, partisan control of the executive, and the strength of extraparliamentary corporatist arrangements. On the other hand, analysts have also employed a wide range of measures of welfare state development, including measures of wage and income inequality and levels of unemployment and of public expenditure on social welfare programs or "welfare state effort," and even some efforts to measure qualitative aspects of these programs (Castles 1982; Hicks and Swank 1982; Friedland and Sanders 1985; Myles 1984).

With these more complex models in hand, a formidable array of comparative quantitative studies has been published in just the past few years, examining the impact of various measures of working class strength in electoral representative institutions on measures of welfare state accomplishments. And despite internal debates over the relative significance of various measures of working class political strength or of welfare state outcomes, and over the relation of political variables to underlying differences in national economies, these studies tend to buttress the general claim that political democracy is the main arena of class struggle and that variations in welfare state outcomes are a good measure of the success of that struggle.

Still, although cross-national statistical comparisons inevitably give the appearance of weighty scientific stuff, the limitations of this method are great, as some of the participants in the enterprise are coming to agree. For one, since the argument applies only to advanced industrial nations with democratic political systems, investigations of the interaction of an increasing array of variables is limited to a universe of perhaps 15 to 20 countries (usually the 18 OECD countries for which data are readily available), with results that can only be suggestive at best. Moreover, the case for treating European nations as distinctive systems grows steadily weaker as the European community takes on the characteristics of a nation state. At some point, the reasoned basis for cross-national statistical comparisons will collapse.

There is also the persistent and familiar problem of identifying satisfactory statistical measures of welfare state effort. Shalev's recent work, which draws attention to the large role played in some countries by the quasiprivate pension systems that are excluded from measures of public expenditure, is only one illustration of this plaguing problem (Shalev 1987). Its seriousness is suggested by the fact that the United States and Japan rely on employment-based benefits. These countries carry enormous weight in making the social democratic case because they are both the main welfare state laggards and they also have weaker unions and left parties. The inclusion of private benefit programs in analyses may thus simply eliminate much of the distinctiveness of the main cases that make the social democratic argument.

Finally, there is the possibility raised by the work of the European Consortium for Political Research that different measures of welfare state success employed in different studies may well turn out to be trade-offs: where social democratic parties and centralized trade unions succeed in winning greater wage equality, it is by sacrificing public expenditure programs, or vice versa.

Thus, van Arnheim and Schotsman (1982:351) conclude that in advanced capitalist societies, "the situation with respect to the possibilities for equality of income distribution . . . resembles that of a 'zero sum game'" where equality achieved by one set of policies is canceled by another set. Our point is not to categorically dismiss efforts to develop empirical measures of the bearing of working class political strength on welfare state policies, rather it is to remind the reader that the empirical correlations that are sometimes taken as confirmation of the social democratic perspective remain uncertain. On empirical grounds, the jury is still out on the success of "the democratic class struggle."

There are also a number of weaknesses in the theoretical logic underlying this "new political economy." One problem has to do with the failure to develop a reasoned and qualified justification for equating classes formed in productive spheres with the organizations that purport to represent them in political spheres. The social democratic model treats as axiomatic the assumption that trade unions and social democratic parties in fact represent working class interests, as when Korpi (1983:39) proposes that working class power will be greatest where trade unions are centralized and collaborate closely with a socialist party. But to leave it at that is a kind of nominalism: it is to assume the politics of organizations can be understood by the names they give themselves. There are good reasons for being troubled by that assumption. One is the long historical experience demonstrating the tendency of working class organizations to gradually move away from the political interests of their rank and file, as they maneuver for survival and success in an environment dominated by other powerful organizations. This is the tendency toward oligarchy documented and explained by Michels in his work on the German Social Democratic Party, although his critique has generally been acknowledged only to then be ignored.

Another reason to wonder about the nominalistic equation of social democratic parties with working class interests has to do with the compromises forced on the left parties precisely by the effort to advance along the electoral path. Electoral contests constrained left parties to build support over the short run by making appeals for popular support in terms of immediate material improvements. As Przeworski (1985) and others have argued, this constraint forced the social democratic parties into accommodations with the business groups that control investment and the possibility of material improvement. Moreover, the early prediction that the advance of industrial capitalism would create a working class electoral majority was disappointed. The industrial proletariat never achieved majority status, and in most countries it was also deeply fragmented by ethnic and racial divisions, as well as by the sectoral and hierarchical divisions generated by industrial organization. As Offe (1982) has remarked,

There are numerous categories of differentiation—including the distinctions between
the primary and secondary labour markets; skilled versus unskilled labour; gender-based
divisions of wage-labour; differences between traditional proletarians and workers who
have recently come from self-employed families; productive labour versus service labour
(labour that produces not physical products but things like advice which are immediately consumed); and so on.[2]

In any case, as the twentieth century advanced, it became clear that social
democratic parties bidding for state power through electoral processes had
to seek support from other classes. Inevitably, therefore, the agenda and
culture of the left parties tended to become oriented toward extra-working
class voters, or toward coalition with the parties of extra-working class
voters. Thus, Esping-Andersen (1985) emphasizes the historical importance
of coalition with the farmers party in overcoming the minority status of the
Swedish social democratic party, and calls attention to the contemporary
necessity of building support among white collar groups. Korpi (1983:95,
passim) also calls attention to the advance of the socialist parties among
higher levels of salaried employees in recent decades. The point is not that
any of this is reprehensible, or even avoidable (although it is difficult to
escape the sense that the social democratic analysts have become something
of a cheering squad for whatever strategy is employed by the Swedish social
democratic establishment). It is rather that the extent to which social democratic parties (as well as centralized trade unions) do in fact represent working class interests should probably not be taken for granted, but should be
treated as historically contingent and therefore as empirically variable.

There is another problem with the underlying institutional logic of the
social democratic argument. We said earlier that it is an institutional hybrid,
positing that the class interests formed in production relations are expressed
in democratic politics. But once class interests are transported into democratic arenas, they assume collective forms influenced by electoral institutions, depend on resources generated by electoral representative arrangements, and must necessarily employ the strategies shaped, if not dictated, by
the electoral system.[3]

In turn, the distinctive collective forms, resources, and strategies arising
from electoral institutions transform the modes of class conflict. Thus, Korpi
(1983:46–47) tells us that with the growing strength of the Swedish social
democratic party, industrial conflicts subsided from the high levels of the
early twentieth century. Myles (1984:90) holds the same view, concluding
that working class political power is inversely related to levels of industrial
conflict and, even more simply, that the quality of citizenship entitlements is
a reflection of party competition and of the size of the dependent population
(Myles, 1984:89, 95. See also Hibbs 1978; Korpi and Shalev 1980, cited in
Myles 1984:90). Considered alone, these propositions express so much
confidence in the vigor of democratic processes as to seem to unhinge the

analysis from its roots in industrial capitalism and class conflict. Of course, this is not the complete argument. Both Myles (1984) and Esping-Andersen (1985) for example, stress the *ultimately* contradictory consequences for capitalism of an expanding welfare state, which Esping-Andersen says entails the "decommodification" of labor power, and which Myles (1984:110–111, 114) says shifts the balance of power between capital and labor (1985, especially chapter 6).

We have no quarrel with giving electoral politics its due. Our query has to do rather with the apparently arbitrary movement between economic and political spheres in explaining different facets of the political dynamics of the welfare state. Thus, great weight is assigned to political democracy in determining the resources for political conflict, and in shaping the collective forms and strategies of conflict. But the underlying interests that structure the conflict are assumed to reflect class interests formed in production relations.[4] If political democracy can be so powerfully formative of the strategies of class conflict, then what theoretical barrier prohibits the possibility that democratic political institutions also create underlying interests, and not merely the resources, forms, and strategies through which class interests are expressed? Public employee unions and senior citizen groups, for example, are demonstrably powerful interests, formed by political relations rather than production relations, and specifically by the relations of the welfare state.

STATE-CENTERED INTERPRETATIONS OF THE (MAINLY AMERICAN) WELFARE STATE

Theda Skocpol and her students propose that the main institutional environment that structures the politics of the welfare state is not the economy, or electoral representative arrangements as such, or the family, but mainly the state bureaucracies and the reform groups and congressional actors to which they are connected (Orloff and Skocpol 1984; Weir and Skocpol 1985; Ikenberry and Skocpol 1987; Skocpol 1988). Most of the work promoting this "state-centered" approach is recent (although its line of argument is strongly linked to both the professional social welfare interpretations referred to at the outset, and to the once-favored outlook of the field of public administration). But the state-centered perspective was not launched with reference to either of its intellectual precedents. On the contrary, its proponents are oriented to the varieties of Neo-Marxist theory that gained ascendance in some quarters in the 1970s. The state-centered approach set out to deal with a quandary created by interpretations that posited the "relative autonomy" of the state, but then invariably explained state policies by reference to the systemic imperatives or political forces generated by capitalist economies, if only in the "last instance." There is, in truth, not much autonomy in relative autonomy theories.

The advocates of the statist approach promised to provide a theoretical remedy. They would concentrate on the distinctive organizational environment of state decision-makers, and show how features of that state environment, and the opportunities, constraints, and incentives generated within it, informed the practices of state actors. This was not, at the outset, promoted as an alternative to interpretations that rooted the politics of the welfare state in the capitalist economy, but rather as a mode of interpretation that would complement neo-Marxist explanations by adding another institutional dimension to the analysis.

As the work of the state-centered advocates developed, however, their mission changed: they fastened singularly on state actors responding to influences generated by state structures, to the point of denying the significance of economic forces, and especially denying the significance of class forces. It is bureaucrats, it turns out, who are the main actors in the formation of welfare state policy, and occasionally legislators, interacting with experts and reform organizations. In their exposition of the evolution of the American social welfare policy in the early twentieth century, for example, Orloff and Skocpol (1984) explicitly dismiss the significance of business as a source of influence; business groups are merely part of a larger network of reform groups, without distinctive interests of their own that might be derived from economic relationships. The reform network as a whole is composed of groups that are described as if they were divorced from economic and class forces (despite the indisputable evidence of the large role played by industrialists and financiers in these reform organizations). Nor are the reformers concerned with economic relationships, and this despite the serious economic disturbances that wracked the country during the early part of this century. Rather the reformers who exerted a determining influence in preventing the establishment of income protections did what they did because they were "wracked" with worry over the patronage abuses that social welfare programs might permit (Orloff and Skocpol 1984). Similarly, in accounting for the development of American welfare state policies in the 1930s, Skocpol (1988) provides an account that simply deletes the popular movements of the unemployed, the aged, and industrial workers, and deletes business influences as well, again in favor of bureaucratic actors influenced by bureaucratic constraints and their reform allies.[5]

The state-centered approach rests on a number of propositions asserting the predominant influence of state structures and state actors at key moments in the evolution of American social welfare policy. Each of these propositions can be challenged on historical grounds. First, the approach emphasizes the formative influence of preexisting state structures on social welfare innovations. Thus, the devolution of the Unemployment Insurance program to the states in the 1930s is said to reflect the historical fact that there already existed state-run unemployment benefit programs. Similarly, the large role assigned to the states in setting benefit and eligibility criteria in the Aid to Dependent Children program is said to reflect the fact the Mothers' Pensions programs already existed in many of the states.

Now there is no question but that preexisting state programs do influence and constrain subsequent policy initiatives. What is at issue is whether this influence is singular and predominant. In fact, only a few states had unemployment benefit programs, and these were new programs at that. Can a few small state programs really carry the burden of explanation attributed to them? Similarly, is it reasonable to give such weighty influence to the puny Mothers' Pensions programs? Notice how easily, and without a stir of political opposition, a whole battery of much larger categorical aid programs was federalized in 1974 with the adoption of the Suplementary Security Income program. In this and other cases, the very informality of the historical comparative method is clearly a danger, for it makes possible the selective use of events to serve the purposes of argument rather than illumination.

The issue can perhaps be illuminated by scrutinizing the historical evidence to discover just who it was that clamored to protect these rather puny policy precedents—to reserve authority over the unemployment insurance or the Dependent Children programs to the states, for example. In our opinion, a far better case can be made for the determining influence of agricultural and business interests who wanted state-run programs to ensure that income protections would not undermine regional wage disparities (see Piven and Cloward 1971; Quadagno 1984; Alston and Ferrie 1985). The more general point is this: The influence of prexisting state structures cannot be understood apart from the social and economic context in which they are embedded.[6] They cannot be understood apart from the interests, including the class interests, that develop a stake in the agency and its policies, and help to determine the direction of bureaucratic interests, and whether bureaucratic interests prevail in political contests. For this reason, bureaucracies are not created equal. As Block (1987) has pointed out, the British Treasury is not just a bureaucracy. It is a bureaucracy tied to British finance.[7] The influence of the Treasury or of any other bureaucracy has to be understood in terms of the economic and social interests with which it is intertwined, and which develop a stake in the agency and its policies. Otherwise, we contemplate the ludicrous prospect of treating bureaucracies as influential because they are bureaucracies, and thus of equating the influence of a treasury agency or a national bank with a program for orphaned children.

Much the same point can be made about the emphasis in state-centered interpretations on the role of experts and reform organizations, to whom state actors are linked. To be sure, there are always experts and reform organizations, and they can always be found to be busy working on the politics of welfare state policies. There is reason to think, in other words, that experts and reformers are more or less ubiquitous. But although experts and reformers may always be busy, their influence rises and falls, and the influence of different experts and reformers rises and falls with changes in political context. Thus, Michael Harrington's book The Other America is widely said to have carried great weight in the formulation of the social welfare policies of the 1960s (Harrington 1962). George Gilder (1981) and Charles Murray (1984) are sometimes said to carry similar weight in the 1980s. To give weight to experts tells us nothing about the widely different political constellations that made these very different experts significant at different historical junctures.

And then there is the proposition that state policies constitute not only a set of structures that delimits future policy developments, but a policy heritage, a set of ideas. This too is almost surely true. But the significance of these ideas is far too narrowly construed when the focus is placed mainly on state actors. The pattern of established state policies has very broad effects on political culture, on the expectations of the citizenry, and on interpretations of the proper relationship of the state to other social institutions, and the "policy heritage" also has effects on the formation and organization of political interest groups, and even on the relations between classes.

Finally, we should note that state-centered interpretations have made broad claims about being engaged in an effort to theorize the state. However, in the main these interpretations have ignored the coercive, judicial, and extractive agencies of the state and concentrated instead on a narrow range of bureaucracies. It is that narrower bureaucratic concentration that explains the emphasis in much of this work on problems of coordination, planning, centralization, policy precedents, expertise, and so on.

Of course, we do have to understand the welfare state as a bureaucratic apparatus, and the renewed attention to it is in this sense all to the good. A decade or so ago, at a time when many of us were enthralled by the functionalist Marxist notions of systemic imperatives, Wolfdeiter Narr enjoined us to try to unravel "the function of the functions." Renewed attention to the welfare bureaucracies could permit us to do just that, to understand how the state bureaucracies work. But that result is unlikely when analysts insist that bureaucracy and its paraphernelia constitute the singular and preeminent institutional determinant of state policy.

FAMILY AND THE POLITICS OF THE WELFARE STATE

The focus on the institutional context of the family has emerged from the work of feminists calling for a specifically gender analysis of broad areas of social life.[8] The study of society has been distorted by the (motivated) failure to pay heed to gender as a category in the construction of social life. Concretely, this has meant attending to the sexual division of labor, to women as political actors, and to the institutional sphere of the family where gender roles are formed and where women's activities have historically been concentrated. And applied to the emergence and evolution of welfare state policies, this orientation has produced substantially new and different interpretations.

Where most of the work on the welfare state emphasizes industrial capitalism, or the capitalist system of production, as the core institutional sphere, much of feminist work emphasizes the family, or reproduction, as the dominant institutional sphere. Welfare state programs can best be understood as enforcing or supporting the male-headed nuclear family, and enforcing or supporting women's several roles as unpaid domestic laborers, as providers of sexual and reproductive services, and as consumers.[9] Welfare state programs also ensure that when women do participate in the labor market, they are concentrated in occupations where they are subordinate to men, and perform "women's work" consistent with family roles. Finally, some feminists assert that a preoccupation with economy, economic classes, and class actors distorts our understanding of the political history of the welfare state. It leads us to ignore the large role of women, informed by family values and acting to defend family roles, as major actors in the origin and evolution of welfare state programs (see Gordon 1988; Shaver 1987).

All of this is provocative and appealing, for obvious reasons. It gives a large role to people who do not usually figure in conceptions of history, and to an institution that does not figure much in the explanation of history. Still, the argument does not stand up well to the evidence. In the history of the United States, market concerns and market actors were overwhelmingly determining in the politics of the welfare state programs. Moreover, we think the same generalization holds for Europe. Rose's (1986) assertion that the English welfare state, including the programs specifically for women and children, was an uneven accommodation between capital and a male-dominated labor movement might as well describe the United States.

This is not to deny that middle-class and upper-class women were active in organizing charities ostensibly dedicated to improving working class family life or socializing working-class children. They were, and their efforts have to be understood as in some sense political, as intended to shape part of the world according to the standards of middle-class women. Similarly, as Gordon (1988) has shown, the stratagems by which working-class women tried to turn these interventions to their own purposes ought also be understood as political efforts. Voluntary service activities are interesting precisely because they reveal something about the attempts of subordinate groups— middle-class and immigrant working-class women alike—to exercise power. But the effort to exercise power under enormously constrained conditions is one thing, and the achievement of power quite another. Overall, in the political history that shaped the main welfare state interventions, no one who mattered, no one who had power, cared much at all about families.

At first glance, there is an abundance of evidence that appears to contradict this proposition. The historical record is studded with expressions of concern about the preservation of the family, about the proper rearing of children, and about family and sexual morality. Moreover, women appear to have been the objects of at least some programs, such as Mothers Pensions and Aid to Dependent Children. And women were sometimes actors as well. Think only of the large role played by late nineteenth-century women reformers, including such historic figures as Jane Addams and Florence Kelly, in campaigns to limit child labor, or to regulate the working conditions of women to prevent any injury to their reproductive capacities, or to prohibit gambling, drunkenness, and prostitution so as to protect family life. What such a cursory overview neglects, however, is the final tally. In the clash with the forces of industrial capitalism, and with the imperatives of industrial capitalism, concerns with the family always gave way, and women reformers were always defeated.

We need to look more closely at the practices that accompanied sanctimonious rhetoric about family life and at the actors who were actually influential in shaping these practices. Consider a relatively early phase in the movement from the old poor law to a modern welfare state—the rise of the scientific charity movement in the 1870s. True, there were some women leaders in the Charity Organization Societies (COS) that led the movement. Josephine Shaw Lowell is a prominent example. But Lowell was hardly a defender of the family when she campaigned fiercely against outdoor relief and advocated leaving people "to the hard working of natural laws" (1972:6). In any case, the COS governing boards were not dominated by women, no matter what their attitudes, but by the corporate and financial magnates who led the post-Civil War rush to industrialize. Their principles, as Zaretsky (1982) says, were not paternalistic or familistic, but individualistic and *laissez-faire*. And their principles matched their interests in increasing the pool of proletarianized labor available to work the expanding railroads and burgeoning manufacturing enterprises. If anything, families might offer some protection against proletarianization. Accordingly, the leaders of scientific charity advocated disrupting impoverished working class families in their war against idleness. The New York Association for the Improvement of the Condition of the Poor summed up the doctrine:

> To keep such families together either by occasional relief or employment, is to encourage their depravity. . . . These nurseries of indolence, debauchery, and intemperance, are moral pests of society and should be broken up. The inmates . . . should be sent to the

Alms-House . . . the children to be educated and apprenticed, and the able-bodied adults sent to work, under such discipline and regulation as would tend to correct their habits, and oblige them to earn their own subsistence.[10]

Or consider the "child saving" campaign of the 1890s. The campaign gave rise to a veritable floodtide of sentimental rhetoric about home and family as the core of civilized society. All of this rhetoric followed quickly, however, on the heels of the successful elimination of outdoor relief in every major city in the country, a reform that was part of a larger effort by industrialists to overcome resistance by workers to mechanization and to the elimination of the role of skilled workers in the production process (Gordon et al. 1982:106 and passim; Piven and Cloward, 1987:14). Inevitably, with the loss of the bit of food and coal provided to some of the unemployed by outdoor relief agencies, workers knuckled under more quickly to the new terms of factory labor. And inevitably, some working-class families, particularly families with only one parent, found themselves unable to care for their children, no matter how loudly the child savers might proclaim their new appreciation of the sanctity of the family. As a result, Katz (1986) reports that 247 new orphanages were incorporated in the 1890s at the peak of the child saving movement.[11] Many of the children in these institutions did in fact have at least one living parent.

Or consider the "mothers pensions" programs that were introduced in many states around the turn of the century. At first glance, this program also seemed to provide evidence for the feminist and family-centered perspective on social welfare (see, for example, Libba Gabe Moore 1986; Abramovitz 1988). After all, women and mothers were the exclusive objects of the programs; the programs were widely promoted specifically because they would make it possible for mothers to keep their children, in contrast to the prior practice of institutionalizing children so that widowed or single mothers could be kept in the labor market; and the specific regulations developed by the states frequently revealed a preoccupation with the proper family and sexual conduct of prospective beneficiaries. Finally, a case can be made that women were important political actors, since reform-oriented middle class women's organizations were active in the state campaigns for pension legislation. These sorts of observations are at least consistent with an interpretation of the mothers' pensions programs in which family roles are of central concern, and women are central actors. Still, the main fact about the mothers' pension programs remains. It is simply that hardly anyone ever got pensions. By 1921, when the programs were reasonably well established, the Childrens Bureau reported that only 55,000 families were receiving pensions in the entire country. Clearly, mothers' pensions did not matter much. Moreover, the grants given to these few women were fixed below wage rates, and were closely calibrated with regional differences in wage rates.[12] The late nineteenth-century policy of eliminating income protections that might relax the discipline of the labor market was clearly still in command, family concerns notwithstanding.

The decades-long fight for child labor laws provides another instance of the clash between families and women on the one hand, and labor market interests on the other. Once more, market interests prevailed. The campaign for laws limiting child labor was waged by women reformers, settlement house workers, some of the clergy, and organized male workers (who wanted to limit competition from cheap and vulnerable child workers). This motley coalition was pitted against southern planters who relied on children in the fields, and against a good many industrialists who also used child labor. And although there were moments when the child advocates seemed to be on the verge of success (the Wicks Bill actually passed the Congress in 1916, only to be declared unconstitutional), it was in fact not until the New Deal that national legislation was enacted that limited the employment of children. It is perhaps needless to add that the 1933 child labor provisions of the National Industrial Recovery Act were more a reflection of the rising influence of organized labor, and of its concern with flooded labor markets, than of the influence of women and of their concern with families.

The 1935 Social Security Act that established the legislative framework of the modern American welfare state was also forged by market forces, and by sharply conflictual market forces. On the one hand, the unemployment and pension provisions of the Act emerged out of the depths of the Depression, and were prompted by the protest movements of the unemployed, industrial workers, and the elderly demanding protection from the vicissitudes of unemployment and extreme destitution. On the other hand, the Act was shaped by businessmen who, once their manifest panic at market collapse and rising street protest during the early 1930s had subsided, were concerned that relatively liberally administered emergency relief programs would erode the discipline of the labor market. True, the legislation that resulted largely took for granted the family wage; coverage and benefits were mainly deter-mined by the work history of typically male heads of households. Relief programs thus reflected and to an extent reiterated dominant family forms, which is of course evidence of how deeply embedded the family wage system was. But it is not evidence that relief programs can be understood as an effort to construct and sustain those forms. Certainly family structure was not at issue in the debates over the legislation. What was at issue was the categories of workers who would be protected, the levels of protection, and the condi-tions attached to those protections. These issues were keenly debated be-cause they affected the relative labor market power of workers and employers, and not because they affected families, which they surely did. In the series of compromises incorporated in the legislation, many workers did win some protection from the uncertainties and hardships that afflict wage workers, including unemployment, disability, and old age. These protections were strictly circumscribed, however. Certain categories of low wage workers were simply excluded from coverage, such as domestic workers and farm laborers (which included many women). And receipt of benefits was conditional on a history of stable participation in the workforce, a restriction intended to shore up market discipline (and one that also worked against women whose work patterns were more likely to be irregular).

For women and children unconnected with men in covered categories, the Act established the Aid to Dependent Children program [later called Aid to Families with Dependent Children (AFDC)]. Much in the history of that program seems to reflect concerns with proper family life. For example, in the 1950s, a number of southern states passed "suitable homes" laws that denied aid to women with illegitimate children. Similarly, many states had varieties of "man-in-the-house" rules that denied aid to women living with men, or even to women known to be consorting with men, and enforced those rules with notorious midnight raids on the homes of AFDC recipients.

But this apparent preoccupation with family morality is deceptive. The main features of the AFDC program were shaped by labor market not family structure concerns. It was to ensure that the program meshed with the disparate requirements of regional labor markets, and particularly with the requirements of regions that relied on large numbers of low wage workers, including women and children workers, that the federal program ceded authority over grant levels and eligibility criteria to the states (Bensel 1984; Piven and Cloward 1971:chapters 4–5). The states then used that authority to implement such provisions as "man-in-the-house" rules, which were almost surely intended to prevent nonmarket income from reaching men in the low wage labor pool. And it was, after all, the southern planters who employed women and children in the fields who were most concerned about the immorality of families on AFDC. Moreover, the solutions to ostensible problems of proper family behavior invariably took market forms. Women cut off the rolls because of their unsuitable homes were forced into the cotten fields, at wages lower than AFDC benefit levels.

The contemporary campaign for welfare reform reveals the same dualistic relationship between a rhetoric dominated by family concerns and actual program changes shaped by labor market concerns. Much of the political rhetoric about the need for welfare reform emphasizes the ostensibly destructive impact of AFDC on patriarchal family forms. Thus, there is said to be a need for reform because AFDC is leading to rising rates of marital breakup and an epidemic of illegitimate births. Neither of these constantly reiterated charges has so far been confirmed by the endless series of studies of the relationship of AFDC to marital stability and illegitimacy rates. Indeed, even the notion of an epidemic of illegimate births turns out on scrutiny to be very much a socially constructed phenomenon. But the uses of family rhetoric in the politics of welfare reform has never depended on empirical evidence.

Meanwhile, as always, the programmatic solutions that accompany this tide of family rhetoric are focused on work, not on the family. Indeed, if the erosion of the patriarchal family is the problem, the remedy is to weaken the matriarchal family as well, by forcing the mothers of young children into the labor market or, if they fail to get jobs, into supervised work regimens. These state "workfare" programs are likely to expand as a result of the passage of legislation in 1988 entitled, consistently enough, "The Family Support Act." The Act will require a good many mothers to place their infant children in some sort of child care while they participate in mandatory job search, training, or work routines. Whatever one thinks of such "reforms, their impact can hardly be to restore the two-parent patriarchal family. And rhetoric aside, it is scarcely the intent of the proponents of such work-enforcing measures to restore that family system. Contemporary welfare reforms are merely a replay of a history of social welfare initiatives in which intensely felt popular concerns with family are evoked to justify programs that shore up labor market discipline. And in the current act of this endless drama, more punitive welfare policies for women are likely to have a large labor market effect because they will drive substantial numbers of women to compete for low wage jobs.

None of this is to deny that there is a politics shaped by family concerns, and that historically women have been preoccupied with the family. But family concerns and family politics have not determined the shape of the main welfare state programs. To the contrary, in the clash with market interests, family interests have consistently given way, and in the clash with market actors, women championing family interests have consistently been defeated.

On the other hand, there are reasons to think that the future may be different. The increased politicization of women together with their large-scale engagement with the welfare state as workers and beneficiaries could mean that "home" values and women actors will make an increasingly large mark on welfare state programs. There is evidence of a broad politicizing of women both in Europe and the United States, particularly in relation to welfare state issues. Since this is a recent development, a far better case can be made that the welfare state has promoted the politicization of women than that women were a significant force in the emergence and evolution of the welfare state. Perhaps the ideology associated with a developed welfare state underlines and reinforces "home values" of nurturance and security.[13] Furthermore, welfare state programs aggregate women as workers and as clients, and thus create new capacities for collective action.[14] And welfare state organizations may provide opportunities for access and leverage on the political system.[15] As the prominence of women in Swedish and Norwegian electoral politics suggests, a developed welfare state may be "women friendly" (Hernes 1987a; see also Korpi 1983:64–67). And if the welfare state is in fact an institutional domain that promotes the politicization and mobilization of women, then women in turn may become more important—indeed, perhaps even major—actors in the *future* development of the welfare state. But none of this argues that women were major actors in the construction of the welfare state, or that the traditional family was the institutional context that patterned the orientations and capacities of those actors who did matter.

THE PROLIFERATION OF INSTITUTIONAL SITES: BACKWARD TO PLURALISM

The tendency to which we now turn is perhaps implicit in the very multiplication of analyses we have just reviewed, for it is in a way a culminating intellectual development. A number of theorists, particularly those who are concerned to explain and legitimize the diversity of "new social movements," have proposed in effect that no institution is preeminent in the patterning of political conflict, whether with regard to welfare state policies or any other set of issues. Offe's formulation exemplifies the tendency:

> My thesis is that under modern capitalist conditions there is no one central condition that causally determines all other conditions in a base-superstructure or primary-secondary manner. The work role is only partly determinative of social existence. For instance, workers' struggles have no necessary priority over conflicts that in some modern Communist Party doctrines are called "popular democratic struggles. . . ." [T]he wage-labour-capital relationship is not the key determinant of social existence, and . . . the survival of capitalism has become increasingly contingent upon non-capitalist forms of power and conflict . . . generated by consumers, clients, citizens or inhabitants of an ecosystem. (Offe 1984:283–285)

And some theorists go beyond a position that proliferates the institutional sites of conflict to argue that institutions do not pattern political conflict at all. Laclau and Mouffe, in their influential book *Hegemony and Socialist Strategy,* assume an extreme antistructuralist stance in their effort to explain the "highly diverse struggles" by "urban, ecological, anti-authoritarian, anti-institutional, feminist, anti-racist, ethnic, regional or sexual minorities" (Laclau and Mouffe 1985:159). Like Offe, they maintain that no institutional site is privileged as the location of political aggregation and conflict. "[T]here is no *last instance* on the basis of which society can be reconstructed as a rational and intelligible structure" (Laclau and Mouffe 1985:94) and "there is no reason to assume that the working class has a privileged role in the anti-capitalist struggle" (p. 104). Rather "it is necessary to start from a plurality of political and social spaces which do not refer to any ultimate unitarian basis" (p. 140).

But if Laclau and Mouffe (1985) begin by asserting that conflict can emerge in multiple sites, none necessarily more important than another, they end by denying that social structure has much relevance at all, except as it defines a series of superordinate/subordinate relationships. Political conflict is not shaped by the variable and specific features of these structured relationships of superordination/subordination—for example, by the degree to which people on either side of the relationship are aggregated or dispersed. Instead, the emergence of political conflict is determined entirely by the extent to which those in subordinate positions acquire "democratic" or "egalitarian" *ideas* that subvert the legitimacy of their domination. In the language of Laclau and Mouffe (1985:89) "the form and essence of objects are penetrated by a basic instability and precariousness, and that is their most essential possibility." Political conflict and the rise of social movements are thus understood as a consequence of the contagious influence of democratic ideas, of the progressive extension of the "equalitarian imaginary" (p. 160) to whole new sets of relationships.

On the other hand, nonegalitarian ideas may also penetrate these various sites: "All struggles, whether those of workers or other political subjects . . . can be articulated to very different discourses. It is this articulation which gives them their character, not the place they come from" (Laclau and Mouffe 1985:169). In other words, diverse subordinated populations are engulfed by a swirl of competing discourses, and the extent to which one or another discourse achieves hegemony is random, or, at least, the success or failure of one or another discourse is independent of social structure. What we have here is a new sort of radical pluralism in which multiple groups, detached from structuring influences, pursue their subjectively defined interests.

There is a certain appeal in this intellectual position. In effect, it asserts that the possibilities of politics are unlimited by institutional structure, indeed unlimited by anything but human imagination. Political struggle against oppression can take place anywhere, by anyone, in a virtual satyricon of radical pluralism. However, the price in explanatory power exacted by this optimistic perspective is high. If anything is possible, it is precisely because of a full scale retreat from the effort to take account of the institutional constraints on political life, including the institutional sources of the discourses that are said to shape political life.

Still, there is something to be said for the more limited argument that there is a multiplicity of institutional sites from which political action may emerge, including the political action that shapes welfare state programs. After all, social life is made up of more than one system of domination, and political struggles clearly do emerge in a variety of institutional contexts. Variable institutional constraints and opportunities, in turn, require complicated explanations of conflict; the conditions that account for the emergence of conflict in one institutional location will not necessarily account for the conflicts that arise in another. The forms and occasions of conflict will be different from one institutional site to another, including the solidarities and cleavages that form the axis of conflict, the grievances that galvanize participants, their strategies of action, as well as the timing of outbreaks and the variable outcomes. All of which indicates that the acknowledgment of multiple sites increases the problems of structural analysis but surely does not eliminate the need for such analysis.

Furthermore, it is not good enough to say that political conflict may arise in a variety of institutional sites, and leave it at that. Although no institution is privileged as the site of political struggle, some institutions are more important than others, and this bears on an understanding of political conflict in two ways. First, in the complex pattern of institutional interdependencies that constitutes society, some institutions are more powerfully formative of the conditions on which other institutions depend. Economies and states matter largely, and surely more than schools or churches. True, the church and state are each capable of generating a distinctive politics, and the politics of each affects the other. But unless the church forms alliances that yield it command of coercive capacities, the state is more likely to be able to suppress the church than the other way around.

In other words, an emphasis on multiple institutional sites can be misleading because it distracts from the complex hierarchical relations between institutions. Conflicts within philanthropic institutions can be superseded by the dependence of philanthropy on corporate giving, for example; conflicts within local governments can be superseded by the subordination of local to national government. This brings us to the second way in which the hierarchy of institutional determinations patterns political conflict. Dominant institutions can influence the conditions for the very emergence of conflict in other institutions, as when strikes are prevented by fear of state reprisals, or student protests are subdued by fear of sanctions that cloud future employment prospects.

In sum, to agree that there is a plurality of institutional sites that generates the politics of the welfare state is not to adopt a pluralist stance, at least not in the simple sense of an analysis that treats the articulated group as the fundamental unit of politics, unanchored to institutional influences. A plurality of institutional sites does not do away with a need for structural analysis, but rather complicates the problem of structural analysis, in at least two ways. It argues the necessity of understanding the roots of particular political conflicts in particular institutional settings, and thus expands the problem of structural analysis. And it also brings to the fore the problem of disentangling the web of simultaneously hierarchical and interdependent relations among institutions that also pattern political conflict. In other words, the recognition that there is a plurality of sites for political struggles requires more complex and discriminating theories of institutional life. We should not march back toward pluralism.

NOTES

1. See Korpi (1983:209) for a discussion of the Swedish Social Democratic concept of the reformist road to socialism in the period between the World Wars.

2. However, Przeworski and Sprague (1988) argue that socialist party efforts to win the electoral support of allies were in fact less vigorous than an optimal electoral strategy would have dictated.

3. A number of Marxist theorists have also made the point that liberal democracy exerts a decisive influence on working class formations, but draw conclusions quite the opposite of those of the social democratic theorists. Beginning with Rosa Luxemburg (1970:202), Marxists have pointed to the fractionalizing effects of electoral participation, for example. Lukacs (1971:65–66), and later Poulantzas (1973), made the similar argument that capitalist democracy individualizes class relations.

4. We should note Offe's (1987) large difference with this position when he argues that the interaction of changing and especially uncertain economic conditions with liberal democracy has had the effect of splintering solidarities, including class solidarities.

5. For empirical and theoretical challenges to this interpretation of the politics of the Social Security Act see Quadagno (1984), Domhoff (1970), Piven and Cloward (1977), and Ferguson (1983, 1984).

6. Or, as Charles Noble writes in another recent critique of the state-centered approach, "Skocpol and associates [refuse] to ground their account . . . within some determinate socioeconomic space" (1988:22).

7. Block's comments (1987) are in reference to Weir and Skocpol 1985.

8. The argument in this section was initially put forward in our debate with Linda Gordon which appears in the Winter 1988 issue of *Social Research*.

9. Various formulations of this argument can be found in Brown (1980), Fraser (1987), and Shaver (1987). On consumption specifically, see Smith (1987). See also Barrett (1983), Boris and Bardaglio (1983), Eisenstein (1981, 1983), McIntosh (1978), Polan (1982), and Wilson (1977).

10. NYAICP, 8th Annual Report, 1851, cited in Abramovitz (1988:145). "True charity," opined a leader in these efforts in 1888, "must seek not only to rescue the home from all base conditions, but often must break-up the unworthy family" (Abramovitz 1988:167).

11. See also Gordon (1988:43–45) for a discussion of commercialized infanticide during this period of "child-saving."

12. Abramovitz (1988:204) reports that in 1931, the average monthly grant ranged from $4.33 in Arkansas to $69.31 in Massachusetts.

13. The emergence of a large attitudinal "gender gap" is perhaps evidence of this sort of confluence between traditional female orientations and the influence of the welfare state. See Piven (1985) for a discussion of this thesis. For survey evidence of the gender gap, see Kenski (1988), Morris (1988), Meuller (1988), Miller (1988), Klein (1985).

14. On the employment of women by welfare state agencies, see Erie and Rein (1988), Erie et al. (1983), and Erie (1983). For a general discussion of the involvement of women with welfare state programs, see Ehrenreich and Piven (1984).

15. For some the recent work on the ideological and political resources yielded women by the welfare state, see Balbo (1987), Borchorst and Siim (1987), Dahlerup (1987), Ergas (1983), Hernes (1987b), Rossi (1983), and Piven (1985).

REFERENCES

Abramovitz, Mimi. 1988. *Regulating the Lives of Women: Social Welfare Policy from Colonial Times to the Present.* Boston: South End Press

Alston, Lee J. and Joseph P. Ferrie. 1985. "Labor Costs, Paternalism, and Loyality in Southern Agriculture: A Constraint on the Growth of the Welfare State." *Journal of Economic History* XIV(1):95–117.

Balbo, Laura. 1987. "Crazy Quilts: Rethinking the Welfare State from a Women's Point of View." Pp. 45–71 in *Women and the State,* edited by Anne Sassoon. London: Hutchinson.

Barrett, Nancy. 1983. "The Welfare System as State Paternalism." Paper presented to Conference on Women and Structural Transformation, Institute for Research on Women, Rutgers University.

Bensel, Richard. 1984. *Sectionalism and American Political Development, 1880–1980.* Madison: University of Wisconsin Press.

Block, Fred. 1987. *Reviewing State Theory.* Philadelphia: Temple University Press.

Borchorst, Ann and Birte Siim. 1987. "Women and the Advanced Welfare State—A New Kind of Patriarchal Power?" Pp. 128–157 in *Women and the State,* edited by A. Sassoon. London: Hutchinson.

Boris, Eileen and Peter Bardaglio. 1983. "The Transformation of Patriarchy: The Historic Role of the State." Pp. 70–93 in *Families, Politics, and Public Policy,* edited by Irene Diamond. New York: Longman, Green.

Brown, Carol. 1980. "Mothers, Fathers, and Children: From Private to Public Patriarchy." Pp. 239–267 in *Women and Revolution,* edited by Lydia Sargent. Boston: Southwood Press.

Cameron, David. 1978. "The Expansion of the Public Economy: A Comparative Analysis." *American Political Science Review* 72(4) (December):1243–1261.

Castles, Francis G. 1982. *The Impact of Parties: Politics and Policies in Democratic Capitalist States.* Berkeley, CA: Sage Publications.

Dahlerup, Drude. 1987. "Confusing Concepts—Confusing Reality: A Theoretical Discussion of the Patriarchal State." Pp. 93–127 in *Women and the State,* edited by Anne Sassoon. London: Hutchinson.

Domhoff, G. William. 1970. *The Higher Circle.* New York: Random House.

Ehrenreich, Barbara and Frances Fox Piven. 1984. "The Feminization of Poverty: When the 'Family-Wage System' Breaks Down." *Dissent* (Spring):162–170.

Eisenstein, Zillah. 1981. *The Radical Future of Liberal Feminism.* New York: Longman, Green.

———. 1983. "The State, the Patriarchal Family, and Working Mothers." Pp. 41–58 in *Families, Politics, and Public Policy,* edited by Irene Diamond. New York: Longman, Green.

Ergas, Yasmine. 1983. "The Disintegrative Revolution: Welfare Politics and Emergent Collective Identities." Paper presented to the Conference on the Transformation of the Welfare State: Dangers and Potentialities for Women, Bellagio, Italy.

Erie, Steve. 1983. "Women, Reagan and the Welfare State." Paper presented to the Women's Caucus for Political Science, Chicago, Illinois, September 1–4.

Erie, Steve and Martin Rein. 1988. "Women and the Welfare State." Pp. 173–191 in *The Politics of the Gender Gap: The Social Construction of Political Influence,* edited by Carol Mueller. Berkeley, CA: Sage Publications.

Erie, Steve, Martin Rein, and B. Wiget. 1983. "Women and the Reagan Revolution: Thermidor for the Social Welfare Economy." Pp. 94–119 in *Families, Politics, and Public Policy,* edited by Irene Diamond. New York: Longman, Green.

Esping-Andersen, Gosta. 1985. *Politics against Markets*. Princeton: Princeton University Press.

Flora, Peter and Arnold Heidenheimer. 1981. *The Development of the Welfare State in Europe and America*. New Brunswick, NJ: Transaction Books.

Fraser, Nancy. 1987. "Women, Welfare and the Politics of Need Interpretation." *Thesis Eleven* 17.

Ferguson, Thomas. 1983. "Party Realignment and American Industrial Structure: The Investment Theory of Political Parties in Historical Perspective." Pp. 1–82 in *Research in Political Economy,* edited by Paul Zarembka. Greenwich, CT: JAI Press.

———. 1984. "From Normalcy to New Deal: Industrial Structure, Party Competition, and American Public Policy in the Great Depression." *International Organization* 38(1):41–94.

Friedland, Roger and Jimy Sanders. 1985. "The Public Economy and Economic Growth in Western Market Economies." *American Sociological Review* 50:4.

Gilder, George. 1981. *Wealth and Poverty.* New York: Basic Books.

Gordon, David, Richard Edwards, and Michael Reich. 1982. *Segmented Work, Divided Workers*. London: Cambridge University Press.

Gordon, Linda. 1988. *Heroes of Their Own Lives.* New York: Viking.

Gough, Ian. 1979. *The Political Economy of the Welfare State.* London: Macmillan.

Harrington, Michael. 1962. *The Other America.* New York: Macmillan.

Heclo, Hugh. 1981. "Toward a New Welfare State?" Pp. 383–406 in *The Development of Welfare States in Europe and America,* edited by Peter Flora and Arnold J. Heiderheimer. New Brunswick, NJ: Transaction Books.

Hibbs, Douglas. 1977. "Political Parties and Macroeconomic Policy." *American Political Science Review* 71(4) (December):1467–1487.

Heclo, Hugh. 1974. *Modern Social Politics in Britain and Sweden: From Relief to Income Maintenance.* New Haven, CT: Yale University Press.

Hernes, Helga. 1987a. *Welfare State and Woman Power.* Norwegian University Press.

———. 1987b. "Women and the Welfare State: The Transition from Private to Public Dependence." Pp. 72–92 in *Women and the State,* edited by Anne Sassoon. London: Hutchinson.

Hibbs, Douglas. 1978. "On the Political Economy of Long-Run Trends of Strike Activity." *British Journal of Political Science* 8:153–75.

Hicks, Alexander and Duane Swank. 1982. "The Domestic and International Political Economy of Welfare Expansion: The Case of 17 OECD Nations, 1960–1971." Paper presented at the annual meeting of the American Political Science Association, St. Louis, MO.

Ikenberry, G. John and Theda Skocpol. 1987. "Expanding Social Benefits: The Role of Social Security." *Political Science Quarterly* 102(3):389–416.

Katz, Michael. 1986. *In the Shadow of the Poor House: A Social History of Welfare in America.* New York: Basic Books.

Kenski, H. 1988. "The Gender Factor in a Changing Electorate." Pp. 38–60 in *The Politics of the Gender Gap: The Social Construction of Political Influence,* Vol. 12, Sage Yearbooks in Women's Policy Studies, edited by Carol Mueller. Beverley Hills, CA: Sage Publications.

Korpi, Walter. 1983. *The Democratic Class Struggle*. London: Routledge & Kegan Paul.

Korpi, Walter and Michael Shalev. 1980. "Strikes, Power and Politics in the Western Nations, 1900–1976." Pp. 301–334 in *Political Power and Social Theory*, Vol. 1, edited by Maurice Zeitlin. Greenwich, CT: JAI Press.

Laclau, Ernesto and Chantal Mouffe. 1985. *Hegemony and Socialist Strategy: Towards a Radical Democratic Politics*. London: The Thetford Press.

Lowell, Josephine Shaw. 1972. "The Friendly Visitor." Pp. 3–10 in *On their Own: The Poor in America*, edited by Rothman, David J., and Sheila M. Rothman. Reading, MA.: Addison-Wesley Publishing Company.

Lukac, Georg. 1971. *History and Class Consciousness*. London: Merlin Press.

McIntosh, Mary. 1978. "The State and the Repression of Women." Pp. 254–289 in *Feminism and Materialism*, edited by A. Kuhn and A. Wolpe. London: Routledge and Kegan Paul.

Myles, John. 1984. *Old Age and the Welfare State: The Political Economy of Public Pensions*. Boston: Little Brown.

Moore, Libba Gabe. 1986. "Mother's Pensions: The Origins of the Relationship between Women and the Welfare State." Unpublished doctoral dissertation, Graduate School, University of Massachusetts.

Morris, Pippa. 1988. "The Gender Gap: A Cross-National Trend?" Pp. 217–234 in *The Politics of the Gender Gap: The Social Construction of Political Influence*. Vol. 12, Sage Yearbooks in Women's Policy Studies, edited by Carol Mueller. Beverley Hills, CA: Sage Publications.

Mueller, Carroll. 1988. "The Empowerment of Women: Polling and the Women's Bloc." Pp. 100–125 in *The Politics of the Gender Gap: The Social Construction of Political Influence*, edited by C. Mueller. Berkeley, Sage Publications.

Murray, Charles. 1984. *Losing Ground*. New York: Basic Books.

Noble, Charles. 1988. "State and Class? Notes on Two Recent Views of the Welfare State." Paper presented at the annual meeting of the American Political Science Association, Washington, D.C.

O'Connor, James. 1973. *The Fiscal Crisis of the State*. New York: St. Martin's Press.

Offe, Claus. 1972. "Advanced Capitalism and the Welfare State." *Politics and Society* 2:4.

———. 1982. *Contradictions of the Welfare States*. Cambridge, MA: MIT press.

———. 1984. "Societal Preconditions of Corporatism and Some Current Dilemmas of Democratic Theory." Working Paper of the Helen Kellogg Institute for International Studies, University of Notre Dame.

———. 1987. "Democracy against the Welfare State: Structural Foundations of Neo-Conservative Political Opportunities." Unpublished, Department of Sociology, University of Bielefeld, Bielefeld.

Orloff, Ann Shola and Theda Skocpol. 1984. "Explaining the Politics of Public Social Spending." *American Sociological Review* 49(6) (December).

Piven, Frances Fox. 1985. "Women and the State: Ideology, Power and the Welfare State." Pp. 265–287 in *Gender and the Life Course*, edited by Alice Rossi. Hawthorne, NY: Aldine.

Piven, Frances Fox and Richard A. Cloward. 1971. *Regulating the Poor: The Functions of Public Welfare*. New York: Pantheon.

————. 1977. *Poor People's Movements*. New York: Pantheon.

————. 1985. *The New Class War*, revised and enlarged edition. New York: Pantheon.

————. 1987. "The Historical Sources of the Contemporary Relief Debate." Pp. 3–44 in *The Mean Season: The Attack on the Welfare State*, Fred Block, Richard A. Cloward, Barbara Ehrenreich, and Frances Fox Piven. New York: Pantheon.

Polan, D. 1982. "Toward a Theory of Law and Patriarchy." Pp. 294–303 in *The Politics of Law*, edited by D. Kairys. New York: Pantheon.

Poulantzas, Nicos. 1973. *Political Power and Social Classes*. London: Nw Left Books.

Przeworski, Adam. 1985. *Capitalism and Social Democracy*. London: Cambridge University Press.

Przeworski, Adam and John Sprague. 1988. *Paper Stones: A History of Electoral Socialism*. Chicago: The University of Chicago Press.

Quadagno, Jill. 1984. "Welfare Capitalism and the Social Security Act of 1935." *American Sociological Review* 49(5):632–647.

Rose, Hilary. 1986. "Women and the Restructuring of the Welfare State." Pp. 80–95 in *Comparing Welfare States and their Futures*, edited by Else Oyen. Aldersdhot, Hants: Gower.

Rossi, Alice. 1983. "Beyond the Gender Gap: Women's Bid for Political Power." *Social Science Quarterly* 64:718–733.

Shalev, Michael. 1983. "The Social Democratic Model and Beyond: Two Generations of Comparative Research on the Welfare State." *Comparative Social Research* 6:315–351.

————. 1987. "The Political Economy of Employment-Based Social Protection in Israel." Unpublished, Department of Sociology and Anthropology, The Hebrew University of Jerusalem.

Shaver, Sheila. 1987. "Gender, Class and the Welfare State: The Case of Income Security." Unpublished, Sociology Program, Graduate Center, City University of New York.

Skocpol, Theda. 1988. "The Limits of the New Deal System and the Roots of Contemporary Welfare Dilemmas." Pp. 293–311 in *The Politics of Social Welfare in the United States*, edited by Margaret Weir, Ann Shola Orloff, and Theda Skocpol. Princeton: Princeton University Press.

Smith, Joan. 1987. "Transforming Households: Working-Class Women and Economic Crisis." *Social Problems* 34:416–436.

van Arnhem, J. Corinia M., and Geurt J. Schotsman. 1982. "Do Parties Affect the Distribution of Incomes? The Case of the Advanced Capitalist Democracies." Pp. 283–364 in *The Impact of Parties: Politics and Policies in Democratic Capitalist States*, edited by Francis G. Castles. Berkeley: Sage.

Weir, Margaret and Theda Skocpol. 1985. "State Structures and the Possibilities for 'Keynesian' Responses to the Great Depression in Sweden, Britain, and the United States." Pp. 107–163 in *Bringing the State Back In*, edited by Peter B. Evans, Dietrich Rueschemeyer, and Theda Skocpol. London: Cambridge University Press.

Wilensky, Harold I. 1975. *The Welfare State and Equality: Structural and Ideological Roots of Public Expenditures*. Berkeley: University of California Press.

Wilensky, H. and C. Lebeaux. 1965. *Industrial Society and Social Welfare*. Glencoe, IL: Free Press.

Wilson, Elizabeth. 1977. *Women and the Welfare State*. London: Tavistock.

Zaretsky, Eli. 1982. "The Place of the Family in the Origins of the Welfare State." Pp. 188–224 in *Rethinking the Family*, edited by Barrie Thorne and Marilyn Yalom. New York: Longman.

John Myles

In the twentieth century, what it means to be young, middle-aged, or old, indeed what it means to be a man or a woman, has continuously been redefined by labor markets and states. Changing practices of labor force management and the rise of welfare states have altered the way individuals and families articulate their lives with both the economy and society. With the advent of industrial capitalism and the expansion of labor markets, the life course of most people became linked to the wage–work contract.[1] The result is that as capitalism evolves and the structure of labor demand changes, the flow of events and life transitions we call the life course (Hagestad and Neugarten 1985) changes as well.

Two major events of the twentieth century illustrate this claim. The first was the social construction of retirement as a way of managing the labor force of an *industrial* economy and the resulting transformation of old age into a social category to which one gains access on reaching an officially prescribed pensionable age (Graebner 1980; Myles 1984). The second, more recent, change is the incorporation of women into the paid work force as a way of managing the labor requirements of a postindustrial labor market and a *service* economy. Both changes required the involvement of states. Whether one is allowed to become "old"—that is, to retire—at age 60 or 65 and how well one lives thereafter are matters largely determined by public policy. Similarly, public policy determines the ease with which women enter the wage labor force as well as the quality of jobs and wage levels available to them.

If, then, life courses—and even identities—are constructed at the intersection of labor markets and states, this implies that the kinds of research questions we will be called on to address over the next decade depend on emergent trends in both spheres. But emergent trends are notoriously difficult to identify. First, they are difficult to measure since large historical shifts are usually the accretion of many small changes that are difficult to detect empirically. Second, once they are observed, it is generally impossible to know whether what one is observing is an emergent trend, a blip in a cycle, or simply random noise in the process of world historical change.

Identifying trends in labor markets, states, and life cycles is difficult, but identifying the nature of their intersection—the relationships among these spheres—is hazardous. Few would disagree that "politics matters" in the social construction of the life course or that an "economics of the life course" is a necessary ingredient for understanding the way we live out our lives. It is when we attempt to unravel the nature of the intersection between the political and the economic—the domain of *political economy*—that theoretical tempers begin to flare. Neoclassical and marxist economists, institutional sociologists, and their many related schools of thought differ sharply over these matters. Nevertheless, it is important to make the effort, even if we are often wrong, for normative as well as analytical reasons. Some trends, after all, should never be allowed to emerge, and early detection—before a pattern becomes institutionalized—increases the chances for a successful cure. Many of my examples and empirical observations are based on recent Canadian experience. These observations are often placed in comparative context but I have made no special effort to "Americanize" my discussion. By and large the patterns in the two countries differ more in detail and political rhetoric than they do in substance.[2] Comparative evidence is drawn on to illustrate variations in trends and to identify alternative possible outcomes of these developments.

Though based on empirical studies conducted in all three areas over the last decade, my purpose in this paper is reflective and speculative. One way of going about such an exercise is to begin with a general theory and in a rigorous deductive way let it tell us what *should* be happening under the present circumstances. Among my major assumptions, however, is that we are in a period of transition, a time when "the parameters that create regularity in routine periods are themselves in flux and unsettled, and consequently behavior becomes unpredictable" (Cohen and Zysman 1987:88). Under these conditions outcomes cannot be deduced. As Mahon (1989:1) concludes: "[T]he best that scholars can do is to attempt to discern the broad outlines of possible alternatives from the contradictory tendencies at work, and indicate the possible consequences associated therewith."

This paper deals with two of these apparent tendencies: the so-called "crisis of the welfare state" and ongoing transformations in the labor market that, in the North American context, have been captured in the metaphor of "the declining middle class." The first tendency has to do with states and the second with labor markets. Typically, discussions and debates over these developments have been conducted independently of one another. One of my objectives is to establish the links between them.

The *consequence* that gives the paper its focus is the life cycle and especially the gendered character of the life cycle. The ideal-typical fordist life cycle I describe below was initially constructed with men in mind. Now a variety of alternatives lie before us. The selection among these alternatives is particularly consequential for the way relationships between men and women will be constructed in the future. Before leaping into the future, however, it is necessary to return to the (very recent) past.

CONSTRUCTING THE FORDIST LIFE CYCLE

As developed by the French regulation theorists (Aglietta, Boyer, and Lipietz) and those who draw on this perspective, fordism was a form of capitalism that emerged out of the Depression and World War II based on mass production technologies, on the one hand, and the extension of mass consumption on the other (Jenson 1989). The distinguishing features of regulation theory are its emphases on the historically contingent character of particular sets of institutional arrangements that stabilize or "regulate" (contradictory) social relations and the interconnectedness of new forms of economic organization with other social and political institutions (Lipietz 1988). History is filled with "branching points" (Piore and Sabel 1984:38) not inevitability. Thus, "fordism" was a contingent not a necessary development in modern capitalism. And its adoption brought with it new ways of organizing both political and social life to accommodate it.

Because of the high fixed overhead costs and inflexibility of production techniques associated with mass production, firms investing in these technologies require stable and growing markets to absorb their output. The key to investment is consumer demand rather than changes in the cost of labor and other factor inputs (Piore and Sabel 1984:76–77). The solution to this problem was the so-called fordist mode of regulation: by linking wage increases to rising real rates of productivity, the working class would be able to consume what it produced. In the United States, the prototype for this arrangement was the wage-setting formula negotiated between General Motors and the UAW in 1948.

The fordist wage relation was not just a way of regulating wage conflict at a point in time. By itself, this would have solved nothing. The object was not to maintain demand in the short term but to stabilize product markets over the long term. Rather, it involved the creation of a system of *wage stabilization* to smooth the flow of income to workers over the life course and the flow of profits to corporations over the ups and downs of the business cycle. This was accomplished with

1. historically high (and rising) real wage rates;
2. public, corporate, and union policies to ensure stability of employment;

3. public, corporate, and union policies to provide high levels of wage
    replacement during labor force interruptions associated with illness
    and unemployment;
4. an extensive period of retirement with a "retirement wage" sufficient
    to maintain past living standards.

The fordist life cycle was constructed around a system of wage stabilization
at historically high standards of living that eliminated the "cycle of poverty"
(Rowntree 1901) traditionally associated with the working class life course.[3]
In the history of western capitalism, this "embourgeoisement" of the working class—the extension of living standards and income security traditionally associated with civil servants and salaried white-collar workers to
the industrial working class—was a development of major historical significance. At its construction, it was seen as bringing the "end of ideology" (Bell
1960) and with it an end to class conflict.

The construction of the fordist life cycle depended on transformations not
only in industrial relations practices but also in state policy. Traditional
welfare states designed to provide *social assistance* to the "poor" were not
enough. The purpose of the postwar *social security* welfare state became
that of providing income security—that is, wage replacement—to a now
high wage working class and to a growing strata of white-collar professional,
technical, and managerial workers. Similarly, the state, not employers, acquired responsibility for ensuring high and stable levels of employment.

State policy, and politics more generally, also established the extent to
which the fordist life cycle was made widely available. Where organized
labor was strong, as in Scandinavia, states tended to intervene more in the
wage-setting process and in organizing income and labor market security
programs (Panitch 1981). Where organized labor was weak, as in Canada and
the United States, the full benefits of the fordist life cycle were made available
to part but not all of the labor force—workers in the "core" mass production
industries, state sector workers, and the professionals and managers of an
expanding "new middle class." For workers not located in the core, the
postwar welfare state is in many respects very much like the "social assistance" welfare state of the prewar era.[4] This "dual labor market" welfare
state characteristic of the Anglo-American democracies (Kahn and Kamerman 1983–84; Myles 1988a; Esping-Andersen 1989) means that to have full
and direct access to the fordist life cycle, it is not sufficient to be a citizen. One
also has to be a member of the primary or core sector of the economy where in
addition to public social benefits one has access to employer-sponsored but
state-subsidized "private" insurance plans and other fringe benefits.

At its inception, this fordist life cycle was considered to be a life cycle for
adult males. Men would have high levels of employment at high wages and
be allowed to retire with a retirement wage. Women and children would live

mainly from the wages and be supported by the income security programs made available to men. These programs would often be supplemented to take account of the presence of an economically dependent female at home.

THE RISE AND DEMISE OF THE FORDIST LIFE CYCLE

The period since World War II has been made up of a set of countervailing trends, but at least until the end of the 1960s the fordist life cycle was in the ascendancy. Employment in the manufacturing sector, where the fordist life cycle was constructed, was in *relative* decline almost from the beginning but, until the 1980s, it was not in decline in any absolute sense. Rather, employment in manufacturing was not increasing as rapidly as employment in services (Picot 1986). This meant that until the 1980s, there continued to be opportunities for young males—especially uncredentialled young males—to gain access to high paying jobs in traditional mass production industries.

Through the 1950s and 1960s, the shift to service employment also spread the fordist life cycle. The major change in this period was the growth of state sector employment—public administration in the 1950s and the "welfare state" industries (health education and welfare) in the 1960s. As O'Connor (1973) pointed out, wage and employment patterns in this sector tended to mimic those in the core—they were constructed around the pattern of the fordist life cycle of high wages, income security, employment stability, and a retirement wage. (A more historically accurate statement is that the fordist life cycle initially mimicked wage and employment patterns traditionally available to state workers.) This was extremely important since it made a fordist life cycle available to many women (indeed this is the only place it is made available to women on a large scale) and to a growing pool of credentialled males. Finally, the social security benefits of the welfare state were being extended to a growing share of the labor force and to the population as a whole.

The countervailing trends and their development are also familiar. At its inception, the fordist life cycle was considered to be a life cycle for adult males. But as mass production industries became more efficient, rising real incomes created a demand for more services.[5] This in turn opened the way for the rapid growth of female employment, a trend enhanced by the greater potential for productivity growth in the machine-based industries. As women gained financial independence through the labor market, it became possible for more of them to achieve sexual independence as well, that is, to live independently of a male "bread-winner." The result is that the implicit social model for fordist *reproduction*—the famous suburban nuclear family of the 1950s—became less common and the social and economic institutions that were premised on such a model less viable. The consequence, however, is the growing pauperization of women and children (Ross and Sawhill 1975). As women gain access to independent incomes, the probability they will exit from abusive or undesirable relationships rises dramatically. However, these incomes typically provide comparatively low living standards relative to those of men. In the past, the economic subordination of women was "hidden in the household," concealed by the practice of incorporating the wages of male partners into the measurement of women's economic status. As family forms have changed, however, this economic subordination has become more visible.

Second, at the end of the 1960s public sector expansion, the major source of good jobs in the service sector came to an end. Thereafter, service sector growth shifted to the low wage, low skill consumer services and to business services (a more polarized sector providing a mix of both "good" and "bad" jobs).[6] The major impact of this was on new entrants to the labor force. Unlike the 1960s, when young workers shared in the expansion of professional, technical, and managerial jobs, young workers in Canada actually lost ground in the 1970s despite rising educational credentials. This was reflected both in a declining share of young people in professional occupations (Myles 1988b) and a shift in the age–earnings profile (Kennedy 1987) to the detriment of young workers.

The 1980s also brought a genuine process of "deindustrialization." Employment in manufacturing began to decline not just as a share of total employment but in absolute terms as well. The manufacturing jobs lost during the deep recession of the early 1980s were not recovered when the economy moved out of recession after 1983. Over 1981–1986 the pattern of job creation was that captured in Kuttner's (1983) evocative imagery of the "declining middle class": There was growth at the bottom and the top of the wage distribution but decline in the middle.[7] The most disturbing element was the continuing deterioration in the position of the young who absorbed almost all of the bad jobs added to the economy.[8]

The 1970s also brought "the crisis of the welfare state," the political foundation of the fordist life cycle. The main symptom of the "crisis" was the breakdown of the Phillips curve trade-off between inflation and unemployment. Traditionally, when labor demand was strong enough to create inflation-generating wage pressure, discipline was restored with restrictive fiscal policies to raise unemployment levels. In the 1970s, it appeared this strategy was no longer working. The result was "stagflation": wage pressure, inflation, and unemployment could all rise together.

The welfare state was thought to be implicated in this development. Welfare states—or at least the social security side of welfare states—immunize workers from market forces, increase their bargaining power, and generally skew the capital–labor relation in favor of labor. Because of unemployment insurance and other benefits, the impact of rising unemployment on wage demands and labor militancy is muted. The result is continued wage pressure, inflation, and a profit squeeze. Since the welfare state was part of the problem, it was thought that dismantling the welfare state must be part of the solution.

It is now fairly clear, however, that the welfare state is unlikely to be dismantled overnight. Even the most determined ideologues (Reagan, Thatcher) have demonstrated their inability to do this. But it is less evident that we have not begun a long, slow process of welfare state erosion—a sort of incrementalism in reverse. Welfare state expenditures have continued to rise in all capitalist democracies (Banting 1987) but at a decelerating rate over a period when demand for assistance in many countries and regions has been growing (Moscovitch 1986). And though the welfare state has not been submitted to radical surgery, it has undergone a great deal of what Wolfson (1987) calls "modest tinkering." In particular, there has been a significant shift of the tax burden for the welfare state into the lower end of the income distribution in Canada, Britain, and the United States.

More significant is the fact that the once expected convergence in welfare state structures and programs failed to materialize. In the early to mid-1970s, welfare state innovation came to a halt in virtually all capitalist democracies. Countries that did not have major welfare state institutions in place (e.g., health care in the United States) do not have them today. Institutions that were seriously underdeveloped (e.g., old age pensions in Canada) have not been improved even in the face of broad consensus on the need for reform. The comparative lethargy in welfare state reform is even more problematic in light of the emergent labor market and family trends identified above. As new problems have arisen (e.g., the growth in single parent families), the welfare state has not responded with new programs or strategies to meet them.

In sum, the labor market institutions, family arrangements, and state policies on which the fordist life cycle was constructed appear to be threatened. The relative decline of the fordist life cycle, the fact that there is the possibility that in the future it will be a privilege of the few rather than of the many, has produced a variety of responses. Conservatives have welcomed this development; many liberals see it as inevitable. In view of prevailing forms of family organization, emergent labor market trends, and the growing importance of competing in international markets, it is unrealistic, many argue, to expect the labor market to provide everyone with the high and rising real wage levels we came to expect in the past. Under these conditions, the state cannot afford to "waste" scarce transfer dollars on the middle classes (i.e., on social insurance and public services). A fundamental requirement of the welfare state of the 1990s and beyond, according to the Canadian Council on Social Development (1987:5), a major antipoverty lobby, is "to find acceptable ways of accommodating this form of economic development." The welfare state must be adjusted to the new reality of a service economy, single-parent families, and flexible, low wage, labor market through better targeting of benefits for the poor. Instead of a universal system of income security for a nation of high wage workers, the welfare state of the future will have to provide subsistence to a growing number of low wage workers.

So, it seems, we are moving naturally, almost inevitably, toward a new kind of labor market, a new kind of welfare state and, as a result, a new kind of modal life cycle for many and perhaps the majority. Instead of the predictable, orderly pattern that life course implied, it is now claimed that the life course is becoming increasing disorderly and fragmented.[9] Instead of representing a way of life that would soon be accessible to all, the security, stability, and affluence associated with the fordist life cycle, it is argued, is becoming the privilege of the few. The scenario appears to be one of increasing polarization. Mike Davis' (1984:27) depiction of a future America polarized between the masses "huddled around their K-Marts" and the minority consuming designer clothes, sports cars, and posh restaurants is just one of the more vivid.

Such scenarios are undoubtedly *possible* outcomes of the current transition and in some countries (e.g., Canada and the United States) may even be the most probable (Mahon 1987). But they do not represent the only alternatives available and in some countries (e.g., Sweden) appear highly unlikely. To determine these alternatives, it is necessary to outline the nature of the transition underlying these trends.

The argument has two parts. The first concerns the "crisis of the welfare state." Departing from much of the conventional "crisis" literature, I argue that the symptoms of crisis that began to appear in the 1970s did not mark the beginning of the end of the welfare state. Rather, the particular welfare state regime put in place in Canada, the United States, and the other Anglo-American democracies after World War II has reached an impasse. Welfare states are ensembles of social practices and strategic understandings designed to resolve historically specific problems of harmonizing the production of wealth with its distribution. Welfare states become *stuck,* unable to go forward or backward, when they no longer provide such solutions.

My second purpose is to locate the problems that current welfare state practice is unable to resolve. Here my argument is that symptoms of "crisis" in the welfare state and the broader labor market trends I have described are products of a period of postindustrial transition. Though such an argument privileges the "economic" over the political, it does so in a particular way. The "economic" defines the possibilities and alternatives that are open to the future but does not determine the choice among them. The selection process is a function of politics, a point to which I return in the conclusion.

The Impasse of the Welfare State[10]

Since the 1970s, it has been commonplace on both the left and the right to describe the welfare state and the capitalist state more generally as being in crisis. The crisis metaphor was invoked not to describe a particular state of the welfare state, such as a situation in which the gap between revenues and expenditures was growing (Block 1981). Rather, the term was used by O'Connor (1973) and others to describe a process that is self-destructive. A system may said to be in crisis in this sense when doing those things that are imperative for the system's reproduction sets in motion processes and events that destroy the conditions necessary for the system's own survival.[11] As Hernes (1976) shows, both nature and history are replete with such processes. Well known examples include Marx's analysis of the transition from feudalism to capitalism and biological and social models of ecological succession. The question is whether this sort of model is the appropriate one for describing the current situation? For a variety of reasons, I think the answer is no.

First, dismantling the welfare state has not been necessary. This is because the problem in which the welfare state was implicated—inflation-generating wage pressure—was successfully tamed through accentuated use of more traditional monetary, fiscal, and labor policies.[12] Second, as conservatives learned when they come to power, dismantling those sectors of the welfare state that incorporate the middle classes (such as Social Security in the United States) is extremely difficult and unlikely to lead to continued electoral success. Third, and most important, even conservatives now seem to recognize that returning to Adam Smith's heaven of a pure self-regulating market without any welfare state at all is at best a utopian fantasy (we cannot "go back") and, at worst, destructive. As Polanyi (1944) pointed out, markets need welfare states or people will die, revolt, or both. It is not a question of having a welfare state or not but rather what *kind* of welfare state.

If the welfare state is not in crisis in the conventional sense, this does not mean nothing has changed. In Michael Mendelson's (1986) provocative formulation, it would appear that sometime in the mid-1970s social policy "died." He does not mean that national social programs are dead or that the cost-cutters have won the battle. Nor does he mean that social policy questions are no longer of interest. Rather he is drawing an analogy to a dispute of the 1960s in which philosophers and theologians debated the question: "Is God dead?" The dispute was neither about the biological demise of God nor about whether religious belief was declining but whether there was a meaningful role for God in the context of a highly educated scientific society. What stimulated the debate was not a failure in belief or declining attendance at churches; rather it was the failure to find any relevant applications for religious ideas in an age of science.

Mendelson's point is that social policy is dead in precisely the same way. It is not a matter of whether people are undertaking policy research or whether social policy is of interest to the popular media. Rather it is a question of relevant application: How useful is social policy in helping us decide what kind of society we will have in the future? The answer, according to Mendelson, is not very much. The liberal reformist paradigm is exhausted: new and better social programs that will make us healthier or more equal no longer seem part of the *general* strategy to solve the problems that confront us but merely an expression of do-gooder sentiment. The conservative agenda is utopian in the sense that for both political and theoretical reasons it can neither be tested nor implemented. Hence, it is of no practical relevance to the current situation. The result is that we are at an impasse. Both sides have won a few and lost a few in the past several years but, on balance, we have gone nowhere.

A situation like this may be thought of as analogous to Kuhn's (1962) description of the way paradigms eventually break down and are transcended in science. An established paradigm allows "normal science" to proceed for a while but eventually begins to generate problems or encounter questions for which it has no answer. Solving the problem requires more than additive adjustment to the theory: the scientist has to come to view the world in a fundamentally different way. Hernes (1976:536–540) shows that many social processes, as well as the history of science, can be characterized as "problem-generating structures" of this sort. The notion here is that a particular form of social organization (or social paradigm) may solve old problems and generate new ones simultaneously.

Welfare states are like this. The history of welfare states is not one of linear evolution but of rearrangements of the ways states intervene to organize the distribution of wealth and income. And particular welfare state regimes have generally been introduced as particular responses to specific historical problems related to production. In the nineteenth century, the "poorhouse welfare state" was created to encourage a reluctant population to enter a nascent industrial labor force (Bendix 1956; Piven and Cloward 1971). In the mid-twentieth century the big problem was not creating labor markets but stabilizing product markets for mass-produced consumer goods. Systems of wage stabilization—the social security welfare state—helped to solve this problem. The fact that social policy seems to be "dead," that countries such as Canada and the United States with incomplete and underdeveloped social security systems are not bringing them to maturity suggests this particular strategy for harmonizing the production of wealth with its distribution is no longer working. This in turn has generated a search for a new paradigm, a new kind of welfare state regime that would be compatible with a new wave of productivity, growth, and accumulation. Welfare states are designed to solve distributional problems of course, but in ways that simultaneously solve new problems of production and accumulation or are at least compatible with such solutions. So what are the sorts of problems the next welfare state must address? My argument, like Block's (1987a:27), is that "the exhaustion of the traditional repertoire of policy responses can best be understood as products of a period of postindustrial transition."

THE TRANSITION TO POSTINDUSTRIALISM

In its original incarnation, the concept of postindustrialism was deployed by mainstream practitioners of what Giddens (1976) calls "industrialization" theory to make sense of emergent trends and patterns that were inconsistent with the conventional concepts and categories of this perspective. If emergent trends could not be adequately understood with a theory derived from "the logic of industrialism" (Kerr et al. 1964), then presumably a theory based on "the logic of postindustrialism" was necessary (Bell 1973).

My use of the term is less ambitious. As Block (1987a:27) observes, the concept of *postindustrialism* (like post-Keynesian or post-Fordist) is a negative one. It does not designate the kind of economy or society we are moving toward but only the kind of economy and society we are leaving behind. It means simply that societies have moved beyond "industrialism"—an historical not a logical category. But my use of the term also differs from Block's for whom postindustrialism represents "the development of new productive forces that come into conflict with capitalist social relations" (Block 1987a:107). It is not *capitalist* social relations per se that are threatened by postindustrialism but a particular historical form of those relations. The fordist model of industrialization and mode of regulation that is now breaking down describes a particular period of capitalist development.

By itself, however, the empirical terrain subsumed by the fordist metaphor is too narrow. As Mahon (1987) observes, the analyses of postwar labor markets that derive from this perspective (e.g., Piore and Sabel 1984) have been constructed largely around blue-collar work in manufacturing. The distinctive feature of advanced capitalist labor markets, however, is the fact that most employment is now in the service sector, a result of the greater potential for productivity growth in the machine-based industries. This dimension of the transition has been captured in the concept of the "service economy"; but it too is limited in scope, suggesting that manufacturing no longer matters. Manufacturing does matter both as a generator of wealth and of employment (Cohen and Zysman 1987). The point is rather that manufacturing now generates more information and data-based occupations (engineers, lawyers, accountants, designers, clerks) and the "direct producers"—craft workers and factory operatives—continue to decline. The concept of postindustrialism is sufficient to capture both the changing nature of goods production and the rise in employment in services. But, more importantly, it captures in historical terms the process underlying these tendencies; and, here, I return to Block.

The key insight of the "postindustrial" metaphor is that "most developed societies—both capitalist and state Socialist—face a transition from industrial society, organized around the production of goods, to postindustrial society, organized around the provision of services and advanced technologies that release labor from direct production" (Block 1987a:99–100). The implication is that we now face (indeed have been facing for some time) a transition directly analogous to the transition from an agricultural to an industrial economy. Traditionally, 50–70% of the adult male labor force was required to produce the food required for societal survival. Today that figure has fallen to 3–4% of the labor force.

The trend in manufacturing has been similar. In Canada, where the shift to a "service economy" is most advanced, less than 20% of the labor force is now directly engaged in manufacturing and 30% in the entire goods sector (agriculture, manufacturing, resource extraction, construction) of the economy. In the brief period between 1981 and 1986, the percentage of full time equivalent jobs in processing, fabricating, and machining occupations declined from 17.7% to 14.9% of all jobs (Myles et al. 1988:52). In turn, rising productivity in goods production is releasing labor for other things. This includes not only increasing employment in services but also the possibility of less employment and, as a result, the possibility for the construction of a new kind of life cycle. In short, rising productivity raises the issue of how the labor time that is released from goods production will be organized.

Postindustrialism, then, highlights three critical dimensions of the current transition: a transformation in the character of goods production, the growth of employment in services, and changes in the volume of paid labor time. In the following sections, I consider each in turn. My purpose is a modest one: to lay out the alternatives before us. To do this I draw ideal types that both exaggerate and simplify the contrasts. The justification is that such an exercise aids clarification.

Flexibility: The Slogan of the Transition

To begin, we can consider Piore and Sabel's (1984) conclusion that for a whole series of reasons the Fordist mass production–mass consumption paradigm has broken down, at least for the first world. Mass production is based on combining semiskilled labor with product-specific machinery to produce a large volume of standardized goods for homogeneous markets. As Mahon (1989:5) writes: "The fordist regime of accumulation centered on the mutually reinforcing (at least for a while) connection between productivity rises associated with the system of mass production and mass consumption, including the working class's ability to consume what it produced." The "crisis" of fordism refers to the fact that this virtuous circle between consumption and production is breaking down. The emergent and increasingly successful technologies (specialty steels in Germany, textiles in Italy) combine skilled labor with general purpose machinery to produce small batches for specialized markets. New technologies allow producers to realize "economies of scope"—volume production of a *variety* of goods—rather than "economies of scale"—volume production of a single good (Cohen and Zysman 1987:130). The system of "flexible specialization" that results from this strategy is the antithesis of the rigidities (i.e., stability) embedded in the mass production model.

Piore and Sabel's analysis bears a striking resemblance to another, more famous, diagnosis of our present situation. The contrast they draw between the "rigidities" and "inflexibilities" of the Fordist system sounds remarkably like the complaints of conservatives who seek less regulation and more "flexible" labor markets by limiting the rights of labor unions and adjusting the welfare state to "improve" labor response to the price mechanism. Indeed, Cohen and Zysman observe (1987:156), *flexibility* has become the slogan of the current transition. Despite disagreement over causes and solutions, the implication is that the emergent production problem is the capacity of an economy to handle change; not just to absorb change but to stimulate it. The strategic choice now faced in manufacturing is not *whether* but *how* to adapt to this new situation.

The conservative solution to the problem of "flexibility is well known. The fordist institutions that encourage stability also introduce rigidities both in the labor market and on the shop floor. The welfare state, by stabilizing wages, immunizes workers from market forces reducing "response time" to market signals. Welfare states, regulations, and unions, create sticky wages at the bottom of the labor market (preventing the creation of low wage jobs) and too much wage equality (limiting mobility between regions and industries). In sum, the security and equality afforded by the welfare state are obstacles to innovation. Both the Reagan and Thatcher "revolutions" have been experiments in the application of this analysis. But it is not the only strategy available.

The solution traditionally offered by social democrats and by a growing number of neoinstitutional economists and economic sociologists is a welfare state that provides more equality and more security for workers (see especially Aberg 1984, 1986). At least since the Myrdals, it has been part of social democratic lore that the welfare-efficiency "trade-off" would be a positive sum precisely because of the labor flexibility and responsiveness to innovation more equality and security would bring (Esping-Andersen 1989). Insecure workers threatened by job loss or a shift from high to low wage work will naturally (and correctly) resist innovation. In contrast, workers confronted with an egalitarian wage distribution and security of employment will welcome and promote structural change. A growing body of neoinstitutionalist economic analysis suggests that this is indeed the case.[13] Streeck, for example, concludes that flexible specialization is not only facilitated by but requires a high wage, full employment economy.[14] It is also the strategy that has been followed for many years by firms such as IBM in their internal labor markets.

It seems we are confronted by a contradiction or at least a paradox. On the one hand, neoclassical orthodoxy asserts that flexible labor markets require workers to be exposed to market forces and, on the other, the neoinstitutionalists and social democrats argue that innovation and flexibility are enhanced by security and equality. The paradox, however, rests on two rather different notions of flexibility. The capacity to change and innovate *may* mean that skilled workers equipped with the appropriate technologies are able to apply these skills and technologies on a *continuous* basis to improve product quality, to change products to accommodate changing markets, and to adopt—even to create—new technologies. But flexibility may also mean the ability to lay off workers, lower wages, and contract out to nonunionized firms. The first—dynamic flexibility—is defined by Cohen and Zysman (1987:131) as the ability to increase productivity steadily through improvements in production processes and innovation. The second—static flexibility—is defined as the ability of firms to adjust operations (release workers, raise or lower wages) at any moment to shifting conditions in the market. Whereas the former strategy requires a high skill, high wage work force with security of employment, the latter requires a low wage, unskilled, disposable labor force. The flexibility it offers is characterized as "static" for two reasons. First there is a tendency to adopt new technologies at a slower rate (low labor costs reduce incentives to innovate) and, second, innovation occurs in a series of successive plateaus rather than on a continuous basis. The point, of course, is that there is nothing inherent in the new technologies that determines a priori which of these forms will prevail. Microchips can be adapted to either set of conditions.

The fordist strategy for combining labor and technology was based on a paradox: a combination of low skill work with high (and secure) wages.[15] The alternative strategies I have described above amount to a choice between two ways of bringing wages and skills into line with one another. In the first, the strategy is to achieve flexibility by increasing wage competition and insecurity. The second strategy involves eliminating the contradiction at the core of fordist relations—the fact that the taylorist forms of work organization exclude the majority of production workers from the battle for productivity and confine the work of innovation and change to the designers and technicians of the operations and methods office (Leborgne and Lipietz

1987). "Flexible specialization" requires a skilled labor force capable not only of adapting to change but also of contributing to it.

The choice of strategies clearly has enormous implications for the future structuring of the life cycle. The first strategy involves exposing workers to market forces by eliminating the institutions and practices that have provided the stability, security, and regularity of the fordist life cycle. The second strategy requires maintaining, even expanding, the life cycle "stabilizers" associated with fordism and the welfare state to even out the distribution of costs and benefits that results from economic change. Whichever strategy is chosen will affect only a minority of workers, however—the declining share employed directly in goods production. For the majority, especially the majority of women, the organization of the life cycle in a postindustrial labor market depends far more directly on the structure of employment in services. Here too there are alternatives to consider.

The Structure of the Service Economy

As traditional manufacturing jobs decline, what kinds of jobs will replace them? The shift to services has been associated with two very different images of the skill and wage mix in postindustrial labor markets. On the one hand, there are optimistic views associated with Bell (1973) and others who emphasize the knowledge-intensive character of work in a postindustrial economy. On the other, there are the pessimistic accounts (Braverman 1974; Kuttner 1983) that highlight the rapid growth in the low wage, low skill personal service industries. Both views contain a germ of truth. What we globally label as "services" is a mixture of industries employing skilled, well-paid labor and industries that employ unskilled, poorly paid labor (Myles 1988b; Myles et al. 1988; Myles and Eno 1989). Public services and consumer services represent the two extremes of the service economy.

1. The "welfare state" industries (health, education, and welfare) and public administration provide jobs with high skill requirements and high wages relative to jobs in goods production.
2. Consumer services including the "servant" industries (cleaning, food, accommodation services) and retail trade have very low skill requirements and low wages.
3. Business (financial, legal, engineering etc.) services provide a mixed, sex-specific, picture. For males, they provide high wage, high skill jobs; females tend to be in the middle (clerical) to lower (bank tellers) end of the industries in this sector.
4. Wage and skill patterns in distributive services (transportation, communication, utilities, wholesale trade) are similar to those in goods production. Historically, these industries along with industrial man-

ufacturing are often considered synonymous with the "industrial revolution" (e.g., railways).

Esping-Andersen (1987) and Elfring (1988) have shown, however, that postindustrial labor markets differ enormously in both the level and mix of
service employment. In Germany, productivity growth in manufacturing has
resulted in "jobless growth" and employment patterns differ little from those
of a traditional "industrial" economy. Where service employment has
grown, the mix of services differs considerably. These differences are illustrated is in Table 1 with data from the Comparative Class Structure surveys
for the Nordic (Finland, Norway, Sweden) and North American (Canada,
United States) labor markets.[16] The distinctive feature of the Canadian and
U.S. labor markets is the large share of employment in the low wage, low
skill consumer services (see also Esping-Andersen 1987). The distinctive
feature of the Nordic countries (especially Sweden) is the large share of
employment in the comparatively high skill, high wage welfare state industries. There are also substantial differences in the share of employment in
business services—11% in Canada and the United States compared to 4–
6% in the Nordic countries. The mix of services is not the product of some
ineluctable "logic of postindustrialism." As Esping-Andersen (1987) argues,
the "welfare state," in its capacity as employer, can play a particularly
critical role in shaping the structure of employment in the service economy.

The consequences of these national differences in the composition of
services are experienced mainly by women (Table 2). Goods production,

Table 1. Nonagricultural Labor Force by Industry Sector[a]

Industry	Canada (1982/83) (%)	United States (1980) (%)	Sweden (1980) (%)	Norway (1982) (%)	Finland (1981) (%)
Goods	30.4	32.0	36.5	31.8	41.3
Distributive services	11.9	10.7	11.1	14.3	11.8
Consumer services	21.0	22.5	12.0	17.5	14.9
Business services	10.9	11.2	4.3	6.2	4.7
Health, education, and welfare	18.7	17.3	30.5	23.4	21.3
Public administration	7.1	6.4	5.6	6.9	6.0
Total	100.0	100.0	100.0	100.0	100.0
N	1982	1407	1148	1609	967

[a]Source: Comparative Class Structure Project.

Table 2. Nonagricultural Labor Force by Industry Sector and Sex[a]

	Canada (1982/83) (%)	United States (1980) (%)	Sweden (1980) (%)	Norway (1982) (%)	Finland (1981) (%)
Males					
Goods	42.9	41.8	51.9	42.9	53.0
Distributive services	15.1	14.2	15.2	18.6	16.0
Consumer services	15.7	18.2	8.3	14.4	11.5
Business services	8.1	8.7	4.8	6.1	5.5
Health, education, and welfare	10.2	9.9	15.0	12.5	9.0
Public administration	8.1	7.3	4.8	7.5	5.5
Total	100.0	100.0	100.0	100.0	100.0
Females					
Goods	17.4	21.0	17.1	18.2	28.9
Distributive services	7.7	6.7	6.1	7.9	7.3
Consumer services	27.9	27.3	16.7	21.9	18.5
Business services	14.6	14.0	3.7	6.2	4.0
Health, education, and welfare	29.8	25.7	50.0	39.7	34.4
Public administration	5.9	5.3	6.5	6.0	5.5
Total	100.0	100.0	100.0	100.0	100.0

[a]*Source:* Comparative Class Structure Project.

distributive services, and public administration tend to be "male" industries. Consumer, business, and social services—where national differences are most pronounced—are "female" industries. Among these, social services is the only sector in which women have access to a large number of middle and high level jobs as measured by both wages and skills (Myles et al. 1988; Myles and Eno 1989). The quality of female employment is directly related to the share of jobs in health, education, and welfare and inversely related to the level of employment in consumer and business services. As a result, the shift to a "service economy" means something far different to Swedish than to North American women.

Alternative designs for the service economy are to be found not just in the mix of services but also in the skill and wage mix *within* service industries. The same service can be provided in radically different ways. For example, there are two alternative models available for the day-care industry to emulate in its labor mix: low wage, unskilled baby-sitting services or high wage, skilled, educational services. Day-care can be provided by highly qualified teachers with advanced degrees in child development or by minimum-wage child-minders. As with the new technologies in manufacturing, there is nothing "technical" about the care of young children to dictate the choice.

In sum, there is nothing intrinsic to a service economy dictating that it will be dominated by low wage, low skill jobs and intermittent employment. And rather than being a problem, the welfare state, particularly one emphasizing employment rather than distribution, may provide the solution. But let us assume an optimistic outcome: That future employment in both manufacturing and services is "biased" toward the high wage, high skill end of the labor market. What then? Will the fordist life cycle simply be reproduced on a larger scale and universalized to include women. This is one possible outcome but not the only one. Just as critical as the quality of future employment is its level and distribution.

The Future of Employment

The motor of postindustrialism throughout the twentieth century has been the production revolution in food and goods production. As Schulz (1989:8) observes: "In each country, the expansion of productive potential has brought with it the opportunity to either increase the amount of goods and services available or to produce the current amount of output but with less labor." In practice, he concludes, industrializing countries have opted for both. There has been both rising output and reductions in working time throughout the twentieth century.

The capitalist democracies, as Therborn (1986) reminds us, however, vary enormously in the way these arrangements have been made. Whereas four-fifths of the adult Swedish population is in paid work, the same is true of about half of the Dutch population (Therborn 1986:70). Female participation rates vary even more, ranging from 39% in Holland to 77% in Sweden. The volume and distribution of employment matter because it is through the wage contract, either directly or through another family member, that the majority of people have had access to many of the key institutions of the fordist life cycle.

Since the early 1970s, many European countries have experienced absolute reductions in employment levels (Therborn 1986:70). This had led to the reflection by many on the left (Gorz, Offe, Keane, Owens) that it is neither feasible nor desirable to attempt a return to full employment and that instead we should move toward a postemployment society.[17] In the postemployment, postwork vision of the world, less human activity would take the form of monetized exchange and more would be in the form of a direct exchange of use values. We may look after one another's children but this will not be in the context of paid employment, that is, a job. The time has come to sever the link between the life-course and the wage–work contract.

Left and right often converge in curious ways and the discussion of the postemployment or postwork society is one of them. Conservatives, of course, do not speak of a postwork society but they are generally dubious about the capacity of the economy to create good jobs for everyone who wants them. And since the invention of the concept of the NAIRU (the Non-Accelerating Inflationary Rate of Unemployment), many no longer see it as desirable: market economies need large numbers of unemployed persons to contain wage pressure. There is a critical difference between left and right on this of course. For the left theorists of the postemployment society, the challenge is defined as increasing the volume of *nonemployment*—making it possible for more people to spend more of their time outside of the labor market and able to live independently of the wage–work contract. For the right, the issue is one of *unemployment*—ensuring there are enough people in the labor market but without jobs to contain wage pressure.

The postemployment view of the future also raises serious concerns however. The problem lies not in the reduction of the socially necessary labor time to produce a given standard of living. For Marx this was the whole point of revolutionizing the productive forces. Rather, the issue is the way the resulting "free time" or nonemployment is distributed and the nonemployed are remunerated.

One strategy for allocating employment is to limit the pool of employables on the basis of age, gender, immigrant status, or family status. All these strategies have been used in the past and have been used with increasing intensity in many countries over the past decade and a half. In the United States, the burden of unemployment has fallen particularly hard on Hispanics and Blacks, in Italy on women, and in Switzerland noncitizens (immigrants) have been sent home to their country of origin (Therborn 1986:69–83).

An alternative to reducing employment levels is to reduce the working time of the employed. Instead of reducing total working time by reinforcing old (or creating new) divisions between those who are and are not employed, the "socially compulsory" labor time of everyone is reduced. In the past this has been done mainly by shortening the work week. But the alternatives also include expanding opportunities for extended work leaves (for retraining or child rearing), vacation time, and paid "sick leave" to care for dependents. This, Block (1987a:115) argues, represents the "positive moment" of the postindustrial transition, the opportunity to construct a flexible life course where periods of work are interspersed with periods of nonwork.

There are decided advantages to such a strategy. All of these examples are forms of reducing work time by increasing periods of nonwork in the form of *paid absences* from work, that is, in the form of benefits provided within the context of an *employment relation*. For the postemployment theorists, in contrast, the strategy is to break the wage–work link and establish some form of guaranteed income or social wage and the creation of a class of nonworkers. As McBride (1987:145) concludes, however, "there is no reason to suspect that such a society would resemble anything than the universalization of Liverpool's experience." Western societies have had long historical experience with the way in which classes of "nonworkers" (e.g., welfare mothers) are treated in capitalist societies. As in the past, such strategies are likely to create a permanent underclass of the unemployed and underemployed. To finance a luxurious social wage or guaranteed income would require very high taxes on those who work, with the result that the income gap between workers and nonworkers would be quite small. This implies there would have to be enormous nonmonetary rewards to the employed to maintain the supply of workers. If this reward were the chance to do truly "creative" work, nonworkers would have to be denied chances to do creative work; if it were power, status, or respect these would have to be denied to nonworkers.

Examples of both strategies—reducing employment levels and reducing the working time of the employed—are already available for evaluation. Employment levels of older adults (55–64) have declined in all advanced capitalist countries since the early 1970s and with particular intensity in France, Germany, Austria, and the Netherlands (Therborn 1986; Guillemard 1988). In part, these shifts can be attributed to a downward drift of the boundaries defining *chronological* old age, a result of lowering the age of eligibility for pension and retirement benefits. But, Guillemard argues, closer inspection indicates something more fundamental is happening—a "dechronologizing" of the life course and a reorganization of old age around definitions of functional capacity in the market place. In Germany, France, and the Netherlands, early labor force exits are not organized by the pension system but by unemployment and disability insurance programs—where "disability" is defined by economic not physiological criteria. As a result, the timing of labor force exits has become increasingly arbitrary and subject to employer discretion.

Sweden is the exception to the sharp upward trend in early retirement. However, high labor force participation rates in Sweden do not mean more work is done. In 1983, the level of actual annual working hours per worker stood at 1596 in Sweden, 1986 in the United States, and 2061 in Japan (Therborn, 1986:75). In part, the Swedish figure represents the high percentage of part-time work (at full time rates and benefits) among Swedish women and in part the high level of paid absences from work. In 1980, hours of paid absence as a percentage of total hours actually worked stood at 11.2 in Sweden compared to 6.6 in France (Esping-Andersen 1985:11). No comparable figure is available for the United States, but if we compare paid absences for sickness alone, the figure for Sweden was 4.4, for France 5.1, and for the United States 1.3. The Swedish strategy has been to reduce working hours rather than employment, a consequence of a welfare state strategy emphasizing employment rather than transfers (Esping-Andersen 1987).

For women, the choice among these alternatives is likely to be quite significant as the growing underclass of "welfare mothers" in many countries shows (Smeeding and Torrey 1988). But there are also problems with the high employment strategy. It is quite conceivable, even probable, that paid absences (including a reduced working day) to care for dependents will be taken by women and paid absences for retraining appropriated by men. By itself, universalizing the employment relation to include women, even at high wages, is not sufficient to "degender" social relations, as the Swedish experience—where child leave is taken almost universally by women—indicates.

Does this mean it is necessary to reconsider the "high employment" strategy? Not necessarily. Instead it requires that we refine our notions of work and nonwork and monetize more, not less, human activity. Economists traditionally formulate the problem of whether to take productivity gains in the form of more goods and services or less working time in terms of a "labor–leisure" trade-off. To many women who work for wages on a part-time basis or struggle to reduce their paid working hours to do domestic labor and child care, such a formulation must seem to be a particularly cruel joke. The solution, however, is to take the "labor–leisure" formulation seriously and monetize all socially necessary labor including care-giving. On the one hand, this would involve an expansion of such "welfare state" services as child care, home services, and respite care and, on the other, to distinguish paid absences for *work* (child care, retraining etc.) from paid absences for leisure (longer vacations, shorter work weeks for everyone). The growth of a service economy has been in part a monetization of human labor previously done outside of the labor market and in part an increase in the volume of such activity. The alternatives opened by this development offers new problems to be resolved but also new solutions to old problems.

CONCLUSION: THE POLITICS OF POSTINDUSTRIALISM

The fordist life cycle constructed in virtually all postwar capitalist democracies after World War II (with the possible exception of the United Kingdom) now appears to be threatened by both politics (the impasse of the welfare state) and markets (declining labor demand, the changing character of goods production, and the shift of employment to low wage sectors of the service economy). Yet in all three areas this postindustrial transition offers alternatives, not inevitability. In broad terms, the "choices" include a future constructed around:

1. a high wage, high skill labor force in an economy characterized by full and high levels of employment; and
2. one polarized between a core of well-paid technicians and managers, on the one hand, and a larger mass composed of a mixture of underemployed low wage workers and an underclass of state dependents.

These ideal-typical alternatives are of course extremes and the alternatives before us undoubtedly include a variety of combinations of these outcomes. Full employment does not mean high employment, for example. Full employment is compatible with an economy in which large sectors of society (the young, the elderly, women) are simply kept out of the labor market and are remunerated not through an employment relation but maintained through dependency relations on those in the market or through social assistance.

Under neither scenario will the now eroding fordist life cycle be reconstructed. In the first, declining demand for labor that results from further increases in productivity will be realized in the form of a flexible life course built around the need for continuous retraining (Block, 1987a:115) and the work of reproduction (child rearing, the care of dependent elders [Kamerman and Kahn 1987]). In the second, the life course of many becomes more disorderly and less secure. In this scenario:

> Working lives of men become much shorter by delayed entry, more interruptions and early retirement. Women's employment while becoming more continuous over the working life is still frequently marginal and in unqualified jobs . . . employment trajectories become more disorderly, less career like with more job shifts, more shifts of employers, more shifts of occupation and more shifts out of the labor force and back. (Meyer 1988:14)

The future life course of women is especially sensitive to these shifts— whether employment growth occurs in high end or low end services, the types of human activity that are monetized, and whether future patterns of work reduction take the form of paid work absence as opposed to nonemployment and social assistance.

Merely considering "alternatives," however, takes us into the world of what is possible, not what is probable. The "choices" that will be made among these alternatives depend on more than "political will." The institutionalized power relations inherited from the past—between classes, between men and women—are embedded in our social, political, and economic institutions and condition the everyday common sense of elites and publics of what is both possible and probable. The selection process is therefore determined by "politics." "Politics" cannot be reduced to "states" but what states do and do not do will be critical in shaping the outcome of the current transition. Not all states will pursue an "industrial strategy" to direct their economies through the transition and may leave the choices we face up to markets. But that will be a political choice and the outcomes that follow will certainly differ from those in which a strategy and set of decisions are made on these matters.

The American debate on these issues has mainly concerned *industrial strategy* (Thompson 1987). But as we have seen, future employment growth, for both men and women, will be mainly in services and, here, the role of the state is even more critical, especially in its capacity as employer. The "welfare state" industries have been the main supplier of "good" service sector jobs and "big" welfare states, such as the Swedish, also tend to crowd out low wage service sector employers. The state will also be critical in determining future trends in employment levels, and the forms that are realized in the "labor–leisure" trade-off.

What states do, however, are also shaped by "politics" in the larger sense—by the institutionalized capacities of elites and publics to set parameters on the choices made by elected and unelected state officials. Historically, the "politics" of capitalist societies have been driven by the structure of alliances within and between classes and between classes and the state (Esping-Andersen 1989). In particular, a strong labor movement capable of resisting strategies emphasizing wage competition and employment reduction can be an important ingredient forcing employers to look for other ways to respond to change (Mahon 1987).

One of the features of "postindustrialism" is the emergence of "new social movements" (of women, minorities, peace and ecological groups) alongside of the traditional class divisions and alliances constructed during the period of "industrialism." The new social movements have not supplanted traditional class divisions but they have opened new possibilities for publics (but also elites) to direct the future course of events and for new kinds of interclass and intraclass alliances and divisions.

Viewing these large macro changes in labor markets and states through the window of individual life cycles serves a useful function both analytically and normatively. Analytically, the life cycle provides an empirical tool with which to map these changes; normatively, it provides us with a tool for evaluating alternatives. There is nothing new about this sort of research strategy of course. As ever, the task of the "sociological imagination" is to establish the link between "personal troubles of milieux" and "public issues of social structure" (Mills 1959).

ACKNOWLEDGMENTS

Thanks go to Jane Jenson, Theda Skocpol, Jill Quadagno, and students in the weekly seminar of the Centre for Reasearch on Political and Social Organization, Department of Sociology, Harvard University for their comments and criticisms on an earlier draft of this paper.

NOTES

1. I owe this formulation to Melissa Hardy.

2. This is especially true with respect to the labor market and wage trends discussed in the text, a result of the high degree of linkage between the two economies. In the area of public policy, matters are more complex. In a few areas (health care, unemployment insurance) Canada has a distinctly more developed welfare state and is less developed in others (old age insurance). Overall, however, spending levels on social programs and the general orientation of fiscal and monetary policy are quite similar when put into a broad comparative perspective. One major difference has been the failure of the neoconservative rhetoric of Thatcher or Reagan to took root in Canada during the 1980s.

3. Rowntree's classic study of working class life at the turn of the century demonstrated that the typical career of a family had the form of a "cycle of poverty" that fluctuated over the life course. The highest risks of poverty were associated with periods of child rearing (extensive under conditions of high fertility) and old age.

4. Health care in the United States provides a stunning, if exceptional, example. There is "social security" (from corporate health plans) with respect to illness for the new middle class and core sector workers but "social assistance" (Medicaid) for the rest. The example of old age security, the largest and most important component of the postwar welfare state, is more typical. In Canada, the United Kingdom, the United States, and Australia, income security in old age hinges critically on access to employer-sponsored pension schemes. Public sector programs may bring people up to or even above poverty levels but real income security in old age requires a combination of public and private coverage in all four countries.

5. The premise of most economists, based on Engel's Law, is that as nations become richer, consumption will shift from necessities to "luxuries" such as leisure and services (Esping-Andersen 1987).

6. Food, accommodation, and related "servant" industries were among the fastest growing sectors over the entire period. They began from a very low base, however, so that the impact of this growth on employment shares was muted until recently.

7. For an extensive review of the relevant American literature on the "declining middle" see Loveman and Tilly (1988).

8. In Canada, the major axis of change was across age groups and was economy-wide, not simply the result of changes in industry composition. The good jobs went to the middle aged and almost all of the expansion in bad jobs to the young. The real wages of workers under 35 declined while that of workers over 35 improved. This is not surprising. Once launched into a job trajectory, the main characteristic of job careers is stability, with the result that changes in the structure of employment and the wage mix are most likely to show among new entrants to the labor force and those who have not accumulated seniority rights. The largest change was the decline of the relative wages of the young workers (age 16–24). But it is difficult to attribute this to demography. Over this period the supply of workers declined substantially. There were almost half a million fewer Canadians aged 15–24 in 1986 (4.2 million) than there were in 1981 (4.7 million), young people were less likely to be in the labor market, and their average age had risen.

9. See Mayer (1988) for a summary statement on these views.

10. This section draws extensively from Myles (1988a).

11. As Block (1981) observes, O'Connor's fiscal crisis is not defined simply by a budgetary gap between expenditures and revenues; strictly speaking, a state of fiscal crisis can exist even when they are in balance. Instead, a situation of fiscal crisis exists in "those situations in which governments find it impossible to finance the expenditures necessary for maintaining the capitalist accumulation process without pursuing policies that either would damage the long-term health of the economy or to impair the state's capacity to generate adequate revenues" (Block 1981:4).

12. The main symptom of the "crisis" as it became defined in the 1970s was the breakdown of the Phillips curve trade-off between inflation and unemployment. Traditionally, when labor became strong enough to create inflation-generating wage pressure, discipline was restored with restrictive fiscal policies that raised unemployment levels. In the 1970s, it appeared this strategy was no longer working: wage pressure, inflation, and unemployment could all rise together and the result was "stagflation." The welfare state was thought to be implicated in this development. Welfare states—or at least the social security side of welfare states—immunize workers from market forces, increase their bargaining power, and generally skew the capital–labor relation in favor of labor. Because of unemployment insurance and other benefits, the impact of rising unemployment on wage demands and labor militancy is muted. The result is continued wage pressure, inflation, and a profit squeeze. Since the welfare state was part of the problem, it was thought that dismantling the welfare state must be part of the solution. But as the past decade has shown, there is a variety of ways of bringing labor to heel. See Myles (1988) for an analysis of the Canadian experience in this respect.

13. The characterization of this literature as "neoinstitutionalist" is suggested by Fred Block's (1987b) review of John Goldthorpe's (1985) collection of articles by a number of authors writing in this tradition.

14. As cited in Mahon (1987:16–18).

15. The paradox is evident when we compare the "deskilling" debates (Braverman 1974) of the 1970s with the "deindustrialization" debates (Bluestone and Harrison 1982) of the 1980s. For Braverman, the *semiskilled* factory operative symbolizes the destructive aspect of modern capitalism. For Bluestone and Harrison, the demise of the very same *well-paid* factory operative is the threat that now confronts us.

16. The data were collected in the early 1980s by independent research teams in the five countries. Results presented here are from the Five Nation Tape distributed by the Inter-university Consortium for Political and Social Research, Ann Arbor, Michigan.

17. For a review of this literature see McBride (1987).

REFERENCES

Aberg, Rune. 1984. "Market-Independent Income Distribution: Efficiency and Legitimacy." Pp. 209–230 in *Order and Conflict in Contemporary Capitalism* edited by J. Goldthorpe. Oxford: Clarendon.

———. 1986. "Economic Incentives and Labor Market Efficiency in Sweden." Paper presented to the conference on "Prospects for Active Labour Market Policies in Sweden," York University, December.

Banting, Keith. 1987. "The Welfare State and Inequality in the 1980s." *Canadian Review of Sociology and Anthropology* 24(3):311–338.

Bell, Daniel. 1960. *The End of Ideology.* Glencoe, IL: Free Press.

———. 1973. *The Coming of Post-Industrial Society.* New York: Basic Books.

Bendix, Reinhard. 1956. *Work and Authority in Industry.* Berkeley: University of California Press.

Block, Fred. 1981. "The Fiscal Crisis of the Capitalist State." *Annual Review of Sociology* 7:1–27.

———. 1987a. *Revising State Theory: Essays in Politics and Postindustrialism.* Philadelphia: Temple University Press.

———. 1987b. "Economic Sociology: Progress and Regression." *Contemporary Sociology* 16:476–478.

Bluestone, Barry and Bennett Harrison. 1982. *The Deindustrialization of America.*
    Basic Books: New York.
Braverman, Harry. 1974. *Labor and Monopoly Capital: The Degradation of Work in
    the Twentieth Century.* New York: Monthly Review Press.
Canadian Council on Social Development. 1987. *Proposals for Discussion: Phase
    One—Income Security Reform.* Work and Income in the Nineties (WIN), Work-
    ing Paper No. 8, August.
Cohen, Stephen and John Zysman. 1987. *Manufacturing Matters: The Myth of the
    Post-Industrial Economy.* New York: Basic.
Davis, Mike. 1984. "The Political Economy of Late-Imperial America." *New Left
    Review* 143 (January–February):6–38.
Elfring, Tom. 1988. *Service Sector Employment in Advanced Economies.* Aldershot:
    Avebury Press.
Esping-Andersen, Gosta. 1985. *Welfare Policy Regimes and Permanent Disemploy-
    ment.* Berlin: Wissenshaftszentrum.
———. 1987. "Post-Industrial Employment Trajectories: Germany, Sweden and the
    United States." Department of Politics, European University, Florence.
———. 1989. "The Three Political Economies of the Welfare State." *Canadian Re-
    view of Sociology and Anthropology* 26:10–36.
Giddens, Anthony. 1976. "Classical Social Theory and the Origins of Modern Social
    Theory." *American Journal of Sociology* 81:703–729.
Graebner, William. 1980. *A History of Retirement.* New Haven, CT: Yale University
    Press.
Guillemard, Anne-Marie. 1988. "Changes in Withdrawal from the Labour Force
    seen from an International Vantage Point: Reassessing Retirement." Mimeo,
    Paris: Centre d'Etudes des Movements Sociaux.
Hagestad, Gunhild and Bernice Neugarten. 1985. "Age and the Life Course." Pp.
    35–61 in *Handbook of Aging and the Social Sciences,* edited by Robert Binstock
    and Ethel Shanas. New York: Van Nostrand Reinhold.
Hernes, Gudmund. 1976. "Structural Change in Social Processes." *American Jour-
    nal of Sociology* 32:513–547.
Jenson, Jane. 1989. "'Different' But Not 'Exceptional': Canada's Permeable Ford-
    ism." *Canadian Review of Sociology and Anthropology* 26:69–94.
Kahn, Alfred and Sheila Kamerman. 1983–84. "Social Assistance: An Eight-Country
    Overview." *The Journal* 8:93–112.
Kamerman, Sheila and Alfred Kahn. 1987. *The Responsive Workplace: Employers
    and a Changing Labor Force.* New York: Columbia University Press.
Kennedy, Bruce. 1987. "Age, sex, time and earnings." Joint working paper of the
    Institute for Research on Public Policy and the Social and Economic Studies
    Division, Statistics Canada, Halifax and Ottawa.
Kerr, Clark, J. T. Dunlop, F. Harbison, and C. Myers. 1964. *Industrialism and Indus-
    trial Man.* New York: Oxford University Press.
Kuhn, Thomas. 1962. *The Structure of Scientific Revolutions.* Chicago: University of
    Chicago Press.
Kuttner, Bob. 1983. "The Declining Middle." *The Atlantic Monthly* (July):60–72.
Leborgne, D. and A. Lipietz. 1987. "New Technologies, New Modes of Regulation:
    Some Spatial Implications." Presented at the conference on Technology, Re-
    structuring and Urban/Regional Development, Dubrovnik, June.

Lipietz, Alain. 1988. "Reflections on a Tale: The Marxist Foundations of the Concepts of Regulation and Accumulation." *Studies in Political Economy* 26:1–36.

Loveman, Gary and Chris Tilly. 1988. "Good Jobs or Bad Jobs: What Does the Evidence Say." *New England Economic Review* (Jan.–Feb.):46–65.

Mahon, Rianne. 1987. "From Fordism to ?: New Technology, Labour Markets and Unions." *Economic and Industrial Democracy* 8:5–60.

———. 1989. "Post-Fordism, Canada and the FTA: Is There Room for the Left to Manoeuvre?" Prepared for the conference on Export-Led Growth, Uneven Development and State Policy: Canada and Italy, University of Pisa, April.

Mayer, Karl Urlich. 1988. "The Life Cycle and Work." Paper presented to the Symposium on Population Change and European Society, European University Institute, Florence, December.

McBride, Steven. 1987. "The state and labour markets: towards a comparative political economy of Unemployment." *Studies in Political Economy* 23:141–154.

Mendelson, Michael. 1986. "Is social Policy Dead?" Paper presented to the Seminar Series on Public Policy, Department of Political Science, University of Toronto, February.

Mills, C. Wright. 1959. *The Sociological Imagination.* New York: Oxford University Press.

Moscovitch, Allan. 1986. "The Welfare State Since 1975." *Journal of Canadian Studies* 21:2 (Summer:77–95.

Myles, John. 1984. *Old Age in the Welfare State: The Political Economy of Public Pensions.* Boston: Little Brown.

———. 1988a. "Decline or Impasse: The Current State of the Welfare State." *Studies in Political Economy* 26:73–107.

———. 1988b. "The Expanding Middle: Some Canadian Evidence on the Deskilling Debate." *Canadian Review of Sociology and Anthropology* 25:335–364.

Myles, John and Gail Eno. 1989. *Job Skills and the Service Economy.* Ottawa: Economic Council of Canada.

Myles, John, Garnett Picot, and Ted Wannell. 1988. "Wages and Jobs in the Eighties: Changing Youth Wages and the Declining Middle." Research Paper No. 17, Analytical Studies Branch, Statistics Canada, Ottawa.

O'Connor, James. 1973. *The Fiscal Crisis of the State.* New York: St. Martin's Press.

Panitch, Leo. 1981. "Trade Unions and the Capitalist State." *New Left Review* 125:21–43.

Picot, W. Garnett. 1986. *Canada's Industries: Growth in Jobs Over Three Decades.* Ottawa: Statistics Canada.

Piore, Michael and Charles Sabel. 1984. *The Second Industrial Divide.* New York: Basic Books.

Piven, Frances and Richard Cloward. 1971. *Regulating the Poor.* New York: Vantage Books.

Polanyi, Karl. 1944. *The Great Transformation.* Boston: Beacon Press.

Ross, H. and I. Sawhill. 1975. *Time of Transition.* Washington D.C.: The Urban Institute.

Rowntree, S. 1901. *Poverty: A Study of Town Life.* London: Macmillan.

Schulz, James. 1989. "The Buffer Years: Market Incentives and Evolving Retirement Policies." Paper presented to the International Conference on Aging, Florida State University, March.

Smeeding, Timothy and Barbara Torrey. 1988. "Poor Children in Rich Countries." *Science* 242:873–877.

Therborn, Goran, 1986. *Why Some People are More Unemployed than Others: The Strange Paradox of Growth and Unemployment.* London: New Left Books.

Thompson, G. 1987. "The American Industrial Policy Debate: Any Lessons for the U.K.?" *Economy and Society* 16(1):1–74.

Wolfson, Michael. 1987. "The Arithmetic of Income Security Reform." Pp. 41–85 in *Approaches to Income Security Reform,* edited by S. Seward and M. Iacobacci. Ottawa: Institute for Research on Public Policy.

MARKETS AS SOCIETY _____ V

The Transformation of
Organizational Forms:
How Useful Is Organization Theory
in Accounting for Social Change?

11

Walter W. Powell

This is a period of considerable experimentation worldwide in the production of goods and the delivery of services. Capitalist and socialist countries alike are searching for new ways to stimulate their economies and alternative methods to provide public services. The quest for new answers is also spurred by a reaction to much greater international competitive pressures, brought on by the spectacular rise of Pacific rim nations from backward economies to industrial powerhouses.

Organizations play a crucial role in these efforts at reform. Solutions to economic problems are embedded in organizational policies and structures. Technological innovation and workplace reform are both organizational phenomena. The pace and success of social change depend, in large part, on organizational performance. Struggles for power and fights over the allocation of resources in modern societies take the form of contests both within and among organizations. The state—that master noun of modern political discourse (Geertz 1981)—is itself a large organizational apparatus. Changes in organizational forms are even reshaping the international political economy. International business alliances (e.g., AT&T and Olivetti or Toyota and GM) span national boundaries, and business–government collaborations (e.g., Sematech—the semiconductor research consortium) blur the distinction between public and private.

Changes in the organization of business and government are typically treated as problems of applied political economy. But I want to suggest that current debates about the design of economic and political institutions could be enhanced by attending to recent work in organizational theory. If social change and organizational performance are closely intertwined, then organizational analysis should provide insight into the speed and direction of social change. Organization theory can help us understand why some firms have been ponderous in responding to shifting conditions and why others are lighter on their feet. Why have some industrial sectors and/or regions been more responsive to change than others? Why are some organizational practices more generalizable than others?

This chapter thus has a dual purpose:

1. To highlight a series of important changes in organizational forms—to shed light on these new developments so that they become the focus of more systematic attention and to frame the discussion in a manner that underscores which aspects of these recent changes are novel and which are enduring puzzles of social organization.
2. To assess the utility of organization theory in explaining these changes—to point out which ideas are most serviceable and which ones are in need of revision or further development.

My argument is highly speculative. I assert that four kinds of modifications in organizational forms are underway and that these changes are extensive in scope and broad in their ramifications. By organizational form, I refer to the policies, procedures, and structural arrangements utilized by organizations. An organizational form is, in a general way, a blueprint for organizing. I offer, however, no metric or scale for assessing the frequency or the ecology of these developments. And I submit that we know even less about the consequences of these processes. Nevertheless, I think there is a general consensus that the following transformations are well underway:

1. the widespread transfer of activities from the public sector to the private sphere;
2. serious efforts at reforming state socialist economies;
3. the "down-sizing" of large-scale enterprises in capitalist economies;
4. the proliferation of "soft contracting," represented by nommarket, nonhierarchical, network forms of exchange.

Three lines of argument are at the forefront of current research and debate in organization theory—transaction costs economics (Williamson, 1975; 1985), population ecology (Hannan and Freeman 1977, 1984, 1989), and institutional analysis (Meyer and Rowan 1977; Meyer and Scott 1983; Di-Maggio and Powell 1983; Zucker 1983). To be sure, these approaches by no means exhaust the universe of organizational research, but interest in these arguments is considerable and research efforts are extensive. I assume that the reader has a general familiarity with this work, so I provide only a brief sketch of the respective arguments.

Transaction cost economics, associated with the pioneering insights of Coase (1938) and the more recent work of Oliver Williamson (1975, 1985), focuses on transactions—the exchange of goods or services among individuals or departments or across organizational boundaries—as the primary unit of analysis. The core question, as posed by Coase, is whether a set of transactions ought to take place in the marketplace or within the boundaries of a firm. The key insight is that markets and firms represent alternative ways of organizing economic exchanges.

The main thrust of Williamson's (1975, 1985) argument is that transactions that involve uncertainty about their outcome, that recur frequently, and require substantial "transaction-specific investments"—of money, time, or energy that cannot be easily transferred—are more likely to take place within hierarchically organized firms. Exchanges that are straightforward, nonrepetitive, and require few transaction-specific investments will take place across a market interface. Hence, exchanges are moved out of markets into hierarchies as knowledge that is relevant to the transaction (asset specificity) builds up. When this occurs, the inefficiencies of bureaucratic organization will be preferred to the relatively greater costs of market transactions. There are two behavioral reasons for this: (1) bounded rationality—the inability of economic actors to write contracts that cover all possible contingencies (when transactions are internalized, there is little need to anticipate such contingencies since they can be handled within the firm's "governance structure"); and (2) "opportunism"—the rational pursuit by economic actors of their own advantage, with every means at their disposal, including guile and deceit (opportunism is mitigated by authority relations and by the stronger identification that parties presumably have when they are joined under a common roof).

These behavioral assumptions are combined with two environmental characteristics: uncertainty and small numbers bargaining. As uncertainty increases, it becomes difficult for parties to an exchange to anticipate all of the potential consequences of their relationship. The existence of a small number of parties to the exchange both increases their mutual dependence on one another, and raises the possibility and costs of opportunistic behavior. As a result, uncertainty and small numbers bargaining both favor internal organization over market exchange.

An ecological perspective (Hannan and Freeman 1977, 1984, 1989; Carroll 1984) seeks to understand how social conditions affect the rates at which new organizations and new organizational forms arise, and the rates at which these organizations and forms die out. To accomplish this, ecologists highlight two processes: how changes in the larger society affect the mix of organizations, and how the dynamics of organizational populations (i.e., such vital rates as foundings, mergers, and disbandings) shape the demography of organizations.

The unit of analysis in ecological research is an organizational population, an aggregate of organizations that is alike in some key respects. The motivating assumption is that change occurs primarily at the population level, that is, when environmental conditions and competitive relations change, opportunities for new organizational forms are created and these new forms replace outmoded older ones. So rather than emphasizing organization adaptation, ecologists highlight selection processes. They argue that most of the variability in organizational arrangements occurs as a result of the creation of new organizations and the replacement of older forms. Thus, the goal of ecological analysis is to explain why certain forms of organizations survive and proliferate while others languish and decline. Ecologists emphasize, however, that processes of selection do not depend on optimization or efficiency assumptions, selection processes may be driven by a broad range of factors.

Why do ecologists contend that adaptation by individual organizations is so difficult? In part they believe that there is a mismatch between an organization's ability to learn about its environment and the speed at which environmental change occurs. The key reason for this is that the inertial properties of organizations are quite strong. There are important constraints—physical, political, psychological, and institutional—on an organization's ability to change. Indeed, as Hannan and Freeman (1984) have argued, accountability and reliability may well be the cornerstones of organizational success. Thus, ecological analysis is most appropriate when organizations are subject to strong inertial pressures and at the same time face changeable, uncertain environments (Hannan and Freeman 1989).

A different aspect of the environment—the rules and beliefs systems as well as the relational networks that arise within organizational fields—has been emphasized by scholars who are associated with an institutional approach to organization–environment relations (Meyer and Rowan 1977; DiMaggio and Powell 1983). In modern societies an important category of the rules and belief systems that arise is sets of "rational myths" (Meyer and Rowan 1977). The beliefs are rational in the sense that they identify specific social purposes and then specify in a rule-like manner either what activities are to be carried out or what types of actors must be employed to achieve them. These beliefs are myths in the sense that they depend for their efficacy on the fact that they are widely shared or are promulgated by individuals or groups that have been granted the right to determine such matters. These institutional beliefs are not merely constraints on action; they can also be employed to legitimate new courses of action. In this fashion, institutionalized practices are always both constraining and enabling. Similarly, new forms of organization can be created as a result of changes in the institutional fabric of the broader society.

A number of important changes in perspective are suggested by the institutional approach. Environments are viewed as comprised not only of bundles of resources and patterns of exchange, but also of cultural elements—symbols, belief systems, professional claims—and the sources of these elements. DiMaggio and Powell (1983:150) state this view clearly: "Organizations compete not just for resources and customers, but for political power and institutional legitimacy, for social as well as economic fitness." Meyer and Rowan (1977) point out that there are multiple and diverse sources of "rational myths": public opinion, educational systems, laws, courts, professions, ideologies, regulatory structures, certification and accreditation bodies, and governmental requirements. The institutional perspective directs attention away from narrow concerns with the location of resources, the availability of customers, or the number of competitors to call attention to the broader role played by the state, the legal system, and the professions in shaping organizational life, both directly by imposing constraints and creating opportunities and indirectly by promulgating new "rational myths." Modern societies contain all kinds of institutionalized rules and patterns that provide a framework for the creation and development of formal organization. These building blocks are not merely general values, however; they often take on highly specific forms—as professional expertise, government mandate, or procedural requirements.

Each of these approaches claims a particular competence for explaining organizational change. Williamson (1985:408) holds that "microeconomic institutions play a crucial, subtle, and relatively neglected role in explaining differential economic performance—over time, within and between industries, within and between nation states and sociopolitical systems." Ecologists (Carroll 1984; Hannan and Freeman 1989) maintain that organizations play a key role in broad processes of social change. Institutionalists contend that the "engine of rationalization and bureaucratization has moved from the competitive marketplace to the state and the professions" (DiMaggio and Powell 1983:147), a claim that implies generality to a wide range of organizational settings.

These approaches share several common assumptions, and also display sharp differences in the factors that are given the most explanatory weight. All three emphasize that organizational form matters a great deal—in determining whether activities are handled efficiently, in shaping survival chances, and in dictating whether a given activity is regarded as accountable or legitimate. Both institutional and ecological arguments focus on how changes in the environment influence organizational behavior, while transaction costs economics asserts that methods of organizing, that is, realigning the boundaries of the firm, make a difference for performance. As Hannan and Freeman (1989) have observed, both institutional and ecological accounts deny the primacy of efficiency as a rationale for explaining organizational variability, a primacy that transaction costs economics holds dear.

Researchers in each of the three camps will undoubtedly challenge some of my explanations. My purpose, however, is not to generate rival falsifiable hypotheses, rather I seek to show that organization theories can be highly useful in accounting for patterns of social change. In my view, the greatest contribution that these theoretical perspectives have to offer is not explicit hypotheses about the broad social transformations that are underway, but in more general metatheoretical conceptualizations about how to view these phenomena. We turn now from the realm of theory to the world of practice.

PRIVATIZATION, OR THE SHIFTING BOUNDARIES OF PUBLIC AND PRIVATE

The current enthusiasm for privatization appears to be boundless. Britain has sold off its telephone system, British Airways, and even its prize among the Crown's jewels, the Rolls Royce Motor Company. France has sold the country's largest television station. Soon, the Japanese telephone system may be in private hands. Brazil and Mexico have government-owned assets up for sale. Everywhere, nations are deregulating their financial systems, relaxing constraints on banks and investment houses, and creating new financial options and new organizational entities to market them. In the United States, we hear of private provision of public services such as fire protection, garbage collection, and prisons. In Minnesota, school districts now contract with private-practice teachers, and voucher-like experiments, which allow parents to send their children to the school of their choice, are being labeled a success. Railroads, housing projects, airports, and electric utilities are up for sale. What is going on?

The historical etiology of the public/private split reminds us that there is no clear dualism, rather there has long been a sense of fuzzily separable worlds.[1] Indeed, the American government played a crucial role in the creation of the private corporation. The state provided the legal underpinnings of the corporate form of property, offered financial assistance to fledgling corporations, removed barriers to a national market, and helped dampen the opposition of anticorporate forces. Although it may be more comfortable to conceive of public and private as independent realities, which engender turbulence like conflicting tides, the reality is that social organization is often an incoherent tangle of historical accidents and cross-purposes. The clean rubric of privatization masks, in the United States at least, a great diversity of organizational arrangements.

Not surprisingly, there are many uses of the term privatization. To some it means turning over public sector enterprises to private industry. But in the United States, unlike Western Europe or the Third World, direct government ownership of "commercial" activities has been rare. As a result, privatization efforts in the United States tend to involve the private provision of some public services. In a very useful overview, Pack (1987) suggests that the public sector has three main elements—finance, production, and regulation. Hence the three principal forms of privatization are the divestiture or deevolution of the public function, maintaining public finance but shifting the locus of production out of the public sector, and deregulation. A city, for example, could get out of the business of sanitation altogether by taking the function out of the city budget, or the city might decide to finance trash collection by contracting with private companies (either for-profit or non-profit) to provide the service. Sanitation then remains in the city budget, but the city no longer maintains a sanitation department (Pack 1987:524).

The actual range of privatization experiments in the United States is extensive, resulting in complex gradations of public, private, and nonprofit. For example, we can identify the following kinds of arrangements:

1. Divestiture or withdrawal of a public service, which is supplanted by either private provision or voluntary associations.
2. Government contracts with for-profit or nonprofit services to provide public goods. (Following Salamon 1987, I would argue that in most fields other than defense, the standard form of "third party government" involves private nonprofit organizations using federal monies to provide health care, education, the arts, social service, research and development, and so on.)
3. Purposeful attempts to stimulate competition among public agencies, voluntary associations, and private firms by selling off only minority shares of public enterprises, or contracting out for only a portion of the services.
4. Private firms spring up to capture dissatisfaction with public services (the proliferation of private postal services was not initiated by government, but rather reflected unmet needs in the provision of postal services).
5. Private firms develop where formerly nonprofit, volunteer associations dominated (Rural/Metro fire service, my own provider of protection against fires and rattlesnakes as well, is the largest private provider of fire services, yet it has never displaced a municipal service—it evolved when suburban sprawl rendered voluntary fire departments unfeasible).

What underlies the current movement toward some form of privatization? Is it motivated by economic evidence about the inefficiency with which public goods and services are produced? Does it reflect a widespread belief that the public sector has grown too large? Or have we reached a policy impasse—a loss of faith in the government's ability to solve highly complex social and technical problems—transportation, education, pollution, crime, and soon—and a willingness to try any other alternative? If the latter is the motivation, does the purported failure of the public sector provide us with any evidence that the private or nonprofit sectors can do a better job? There is ample political and economic theory on the respective roles of the market and government. Indeed, much of Western orthodox social thought is "inextricably connected with the articulation of the virtues of private enterprise" (Nelson 1981). As Nelson (1981, 1987) has persuasively argued, however, market failure analysis and modern public choice theory—the standard analytical tools for examining the appropriate roles of the public and private sectors—provide very little rationale for *either* public *or* private actions.

Private enterprise is typically regarded as more responsive than public bureaucracies. Ever since Adam Smith, economists have suspected that public administration was wasteful because public employees do not have a direct interest in the commercial consequences of their actions. In contrast, private owners face important incentives that make it desirable to monitor employee behavior and to be responsive to consumer demand. Hence private firms are thought to be faster on their feet because there is greater incentive to modify decision rules and organizational procedures so as to better deal with changing environments. But the past decade has shown how difficult it can be for private firms to realign their entrenched methods, even in the face of considerable competitive pressures. And, as Nelson (1981) has pointed out, fast response is one thing, well-directed response another. The argument that private firms are quicker to respond and more sensitive to changes is plausible, but when one examines the quality and direction of these responses, the case for private enterprise is much less impressive (Nelson 1981; Hannan and Freeman 1984). Moreover, many of the inefficiencies of the public sector are built in deliberately through our system of checks and balances. Nelson (1987) even suggests the currently heretical notion that many things presently done largely privately, such as research and development or job training, might be done more effectively if we could agree to a an expanded governmental role.

The nonprofit sector in the United States consists of private activity that ostensibly contributes to some common good, organized in a fashion that does not allow for the retainment of profits by employees or investors. It is not public, in the sense of being open to all. It is voluntary, hence often regarded as more trustworthy than for-profit firms because of its eleemosynary character (Hansmann 1987). One of the benefits of the nonprofit sector is to provide a blanket of trust for poorly informed consumers, especially in areas such as nursing homes and day-care (Weisbrod, 1988). Nonprofits are regarded as more flexible and adaptive than public organizations because of their smaller, more localized scale. But an examination of the ecology of the sector suggests that some nonprofit organizations are little more than creatures of the tax code, while others are bastions of elite prestige, and highly particularistic (see the various essays in Powell 1987a).

What insights can organizational theories offer into the institutional complexity that characterizes modern mixed economies? The very nature of American governmental processes—the system of overlapping responsibilities, multiple levels of decision-making, and an absence of centralized authority—produces high transaction costs (North 1984). The federalist system, the explicit establishment of independent authorities with both separate responsibilities and overlapping jurisdictions, poses all kinds of difficulties from a cost minimization perspective. Transaction cost reasoning may be useful in helping public officials determine which kind of services might be most effectively turned over to private firms. One goal of transaction costs economics is to specify what types of contracts are best suited to particular kinds of transactions. Following Williamson's logic, those activities that are generally well-defined, which have a hard, tangible quality to them, and for which there are alternative sources—be they nonprofit or private—are the best candidates for contracting out. For example, vouchers may work well when there is an ample supply of vendors and an abundance of product— the best example is food stamps, which is one of the few vouchers with buying power as good as hard cash. The fact that many current privatization efforts involve intermediate inputs, such as various maintenance functions (Pack 1987), is supportive of the transaction costs position. On the other hand, transaction costs thinking also suggests a rationale for public or common ownership in a number of circumstances. As Sappington and Stiglitz (1987) suggest, the more complex the good or service, the more uncertain the technology, the harder it is to measure and monitor outputs, thus the higher the transaction costs. In these cases it would be more difficult to turn such activities over to private firms, without encountering problems of shirking, poor quality, and insufficient service to poorer consumers. Indeed, as Weisbrod (1988) argues, one of the reasons that services such as education get assigned to government or the nonprofit sector in the first place is because it is difficult to assess their quality.

Ecologists argue that the relaxation of constraints, which create boundaries among organizations, often unleashes a competitive struggle between populations that were not previously antagonists. The loosening of boundaries between public and private activities results in a more diverse population of organizations entering into competition with one another. This competition forces firms to reduce slack and redundant operations. These arguments provide a theoretical rationale for a common observation: public agencies that operate in an environment in which they are forced to compete with private and nonprofit bidders often realize significant cost savings. Or as a front page story in *The New York Times* (April 27, 1988) concluded, "the way to efficient public services is not replacing government agencies but pitting them against companies in continual competition." These journalistic reports lend support to the argument that organizational performance depends substantially on the mix of organizational forms within a particular industry.

An institutional perspective might begin with the observation that patterns of public and private ownership reflect the accidents of history and the

peculiarities of politics more than any "logical" model of relative competence. For example, how do we explain the enormous differences that exist
cross-nationally in the organization of various key industries? There are but a
few commonalities: throughout the western industrial nations, the post office, the railways, and the utilities tend to be public sector enterprises,
although each may be supplemented by some degree of for-profit competition. But the convergence ends there, and in industries such as gas, pe-
troleum, coal, the airlines, autos, steel, and shipbuilding, we find a highly
variegated pattern of ownership (McCraw 1984). Neither ecological nor
economic arguments appear to shed much light on this diversity. Institutionalists, however, would explain these divergent patterns by examining the
historical role played by the state in each society. A variety of sociopolitical
factors—such as the perceived legitimacy, or lack thereof, accorded to public authority, the presence of an elite civil service, extensive contacts among
business, labor, and government, political ideology, policies that favor infant
industries, and the stage of development—would help account for distinctive combinations of public and private ownership.

ECONOMIC REFORMS IN STATE-SOCIALIST SECTORS

Some of the most widely discussed changes in organizational forms are
underway in socialist societies. These reforms have been most pronounced
in Hungary; but more recently, worldwide attention has focused on nascent
efforts at restructuring (*perestroika*) all spheres of social and economic life in
the U.S.S.R. Similarly, thoroughgoing changes are being pursued in Czechoslovakia and Poland.[2]

Stylized models of the capitalist firm highlight its dependence on profits
taken in competition with other firms in the marketplace. Companion models
of socialist enterprise define viability in terms of success achieved through
bargaining with the state. Thus, the success of a socialist enterprise depends
less on its efficient production processes than on its bargaining power with the
central government (Kornai 1986a,b). Much of the discussion of, and attempts
at, economic restructuring in the planned economies focuses on changing
some of the economic institutions of socialism by introducing new management techniques, new methods of financing and accounting, and various
kinds of market mechanisms of exchange. Such efforts may involve the
elimination of mandatory planning and the centralized allocation of resources, as well as the creation of incentives for managers and investors
(Bauer 1988b). The goal is to create a system of market socialism (Brus
1987)—a system in which the means of production (capital) are publicly or
collectively owned, and the allocation of resources follows the rules of the
market. Or, as a leading Soviet academic puts it, "The essence of these

revolutionary changes is a transition from an excessively stable and rigid economic system to one which is more flexible" (Makarov 1988:459).

The logic behind these reforms is centered on the belief that overconcentration of decision-making power is the primary shortcoming of traditional socialist economic systems. The allocation of resources solely through administrative commands is purported to necessarily entail the inefficient use of resources. By turning some, though by no means all, activities over to private initiative, it is hoped that economic performance and innovation will be enhanced. The goal appears to be one of retaining central planning for important strategic developments, and allowing day-to-day operations to be controlled via the market.[3]

The centralization of economic power is not the only obstacle, however. Indeed, efforts at reforming large state-run enterprises have met with limited success. Much more attention has been devoted to the expansion of the "second economy." In part, this is a response to political ferment, as well as a recognition that various informal or subterranean practices have become exceedingly widespread.

The second economy consists of income-producing activities that occur outside of employment in the state-run enterprises of the socialist sector. Private agriculture, retail trade, various personal services, handicrafts, and nonlicensed gray- or black-market activities—particularly in construction and repair services—are the "nucleus" of the second economy (Bauer 1988a). Over the past three decades, Bauer tells us, numerous forms of mixed or semiprivate activities have proliferated in every socialist economy. David Stark (1989) reports that three-fourths of all households in Hungary earn some additional income from the second economy. And as consumers, Hungarians turn to the second sector for everything from bread to computer software. Moshe Lewin (1988), in his sweeping survey of the "Gorbachev phenomenon," argues that informal structures of relations, or "microworlds," have come to characterize everyday urban life in the Soviet Union. These networks, which range from professional associations to the followers and participants of the pop and jazz music scenes to the underground economy, are vital to Soviet citizens' efforts to obtain both basic consumer goods and an occasional luxury. These subterranean practices are "correctives or defensive mechanisms against the tensions and imbalances" that the formal structures of Soviet society fail to overcome. Recent Soviet reforms are forced to come to terms with these unofficial arrangements, often incorporating them in an effort to improve the economy.

In Hungary, a form of inside contracting has emerged, both as an effort to promote organizational flexibility within socialist firms and to augment the incomes of elite urban workers and preempt political discontent.[4] These enterprise business work partnerships, or VGMs, have up to 30 members, are accorded legal status as semiautonomous work units, and negotiate to produce goods or services on their "off" hours using the enterprise's equipment. It is a process, Stark (1986, 1989) explains, whereby aspects of the second economy are incorporated into the very heart of the socialist enterprise. By mid-1986, roughly 1 of every 10 manual workers participated in a VGM. This adds up to more than a quarter of a million workers, scattered across some 21,000 odd partnerships. The VGMs are a contradiction-filled form. They entail new methods of work organization in that they involve considerable restructuring of work roles, freer expression, greater autonomy, and a performance-based pay scheme. At the same time, workers experience the failure to incorporate any of these reforms into the regular hours of work as highly frustrating. Employees encounter two discordant organizational forms on a daily basis. Unlike the second economy, which operates outside the boundaries of the socialist enterprise, the VGM is located inside its very gates. The future of this innovation is not clear, but it is the subject of much frequent, and highly public, debate.

The outcome of market reforms in socialist societies is not altogether apparent, but these economies appear to be moving toward more mixed—perhaps mongrel is a more apt term—modes of work organization. An expanding second economy combined with modest reforms in the primary sector seems to be the norm. These reforms may create several wider changes: (1) the potential for considerable income redistribution and possible new avenues of social mobility, which will favor successful entrepreneurs and privileged skilled workers at the expense of state managers, and (2) an increasing role and importance for informal networks of market-like relationships.

How much insight do Western organizational theories offer into these developments in socialist societies? Somewhat surprisingly, organization theory appears to travel reasonably well. Population ecology emphasizes the replacement of outmoded organizational forms by new ones when environmental conditions undergo change. Rather than emphasizing the alleged efficiency of organizational reforms, ecologists would point to the advantages that accrue from a diversity of organizational forms. This classic evolutionary viewpoint stresses the advantages of diversity, which provides a higher probability of having an existing solution, or a means to develop one, that is responsive to changing environmental circumstances. The ecological view is consonant with Stark's (1989) contention that the decentralization of decision-making is perhaps not the Hungarian lesson, but instead the diversification of property forms might be the solution to the reconstructing of centrally planned economies.

Williamson's (1975, 1985) market-hierarchy continuum implies that the response to bureaucratic failure will lie in greater reliance on market mechanisms. Certainly much of the rhetoric of reform embraces efforts to introduce the high-powered incentives associated with markets into overly bureaucratic societies. Transaction costs analysis suggests that such changes would encourage higher levels of individual initiative. But transaction cost reasoning is largely silent on the timing of these reforms, and has little to say about whether they will meet with success. For example, Boisot and Child (1988) suggest that so-called market reforms in Communist China have failed to promote a market orientation. The existing institutional infrastructure supports patrimonial values; hence personal relationships are an essential feature of any economic exchange. Impersonal contracting remains uncommon and courts seldom enforce contracts. Control by the central government, never very complete, is now even weaker; but instead of market relations, economic activity is guided by informal trust-based relationships. To Boisot and Child (1988), China is becoming a land of "industrial fiefs," not of market transactions.

These observations would not be surprising to institutional theorists. Efforts at restructuring that involve modifications of existing frameworks or piecemeal efforts to transform current economic mechanisms are likely to be short-lived. This is because serious reform entails a general change in the operating principles of a society. Bauer (1988b) makes this point clearly in his discussion of Hungarian reforms. He suggests that success requires that a package of significant measures be undertaken simultaneously: the creation of thousands of new small enterprises, genuine liberalization of prices, the elimination of subsidies, the creation of competition among banks and an independent capital market, import liberalization, and the assurance of managerial freedom from the party and the state.

An institutional perspective is less concerned with the relative advantages of capitalist or socialist enterprise per se, and more interested in the conditions under which different justifications for organizational behavior are regarded as legitimate. Does the expansion of the second economy have the consequence of making entrepreneurial or self-interested accounts more widely acceptable? Or do the managers of profitable firms use this measure of success to push for larger budgets or increased subsidies? The discourse associated with reform may reveal a great deal about whether the institutions of socialism are undergoing change.

An institutional argument would also help account for why reform policies have typically turned toward concessions to private initiative instead of thorough-going changes in large-scale, socialist enterprises. State ownership enhances the power of the state managers. As Szelenyi (1982) has observed, the dominant class in state-socialist societies includes the bureaucrats who control resource allocation processes and the elite workers and intelligentsia who benefit from state policies. Institutionalists contend that the state is the great rationalizer of the twentieth century, and its agents are typically loathe to relinquish their power and influence (DiMaggio and Powell 1983). Any restructuring of state enterprises is a threat to the power of state bureaucrats, so it is not surprising that reforms in the second economy will be more tolerated and expansive than changes in the primary sector.

THE DECENTRALIZATION OF LARGE-SCALE ENTERPRISES

The decade of the 1980s has been a sobering one for U.S. businesses. Sluggish productivity, foreign competition, and hostile takeovers are but a few of the threats that have fostered a reexamination of business practices and led to the search for new ways of organizing the workplace. In one variant of these developments, firms have rediscovered the competitive marketplace, the hostile world of arms'-length relationships that characterizes the competitive model of microeconomic theory. Associated with this rediscovery are draconian efforts at cost cutting, fewer restrictions on managerial freedom in the deployment of labor, and intense lobbying to reduce government regulations. These changes are intended to make firms "lean and mean" to help them survive intensified competition for jobs and contracts. In another variant of this trend, firms seek to become more competitive and flexible by reorganizing the nature of production, in some cases by developing entirely new methods for organizing competition. These firms are responding to competition not so much by eliminating workers, but by tying some portion of employee wages to company performance and by engaging workers more actively in the operations of the company (Weitzman 1984; Walton 1985). Both of these responses entail some form of vertical disaggregation, or the "down-sizing" of large corporate hierarchies.

In an era when the pace of technological change was relatively slow, and production runs turned out large numbers of similar products, vertical integration was a highly successful strategy. But the disadvantages of large-scale vertical integration can become acute when the pace of technological change quickens, product life cycles shorten, and markets become more specialized. Firms are trying to cope with these new pressures either by explicitly limiting the size of work units, by contracting work out, or through more collaborative ventures with suppliers and distributors.

The United States is not alone in this respect: in many industrial nations firms are choosing to shrink their operations in response to the liabilities of large-scale organization. For example, Mariotti and Cainarca (1986) describe a pattern of disaggregation in the Italian textile industry, where there has been a decline in the number of vertically integrated firms and growth in various kinds of interfirm agreements. They attribute this development to three problems that plague large vertically integrated firms: an inability to respond quickly to competitive changes in international markets, opposition to process innovations that alter the relationship between different stages of the production process, and systematic resistance to the introduction of new products. Wilkinson (1983) details related developments in Britain, where retailing, clothing, shoemaking, printing, and foodstuffs have undergone vertical disintegration, with the subsequent rise of small firms and numerous subcontracting relationships.

Another common way in which large firms are growing "smaller" is through the use of subcontractors and temporary employees. To be sure, neither the use of part-time workers nor contracting for various business services as needed is a new addition to the repertoire of organizations. But these methods of accomplishing tasks have recently grown in importance (Pfeffer and Baron 1987; Abraham 1987, 1988; Mangum et al. 1985; Carey and Hazelbacker 1986). We do not yet know if these trends are merely a reaction to a difficult economic period or part of a fundamental change in the organization of work. The answer is not clear, because practices such as subcontracting have a double edge: they may represent a move toward relational contracting (Macneil 1978), with greater emphasis on security and quality, or they could be a rediscovery of the nineteenth century putting out system, an effort to slash labor costs, and limit the power of unions even further.

The U.S. auto industry provides a good example of the crossroads many firms are at as they encounter the limits of vertical integration. The auto industry—both domestic and international—has undergone a profound shake-up. Prior to the mid-1970s, the big three U.S. automakers operated in a comfortable environment with little competitive pressure and scant customer demands for gas-efficient, high quality cars. The auto companies pursued a strategy of tight integration of production, which provided a means of guaranteeing supplies during periods of peak demand, and afforded protection to annual styling changes. Vertical integration also kept down the prices of the independent parts suppliers with whom the companies traded. There was neither any give and take nor trust between the automakers and the subcontractors. Contracts were lost because a supplier bid 0.01 cents per item higher than a competitor (Porter 1983). Automakers rigorously inspected supplier facilities, quality control procedures, stability of raw material sources, cost data, and management quality and depth (Porter 1983:278). They were reluctant to permit a supplier to manufacture a complete system. Instead, automakers preferred a competitive situation in which several firms supplied various components and the final assembly was done in-house.

Today this old system has crumbled in the face of international competition and fallen prey to the contradictions and short-term logic of the regime of competitive supplier relations. Heightened competition exposed a number of serious defects in this system. Abernathy (1978) has argued that vertical integration in the auto industry led to inflexibility. One consequence of tight technological interdependence is that change in any one part means the entire process must be altered. Pursuit of a cost-minimization strategy also reduced the automakers' ability to innovate. Susan Helper (1987), in an excellent analysis of supplier relations in the auto industry, observes that the old methods prevented suppliers from developing expertise, thereby reducing the skill requirements of their employees. This made it hard for them to develop any nonautomotive contracts and kept them dependent on the auto companies. It also had a chilling effect on innovation. There was neither any incentive nor capability for the suppliers to update equipment, suggest technological changes, or make long-range plans.

Because of their loss of market share and declining profits, the automakers began to experiment with new subcontracting policies (Helper 1987). The length of contracts has been expanded, from one to three to five years. More joint design work is being undertaken and sole-sourcing agreements are becoming more common. These new collaborative arrangements involve less monitoring and costly inspections, yet defect rates are much reduced. The automakers are becoming more dependent on the technological expertise of the suppliers, whose long-run health is now a factor in the automakers' profits.

At the same time, however, the automakers are pursuing a second strategy: outsourcing to low wage areas. They are simultaneously deciding which suppliers are worth investing in a long-term relationship with and determining which components can be obtained on the basis of price rather than quality. In these cases, there is little concern for collaboration or supplier design work; instead, the effort is aimed at finding third-world suppliers that can provide parts at the lowest possible price.

At first inspection, none of the theories appears to be particularly well equipped to explain this trend. Ecologists argue that large established organizations rarely change their strategy and structure quickly enough to keep pace with the demands of changing environments. Similarly, institutional theory conceives of organizations as creatures of habit and routine. As a result, organizations tend to resist attempts at change. They are not highly malleable, adaptive institutions. The recent efforts of large vertically integrated firms to down-size thus run counter to the assumptions of both these approaches. Still, these moves have been halting, controversial, and, in some cases, last-ditch responses to alterations in the economic environment. The view of large organizations as ponderous entities is not altogether inaccurate; what is missing in these theories is any notion of just how dramatic the changes in the larger environment must be to provoke a response on the part of organizations.

Ecological and institutional theories view change as episodic rather than gradual. When adjustments in organizational strategies and structures do occur, they are likely to do so in periods of crisis, which are then followed by longer periods of consolidation and stability. This suggests that these recent organizational realignments may set the course for a new path of development. Once the shift to new forms of organization is underway, institutional theory has much to say about how new practices are diffused. DiMaggio and Powell (1983) suggests that organizational reforms are spread through personnel transfers, via professional training workshops and executive education courses, and with the assistance of consulting firms.

Nor does transaction costs economics offer a very plausible explanation either. Indeed, the primary focus of this approach is directed at explaining market failure, or the conditions that give rise to the establishment of hierarchical forms. Very little attention has been paid to the liabilities of vertical integration.[5] Williamson (1985) laments that the study of bureaucratic failure is "very primitive." (There is, of course, an extensive literature in sociology on bureaucratic pathologies, but for several reasons this work is not easily incorporated into a transaction costs framework.[6])

But what about the choice that many firms confront between moving transactions back into the marketplace, and creating modern variants of the old putting out system, or establishing long-term, give-and-take relationships among more or less autonomous parties? Here transaction costs thinking may be more helpful. My reading of Williamson (1985) and Macneil (1978) suggests that when tasks involve relatively standardized activities that require little asset specificity, or when demand for a product is highly uncertain, firms are likely to turn to market relationships. But when tasks require knowledge and skill, demand is steady, and quality is important, firms are more likely to rely on relational contracting, on the long-term give-and-take relationships that rely on personal contact and some degree of trust.

THE PROLIFERATION OF NETWORK FORMS OF ORGANIZATION

In a number of key respects, networks represent a modern version of a centuries-old means of allocating goods and services, a method that Polanyi (1957) termed "generalized reciprocity." In this model of resource allocation, transactions occur neither through discrete exchanges nor by administrative fiat, but through networks of individuals engaged in reciprocal, preferential, mutually supportive actions. In network forms of organization, individual units exist not by themselves, but in relationship to other units.

In many network-like settings, there is scant separation of formal business roles and personal social roles. One's standing in one arena often determines one's place in the other. As a result, there is little need for hierarchical oversight, because the desire for continued participation successfully discourages opportunism. Monitoring is generally easier and more effective when done by peers than when done by superiors. Performance evaluation takes place through the kind of subtle reading of signals that is possible only among intimate co-workers but that cannot be translated into explicit, verifiable measures. Consensual ideologies substitute for formal rules and compliance procedures.

The examples presented below suggest that the conditions that give rise to network forms are quite diverse. The immediate causes, to the extent that they can be discerned, reveal a wide variety of reasons for the proliferation of network-like arrangements. The origins and development of network forms seldom reveal a simple chain of events. In some cases, the formation of networks anticipates the need for this particular form of exchange; in other situations, there is a slow pattern of development that ultimately justifies the form; and in still other circumstances, networks are a response to the demand for a mode of exchange that resolves exigencies that other forms are ill equipped to handle. The network story, then, is a complex one of contingent development, tempered by an adjustment to the social and economic conditions of the time. Some of the more common examples of networks include the following:

1. The vigorous growth of informal enterprise (e.g., in consumer services, light industries, the garment and construction trades, etc.) in developed nations, and the persistence of the informal economy in developing nations, long after the point at which these activities were predicted to subside (Portes and Sassen-Koob 1987).
2. The stability of quasifirms or hybrid forms in such craft-based industries as construction (Eccles 1981), book publishing (Powell 1985), cultural industries, and research and knowledge production.
3. Alliances and partnerships that join together small firm innovativeness with large firm distribution and marketing clout.
4. The global resurgence of regional economies, in high technology sectors in the United States, in intermediate product markets in Sweden, and in the "third Italy," where flexible craft production has expanded dramatically (Sabel 1989).

For the purposes of discussion, I focus on these last two developments. (For a more detailed discussion of a wide range of network arrangements, see Powell 1990.)

Strategic Partnering

There is considerable experimentation with various new kinds of interfirm agreements, collaborations, and partnerships—in some industries, these practices have mushroomed in an unprecedented fashion (Friar and Horwitch 1985; Teece 1986; Zagnoli 1987). Firms are seeking to combine their strengths and overcome weaknesses in a collaboration that is much broader and deeper than the typical marketing joint ventures and technology licensing that were used previously. These new ventures may take the form of new cooperative relationships with suppliers, or confederations among small firms that facilitate research and new product development. More generally, internally generated and financed research is giving way to new forms of external R&D partnerships among previously unaffiliated enterprises. Indeed, in some industries, there appears to be a wholesale stampede into various alliance-type combinations that link large generalist firms and specialized entrepreneurial start-ups. Nor are these simply new means to pursue research and development; the new arrangements also extend to production, marketing, and distribution. And, in some circumstances, large firms are joining together to create "global strategic partnerships" (Perlmutter and Heenan 1986) that shift the very basis of competition to a new level—from firm vs. firm to rival transnational alliances.

These developments, not surprisingly, are particularly common in high technology industries (Mariti and Smiley 1983; Zagnoli 1987). Both the motivations for collaboration and the organizational forms that result are quite varied. Firms pursue cooperative agreements to gain fast access to new technologies or new markets, to benefit from economies of scale in joint research and/or production, to tap into sources of know-how located outside the boundaries of the firm, to share the risks for activities that are beyond the scope or capability of a single organization, and to contract for complementary skills. The ensuing organizational arrangements include joint ventures, strategic alliances, equity partnerships, collaborative research pacts or large-scale research consortia, licensing agreements, reciprocity deals, and satellite organizations. There is no clear-cut relationship between the legal form of the cooperative agreements and the purposes they are intended to achieve. The form of the agreement appears to be individually tailored to the needs of the respective parties, and to tax and regulatory considerations.

High technology industries, such as microelectronics and biotechnology, are graphic examples both of the range of different possible ways of organizing and allocating tasks and of their sharp divergence from traditional patterns of industrial organization. In these process-oriented fields, timing considerations and access to know-how are paramount concerns. Teece and Pisano (1987) suggest that, increasingly, the most qualified centers of excellence in the relevant know-how are located outside the boundaries of the large corporation. Whether it is the case that one firm's technological competence has outdistanced others, or that innovations would be hard to replicate internally (as suggested by the growing reliance on external sources of research and development—see the articles by Friar and Horwitch, and by Graham in the special issue of *Technology in Society*, 1985), network forms represent a fast means of gaining access to know-how that cannot be produced internally. The network-like configurations that have evolved in high technology can process information in multiple directions. They create complex webs of communication and mutual obligation. By enhancing the spread of information, they sustain the conditions for further innovation by bringing together different logics and novel combinations of information.

Regional Economies

Competition and uncertainty have also created, or perhaps recreated is a better word, new forms of collaboration among firms outside of high technology fields. This rediscovery or reinvigoration of nineteenth-century industrial districts points to the advantages of agglomeration, in which firms choose to locate in an area not because of the presence of an untapped market, but because of the existence of a dense, overlapping cluster of firms, skilled laborers, and an institutional infrastructure (Arthur 1987).[7]

Charles Sabel and his colleagues (1987) describe the German textile industry, centered in the prosperous state of Baden-Wurttemberg in southwestern Germany, as an "association of specialists, each with unmatched expertise and flexibility in a particular phase or type of production." This flourishing traditional craft industry employs a highly refined system of production that links small and medium-sized firms with a wide range of institutional arrangements that further the well-being of the industry as a whole. These support services include industry research institutes, vocational training centers, consulting firms, and marketing agencies. Most textile producers are highly specialized, and, as Sabel et al. argue, the more distinctive each firm is, the more it depends on the success of other firms' products that complement its own. This production system depends on an extensive subcontracting system in which key technologies are developed in collaboration. The subcontractors are also connected to overlapping interindustry supplier networks. These linkages allow textile makers to benefit from the subcontractors' experiences with customers in other industries, and the suppliers are, in turn, buffered from downturns in any one industry. All of these arrangements strengthen the social structure in which textile firms are embedded and encourage cooperative relations that attenuate the more destructive aspects of competition.

Ronald Dore (1983) argues that networks of preferential, stable trading relationships are a viable alternative to vertical integration. His work on the regionally concentrated Japanese textile industry, particularly its weaving segment, aptly illustrates this point. The industry was dominated in the 1950s by large mills, most of which were vertically integrated enterprises with cotton-importing, spinning, and finishing operations. By 1980 the larger mills had closed and the integrated firms had divested and returned to their original base in spinning. This "devolution" has led to a series of stable relationships among firms of different sizes. The key to this system is mutual assistance. Dore gives the example of a finisher who reequips with a more efficient process, which gives him a cost advantage. This finisher, however, does not win much new business by offering a lower price. The more common consequence is that merchants go to their own finishers and say: "Look how X has got his price down. We hope you can do the same because we really would have to reconsider our position if the price difference goes on for months. If you need bank financing to get the new type of vat we can probably help by guaranteeing the loan." This type of relationship is, of course, not limited to the Japanese textile industry; similar patterns of reciprocal ties are found in many other sectors of the Japanese economy.

What are the performance consequences of these kinds of extended trading relationships? Dore suggests that the security of the relationship encourages investment by suppliers, as the spread of robotics among Japan's engineering subcontractors amply attests. Trust and mutual obligation result in a more rapid flow of information. In textiles, changes in consumer markets are passed quickly upstream to weavers, and technical changes in production also flow downstream rapidly. There is, Dore asserts, a general emphasis on quality. One would not terminate a relationship when a party cannot deliver the lowest price, but it is perfectly proper to sever an agreement when someone is not maintaining quality standards.

These cases are more than mere illustrations, because taken together, they represent a number of highly competitive and/or resurgent industries, and they tell a consistent story. The common theme is one of how cooperation can be sustained over the long run. Networks represent a different model of production, one in which rapid access to information is utilized to alter the relationship between production and strategy. Networks allow ideas to be put into action more quickly than is the case for markets or hierarchies.[8]

How well do our theories of organization account for the growing importance of network forms? The absence of a clear developmental pattern and the recognition that network forms have multiple causes and varied historical trajectories suggest that no single explanation is satisfactory. Economizing is obviously a relevant concern in many instances, especially in infant industries where competitive preserves are strong. But it alone is not a particularly robust story, it is but one among a number of theoretically possible motives for action—all of which are consonant with a broad view of self-interest. Clearly many of the arrangements discussed above actually increase transaction costs, but in return they provide concrete benefits or intangible assets that are far more valuable. The reduction of uncertainty, fast access to information, reliability, and responsiveness are critical concerns that motivate the participants in exchange networks.

Network arrangements are common in high technology industries, which are relatively young and early in their product life cycles. Consequently, population ecology has much to offer in explaining the proliferation of this form. Ecologists argue that key changes or strategic innovations occur early in the life history of individual organizations and of organizational populations. Moreover, ecologists would be comfortable with the argument that rapid structural changes in the world economy create movement both away from an older set of industries (thus causing firms in these industries to shrink) and toward a new set of industries (in which most firms are still in a youthful stage).

Partnerships or alliances reflect the differential abilities of small and large firms. They represent a quintessential case of the combination of specialist and generalist firms (Hannan and Freeman 1977). The movement in large companies away from in-house development to partial ownership or collaboration reflects an awareness that small firms are much faster at, and more capable of, innovation and product development, and that outright takeover or merger, the previously most common means of acquiring new capabilities, tends to dampen the contributions of the small, technology-driven firms.

An institutional explanation for the spread of networks would focus on the features of the context in which networks emerge, and the patterns through which network-like arrangements diffuse. The extent to which economic actors rely on the marketplace, private enterprise, or network forms of relational contracting is determined, to a considerable extent, by state policies. The sociopolitical context plays a key role in the development and spread of networks in certain industries and nations, and not in others. For example, the legal structure of Japanese business, with its relaxed antitrust standards, and the financial structure, which affords a longer term time perspective, are particularly conducive to interorganizational collaborations. The combination of these legal and financial regimes with a government whose key ministry (MITI) plays an active role in linking private firms through R&D networks provides a propitious setting for interfirm relationships.

In the United States, where the larger institutional context is less hospitable, the focus of an institutional argument would be on how the collaborative norms of science are transported to private firms via contacts forged in professional or graduate schools, or through various kinds of professional activities. An institutional analysis would also examine the kind of knowledge that is utilized in network forms of organization. Network arrangements are particularly well suited for a highly skilled labor force, where participants possess fungible knowledge that is not limited to a specific task but applicable to a wide range of activities. Networks complement these human capital skills by providing work roles with multiple responsibilities, and strong ties both across the immediate work team and to members of other organizations.

The human agents who populate transaction costs economics are highly calculative and opportunistic, lacking in compassion. As Williamson (1985:391) notes, this is "plainly not an attractive or even an accurate view of human nature." This narrow view, however, does not preclude the possibility that they will forge alliances or partnerships. Indeed, the literature on credible commitments (Williamson 1985) suggests one set of circumstances under which these relationships might be sustained. There are numerous mechanisms—hostage-taking, collateral arrangements, and the like—for creating mutually reliant and self-enforcing agreements. But by ignoring solidarity and reciprocity, transaction costs arguments will find it difficult to explain collaborative arrangements that are not based on purely self-interested motives. The broader issues of culture and politics are critical to any account of the origins of networks.

In only a minority of instances is it sensible to maintain that the genesis of network forms is driven by a concern for minimizing transaction costs. Strategic considerations—such as efforts to guarantee access to critical resources, to obtain crucial skills that cannot be produced internally, to pacify the concerns of professional communities or national governments, or even, as in the case of global partnerships, to remake the very nature of international competition—certainly seem to outweigh a simple concern with cost minimization. David Teece has shown, however, that transaction cost thinking can both be useful in accounting for when organizations are likely to enter collaborative agreements for the exchange of complementary skills, and helpful in alerting us to which situations are rife for the exploitation of a disproportionate share of the relationship (Teece 1986; Teece and Pisano 1987).

SUMMARY AND IMPLICATIONS

What do these diverse developments tell us about the current strengths and weaknesses of various organizational theories? Not surprisingly, given their divergent roots, these approaches are probably more complementary than oppositional. Each has differential strengths and weaknesses, and evinces a distinctive ability to shed light on particular problems, while at the same time remaining in the shadows when it comes to other matters. Each theoretical perspective is based on different presuppositions, on divergent views about the appropriate unit and level of analysis. Therefore, the various approaches have different standards for what constitutes an appropriate explanation.

Transaction costs economics emphasizes that the study of economic organization must go beyond matters of technology and ownership to include an examination of incentive and governance structures. This approach seems well suited for examining questions of organizational boundaries and issues of appropriability. Why is one kind of collaboration, say research and development, more likely to be enduring than a fee for service arrangement? Transaction costs analysts would tell us that agreements based on contracting for the performance or delivery of various services are likely to be discontinued when one party's internal skills "catch up" with those of the partner. On the other hand, when exchange partners are involved in ongoing, complementary contributions—such as the pooling of research staffs or joint production activities—the relationship is likely to be more enduring.

But once we move beyond the immediate boundaries of the firm, this approach appears to lose some of its force. An exclusive focus on the transaction as the primary unit of analysis appears to be disabling when it comes to explaining broad patterns of organizational change. From either an ecological or an institutional perspective, it makes little sense to separate organizational behavior from its social and historical context. Nor can many of the issues dealt with herein be divorced from the "messy" world of politics.

Institutionalists define organizational fields broadly to include key political and economic agents within the domain of organization theory. Thus, this approach can be revealing about the environmental context that shapes organizational behavior, but of limited utility in accounting for the specific actions of an individual firm. Many of the changes that I have described appear to have a systemic quality to them, that is, they are more than recombinations of existing practices or reshufflings of old themes. As Bauer (1988b) suggested in his analysis of Hungarian reforms, successful implementation requires the simultaneous adoption of a "package" of new organizing principles. More broadly, it appears that these new organizational forms have a certain coherence in that they consist of a number of supporting elements, any of which would be insufficient on its own. Relational contracting, for example, seems to entail some combination of skilled labor, employment security, salaries rather than piece rates, some externally provided means of job training, and relative equality among the various partners.

Institutional theory could make a significant contribution to our understanding of organizational change if it were able to explain what kinds of practices go in tandem. Questions that are at present unanswerable could then be addressed: How much government infrastructure is necessary for private enterprise to flourish? How much collectivist baggage can be loaded onto a private enterprise system? Is it possible to foster economic pluralism in state-socialist societies while maintaining the framework of a one-party regime? At the moment, organization theory cannot respond to these concerns; but if it is going to, I submit that the answers will largely be institutional ones.

An ecological approach is also much more relevant in explaining how broad processes of social change influence organizational populations than in accounting for the actions of individual firms. Population ecology also directs attention away from a focus on connections among organizations. But many questions, firmly within the purview of ecological thinking, remain. How do changes in the environment affect the rate at which new organizational forms are created? How do changes in political and economic systems affect the diversity of organizational populations? How does the ecology of organizational populations shape political and economic development? Volatile environments support a diverse population of organizational forms, while stable environments constrain variety, thus political ferment gives rise to new organizational arrangements. Periods of technological change and social experimentation rob established organizational forms of their influence and bring upstarts to the fore, leading to replacement of older forms by newer ones.

The changes I have described are broad-based. We find them ongoing across industries—in supposedly mature mass production industries, in traditional sectors where craft techniques were never abandoned, and in the new high technology fields, and across nation states—in the state-socialist societies of Eastern Europe and in the industrial democracies of the West. At the same time, these developments are provisional and uncertain. We do not know whether they represent a fundamental leap to a new and different kind of interaction or whether they are merely transitional or cyclical responses to economic downturns and public dissatisfaction. Are new players and new kinds of organizational arrangements taking center stage or are the changes only temporary, and previously dominant incumbents will soon reemerge on top? These issues are far from being resolved, but I hope I have underscored the crosscutting pressures that capitalist and socialist enterprises alike, as well as public agencies and private nonprofits, are facing: circumstances that push them toward sharp-edged competitive practices that entail lower wages and a more intensive pace of work, and equally strong conditions that lead them to search for policies that permit flexibility, promote equality and more collaborative relationships, and provide ready access to sources of know-how.

ACKNOWLEDGMENTS

I am grateful to Glenn Carroll, Paula England, Roger Friedland, David Stark, and Mayer Zald for very helpful comments on an earlier draft.

NOTES

1.   The intermingling of public and private has a very long ancestry. The assignment in the late Roman Empire of public duties involving revenue or construction to private contractors or mercantile companies was but a very early example of a hybrid or mixed organizational form.

Perry Anderson (1974) has argued that the early modern redefinition of property rights and reorganization of political space unleashed both interstate political relations and capitalist production relations. The sales of offices "correspond to the overdetermination of the late feudal state by the swift growth of mercantile and manufacturing capital. The contradictory nexus which it established between public office and private persons reflected medieval conceptions of sovereignty and contract" (Anderson 1974:217). The development of English interior transportation on highways and canals was turned over to profit-seeking private corporations obligated to allow passage to "eligible" vehicles. The eighteenth-century English turnpike trust and the great canal of Languedoc in France were other premodern forms of quasipublic corporations. Similarly, the great trading companies of the sixteenth, seventeenth, and eighteenth centuries, such as the East India Company, are yet another example of how fuzzy the lines are between public and private.

2.   For an excellent general discussion of these reforms, see Nee and Stark (1989).

3.   What are important strategic developments? They appear to vary considerably across socialist countries, but Makarov (1988:458) suggests that in the "reform-minded" USSR, "they will be limited to ensuring supplies for the most important projects in the social sphere, state investment projects, and defense."

4.   This discussion relies extensively on the research of David Stark (1986, 1989).

5.   In a recent paper (Powell 1987b), I suggest that large vertically integrated firms may perform quite well when mass production, strict routines, and well-specified procedures can be used to attack stable and predictable markets. But when organizations are confronted by sharp fluctuations in demand and unanticipated changes, the shortcomings of large scale are exposed. Among the principal disadvantages of bureaucratic forms of organization are a bias toward internal procurement and expansion, problems of structural inertia, risk aversion, and decreased employee satisfaction and commitment.

6.   One reason that work in sociology is subversive of a transaction costs approach is that it does not assume that certain kinds of activities are best suited to specific types of governance structures (see the discussion in Granovetter 1985). Williamson's apt response is that the sociological literature is not always informed by a comparative institutional assessment, that is, insufficient attention is paid to whether certain pathologies are more or less likely to occur in specific kinds of organizational settings.

7.   The discussion of regional economies is developed at much greater length in a very thoughtful paper by Charles Sabel (1989) on changes in the scale of production.

8.   For a more extensive account of the logic of network forms, see Powell (1990).

REFERENCES

Abernathy, William. 1978. *The Productivity Dilemma*. Baltimore: Johns Hopkins University Press.

Abraham, Katherine G. 1987. "Restructuring the Employment Relationship: The Growth of Market-Mediated Work Arrangements." Paper presented at conference on New Developments in Labor Markets and Human Resource Policies, Sloan School, M.I.T.

————. 1988. "The Role of Flexible Staffing Arrangements in Short-Term Workforce Adjustment Strategies." In *Employment, Unemployment, and Labor Utilization*, edited by R. A. Hart. Boston, Unwin Hyman.

Anderson, Perry. 1974. *Lineages of the Absolutist State*. New York: Shocken.

Arthur, Brian. "Urban Systems and Historical Path-Dependence." In *Urban Systems and Infrastructure,* edited by R. Herman and J. Ansubel. NAS/NAE, forthcoming.

Bauer, Tamas. 1988a. "Economic Reforms within and beyond the State Sector." *American Economic Review* 78(2):452–456.

———. 1988b. "Hungarian Economic Reform in East European Perspective." *Eastern European Politics and Societies* 2(3)(Fall):418–432.

Boisot, Max and John Child. 1988. "The Iron Law of Fiefs: Bureaucratic Failure and the Problems of Governance in the Chinese System Reforms." *Administrative Science Quarterly* 33(4)(December):507–528.

Brus, Wlodziemierz. 1988. "Market Socialism." Pp. 337–342 in *The New Palgrave: A Dictionary of Economics,* edited by John Eatwell et al. New York: Stockton Press.

Carey, Max, and Kim Hazelbacker. 1986. "Employment Growth in the Temporary Help Industry." *Monthly Labor Review* April:37–44.

Carroll, Glenn. 1984. "Organizational Ecology." *Annual Review of Sociology* 10:71–93.

Coase, Ronald. 1937. "The Nature of the Firm." *Economica* 4:386–405.

DiMaggio, Paul, and Walter W. Powell. 1983. "The Iron Cage Revisited: Institutional Isomorphism and Collective Rationality in Organizational Fields." *American Sociological Review* 48:147–160.

Dore, Ronald. 1983. "Goodwill and the Spirit of Market Capitalism." *British Journal of Sociology* 34(4)(December):459–482.

Eccles, Robert. 1981. "The Quasifirm in the Construction Industry." *Journal of Economic Behavior and Organization* 2 (December):335–357.

Friar, John, and Mel Horwitch. 1985. "The Emergence of Technology Strategy: A New Dimension of Strategic Management." *Technology in Society* 7(2/3):143–178.

Geertz, Clifford. 1981. *Negara: The Theatre State in Nineteenth Century Bali.* Princeton: Princeton University Press.

Graham, Margaret. 1985. "Corporate Research and Development: The Latest Transformation." *Technology in Society* 7(2/3):179–196.

Granovetter, Mark. 1985. "Economic Action and Social Structure: The Problem of Embeddedness." *American Journal of Sociology* 91:481–510.

Hannan, Michael and John Freeman. 1977. "The Population Ecology of Organizations." *American Journal of Sociology* 92:929–964.

———. 1984. "Structural Inertia and Organizational Change." *American Sociological Review* 49:149–164.

———. 1989. *Organizational Ecology.* Cambridge: Harvard University Press.

Hansmann, Henry. 1987. "Economic Theories of Nonprofit Organization." Pp. 27–42 in *The Nonprofit Sector,* edited by W. W. Powell. New Haven: Yale University Press.

Helper, Susan. 1987. *Supplier Relations and Technical Change.* Ph.D. Dissertation, Department of Economics, Harvard University.

Kornai, Janos. 1986a. "Comments on the Present State and Prospects of the Hungarian Economic Reform." *Journal of Comparative Economics* 7(September):225–252.

————. 1986b. "The Hungarian Reform Process: Visions, Hopes, and Reality." *Journal of Economic Literature* XXIV (December):1687–1737.

Lewin, Moshe. 1988. *The Gorbachev Phenomenon: A Historical Interpretation.* Berkeley: University of California Press.

Macneil, Ian. 1978. "Contracts: Adjustment of Long-term Economic Relations under Classical, Neoclassical, and Relational Contract Law." *Northwestern University Law Review* 72(6):854–905.

Makarov, Valery L. 1988. "On the Strategy for Implementing Economic Reform in the USSR." *American Economic Review* 78(2):457–460.

Mangum, Garth, Donald Mayall, and Kristin Nelson. 1985. "The Temporary Help Industry." *Industrial and Labor Relations Review* 38:599–611.

Mariotti, Sergio, and Gian Carlo Cainarca. 1986. "The Evolution of Transaction Governance in the Textile-Clothing Industry." *Journal of Economic Behavior and Organization* 7:351–374.

Mariti, P. and R. H. Smiley. 1983. "Co-operative Agreements and the Organization of Industry." *Journal of Industrial Economics* 31(4):437–451.

McCraw, Thomas K. 1984. "Business and Government: The Origins of the Adversary Relationship." *California Management Review* 26(2):33–52.

Meyer, John W. and Brian Rowan. 1977. "Institutionalized Organizations: Formal Structure as Myth and Ceremony." *American Journal of Sociology* 83:340–363.

Meyer, John W. and W. Richard Scott. 1983. *Organizational Environments: Ritual and Rationality,* Beverly Hills, CA: Sage.

Nee, Victor and David Stark (eds.). 1989. *Remaking the Economic Institutions of State Socialism.* Stanford: Stanford University Press.

Nelson, Richard R. 1981. "Assessing Private Enterprise: An Exegesis of Tangled Doctrine." *Bell Journal of Economics* 12(1):93–111.

————. 1987. "Roles of Government in a Mixed Economy." *Journal of Policy Analysis and Management* 6(4):541–557.

North, Douglass C. 1984. "Government and the Cost of Exchange in History." *Journal of Economic History* XLIV:255–264.

Pack, Janet Rothenberg. 1987. "Privatization of Public-Sector Services in Theory and Practice." *Journal of Policy Analysis and Management* 6(4):523–540.

Perlmutter, Howard and David Heenan. 1986. "Cooperate to Compete Globally." *Harvard Business Review* April/May:136–152.

Pfeffer, Jeffrey and James Baron. 1987. "Taking the Workers Back Out: Recent Trends in the Structuring of Employment." Pp. 257–304 in *Research in Organizational Behavior,* Vol. 10, edited by B. Staw and L. Cummings. Greenwich, CT: JAI Press.

Polanyi, Karl. 1957. *The Great Transformation.* Boston: Beacon.

Porter, Michael. 1983. *Cases in Competitive Strategy.* New York: Free Press.

Portes, Alejandro and Saskia Sassen-Koob. 1987. "Making it Underground: Comparative Material on the Informal Sector in Western Market Economies." *American Journal of Sociology* 93(1):30–61.

Powell, Walter W. 1985. *Getting into Print: The Decision Making Process in Scholarly Publishing.* Chicago: University of Chicago Press.

————. (ed.) 1987a. *The Nonprofit Sector: A Research Handbook.* New Haven: Yale University Press.

————. 1987b. "Hybrid Organizational Arrangements: New Form or Transitional Development?" *California Management Review* 30(1):67–87.

————. 1990. "Neither Market Nor Hierarchy: Network Forms of Organization." Pp. 295–336 in *Research in Organizational Behavior,* Vol. 12, edited by B. Staw and L. L. Cummings. Greenwich, CT: JAI Press.

Sabel, Charles F. 1989. "Flexible specialization and the Re-emergence of Regional Economies." Pp. 17–71 in *Reversing Industrial Decline?* edited by P. Hirst and J. Zeitlin, Oxford, UK: Berg.

Sabel, Charles F., Gary Herrigel, Richard Kazis, and Richard Deeg. 1987. "How to Keep Mature Industries Innovative." *Technology Review* 90(3):26–35.

Salamon, Lester M. 1987. "Partners in Public Service: The Scope and Theory of Government—Nonprofit Relations." Pp. 99–118 in *The Nonprofit Sector,* edited by W. Powell. New Haven: Yale University Press.

Sappington, David and Joseph E. Stiglitz. 1987. "Privatization, Information, and Incentives." *Journal of Policy Analysis and Management* 6(4):567–581.

Stark, David. 1986. "Rethinking Internal Labor Markets: New Insights from a Comparative Perspective." *American Sociological Review* 51:492–504.

————. 1989. "Coexisting Organizational Forms in Hungary's Mixed Economy." Pp. 137–168 in *Remaking the Economic Institutions of Socialism* edited by V. Nee and D. Stark, Stanford: Stanford University Press.

Szelenyi, Ivan. 1982. "The Intelligentsia in the Class Structure of State-Socialist Societies." Pp. 287–326 in *Marxist Inquiries,* edited by M. Burawoy and T. Skocpol. Chicago: University of Chicago Press.

Teece, David. 1986. "Profiting from Technological Innovation: Implications for Integration, Collaboration, Licensing and Public Policy." *Research Policy* 15(6):785–305.

Teece, David and Gary Pisano. 1987. "Collaborative Arrangements and Technology Strategy." Paper presented at the conference on New Technology and New Intermediaries, Center for European Studies, Stanford.

Walton, Richard. 1985. "From Control to Commitment in the Workplace." *Harvard Business Review* 85(2):76–84.

Weisbrod, Burton. 1988. *The Nonprofit Economy.* Cambridge: Harvard University Press.

Weitzman, Martin. 1984. *The Share Economy.* Cambridge: Harvard University Press.

Wilkinson, Frank. 1983. "Productive Systems." *Cambridge Journal of Economics* 7:413–429.

Williamson, Oliver. 1975. *Markets and Hierarchies.* New York: The Free Press.

————. 1985. *The Economic Institutions of Capitalism.* New York: The Free Press.

Zagnoli, Patrizia. 1987. "Interfirm Agreements as Bilateral Transactions?" Paper presented at the conference on New Technology and New Intermediaries, Center for European Studies, Stanford.

Zucker, Lynne. 1983. "Organizations as Institutions." Pp. 1–47 in *Research in the Sociology of Organizations,* Vol. 2, edited by S. B. Bacharach. Greenwich, CT: JAI Press.

Once More into the Breach between Economic and Cultural Analysis

12

George E. Marcus

A DIFFERENCE STARKLY PUT

It is very striking that the classic technique devised in response to the impossibility of understanding contemporary society from experience, the statistical mode of analysis, had its precise origins within the period of which you are speaking. For without the combination of statistical theory . . . and arrangements for the collection of statistical data . . . the society emerging out of the industrial revolution was literally unknowable. . . . From the industrial revolution onwards, qualitatively altering a permanent problem, there has developed a type of society which is less interpretable from experience. . . . The result is that we have become increasingly conscious of the positive power of techniques of analysis, which at their maximum are capable of interpreting, let us say, the movements of an integrated world economy, and of the negative qualities of a naive observation which can never gain knowledge of realities like these. . . . Experience becomes a forbidden word, whereas what we ought to say about it is that it is a limited word, for there are many kinds of knowledge it will never give us, in any of its ordinary senses.

Raymond Williams
Politics and Letters

The idea of *Economy* (various treatments of capitalism: classical, neoclassical, Marxist) has been perhaps the major space in the modern Western imagination of society for the valorization of universal reason, systemic order, and formal knowledge—in other words, a Utopian dream of control of the unruliness of human life (see, for example, Hirschman's *The Passions and the Interests* 1977) into which the messiness of politics has been more (Marxist) or less (neoclassical theory) admitted. To me (and Raymond Williams), the great value of Western economic analysis has been in its aggregations, in its macrorepresentations of modern societies in their most

331

dynamic dimension—not that these representations are uncontested within economics, but that at least "modern society" became a knowable object for contemplation on a holistic level.

The idea of *Culture* as specifically developed within anthropology has entailed the systematic demonstration of variety and diversity in that which otherwise is more comfortably, or hopefully, viewed as universal, whole, and homogeneous. Cultural analysis presumes a certain methodological relativism, but need not presume an extreme relativism that paralyzes ethical judgment and prohibits statements about the systematic connectedness of the real world or the conscious efforts on the part of some cultures to produce such unified order. Rather, cultural analysis tends to make complex and obstruct any project, however sophisticated technically, that operates on reductionist assumptions and admits complex variation only within those assumptions.

Contemporary anthropology's commitment to developing systematic accounts of diversity derives from a particular method that rests on the researcher's direct and often intimate experience of his or her subjects' conditions of life—fieldwork and ethnography—which increasingly in recent years has accorded an explicit intellectual status to "native" accounts of the phenomena, such as the economy, in which the anthropologist is interested—to the point of granting these accounts an authority equivalent to the specialized frameworks of knowledge of his or her academic community of origin. For some, getting at "the native's point of view" is enough, and a representation of such a perspective is not mere data for further commentary by the anthropologist, but getting this view right is the end of cultural analysis itself, a project often expressed through the metaphor of translation. The distinctive form of life represented is either another case for the archive of diversity the anthropologist has historically accumulated as "cultures" or is tacitly left to stand as an implicit commentary on the practices of the anthropologist's own "local" culture.

For others, representations of "native" thought that parallel one's own modes of thought must play a subordinate, or at least incorporated, role in a project of knowledge that is authoritatively one's own, or at least is a product of Western intellectual life. But at a moment when the grand theoretical paradigms about society and economy that have guided many disciplines in the human sciences since the nineteenth century are being subjected to trenchant critiques of their rhetorics and claims to generality (see Marcus and Fischer 1986), "native" accounts cannot be treated and merely objectified as data, either. So what to do with all the accounts of social reality(ies), each relativized against the other, *and* the nagging awareness that there is, despite all the locally rooted visions of the good life, indeed a global system, an international political economy with profound consequences for the shaping of any particular culture?

The challenge for cultural anthropologists has been to sustain the integrity of local worlds in their descriptions of them, while contributing to the understanding of macrosystems, such as the economy, that has traditionally been the preserve of those who have complexly modeled the world through self-consciously culture-bound limiting rules and assumptions. Given the elevation in intellectual status of "native" discourses, one tantalizing project for cultural analysis, derived from ethnography, is attempts at remodeling the analytic, abstract, and objectified conceptual languages of economic (or systems) analysis, which are essentially external to the discourses of subjects themselves, on the basis of the *internal* languages of subjects.[1] That is, perhaps the formal analytic description of macrosystems can be reformed by being partly derived from the culturally diverse discourses probed by contemporary cultural anthropology. Thus, one concern of this paper is to pose the question of how far cultural analysis can invade the territory of system modelers from the relatively marginal roles that economic anthropology has played in the past (or to use less martial language, how the contributions of ethnography can renegotiate new levels of collaboration with hegemonic forms of theoretical discourse about major Western economic institutions).

In any case, if there is one feature that gives cultural anthropology distinction among the conventional social sciences, it is its signature obsession with "what the other thinks," and the involved debates about how and if this can be known, how it might be represented, and whether such representations are ends or means of research. Engagement with others' categories and discourses in terms of our own has been an organizing issue in virtually every topical arena in which anthropology has participated, including economic anthropology to which I now turn.

A HIGHLY PARTIAL ACCOUNT OF THE CULTURE QUESTION IN ECONOMIC ANTHROPOLOGY

The generic problematic of cultural analysis in anthropology just outlined was played out implicitly in the formalist–substantivist debate that defined a post-World War II subdiscipline known as economic anthropology. It took the form of searching for the "economic" in societies that were small scale and highly undifferentiated institutionally from a Western point of view (societies once called tribal, primitive, or preindustrial—labels now of very questionable value in defining anthropology's special preserve). The formalists tried to establish a distinctive "economic" sphere in the cultures they studied by demonstrating the adequacy of Western economic concepts, how, for example, the value of factors of production could be quantified in a society without an abstract monetary calculus, or to what extent certain media of exchange could be considered money. Although the formalists were unabashedly concerned with their own systematic conceptions of closely observed indigenous behaviors, there is some indication that they thought that our economic categories were universal rational descriptors that made underlying or "meta" sense of indigenous practices and categories. Raymond Firth's (1929) pioneering, even experimental, work on the economics of the New Zealand Maori was an example of what formalist analysis promised.

Although not overtly making the cultural argument by appeal to native discourses or native "theory," the substantivists were in fact developing this argument by other, more sociological, means. Our differentiated way of thinking about economics and the economy simply could not apply to the institutions of preindustrial societies, in which the social, political, and economic could not be distinguished with any integrity. Better just to deal with the embedded characteristics of the institutions as they are found. Rather than dwell on production processes as the formalists tended to do, the substantivists focused on distinctive institutions and practices of exchange, especially characteristic of tribal societies, such as redistribution and reciprocity. However, the substantivists were not cultural analysts in that they did not engage seriously with the internal discourses about these institutions, which they still took to be and wanted, like the formalists, to be shown to be in the realm of *our* sense of the economic and the rational. The substantivists clearly understood that they were dealing with phenomena that were profoundly "other" and different, but they did not yet have the means of cultural analysis to really develop these differences. To compare Malinowski's classic study of the kula trade, *Argonauts of the Western Pacific* (1922), in which he accented the different logic of this Melanesian institution, but still very much within the framework of our sense of economics, with a recent set of restudies (Leach and Leach, 1983) is to reveal the conceptual limits in which the substantivists were operating.

Thus, the substantivists in relation to the formalists were very much homologous to the "soft" side of the American economic profession, dominated by neoclassical formalists. That is, they were like institutional economists who, even in Western society, resisted the disembodiment of economic analysis from social, political, or cultural analysis, but did not have a sufficiently "powerful" (or prestigious) alternative to mainstream theory.

Today, of course, we are far beyond the formalist–substantivist debates, although the styles of work within economic anthropology, much more broadly conceived, have continued along the same lines. On the one hand, anthropologists' involvement with development economics of the 1960s, and, on the other, the impact of French structuralism and theoretical concerns with symbolic analysis during the same period (that raised the study of culture to new levels of sophistication) might be seen as transforming both the object and issues of economic anthropology. Peasants rather than tribesmen, the incorporation of groups that had been represented as isolated and hermetic into larger entities, specifically the penetration of world markets and commerce into local economies, became the predominant concerns of the economic anthropologist. As the ideological underpinnings and theoretical limitations of development economics became clear, especially in the 1970s, Marxist political economy (Godelier 1977; Terray 1972) and related, but extremely influential approaches like Wallerstein's (1973) historic tracing of a modern world system, relocated the reference points of Western theory in terms of which anthropologists' concern with economics defined itself. To be sure, formalist studies continue as one strong strain of economic anthropology, and they have even been strengthened by affinities with agricultural economics, decision and game theory, and a continuing concern with development issues in Third World countries. But in my view, formalism alone has involuted on methodological issues, that although important technically, do not have the interest that the flowering of the substantivist approach into a more explicit and developed cultural analysis of economic phenomena has had. It is the state and potential of this kind of analysis to which I want to devote the rest of this paper.

Paradigmatic of this flowering are Marshall Sahlins' (1972) collected essays in economic anthropology, *Stone-Age Economics*. Unlike Eric Wolf, Sahlins has never been interested in the political economy of the world system, but rather in the nature of the economy in the classic kinds of small-scale, self-contained societies that anthropologists have studied. The earlier essay, "On the Sociology of Primitive Exchange," is a brilliant synthesis of the substantivist approach, and the later one, "The Spirit of the Gift," is pivotal and on the way to Sahlins' cultural critique of the assumptions that constitute Western economic thought (see his *Culture and Practical Reason*, 1976). The key to Sahlins' transformation from substantivist to cultural analyst is the influence of French anthropology on his thought (specifically structuralism, and the French interest in exchange, which was never viewed by them as a narrowly economic phenomenon).

Like the old substantivist position, the cultural approach has generally focused on exchange relations rather than production processes.[2] In the treatment of isolated economies, the meaning of exchange has been explored through internal or native discourses about such practices, in an unprecedentedly deep way; in the political economy of the incorporation of indigenous peoples into capitalist markets as labor and consumers, cultural analysts have focused most on processes of commodification and the shaping of value, taste, and consumer demand (that is, the determination of particular utilities rather than the positing of abstract ones in economic theory). An advanced statement of where this theory that focuses on the cultural analysis of exchange, markets, and commodification stands and what its prospects are is the introduction by Arjun Appadurai (1986) to the volume which he edited, *The Social Life of Things: Commodities in Cultural Perspective.* I will want to return to this statement since it encompasses the directions for the cultural analysis of the economy that I, too, think are most interesting.

In sum, there are two sets of projects that the contemporary development of a cultural analysis of things economic in anthropology has so far done very well. To me, it seems that the specifically economic interest in classic isolated small-scale societies has evaporated, because the increasingly central debate about representations of local discourses and modes of thought to which I referred, has effectively delegitimated or made irrelevant the phrasing of questions about institutions of redistribution or reciprocity in a Western economic frame of reference as opposed to the native's own (which, as has been shown persuasively from ethnography to ethnography, has little to do with the Western idea of the economy). It is when such societies are historically incorporated into capitalist economies that the cultural approach in economic anthropology has produced the richest yield, that is, where it has made common cause with political economy studies of development, mostly within the Marxist tradition. We now have brilliant studies of the transformation of local and regional cultures worldwide [surveyed by Eric Wolf (1983) in his *Europe and the People Without History*]. In particular, there are good cultural analyses of the resistance and accommodation of peoples in various historic situations to the penetration of capitalist institutions, to markets, money, commodification, and proletarianization.

The other set of projects that has come out of the cultural analysis of economic phenomena commonly in the Third World has been trenchant, explicit critiques of Western economic theory. These are powerful examples of the kind of ideology critique that anthropology has always promised, but is delivering systematically only now. Recent major efforts of this sort are Marshall Sahlins' (1976) *Culture and Practical Reason* and Stephen Gudeman's (1986) *Economics As Culture.* The latter is a closely argued statement of cultural anthropology's signature position: that the supposedly universal logical and mathematical schemes on which Western economic models have drawn are themselves local constructions.

What more (or different) does one want, then, from such thriving avenues of inquiry? I would argue that both sets of projects remain limited in a similar way, in that they tend to sustain anthropology's (and thus cultural analysis') marginal position in relation to the terms of debate within other social sciences. Neither has fully taken on, so to speak, our dominant discourses or concepts for representing the economy. Specific ethnographic studies of the transformations of local or regional cultures remain resolutely local. Major world capitalist institutions and processes themselves—particularly the analytic and descriptive practices that constitute their policies and operations—are not deconstructed by the sort of cultural perspective that ethnography offers. Anthropologists indeed are in the habit of thinking beyond the village or urban neighborhood as the specific site of ethnographic research, but what they really know tends to be rooted there. Except as manifested within the framework of this local knowledge, markets, money, commodities—the stuff of macrosystems frameworks on the economy—tend to be left as monolithic constructions, roughly in line with the terms that we analyze and describe as large-scale economic processes. Although cultural analysis in anthropology thus provides rich cases of diversity within the world economy, it also marginalizes itself by not addressing the distinctly nonlocal core institutions of capitalism. In this regard, social and cultural historians who have recently become very interested in the "culture of capitalism" (see, for example, Sewell 1980; Reddy 1984; Hall 1982; Lears 1981), albeit only in the context of EuroAmerican societies, are far more advanced than those working on the cultural side of economic anthropology.

From experience in the study of non-Western economies at local levels, those anthropologists who have offered ambitious critiques of Western economic discourse have also been limited. In a sense, from their distinctive cross-cultural angle, they have merely joined the strong minor key tradition of twentieth-century critical theory that has developed the same sort of trenchant critiques of the assumptions and styles of thought on which the Western idea of the economy has been constructed. Parallel to the hesitation of cultural analysts to actually develop alternative approaches to the study of phenomena such as markets, banking, and commodities, the anthropological cultural critics of Western economic discourse have been hesitant to try to reform or modify its conceptual apparatus. Since it is too powerful to be simply dismissed, the only project that can come out of such distanced critiques, beyond critique itself, is to attempt to find points of collaboration with those who are trying to reconstruct economic discourse from within (see McCloskey 1985). Although agreeing with Raymond Williams' comment in the epigram to this paper about the indispensability of formal techniques and modeling in the representation of modern societies as wholes, I would like to question how limited perspectives on experience ("the negative qualities of a naive observation which can never gain knowledge of realities like these") really must remain in efforts to represent complex systems instead of local, "knowable" communities, the traditional terra firma of ethnography.

Following the tendency of cultural analysis in economic anthropology to focus on relations of exchange rather than production, what would a *cultural* account of complex markets and their politics, or of the changing status of objects in different contexts of exchange, consist of? How might the privileged discourse of economic theory and modeling actually incorporate a cultural component, emphasizing diversity and derived from ethnographic research? These questions, I would argue, set new agendas for cultural approaches to the economy that move them from the margins to challenge and collaborate with the usual terms of discourse with which political economists, policy analysts, and more formal theorists have constructed their common object.

AGENDA SETTING FROM WITHIN THE DISCOURSE OF CULTURAL ANALYSIS

The questions for the future with which the last section ended suggest two major projects that arise from both the strengths and limits of cultural analysis of economic phenomena so far developed within anthropology. One project arises from the sense that cultural representations of basic capitalist institutions in and across different societies are not merely an interesting option for ethnographic research, but essential if anthropology is ever to address itself squarely to the conditions of modernity, if not postmodernity, worldwide (and this direction for anthropology is increasingly not itself just an option, but the pervasive conditions of ethnographic research). That is, market processes and cultural processes in both the most public and most intimate contexts of late twentieth-century societies are tightly interwoven. The performances and productions of contemporary high and popular culture are disseminated through their commodification, even as the former attempt various strategies to escape the implications of the market processes in which they are embedded. What cultural analysts have generally failed to understand is that market processes, the world of abstract monetary exchange, and commodification are themselves cultural processes that share at some level assumptions, symbols, and discourses with what is more conventionally categorized as "cultural"—public ritual, theater, pop music, fashion, and taste generally. Thus, key aims of this project are, first, to demonstrate the "doppelganger" quality of economic processes in relation to cultural processes in that the former (mainly in terms of commodification) assimilate/imitate a version of all forms of cultural expression for the purposes of reproducing and spreading it, and second, to demonstrate the cultural construction of economic processes themselves. This project in no way indicates economic determinism, since there is always an ongoing resistance and accommodation of cultural forms to their economic doppelgangers, and since economic analysis, budgeting, forecasting, and the like reveal themselves to be fields of contestation over cultural values.

Theoretically, the works of Jean Beaudrillard (1988) and Pierre Bourdieu (1984) have led the way in showing the tight interweave between the economic and the cultural in contemporary societies. For me, personally, it was an ethnographic study of wealthy American families/fortunes (see Marcus 1980, 1985, 1986, 1989) that demonstrated the fluid forms that property and wealth take in the contemporary United States, and that these forms, although seeming to fit squarely into our category of the economic, actually encompass a good deal of the cultural discourses and characteristics of their owners. In other words, a much elaborated theory of Marx's commodity fetishism becomes in effect a theory of culture and a paradigm for ethnographic research in contemporary capitalist societies.

The particular value of this project is that it locates social formations and cultural phenomena that are emergent in the contemporary world and otherwise difficult to conceptualize with the increasingly perceived inadequacy of our store of concepts derived from nineteenth-century social theories to grasp descriptively changes in contemporary postindustrial situations of the world economy (see Marcus and Fischer's 1986, positing of a particularly acute crisis of representation; also see Lash and Urry 1987, on the end of organized capitalism). The cultural analysis of core economic processes, that is how things, people, and signs become commodities for markets, thus becomes an essential means of analytically discovering and describing processes that give a social structural context to cultural performances of all kinds.

The other related, "cutting edge" project with which I want to deal goes beyond the mere critique of economic doctrine and theory to suggest ways to reform it, to open it to the cultural, and in the latter's anthropological sense, to the multiple discourses of subjects who participate in economic activities from a variety of social situations. One can actually find this process of critique and transformation occurring in non-Western contexts, for example, the interesting debates in the Islamic world that explore accommodations between Western economic theory and Islamic thought, something that one does not really find as self-consciously in Western contexts, since the economy is conceived to be more natural than cultural. The aim would be to find a common ground between the cultural analysts of capitalism, pursuing the kinds of issues just discussed, and the internal critics of economic theory like McCloskey (1985). This common ground might be the rhetorical critique of the language of economists and economic theory, which has been a touchstone for previously unarticulated senses of something basically wrong with the paradigm of economic discourse among a number of contemporary practitioners. The critique of any field's rhetoric is in fact a powerful form of ideology critique that opens particular modes of thought to conceptual modification. The internal rhetorical critique of economic discourse might be the way "in" for a cultural supplement to the formulation of questions and habits of the now dominant mode of economic thought without sacrificing its technical accomplishments of description.

The remaining sections discuss further these projects for cultural accounts of core economic processes as well as cultural critiques of the dominant form of discourse about the economy through some comments on work that seems to be moving in the same direction and has been particularly evocative for me.

THE SOCIAL LIFE OF THINGS IN THE DECLINE OF ORGANIZED CAPITALISM: A STRATEGY FOR CULTURAL REPRESENTATIONS OF THE CONTEMPORARY ECONOMY

Scott Lash and John Urry's *The End of Organized Capitalism* (1987) stands out from many of the current syntheses attempting to reevaluate classic political economy perspectives in light of ongoing major historic shifts in the structure of the world economy. Unlike most of these other studies, Lash and Urry are boldly deconstructive of macrosystem perspectives, thus making a place for the expositions of cultural diversity that anthropology has to offer, not on the margins, but in the very fabric and composition of "the system." What looked like one complex game (from the vantage point of, say, state-craft, economic theory, or international banking) can actually be productively seen as many games complexly interconnected. There is indeed a system, composed of market hierarchies that map and manipulate just about all cultural forms of life on the globe, but it is composed of complex connections among (culturally) diverse parts.

Lash and Urry's specific task is to revise the classic Marxist theory of the development of capitalism by stages toward the increasing concentration of capital in the face of clear present conditions of fragmenting national and international economies. They define the decline of concentrated capital in a 14-point summary of much of the current research on structural changes in western economies. I will not reproduce this summary here, but three aspects of it are crucial to the remodeling of Marxist political economy in a pluralist direction, through an ethnography of the system. One, they indicate that major processes are no longer distinctively place-focused (p. 6):

> 8. An increase in cultural fragmentation and pluralism, resulting from the commodifica-
> tion of leisure and the development of new political/cultural forms since the 1960s. The
> decodification of some existing cultural forms. The related reductions in time-space
> distanciation (cf. the 'global village') likewise undermine the construction of un-
> problematic national subjects.

> 11. The overlapping effect of new forms of the spatial division of labour has weakened
> the degree to which industries are concentrated within different regions. To a marked
> extent there are no longer 'regional economies' in which social and political relations
> are formed or shaped by a handful of central extractive/manufacturing industries.

The implication is that place-focused, single-site ethnography provides very partial views of social processes with which it might be concerned; that is, such ethnography can no longer be in explanatory or even narrative control of the subject matter it wants to encompass by description. Two, the rise and proliferation of so-called service classes play a large part in Lash and Urry's comparative analyses of the historic entries of the United States, Germany, France, England, and Sweden into the conditions of organized capitalism (pp. 5–6):

> 2. The continued expansion of the number of white-collar workers and particularly of a distinctive service class (of managers, professionals, educators, scientists etc.), which is an effect of organized capitalism, becomes an increasingly significant element which then disorganizes modern capitalism. This results both from the development of an educationally based stratification system which fosters individual achievement and mobility and the growth of new 'social movements' (students', antinuclear, ecological and women's movements etc.) which increasingly draw energy and personnel away from class politics.

> 6. The spread of capitalism into most Third World countries which has involved increased competition in many of the basic extractive/manufacturing industries (such as steel, coal, oil, heavy industry, automobiles) and the export of the jobs of part of the First World proletariat. This in turn has shifted the industrial/occupational structure of First World economies towards 'service' industry and occupations.

Such classes cannot be descriptively harnessed by the analytic power of the class concept as it now exists. The ethnographic exploration of the social and cultural worlds of so-called service classes is a key task for ethnography and a major challenge to its existing strategies of description. Three, Lash and Urry raise the issue of postmodernism, not just as a form of high culture, or academic artifice, but as the conditions of everyday life (p. 7)[3]:

> 14. The appearance and mass distribution of a cultural-ideological configuration of 'postmodernism'; this affects high culture, popular culture and the symbols and discourse of everyday life.

They indeed end their book with a discussion of postmodernist culture, and claim that given the processes of disorganization they describe, issues of identity and cultural production become *the* issues of political economy.

They make two other orienting remarks about culture in disorganized capitalism (pp. 14–15):

> First, domination through cultural forms takes on a significance in disorganized capitalism which is comparable in importance to domination in the sphere of production itself. Second, there is something importantly classless about postmodernism. With its core assumptions about the breakdown of boundaries, postmodernism finds an audience when the boundaries which structure our identities break down, that is, during personal experiences of liminality during which identity is unstable. . . . Middle-class youth and the professions in the service classes are a potential audience for postmodernist culture and potential sources of resistance to domination in disorganized capitalism. This partly explains their overwhelming presence in the so-called 'new social movements.' The point here is that much of such popular culture, whoever consumes it, is

largely 'classless' in content and form, and the radical anti-hierarchical values and practices, the 'anti-authoritarian populism', it can engender are equally not particularly marked by class characteristics.

If social action always involves an intermingling of presence and absence, modern culture permits an extraordinarily heightened presence-availability of social situations, events, myths, and images which cohere around and construct diverse subjects. With the sea change in modern society in which large organizations, workplaces, and cities are of diminishing significance for each individual, the processes of forming, fixing, and reproducing subjects is increasingly cultural, formed in diverse ways out of a myriad of myths and images, of consumer products, of available life-styles not at all based on where one lives or whom one knows, that is, on those who are immediately present.

The challenge is how to redefine the object of ethnography, the vehicle of cultural analysis in anthropology, so as to capture these pervasive (at least in the West) expressions of culture that resist grounding in conventional notions of place and community. One direction is to move toward an ethnography that focuses more centrally on things, as they pass through different valuations in diverse social contexts of production, exchange, and consumption, rather than on persons. A culturally oriented economic anthropology responding to the postmodern conditions of culture described by Lash and Urry, thus, finds a mobile subject in the social life of objects. Here, we return to Arjun Appadurai's (1986) introduction to *The Social Life of Things,* in which he provides the most stimulating, innovative current statement of the mode-of-exchange, substantivist legacy of economic anthropology, discussed earlier.

Appadurai's introduction is wide ranging and comparative; he does not view commodification as a process limited only to modern capitalist societies, nor does he see gift exchanges as central only in preindustrial, so-called tribal societies. It is the full trajectory of things in their various contexts of production, exchange, and consumption that he tracks. He is especially interested in the cultural construction of desire and taste, that is, of demand. In each context of the trajectory of things, Appadurai is interested in asking how and what kind of value attaches to things as they pass through in terms of a specific sort of cultural politics of meaning. Indeed these trajectories, sometimes moving along the paths of institutionalized markets, sometimes moving in much more informal channels, define the minimal element of structure needed to represent ethnographically cultural process that are not encompassed by our conventional stock of notions about social structure.

Although incorporating examples from modern Western economies such as stock markets, the core material comes from the anthropological tradition of studying non-Western small-scale economic systems like the kula trade of the Massim region of Melanesia. He thus holds open the possibility of using the conceptual apparatus invented by anthropologists to provide accounts of specific non-Western cases in rethinking creatively the standard ways we conceptualize the flow of things (as goods or commodities) in the framework of Western economic discourse. For example, Appadurai generalizes the "path and diversion" model of regional exchange in the Massim area (Nancy Munn in Leach and Leach 1983) to good effect as a set of theoretical concepts for thinking about the process of commodification in Western economics. The comparative use of materials from other cultures to comment on our own institutions has been a marker of anthropology's contribution to Western thought. Often, these comparisons have been fanciful or naive because they have been too direct—one cannot just pull a practice from the Trobriand, Samoan, or Japanese context to apply in an American one. It is quite different with the concepts honed in the course of other culture research, and at this level Appadurai's comparative perspective works very well. The analytic concepts created in research elsewhere may be fully adaptable and usable in the modification of frameworks for the study of homegrown institutions that have become problematic.

In sum, Appadurai's essay is a compendium of all the issues that define an analytic approach to commodification. One can use these as a guide in revising ethnography to meet the unconventional conditions of cultural production that Lash and Urry outline (the only limitation of Appadurai is that he keeps pretty much to things, literally, as commodities, whereas the pressing need in the sort of cultural world that Lash and Urry describe is for more studies of the commodification of services and ideas). Ethnography should be thing or object-focused; it should be mobile following the paths and trajectories of things with transforming cultural definitions and values. In so doing, such an ethnography would provide in pursuing its own ends a cultural account of *the* system (now many local systems tied together by the complex connections of the commodification process), as I noted, one of the two major projects to be developed by culturally oriented research in economic anthropology. The other project, to which I now turn, is to bring such a cultural account to bear on the conceptual and methodological apparatus of the discourse of economic theory.

REMODELING THE DISCOURSES OF ECONOMIC MODELING

Within the discipline of economics itself (as in other social science disciplines currently), an internal critique is coming about through a self-awareness about analytic language, exemplified most prominently in the recent work of Donald McCloskey (1985). But that there is any serious reception among economists (as there is) of this critique of rhetoric at the moment is due to a sense among some practitioners that the paradigm itself (of both neoclassical and Marxist economics) is in difficulty. In economics, this is not the same sort of crisis of representation that Fischer and I specified for ethnography, since economists have never claimed to have provided descriptions of full-bodied, complex social reality. Rather, they have always accepted working with systematic, but skewed approximations of reality, that is, models, as long as these models could eventually be tested against statistical registers and indices of reality with rigor and predictability. It is the success of economic models feeding back into a "thick," complex reality that the critique of economists' rhetoric obliquely but powerfully attacks.

The challenge for the critique of rhetoric in any field, however trenchant, is to say what it is good for, what difference it might make to practice, other than to create a crisis of confidence of varying proportions among practitioners who have listened to the critique. After having delivered a critique of, at times, radical proportions, McCloskey backs away from pronouncing any momentous implications for economic theory. As he says (p. 174):

> One thing is clear: the absorption of rhetorical thinking in economics will not precipitate any revolution in the substance of economics. Rhetoric does not claim to provide formulas for scientific advance. It does not believe that science advances by formula. It believes that science advances by healthy conversation, not adherence to a methodology. To claim that theoretical sophistication is a formula for advances in economics would be self-contradictory. Life is not so easy that an economist can be made much better at what he does merely by reading a book.

Just so, and in line with McCloskey's modest style, but ending with conversation, especially *intra*disciplinary conversation is hardly a satisfying resolution of trenchant critique. If there is *inter*disciplinary conversation, then the outcome is not so modest as McCloskey would have it appear, since substantively, research paradigms, projects, and, most importantly, conceptual frameworks of respective disciplines would not at all remain the same. In the case of cultural analysis, which is founded these days on a fine, critical ear for discourses—both of subjects and scholars—the rhetorical critique of a field such as economics is just such a potential opening for the kind of conversation that might lead to marked changes in concepts and methods. The anthropological critiques of economic discourse are not enough—they need projects that concern mainstream economic systems and access to the aggregate modeling capacities of economic analysis. The internal rhetorical critiques of economists' language, which center mainly on economists' idealization and mischaracterization of research practices in the natural sciences, discover failures to contextualize sufficiently or relativize various measures and the use of excessive hedging language in trying to match the results achieved by models to a more complex, real world (see the beginning of McCloskey's Chapter 9 on the measures of price parity). It is at these points that some sort of ethnographic frame of reference, specifying local conditions, might enter otherwise reductionist economic discourse.

Yet, it became clear to me during the seminar for which this paper was

prepared that the critique of the rhetoric of economics as a means of introducing issues raised by cultural analysis is strategically and pragmatically
much less likely to have salience in dialogue with economists themselves,
within their own disciplinary framework, as with other kinds of social scientists and experts who work outside, but in the shadow of disciplinary economics. That is, those whose work can be seen to be derivative from the
conceptual apparatus and grounding rhetoric of the discipline of economics
(e.g., the central concern with rationality and efficiency in the framework of
utilitarian philosophy, and the adherence to methodological individualism
in the construction of theory), whether such work is developed in critical
reaction to or alliance with economics. On the one hand, this work would
include the academic discourses of such specialties as political economy,
economic sociology, rational choice theory, organization theory, and policy
analysis, all of which were well represented by seminar participants. On the
other hand, it would include the economistic discourse in practice of those
in government bureaucracies, firms, and markets, who do the accounting,
budgeting, regulating, forecasting, advising, and policy making.

I leave the treatment of the problems that cultural analysis poses for the
social science specialities constructed through engagement with economics
and its conceptual frameworks to other papers in this volume, especially
Paul DiMaggio's excellent survey. It is clear that such problems are acknowledged and substantially debated among contemporary political economists,
sociologists, and organization theorists (from my own recent reading, I
would merely note Hirsch 1986, Piore and Sabel 1984, and the debate
between Laitin and Wildavsky 1988). What would divide some anthropologists—often referred to as "interpretive" anthropologists—from these efforts
to pull culture and economics closer together is not at all a different sense of
what culture at base is (values, processes of bounding individual and group
identities, shared cognitions, "scripts" for social action, etc.), but rather a
very different orientation to how such cultural phenomena should be studied, involving different conceptual vocabularies and different methods. Indeed, interpretive work is fully in line with the basic insights about the
importance of cultural formulations as expressed by other social scientists—
that not only is the cultural construction of meaning and symbols inherently
a matter of political and economic interests, but the reverse also holds: the
concerns of political economy are inherently about conflicts over meaning
and symbols.[4] Also, certain anthropologists have been either important partners in the attempt to renew cultural analysis within sociology and political
economy (e.g., Mary Douglas' work with Aaron Wildavsky), or, more dis-
tantly, inspirations for this effort (e.g., Clifford Geertz and Victor Turner).

Yet, this move toward an interest in culture outside anthropology tends to
retain a priority focus on behavioral, rather than linguistic, data, on observing
what people do rather than on listening analytically to what they say (as if

doing and saying can be easily distinguished, by such time honored distinctions as the social versus the cultural). Also, it retains a primarily sociological orientation, in which all questions of value, cognition, and symbolic process are linked back to more basic questions of social (and economic) structure. The interpretive approach to culture in anthropology has moved in recent years more toward the study of discourse and narrative as the richest manifestations of culture. This has suited anthropology's signature qualitative method of empirical investigation—ethnography—as well as its concerns with representing "native points of view" in other cultures and other languages, whereas such a move would probably not be as easily assimilated to the methods of the other social sciences, which have been more committed to quantification and hypothesis testing, and less committed to the task of cross-cultural translation. Thus, for the other social sciences, the difference that a culture represents is never radical enough to challenge seriously their own privileged analytic discourse, which attempts to assimilate the cultural to a conceptual apparatus that is already divided into the political, economic, social, and psychological.

This kind of cultural analysis—sometimes referred to as textualism—has been charged with hermeticism, idealism, and a general lack of concern with social action and the operation of institutions. Such a dismissal is hardly fair. The focus on discourse, narrative, text, and the like—a more appropriate covering term is a concern with practices of representation—is an alternative way of constituting social facts. Systematic representations of the world are what social actors are constantly creating, and it is not only the representations that are studied through interpretive approaches to culture but also the practices by which they are systematically produced in social life, as well as the politics by which they are appropriated by different groups and institutions. In other words, the treatment of culture as representations (and these as *social* facts) is an ambitious strategy for the study of economics and politics *as* culture (fully in line, for example, with Friedland and Alford *in press*). Culture is no longer a residual category that affects social and economic action; it, understood as the production of discourse, is indeed fully constitutive of social, political, and economic activity. As such, this kind of cultural analysis, although it is ultimately complementary to the aims of analysis within sociology and political economy, is not easily integrated into the behavioral and sociocentric conceptual rhetorics of these disciplines. It derives instead from a different set of contemporary sources of theory and method.[5]

In concluding, I want to review briefly a case of how the cultural analysis of discourses both critiques and explains economics as cultural practices. For this, I turn to the other category of discourses derived from economics—that of economic analysis and description in use in the operations of governments (as in the following case in point), firms, and markets.

Emery M. Roe's "Deconstructing Budgets" (1988), among other recent papers (n.d., 1987) by him, is a lapidary demonstration of the power of textual criticism in providing a set of analytic categories for apprehending a very important kind of economic discourse (and activity) as a cultural process. Roe, who himself has had eight years of overseas advising experience in Kenya, recasts some of the basic insights of the seminal works on the budgetary process by Aaron Wildavsky (1984, 1986, 1988). He does so through a judicious use of some of the key notions in poststructuralist theories of discourse: the distinction between writerly and readerly versions of a text (derived from the work of Roland Barthes), and the idea of intertextuality (that all single texts are permeated with previous texts). "Deconstruction" as a method of analysis is used generically by Roe. Rather than being derived specifically from the work of Jacques Derrida or the recent American school of literary criticism, with which the term has doctrinally been associated, Roe's deconstructive analysis is more independent and is intended to reveal the actual social and political process by which the model or representation of the economy in the specific discourse of budgeting is constructed. This, of course, could be done for any other economistic discourse in use. His work differs from Wildavsky's precisely by focusing the politics of the budget on the budget itself as an authoritative representation of the economy, which calls into question the very authority of the analytic categories of economics itself (Wildavsky does not go quite this far). Roe begins (as does Wildavsky) by focusing on the textual character of budgets (1988:62):

> The functions and purposes of national budgeting, of course, extend beyond the written word. Budgeting is a way to set priorities, a mechanism for expenditure control, a means of staff coordination, and more. Still, the printed budget and its associated documentation remain central even to these other efforts. The national budget is, in reality, often not just one published text but is dispersed into several or many. The Government of Kenya's budget, for instance, is a set of publications covering annually its development estimates, recurrent estimates, supplementary estimates, ministerial budget speech, revenue estimates, and survey of current and future economic conditions. The US federal budget covers many of the same topics in two documents: the budget and its appendix. In addition, each of the conventional stages of the budget process—compilation, approval, execution, and audit—requires its own important documentation. This more or less dispersed nature of the printed budget within and over its various stages and functions has profound implications for how closely budgets, money, and power are related.

Roe's specific focus is on repetitive budgeting—the reallocation of a national budget several times during a year—that Wildavsky originally explored. Repetitive budgeting was once thought to be an indication of the incompetence of Third world economic management, but is now a standard practice among rich nations, including the United States. The more fragmented and flexible budgetary practices of the Third World, as in the form of the Kenyan budget above, seem to stand as a juxtaposed critique of the fiction of the coherent economy that is presumed in the streamlined U.S. budget as text. Roe proceeds to deconstruct U.S. budgetary discourse guided by a representation or model of the economy as it ideally would like to be seen through the discussion of the following propositions:

> Budget texts increasingly give reality a fictional character. ([p. 62:] National budgets are notorious for trying, by way of figures and statistics, to simplify, quantify, and commodify into commensurable units a reality that frequently resists such reductionism.)

These texts have no author.

> The texts are open to (mis)reading only. ([p. 63:] A host of government departments and decision makers rewrite the budget once it is published. . . . Much of this revision is carried out unofficially and is the result of reintepretation of an existing document: much is also officially sanctioned and represents replacing one written document by an amended one. Both forms of rewriting go by the name of repetitive budgeting.)

> Budgets are by definition intertextual.

> The terms within the text define each other.

> As a result of the above factors, a profound gap exists today between what we have conventionally thought the text to be, and what it is now.

Roe then goes on to consider the important question of how the fragmentation and dispersal of budgetary power affect the distribution of income in a country. He critiques the conventional notion that national budgets of multiple interpretation and revision are more associated with income inequality than budgets of coherent and authoritative determination. He ends with a sympathetic view of repetitive budgeting, one that judges the effectiveness of such budgeting by an ethnographic sense of how governments construct budgets and how tolerant and anticipatory they are of their flexible appropriation (p. 67):

> This "making the budget effective" stands as the polar opposite to the practice of repetitive budgeting with its multiple interpretations. Indeed, many budgeters would probably say such effectiveness criteria are self-evident. Nonetheless, there would be a radical shift in orientation within comparative budgeting were it to recognize that budgetary effectiveness is a kind of *reading* having, as such, less to do with percentages and other indices than is commonly supposed. Budgetary effectiveness as a specific kind of reading starts and ends with the budget documents qua documents. In sum, comparative budgeting should be conceived as more a species of textual or narrative analysis than an exercise in quantification.

This conclusion, from one in an "applied" context who has long observed what might appear from the perspective of official economic theory to be the "perversion" of efficiency, is modest only because it appropriately directs itself to one particular genre of economic discourse. It could be made considerably more provocative in implication if, on a broader canvas, the relationship of the economic discourse of budgeting were systematically mapped and related not only to other economic discourses in use in their considerable diversity, but to the social science discourses based on economic models to which I referred, and ultimately to the preserve of disciplinary economics discourse itself. This mapping of the complex domain of practices for representing the economy in the West and beyond, in all their local varieties, would constitute an ambitious vision of research on economics to which those who practice cultural analysis might aspire.

NOTES

1.   The considerable interest in Michael Taussig's (1980) *The Devil and Commodity Fetishism in South America* raised hopes for this kind of reformation of the privileged analytic framework of the Western economic theorist through the discovery of alternative and substantial conceptions in "native" discourses, promoted to a level of intellectual equivalence with the former. Taussig's study, however, remains merely tantalizing in that he effectively showed the parallel "truths" in classic Marxist commodity/money theory and the more enchanted analytic/belief system in practice among Colombian peasants and proletarians concerning the operation of the economic system into which they had been assimilated. Marxist theory was thus confirmed rather than transformed by the cultural debates concerning commodification within the idiom and scene of ethnographic study.

2.   However, during the interlude of the 1970s when French Marxist approaches (Althusser, Godelier, Terray, among others) held sway over the substantivists in Anglo-American economic anthropology, the focus on modes of production was indeed dominant. In dealing with lineage, tribal, and kin-focused societies, many substantivists came to appreciate the artificial and forced way the mode of production approach was made to fit ethnographic material. Production, as it was conceptually developed in the cultural discourses of the societies in which ethnographers were interested, did not permit the isolation of a level of economic structure, to be distinguished from the superstructural, on which the Marxist approach depended.

3.   The value of debates about the nature of postmodernism is a highly controversial matter among contemporary scientists. Seeing the possibility for theory and research in these debates or passing them off as sterile fantasies marks very important lines of difference in defining common interests and purpose in the contemporary projects of the social sciences, especially in the United States. Although retaining a critical sense about these debates, I tend to see great possibility in them for direly needed conceptual innovations in the way that we analytically represent social, economic, and cultural processes in the late twentieth-century world. For a sample of the range of empirically grounded social scientific projects of research in this domain, see the collected papers in *Theory, Culture and Society,* edited by Featherstone (1988).

4.   In his paper, DiMaggio notes that Friedland and Alford (1989) "argue persuasively that political debates often become contests over the salience of competing "logics" to particular situations, as when feminists seek to economize family relations by placing a dollar value on domestic labor." There is no doubt that particular logics, interests, or values—the stuff of cultural communality and variation—are often articulated in political contests in economistic terms, if only because of the prestige of the discourse of economics, but there are other, parallel, everyday life terms in which the very same logics or values are articulated. One task of interpretive analysis, usually avoided by the sociological treatment of culture, would be to relativize and evaluate the privileged economistic statement of cultural values against its other,

alternative modes of articulation. This analytic exercise, which is minutely concerned with narratives, representations, and linguistic practices, and their consequences for social action and political contests, would be difficult finally to integrate into the frameworks that DiMaggio reviews for the assimilation of cultural issues to the work of economic sociologists and political economists.

5. For accounts of the development of this kind of cultural analysis in anthropology, see Ortner (1984) and Marcus and Fischer (1986). In the emergent interdisciplinary space known as cultural studies (which pulls scholars from a diversity of disciplines, but centrally from history, anthropology, literature, and philosophy), there are many similar statements of a move toward a focal concern with culture as discourses grounded in specifiable social practices. For a particularly clear recent statement see the introduction and first two essays in Chartier (1988). It will be obvious to anyone who ventures into this terrain that the theoretical capital for this kind of cultural analysis is located in major trends of post-World War II French and German social theory.

REFERENCES

Appadurai, Arjun (ed.). 1986. *The Social Life of Things: Commodities in Cultural Perspective*. New York: Cambridge University Press.

Beaudrillard, Jean. 1988. *Selected Writings*, edited by Mark Poster. Stanford: Stanford University Press.

Bourdieu, Pierre. 1984. *Distinction: A Social Critique of the Judgement of Taste*. Cambridge: Harvard University Press.

Chartier, Roger. 1988. *Cultural History: Between Practices and Representations*. Ithaca: Cornell University Press.

Featherstone, Michael. 1988. "Postmodernism, a Special Double Issue." *Theory, Culture and Society* 5(2, 3).

Firth, Raymond. 1929. *Primitive Economics of the New Zealand Maori*. New York: E. P. Dutton.

Friedland, Roger and Robert Alford. in press. "Bringing Society Back In: Symbols, Practices, and Institutional Contradictions." In *The New Institutionalism in Organizational Studies*, edited by Walter Powell and Paul Dimaggio. Chicago: University of Chicago Press.

Godelier, Maurice. 1977. *Perspectives in Marxist Anthropology*. New York: Cambridge University Press.

Gudeman, Stephen. 1986. *Economics as Culture: Models and Metaphors of Livelihood*. Boston: Routledge and Kegan Paul.

Hall, Peter D. 1982. *The Organization of American Culture, 1700–1900: Private Institutions, Elites, and the Origins of American Nationality*. New York: New York University Press.

Hirsch, Paul M. 1986. "From Ambushes to Golden Parachutes: Corporate Takeovers as an Instance of Cultural Framing and Institutional Integration." *American Journal of Sociology* 91:800–837.

Hirschman, Albert O. 1977. *The Passions and the Interests: Political Arguments for Capitalism before Its Triumph*. Princeton: Princeton University Press.

Lash, Scott, and John Urry. 1987. *The End of Organized Capitalism*. Madison: University of Wisconsin Press.

Laitin, David and Aaron Wildavsky. 1988. "Political Culture and Political Preferences. (A debate over Wildavsky's concept of political culture)." *American Political Science Review* 82(2):87–96.

Leach, Jerry W. and Edmund Leach (eds.). 1983. *The Kula: New Perspectives on Massim Exchange*. New York: Cambridge University Press.

Lears, T. J. Jackson. 1981. *No Place of Grace: Anitmodernism and the Transformation of American Culture, 1880–1920*. New York: Pantheon.

McCloskey, Donald N. 1985. *The Rhetoric of Economics*. Madison: University of Wisconsin Press.

Malinowski, Bronislaw. 1922. *Argonauts of the Western Pacific*. London: Routledge and Kegan Paul.

Marcus, George E. and Michael Fischer. 1986. *Anthropology as Cultural Critique*. Chicago: University of Chicago Press.

Marcus, George E. 1980. "Law in the Development of Dynastic Families among American Business Elites: The Domestication of Capital and the Capitalization of Family." *Law and Society Review* 14:858–903.

———. 1985. "Spending: The Hunts, Silver, and Dynastic Families in America." *The European Journal of Sociology* 26:224–259.

———. 1986. "Generation-Skipping Trusts and Problems of Authority: Parent-Child Relations in the Dissolution of American Families of Dynastic Wealth." Pp. 51–70 in *Frailty of Authority*, edited by M. J. Aronoff. New Brunswick: Transaction Books.

———. 1989. "The Problem of the Unseen World of Wealth for the Rich: Toward an Ethnography of Complex Connections." *Ethos*, forthcoming.

Ortner, Sherry B. 1984. "Theory in Anthropology Since the Sixties." *Comparative Studies in Society and History* 26:126–166.

Piore, Michael J. and Charles F. Sabel. 1984. *The Second Industrial Divide*. New York: Basic Books.

Reddy, William. 1984. *The Rise of Market Culture: The Textile Trade and French Society. 1750–1900*. New York: Cambridge University Press.

Roe, Emery M. 1987. "Lantern on the Stern: Policy Analysis, Historical Research, and *Pax Britannica* in Africa." *African Studies Review* 30:45–62.

———. 1988. "Deconstructing Budgets." *Diacritics* 18:61–68.

———. n.d. "Narrative Analysis for the Policy Analyst: A Case Study of the 1980/82 Medfly Controversy in California." *Journal of Policy Analysis and Management*, forthcoming.

Sahlins, Marshall. 1972. *Stone-Age Economics*. Chicago: Aldine.

———. 1976. *Culture and Practical Reason*. Chicago: University of Chicago Press.

Sewell, William. 1980. *Work and Revolution in France: The Language of Labor from the Old Regime to 1848*. New York: Cambridge University Press.

Taussig, Michael. 1980. *The Devil and Commodity Fetishism in South America*. Chapel Hill: University of North Carolina Press.

Terray, Emanuel. 1972. *Marxism and "Primitive" Societies: Two Studies*. New York: Monthly Review Press.

Wallerstein, Immanuel. 1974. *The Modern World-System: Capitalist Agriculture and the Origins of the European World-Economy in the Sixteenth Century*. New York: Academic Press.

Wildavsky, Aaron. 1984. *The Politics of the Budgetary Process,* 4th ed. Boston: Little, Brown.

———. 1986. *Budgeting: A Comparative Theory of Budgetary Processes.* New Brunswick: Transaction.

———. 1988. *The New Politics of the Budgetary Process.* Boston: Scott.

Williams, Raymond, 1981. *Politics and Letters: Interviews with New Left Review.* London: Verso.

Wolf, Eric. 1983. *Europe and the People without History.* Berkeley: University of California Press.

About the Contributors

Richard Cloward is Professor in the Columbia University School of Social Work. With Frances Fox Piven he has written extensively on urban politics and social movements. They are the authors of *Regulating the Poor; Poor People's Movements;* and most recently *Why Americans Don't Vote.* They are currently at work on a study of the politics of rule-making and rule-breaking.

Paul DiMaggio is Associate Professor in the Department of Sociology, the Institution for Social and Policy Studies, and the School of Organization and Management at Yale University. He has edited *Non-Profit Enterprise and the Arts; Structures of Capital: the Social Organization of Economic Life* (with Sharon Zukin); and *The New Institutionalism in Organizational Analysis* (with Walter Powell). He is writing a book on the social organization of high culture in the United States from 1860 to the present.

Paula England is Professor of Sociology at the University of Arizona. She is author of *Comparable Worth: Theories and Evidence* (Aldine, forthcoming) and *Households, Employment and Gender* (Aldine 1986, with George Farkas). She has edited *Industries, Firms, and Jobs: Sociological and Economic Approaches* (1988) with George Farkas.

Robert H. Frank is Professor of Economics at Cornell University, where he has taught since 1972. His books include *Choosing the Right Pond* (1985), and *Passions Within Reason* (1988). A book on *Microeconomics and Behavior* is forthcoming.

Roger Friedland is Professor of Sociology at the University of California, Santa Barbara. He has written on the relationship between state, capitalism and democracy in *Powers of Theory* (1985, with Robert Alford), on the spatial organization of large business firms in the United States (with Donald Palmer), and on the politics of the welfare state and its impact on economic growth and the movement of real and nominal wages (with Jimy Sanders).

He is currently studying conflicts over the organization and meaning of time and space in Jerusalem (with Richard Hecht) and is developing a comparative study of corporate geographies in market economies (with Guido Martinotti).

Mark Granovetter is Professor of Sociology at the State University of New York at Stony Brook. He is the author of *Getting a Job: a Study of Contracts and Careers* (1974), and received the Theory Section Prize of the American Sociological Association for his article on "Economic Action and Social Structure: the Problem of Embeddedness" (*American Journal of Sociology*, 1985). He is currently at work on a book tentatively entitled *Society and Economy: the Social Construction of Economic Institutions*, to be published by Harvard University Press.

Tamara K. Hareven is Unidel Professor of Family Studies and History at the University of Delaware, and member of the Center for Population Studies at Harvard University. She is the founding editor of the *Journal of Family History*. Her best known recent books are *Amoskeag: Life and Work in an American City* (1978), and *Family Time and Industrial Time* (1982). She has edited numerous collections on the family, the life course, and population history, and is currently writing *A Social History of the American Family*. In recent years she has been involved in comparative research on family change in Japan and China, and is completing a study of *The Silk Weavers of Kyoto*.

Keith Hart is the author of *The Political Economy of West African Agriculture* (1982) and numerous articles on economic anthropology, including "Informal Income Opportunities and Urban Employment in Ghana" (Journal of Modern African Studies, 1973). Currently a Lecturer at Cambridge University, he has taught anthropology at Manchester, Yale, McGill, Chicago and Michigan Universities, and most recently at the University of the West Indies in Jamaica.

Barbara Stanek Kilbourne is a doctoral student in Political Economy at the University of Texas at Dallas. She is the author, with Brian J. L. Berry of "West African Urbanization: Where Tolley's Model Fails" (forthcoming in *Urban Geography*). She is currently involved in research using LISREL to study marital solidarity, and in work on determinants of job turnover among young men and women.

George E. Marcus is Professor and Chair in the department of Anthropology at Rice University, Texas. He is co-author, with Michael Fischer, of

Anthropology as Cultural Critique: An Experimental Moment in the Human Sciences. He has been involved in research on noble—commoner relationships in the Kingdom of Tonga, and the perpetuation of dynastic fortunes and families among contemporary U.S. capitalists. He has a broad interest in how cultural analysis, as developed in anthropology, can inform classic modes of ideology critique in social theory, and is currently involved in the study of the systematic relationships between wealth and cultural production in the United States.

John Myles is Professor of Sociology at Carleton University, Ottowa, Canada. He is the author of *Old Age in the Welfare State: the Political Economy of Public Pensions* (2nd Edition, 1989). His recent articles include studies of the impact of industrial restructuring on job skills and wages, and of the contemporary politics of the welfare state. With Jill Quadagno he is currently editing a volume tentatively entitled *Decline or Impasse? The Politics of Old Age in Transition.* With Wallace Clement he is preparing a major research monograph on class organization and class attitudes in the United States, Sweden, Norway and Finland.

Frances Fox Piven is a Professor at the Graduate School of the City University of New York. With Richard Cloward she has written extensively on urban politics and social movements. They are the authors of *Regulating the Poor; Poor People's Movements;* and most recently *Why Americans Don't Vote.* They are currently at work on a study of the politics of rule-making and rule-breaking.

Walter W. Powell is Associate Professor of Sociology and Management at the University of Arizona. He is the editor of and contributor to *The Nonprofit Sector* (Yale University Press, 1987). He and Paul DiMaggio are editors of *The New Institutionalism in Organizational Analysis* (University of Chicago Press, forthcoming). His current research concerns patterns of competition and collaboration in international business alliances.

A. F. (Sandy) Robertson is Professor of Anthropology at the University of California, Santa Barbara. Until 1985 he taught Development Studies and was Director of the African Studies Centre at Cambridge University. Recent books include *People and the State: an Anthropology of Planned Development* (1984), and *The Dynamics of Productive Relationships: African Share Contracts in Comparative Perspective* (1987). A book on *The Social Organization of Human Reproduction* is in press. He has recently embarked on a comparative study of industrialization and reproductive organization in Spain and West Africa.

Michael Wallerstein is an Assistant Professor in the Department of Political Science at the University of California, Los Angeles. He is working with Adam Przeworski on abstract models of class relations, and is also engaged in a study of bargaining structures and unionization in advanced capitalist countries. Among his publications are "The Structure of Class Conflict in Democratic Capitalist Societies" (*American Political Science Review* 1982) and, with Adam Przeworski, "Popular Sovereignty, State Autonomy and Private Property" (forthcoming in *Archives Européennes de Sociologie*).

Index